BOYS OF '67

FROM VIETNAM TO IRAQ, THE EXTRAORDINARY STORY OF A FEW GOOD MEN

CHARLES JONES

Foreword by Gen. Anthony C. Zinni, USMC (Ret.)

STACKPOLE
BOOKS

To my mother and father

ISBN-13: 978-0-8117-0163-1
ISBN-10: 0-8117-0163-8

Table of Contents

Foreword

In 1999, I was privileged to speak at the retirement of Gen. Ray L. Smith, a true friend and colleague for more than twenty years in the Marine Corps. I first met Ray while I was junior major, trying to figure out the business of being a battalion commander. I was blessed to have Ray assigned as my executive. He was a legendary combat leader who taught me a great deal about fighting and leading.

Years later, as Ray left active duty service (like most Marines, he would never truly leave the Corps), another real warrior, Gen. Gary Luck, and I were talking about our mutual friend. "I mean this from the bottom of my heart," Gary said, "if I could only pick one man to be by my side in a firefight, only one, without a doubt, that would be Ray Smith."

I wasn't surprised to hear this, since I felt the same way. I had heard that said about Ray Smith more than any other person I've ever known—soldier, sailor, airman, Marine, past or present. He's everybody's warrior. He's the guy everybody wants on his right flank. And it isn't just because he has guts and he's brave, as his medals attest. It's because of his down-to-earth, practical genius.

That day on the stage at Camp Lejeune, I saw another old friend, Gen. Jim Jones. He was Commandant of the Marine Corps at the time, and because of his own special traits, he later became the first Marine chosen by the president as Supreme Allied Commander, Europe. Jim's intellect, integrity, and dedication to duty clearly stood out for all of us who have had the good fortune to serve with him.

This book tells the story of Ray Smith, Jim Jones, and another Marine officer I came to admire—Martin R. "Marty" Steele, who as a lieutenant general became the highest ranking tank officer in the history of the Corps. Through a twist of fate, Marty Steele was Ray's roommate at The Basic School, the start of a lifelong friendship and service to the Corps. Marty is one of the most passionate leaders I've ever known, and has a reputation for brilliance and innovative thinking.

This trio of Marines started their professional journeys together in The Basic School class of April 5, 1967, and came to embody the traits of some of the best and brightest young Americans who heeded the call to serve in Vietnam and chose to make the Marines a career. Their careers were formed and forged in war and their contributions to a truly remarkable renaissance of our service gave us the powerful Corps we have today.

This is their story. It is also the story of their legacy to Country and Corps.

> Gen. Anthony C. Zinni, USMC (Ret.)
> Former Commander-in-Chief,
> U.S. Central Command

Author's Note

Work on this book began after my father died in 1998. Lt. Gen. William K. Jones was a highly decorated Marine who fought in World War II, Korea, and Vietnam. He also was a kind and forgiving man who never questioned my decision not to follow him into military service. After his passing, I started reflecting on our family's time in and around the U.S. Marine Corps. Growing up on bases around the country, I often felt like a junior member of the Corps, whether it was building trenches with old metal ammo boxes in the swamps of South Carolina or watching in awe as Hawk missiles blew up drone aircraft over the California desert. We lived in our own world, with our own circle of friends and code of loyalty. The Marines seemed a breed apart—self-confident, yet always humbled by the knowledge that they might have to enter combat again. My father and his friends were idealistic, but in a tight-lipped, Gary Cooper way. Along with their wives, they were in the truest sense All-Americans.

Living in and around the Corps helped shaped my worldview and self-image. But ultimately the turmoil of the late 1960s and early 1970s—the Vietnam years—altered my plans to follow in my father's footsteps. Still, with a brother and cousins already serving, the talk around our living room and dinner table always had a distinctively Leatherneck flavor.

After my father's funeral at Arlington Cemetery, I found a new perspective on those often-confusing times. I began reexamining what had happened to the generation of Marines who were almost a decade older than me, guys who faced the hard choice of getting drafted or volunteering for military service. I'd read a number of Vietnam-era books from all sides of the ideological fence about the war. But they didn't seem to capture the humanity and idealism of the people I'd known. One relative in particular helped me better understand his time and place in this chaotic, confusing period. He'd lived with us near Washington, D.C., during his senior year of high school, and I came to know him like a brother. He joined the Corps in 1966, a decision he said was made, at least in part, by my father's inspiration.

That man was James L. Jones Jr. When we started talking in late 1998, Jim had already achieved my father's high rank—lieutenant general—and was serving as the senior military assistant to then-Secretary of Defense William Cohen. This was a remarkable feat, yet one that seemed to have barely registered on my mental radar. After several casual conversations, it finally hit me that my first cousin and friend was playing a key role in the inner circle of the nation's military leadership, where the stakes could reach as high as the Washington Monument. And Jim was on a fast track to attain higher rank and responsibility. In mid-1999, he was promoted to four-star general and became Commandant.

Unfortunately, my father didn't live long enough to see Gen. James L. Jones become the thirty-second commandant in the more than 200 year history of the Corps. I was fortunate to have a front-row seat on his tenure in office, though, and took it on myself to better understand his professional journey. To better understand the other men of his generation, Jim put me in touch with a classmate from The Basic School where the newly minted lieutenants started their professional education on April 5, 1967. That classmate was Maj. Gen. Les Palm. Les, who heads the Marine Corps Association in Quantico, helped me start connecting the dots by contacting active-duty and retired officers, and other enlisted men with close ties to these Marines. Over time, the dots turned into story lines, and a book began to take shape. Gradually, I had to make some hard choices about how to shape their stories into a cohesive narrative, forcing me to leave out some rich and compelling stories in order to keep others.

I concluded that the lives of three men captured the rich flavor and cast of this class of officers. Besides Jones, who remains on active duty as Supreme Allied Commander in Europe and Africa, the other two main characters you'll meet are retired generals—Maj. Gen. Ray L. Smith and Lt. Gen. Martin R. Steele. Smith and Steele blazed their own bright career paths from Quantico to Vietnam to the Middle East to Korea. Each faced unique challenges in war and peace. Their innovative work, often performed in relative obscurity, helped the Corps stay a steady course and prepare for its next battle.

Thomas Hardy wrote "that war makes rattling good history; but Peace is poor reading." This may have been true of the English army, but for the Marines, the lull after Vietnam and through the '80s and '90s held its own rattling good history—though one that, until now, has never been properly recognized. The Marines, in their zeal to be "the tip of the spear" of America's military might, always pride themselves on being the first to fight. It's one thing to talk about it, but quite another to live up to such an ideal. Jones, Steele, and Smith spent years trying to achieve this lofty goal.

Covering the entirety of their extensive, globetrotting careers would take three separate volumes or more. I've done my best to narrate some of the highlights of their lives in and around the Corps. To anyone who has been overlooked, I sincerely apologize. By sharing their most telling stories, and describing the particular challenges of their professional lives, I hope to provide some insight into what drove three highly successful Marines through good times and bad, including one stretch after Vietnam when the Corps' very future hung in the balance. Unlike their fathers and uncles, these Baby Boomer Marines often received little recognition, and even less credit, for their loyalty and courage. They toiled in backwater bases or on often-treacherous foreign shores in ways that mirrored the forgotten soldiers of Kipling's poem: "For it's Tommy this, 'an Tommy that, 'an 'Chuck 'im out, the brute!' But it's 'Savior of 'is country' when the guns begin to shoot."

No real Marine would ever claim to be a national savior. Yet at the outset of my research, I was struck by how little attention the military was getting from the press or other media in late 1998 and early 1999. At that time, the spotlight was on Monicagate and the accumulation of dot.com wealth—two bubbles that burst soon enough. The national amnesia toward the armed services ended for a while after 9/11, when the country was reeling from the first attack on the homeland since Pearl Harbor. Now, it seemed, the American Tommy—and Marine—would get his or her due.

But within a couple of years, military recruiters were struggling to fill quotas as the reality of war filled TV screens. Patriotism was out, "reality TV" was in. Nonetheless, the men and women of the Corps pressed on, knowing from personal experience the wisdom of Horace's dictum that "a wise man in time of peace prepares for war."

This is a story of war, but also the preparations for war. It takes us from the mountains of Vietnam to the back alleys of Beirut, from the shores of Grenada to the snow-capped peaks of northern Iraq. It's told from the ground up—through the eyes and ears and voices of young (and later, middle-aged) warriors trying to make the right decisions in the heat of battle, when, in Napier's words, "the keenest eye cannot always discern the right path."

The right path was not always clear when the bullets were flying and the bombs were falling. In the end, these Marines had to draw on the depth of character and tradition that had first linked them as brothers in arms—*Semper Fidelis*, always faithful.

In that spirit, I have tried to be faithful to the facts as presented to me by scores of participants interviewed in person, by phone, or by e-mail over the last five years. Whenever possible I have sought two or more sources to confirm any significant event. Otherwise, I have tried to make it clear when a particular scene is based on one person's recollections. In a few cases, I have changed a name to protect someone's privacy, or because the correct name can't be verified.

This book is bound together by the colorful threads of the lives of three men with a distinct set of talents and traits—Jones, the cool-headed thinker; Steele, the passionate idealist; and Smith, the courageous combat leader. Their paths sometimes crossed during three decades of active duty, but more often than not, they served in different parts of the world. I have tried to note those rare times they were in each other's professional orbit, but I'm not trying to suggest that they ever constituted a kind of "three amigos" within the Corps. Ray Smith and Marty Steele did remain close for many years and sometimes socialized, but otherwise each had his own circle of confidantes, allies, and mentors.

As an outsider peering into this closely-held brotherhood, I found that these men—and many of their colleagues—displayed a quality of character so eloquently described in Churchill's tribute to Neville Chamberlain: "The only guide to a man is his conscience; the only shield to his memory is the rectitude and sincerity of his actions. It is very imprudent to walk through life without this shield, because we are so often mocked by the failure of our calculation; but with this shield, however the fates may play, we march always in the ranks of honor."

I also discovered that early in their careers as platoon leaders each man was forced to confront the one force that links friend and foe alike in combat. Each had a turning point when they had to face their own mortality and find a way to cope with the grief that any compassionate commander feels at the loss of a comrade. As the American military continues to serve in Iraq, Afghanistan and other hotspots, my hope is that, in some small way, this book provides a measure of insight and inspiration.

"Death, where is thy sting?" Paul asked in his first letter to the Corinthians.

It is a question with no simple or easy answer.

Charles Jones
Richmond, Virginia
November 10, 2005

ONE

The
"Warrior Monks"

In late September 2001, Army general Tommy Franks was asked to stop by the Pentagon office of the Commandant of the Marine Corps to attend a "clear-the-air meeting" with Gen. Jim Jones and Adm. Vern Clark, the Chief of Naval Operations (CNO). The two wanted to ensure that a meeting held the previous day between Franks and the Joint Chiefs of Staff—where Franks had been questioned at length on his plans for the campaign in Afghanistan—had not been misconstrued as being unhelpful in intent. General Franks later dismissed the meeting with the Chiefs as "bullshit."

Franks, in his autobiography, haughtily declared he had no time for high-level interference. He was going to fight a war, and the Joint Chiefs had come across to him "like a mob of Title Ten m-f-ers, not like the Joint Chiefs of Staff."[1] The last thing he needed was the Pentagon four-stars getting in his way when the bullets were about to fly. He recalls, in great detail, telling the Commandant and the CNO exactly where they, too, could get off.

The commander of the U.S. Central Command was well known for his flamboyant behavior, especially in his meetings with the Joint Chiefs. He was also known for regaling his subordinates with colorful tales of how he told the brass a thing or two and how he regularly put them in their place. One of those four-stars he claimed to rebuke was General Jones. A Marine. A combat-tested Marine. A Marine who could smell trouble a mile away—and would walk that much faster to reach it.

Jim Jones certainly recalls Tommy Franks in those tense meetings. Only he remembers things a little differently.

"Tom Franks's 'performances' gave us some humorous moments, for which we were grateful," Jones said, assessing Franks's recollection of the events in his book as "flawed, self-serving, and inaccurate. Tom Franks did not exchange harsh words with either of us in my office." For the man who became the first Marine to be appointed NATO's Supreme Allied Commander, this is a diplomatic way of saying "bullshit."

"Despite the absurdity of his behavior towards us, the Joint Chiefs never lost sight of their role of providing military advice [that Franks benefited from] even as he was doing everything possible to emasculate their influence."

Jones said he offered Franks two Marine Expeditionary Units to help in the campaign in Afghanistan. "Franks accepted this offer at a critical time in the mission, with expressed appreciation. They made him look very good at a critical moment in the campaign. One would never know it now, however."

Franks "did not tolerate being questioned by the Joint Chiefs, whose responsibility, by the way, is to critically examine plans involving the use of the nation's combat forces. His complaints of turf battles and parochialism are both incorrect and absurd."

Jones pointed out that Franks retired from his Central Command post in great haste—certainly before the war ended—and that he "has been fortunate, thus far, in avoiding critical scrutiny of his planning for the war in Iraq. When he took over the Central Command, Tommy Franks said, 'I am not Norman Schwarzkopf.' On that point, I emphatically agree."

Getting into a pissing match with other military men is out of character for the first Marine to be named Supreme Allied Commander of American and NATO forces in Europe and Africa. But Franks's personal shots came at a tense time as Jones's own flesh and blood survived some close calls inside and outside Iraq.

On October 8, 2002, 2nd Lt. Gregory D. Jones was a platoon leader with the 3rd Battalion, 1st Marines, during a training exercise on Kuwait's Faylaka Island in the Persian Gulf. His men had just knocked off from work to get out of the late morning heat and struck up a baseball game near the ocean.

Soon gunfire crackled from the coastal highway. "Holy shit," a Marine hollered, "they're shooting at us!"

A white pickup truck with two Kuwaiti men started taking potshots with AK-47s at the baseball players. One of Greg's lance corporals, Antonio Sledd, died in the drive-by shooting, while his radio operator, Lance Corp. George Simpson, was wounded. As part of their training protocol on foreign soil, the Marines didn't have their weapons loaded. But the company's gunnery sergeant, Wayne Hertz, had the presence of mind to keep some ammo nearby. Several Marines loaded their weapons and coolly picked off the assailants.

In his Pentagon office shortly afterward, Jones reflected: "It does hit home when your son is out there and involved in it. It's something both of us have prepared for," he said, referring to his wife, Diane. "We know it's a dangerous world. I've always said to Marines that they are special targets when they're out there. There is no front line and no rear area."

Six months later, Greg Jones was part of the 1st Marine Division's push toward Baghdad. As reports of house-to-house fighting spread, the general wrote his son a letter that expressed his growing sense of frustration at being on the margins of the fight for the first time in his career. He had been elevated to the position of Supreme Allied Commander, Europe, and Commander, U.S. European Command, by President Bush in early 2003, shortly before the Iraq invasion. Normally, this would have been a time to bask in the historical moment since he was the first Marine appointed to the leadership position first held by the legendary Dwight D. Eisenhower in World War II. His son, now a Marine captain, was to return for a second tour in Iraq less than six months after returning home. The second trip would be no easier for his parents.

"I'm sitting here feeling rather helpless," Jones wrote. "I still can't get used to the idea that one of my children is over there fighting a war. . . . It should be me!" He had been tracking the 1st Marines' movements, "so I have a pretty good idea of where you all are," he continued. "Well done; very impressive performance to date. I'm not surprised that it is tougher than the last time, it always is when the enemy has nowhere to go!"

He noted the ambush of an Army unit—and the taking of the first American POWs—and remarked that he had been in Turkey recently "trying to do a few helpful things to speed things along. It isn't easy, but we're making some headway, I think." Mostly, he wrote as a father to a son, and told him to remember the earlier fatal attack on his platoon on Faylaka Island. "Remember, your island experience should remind you every day . . . there is no front, no rear, and no safe area . . . always watch your six, trust your Marines; even when it's 'over' it never is!"

He concluded, "We love you, take care of yourself and your Marines . . . you are writing history."

This was no idle boast. From the time he began Marine officer training in 1967, Jim Jones found himself putting his own mark on the history of the Corps—starting from the ground up. It had been several decades since he was first thrust into combat in Vietnam, but the faces of his fellow Marines, whose blood flowed into the Asian soil, never left him. The son of a former Marine and nephew of a general, Jim Jones was never one to run from a battle—whether it was taking on a battalion of North Vietnamese regulars or rebutting the ill-chosen remarks of a bellicose Army general.

He also wasn't one to underestimate the enemy. As planning began for the 2003 invasion of Iraq, General Jones emerged as one of the few military commanders willing to openly question the notion—touted by Bush Administration officials—of a quick, surgical victory over Saddam's military and security forces. "Gen. Jones is the latest in a succession of prominent American military figures to issue warnings about the dangers of rushing headlong into war," reported London's *Daily Telegraph.*[2]

The British newspaper was commenting on an interview in the *Washington Times* in which Jones warned against underestimating the resistance American forces surely would face in a country used to war. "The defense of a homeland is hard stuff because they're not going to go anywhere," he said.[3]

Jones managed to voice his concerns without directly challenging his superiors, Defense Secretary Donald Rumsfeld and President Bush. He appeared to use the conservative newspaper to make a point about Iraq that later seemed right on target. "You better have Plan B in your hip pocket," he said, "because when you attack someone who has any kind of well-trained army on their homeland they are going to fight differently than if they engage you, say, in Kuwait."

Despite his cautious warnings to the press, he privately dismissed reports of a rift with his fellow generals and admirals on the six-member Joint Chiefs of Staff, or with others inside the Bush Administration, from Vice President Dick Cheney to Rumsfeld's outspoken deputy, Paul Wolfowitz. Such rumors of in-fighting were overblown, he said. Part of the reason lay in the aftermath of the 9/11 terror attacks, when the military commanders found common cause in going after the state-sponsored fanatics in Afghanistan. This ended, at least for a time, the quarreling that broke out in the early days of the Bush Administration as Rumsfeld tried to retool the Pentagon's massive spending machinery.

"September 11th, for all of its tragedy, had a forcing function inside this building of recalibrating all of us into focusing on those things that are really the most important," Jones said. The heads of the Army, Air Force, Navy, and Marine Corps discovered in the wake of the terrorist attacks "much more of a sense of teamwork and people being focused on a very, very important set of circumstances that deserved our complete attention," he said.

In a November 2002 interview, a full five months before CNN broadcast the ghostly images of Baghdad under aerial attack, Jones shared what he could about the upcoming battle. His office was full of historical artifacts, including a painting of Marines landing on the volcanic ash beaches of Iwo Jima—a stark reminder of how often young Americans are called to fight, and fall, on foreign soil.

Wearing a dark green jacket with four stars per shoulder, he folded his arms and calmly pondered the military situation. He refused to reveal anything said inside the "Tank," the Joint Chiefs' conference room near the river entrance of the Pentagon. He seemed annoyed at the ongoing media reports about the service chiefs, and their alleged differences over war planning. "Those reports are wrong—the reporters are not talking to me or the CNO [Adm. Vern Clark, Chief of Naval Operations], or the Chiefs of Staff of the Army or the Air Force." Reporters were relying on second- or third-tier sources, he said, "and that's when you get down to guessing. Because what goes on in the Tank, stays in the Tank."

Speaking broadly, Jones said the prewar discussions were frank and, guided by the steely-eyed Rumsfeld, intense. "You would expect disagreement, you would expect discussion," Jim said, because Rumsfeld "fosters it—that's his style. The fact that we have those kinds of meetings is to be celebrated." In those prewar days, before Franks published his critical account, Jim sounded positive about his Army counterpart, remarking that he "brings up his plan, it's debated, and we discuss what's the best course of action. Everything is fair game, so it's a healthy process."

The general fell into the Sphinx-like silence of someone used to keeping secrets. This isn't unusual for a man whose colleagues wonder at his ability to seemingly slide behind an invisible shield, an emotional barrier that many say they've never cracked.

Such a protective shield may be necessary for anyone who spends much time near the nexus of national power, where the pitfalls are just a slip of the tongue away. From the outing of "Deep Throat" to the phone calls of Karl Rove, when it comes to keeping state secrets, Washington, D.C., is as leaky as an old row boat. General Jones steers a safer course by keeping his own counsel and disdaining anyone in uniform who leaks stories to the press.

When Greg Jones decided to join the Marines, he expected his father to be ecstatic. He would continue a family tradition that stretched back to 1938, when Jim Jones's uncle, William K. Jones, was first commissioned as a second lieutenant in the Marine reserves, and entered the regular Marine Corps in 1940. Around this time, William Jones's older brother, James Logan Jones, returned from Africa, where he was a salesman for International Harvester, and signed up for officer training in the Corps. The fighting Jones brothers distinguished themselves in combat, and Uncle Bill, as Jim Jones knew him, rose to the rank of lieutenant general and became an integral part of the Corps' leadership of the 1960s and early 1970s. James Logan Jones left the Corps after the war, but became a reserve colonel and steeped his firstborn son in the lore and legends of the men known as Leathernecks.

Yet when the time came for Greg to announce his plans to enter the brotherhood, he found his own father oddly unimpressed. Instead of rising and clapping him on the back and offering a toast, the general sat in his chair in the Commandant's house and looked his son in the eye, asking, "Why?"

His father's dispassionate question surprised and disappointed Greg. Only later did he see why his father might have been so guarded. Jones had seen hundreds of men die in combat and had almost perished himself during one particularly bloody night in Vietnam on a bomb-scarred hilltop called Foxtrot Ridge. He led an undermanned Marine company that was ordered to hold a piece of bombed-out real estate against a heavily armed battalion of North Vietnamese regulars—a poorly conceived assignment that left Lt. Jim Jones up against a unit with more than five times his manpower. Foxtrot Ridge became the crucible that would harden the resolve of the young Marine and shape his thoughts for decades to come. Years later, as he flew in a jet on his way to another ceremony as Commandant, he answered a question about Vietnam by requesting a notebook. He carefully drew a diagram of Foxtrot Ridge to show the battle lines and positions of American and North Vietnamese forces. With meticulous detail, he sketched the place he put his company command post inside a saddle-like depression on the hilltop, and where he placed the rest of his unit that had been depleted by dysentery, attrition, and troop rotations.

There was the valley below with the North Vietnamese battalion, and there the landing zone that served as the Marines' command post. It seemed like it happened only yesterday.

With a sad smile, he recalled how he had once been nicknamed "Bulletproof" by his radio operator, because "I just never thought that I was going to be killed or wounded." In his early twenties, this former basketball sharpshooter saw Vietnam "as a kind of athletic contest."

That night on Foxtrot Ridge, though, blew away the thought of war as competitive sport. Any notions of invulnerability were left simmering on the bomb-blasted hill—along with the backpack containing his letters and pictures from home. All that went up in a napalm bomb's wall of flame, along with his sense of invincibility.

As he sketched the map on an interviewer's notebook, he commented, "I think it took a number of years to realize the impact" of the night-long clash. Afterward, he was amazed to be alive, and knew that only by learning from his experience—and by fighting smarter in the future—would he get himself and his men out of Vietnam alive.

Many of his contemporaries weren't so lucky, and some didn't make it through their first few weeks as platoon commanders in a shadowy war where a friend by day could become a foe by night. Two of Jones's Basic School classmates who did survive, Ray Smith and Marty Steele, did so by never dropping their guard and always keeping their cool in the thick of every firefight. Smith and Steele, roommates at Quantico, rose through the ranks of the Corps together and joined Jones as Marine generals in the 1990s.

Sometimes their career paths crossed, but they could go for years without seeing each other. Yet wherever their orders took them—from the Middle East to Korea to the Marines' training bases on the Atlantic and Pacific coasts—the three Marines demonstrated a shared passion for their chosen profession. Each had a unique leadership style, an uncanny ability to motivate others, and a free spirit.

Steele chose to labor in the prosaic, but vital, field of tanks and armored vehicles. As the Army set the pace for high-tech innovations and maneuver warfare, he embarked on a personal crusade to ensure the Corps didn't get stuck with a fleet of faulty tanks. Despite his best intentions, the hard-driving former runningback from Arkansas often butted heads with authority.

The same could be said of Ray Smith, whose career was marked by critical moments when he challenged authority if it meant protecting his men. A highly decorated hero of two tours in Vietnam, he later played a central role in one of the least-understood chapters of recent Marine history: the aftermath of the 1983 terrorist bombing of the Battalion Landing Team headquarters in Beirut.

In retrospect, Ray Smith clearly was the right man for the hazardous duty of leading a replacement battalion into the smoking ruins of Lebanon, coming on the heels of a victorious sweep of the tiny island of Grenada. He held an unshakable belief in the rightness of his mission from President Reagan to hold the low ground stained with the blood of 241 Marines, soldiers, and sailors.

Notwithstanding his respect for the president, Smith never hesitated to speak his mind to distant theater commanders who seemed willing to risk his men's lives while withholding the authority to fulfill their training and their fate—to attack and kill the enemy.

By the 1980s, Ray's larger-than-life reputation had spread through the ranks of a new generation of lieutenants. They called him "E-Tool" Smith, but only behind his back. It was an honorific that traced its roots back to Vietnam, where, it was said, Smith pummeled a soldier to death with his entrenching tool. Like so many things about the Marine Corps, the legend contained many grains of truth, spiced with a few bits of blarney.

The lives of Jones, Smith, and Steele need no embellishment, though. Their records stand for themselves—not always perfect, perhaps, but always faithful to the Corps' high standards and eagerness to be, in the words of the Marine Hymn, "first to fight for right and freedom, and to keep our honor clean."

Other distinguished classmates at The Basic School included Les Palm, an artillery officer who fought through the siege of Khe Sanh, commanded Marines in Kuwait, and later became a major general. These boys of '67 became men of principle and power who helped shape the identity and course of the modern-day Marine Corps. Unlike the fathers and uncles whose boots they tried to fill, these men faced a series of often confusing conflicts waged in unlikely places—from the Iraqi mountains to the South China Sea—where their missions and outcomes often lacked the clarity and national support of an earlier age.

Today, the question of how to fight—and win—wars in distant, difficult places is as relevant as it was when the class of 1967 boarded planes to begin their odyssey into the jungles of Vietnam. They fought a proxy war against communism, only to return to a native land deeply divided and ultimately hostile to its young people in uniform.

Still, these Marines didn't give up on the Corps or on the country that turned its back on them. Why? What motivated them to keep marching, even when the band stopped playing?

Perhaps part of the answer lies in what Gen. Anthony Zinni has called the "warrior monk" ethic. "For me, joining the Marines was the closest thing to becoming a priest," Zinni said in a 2000 speech at the U.S. Naval Institute. "One way or another, all of us were programmed to believe what we were doing was not a job; not even a profession; but a calling."

When they signed up, the young men of the 1960s left behind the comforts of home to learn the way of the warrior. They traded sports cars for jeeps, left girlfriends for drill instructors, and trusted that if they worked hard, they might survive their trial by fire in Vietnam.

What they couldn't have known at the time, though, was just how much of themselves they would have to leave behind, and how deep they would have to dig, to become a United States Marine.

TWO

The School of Experience

All Marine officers begin their training in Quantico, Virginia. Quantico means "by the large stream," according to Native American lore, and was explored by Capt. John Smith in 1608. It later became a strategic crossroads for the movement of troops and supplies during the Revolutionary and Civil Wars. Located on the Potomac between Washington and Richmond, the River town became a key junction on the 100-mile-long Richmond, Fredericksburg & Potomac Railroad.

During World War I, the Marines used the federal power of eminent domain to acquire 6,000 acres of land to build a training base at Quantico for infantry leaders getting ready to ship out. The topographical convergence in Virginia—with its creeks, woods, ravines, and beaches—allowed officers to practice leading amphibious landings on hostile shores, maneuvering troops through dense woods, and climbing up rocky gullies. With typical understatement, the Corps called its officer training program The Basic School.[1]

In the 1920s, Gen. John Lejeune began to refine the instruction at Quantico to meet the next enemy appearing on the horizon. In 1921, one of Lejeune's planners, Lt. Col. Earl H. Ellis, developed a 50,000-word operational plan predicting a Japanese strike against American forces in the Pacific. "It will be necessary for us to project our fleet and landing forces across the Pacific and wage war in Japanese waters,"[2] Ellis wrote. It would take another twenty years, but his prediction proved prophetic, and the Marine Corps' focus on amphibious landings—with improvements in both battlefield tactics and equipment—would help turn the tide against Japan during the fierce island campaigns of World War II.

Before the challenge of the Rising Sun, however, the Corps was a small sideshow in America's shrinking military. With no imminent threat, the young men who chose to enlist often came from the rural South or the working-class Northeast or Midwest. Given their close proximity to the classic battlefields of the Civil War (or what some southern Marines preferred to call "The War Between the States"), they "amused themselves and official Washington with re-enactments of some of the Civil War battles: Wilderness, Gettysburg, New Market and Antietam," historian Edwin H. Simmons wrote. The traditional Marine Corps dress blue uniform served as the Yankee garb, while Rebel forces proudly wore the Confederate gray of the Virginia Military Institute.

Quantico became known for its strenuous competition in boxing, football, basketball, and baseball.[3] This tradition would last into the 1960s as the Marines could afford to sponsor travel teams, even playing exhibition baseball games against the Washington Senators and New York Yankees.

By 1967, the fun and games were over. America was pursuing a major military buildup to satisfy President Lyndon Johnson's decision to draw a line in the sand against communism in South Vietnam. In response, the Marine Corps was forced to speed up its educational and training rotations to bolster its officer ranks. More than six thousand U.S. soldiers had already been killed in the fighting, and more blood was expected to be shed. Johnson, who worried about appearing soft on communism, vowed in his 1967 State of the Union Address to Congress to "stand firm" in Southeast Asia.[4]

Before the Vietnam buildup, The Basic School had trained about 1,200 newly commissioned second lieutenants per year. In 1967, the number more than doubled as an estimated 2,800 lieutenants entered the program.[5] The training regimen was shrunk from twenty-six weeks to twenty-one weeks.

The Basic School's mission was to educate men "in the high standards of leadership, knowledge and esprit de corps traditional in the Marine Corps in order to prepare them for the duties of a company grade officer in the Fleet Marine Force, with particular emphasis on the duties and responsibilities of the rifle platoon commander."[6]

The school did not act as a screening point for lieutenants, since subpar men were weeded out during the initial training at Quantico in Officer Candidate School (OCS). Unlike the Army or the Navy, The Basic School did not divide its officer ranks into specialists, such as Rangers or submariners. Instead, the Corps trained every officer to lead a rifle platoon. So whether they later led truck convoys or flew jets, every Marine lieutenant knew how to fire a rifle, lead a platoon, and fight at close quarters.

And fight they would. The next stop for most students was the Fleet Marine Force in South Vietnam, where they would be thrust directly into "the school of experience."[7]

Nearly all of The Basic School students of 1967 were college graduates, and most of the rest had logged some time on college campuses around the country. Ray Smith and Marty Steele were in the latter group, starting college in the mid 1960s; for very different reasons, however, they grew impatient with sitting in classrooms and discussing the hypotheticals of life. The world was changing at a dizzying pace—from the war to Civil Rights marches to riots in the streets. It was a time of extremes, from the anger of the Watts rioters shouting "burn, baby, burn!" to the Beatles' calming advice that "all you need is love."

Ray Smith, for his part, found an early and abiding love of the great outdoors. He started college on a practical note, studying engineering at Oklahoma State University, but after a year in school, he decided to explore a growing interest in forestry. Since an older brother was living in Montana, he moved to Missoula and found a summer job with the state forest service. On his first trip out of the plains, Smith marveled at the towering Rocky Mountains: the crisp air, the scenic vistas, the sense of walking the same ground as Sitting Bull and Lewis and Clark.

He savored the solitude of clearing fire trails and building logging roads among the towering loblolly pines of the Lolo National Forest. He dreamed of becoming a forester or park ranger, but those dreams were deferred when he got a letter ordering him to report to the local Selective Service office. Dropping out of college had cost him his student deferment from the military draft.

So at age nineteen, Ray Smith was at a crossroads. Either he could enlist in the Army or join some other branch of the military. That summer in Missoula, a lot of guys his age were finding ways to avoid the draft, by starting families or going to graduate school. Smith had given little thought to military service. He grew up in Shidler, Oklahoma, a small town filled with descendants of oil drillers and cattle ranchers. They had a streak of isolationism in them and felt America would do better keeping to itself and not always jumping into one war or another. His father, Coleman, operated machinery for Skelly Oil Company, a job deemed vital to the nation's defense industry during World War II. This meant Ray Smith, unlike many of his contemporaries, had few role models to draw on when Uncle Sam beckoned him into the military. All he knew for sure was that he couldn't live with himself if he dodged the draft. It would be unpatriotic and irresponsible.

Still, he thought, join the Marines? It was a leap of faith that he couldn't make without considerable assistance—two six packs' worth of assistance, to be exact. Suitably fortified, he stumbled into the recruiting office in Missoula, signed the enlistment papers, and never looked back—at least not until he was staring into the flinty eyes of a drill instructor at the recruit training depot in San Diego, California.

Marty Steele, by contrast, had been inspired to serve. The only question was how soon. His stepfather, Dick Steele, was a hardworking builder and postal official in Fayetteville, Arkansas. As an Army pilot in World War II, he was shot down over France by German antiaircraft fire. He spent months as a prisoner of war and managed to survive until he was liberated by Allied troops. Later, like many World War II veterans, he kept his combat experiences to himself.

On those rare occasions when Dick Steele chose to talk, he did so in a ritualistic way that left an indelible mark on his children's psyches. On each child's eighteenth birthday, they were allowed to miss school, and their father stayed home from work. Pulling up a chair in the kitchen, he poured himself a glass of chocolate milk and said, "Listen closely, because it's the last time you'll hear anything from me about the war."

Then for eight straight hours, Dick Steele talked about the war: how he flew P-47 Thunderbolt fighters, bombing and strafing German infantry and Panzer forces retreating in France toward the Rhine after the Allied invasion of June 6, 1944; how he was shot down on his thirteenth mission; how he hid for weeks in the countryside, evading the Nazis with the help of the French underground.

Marty Steele sat mesmerized. This quiet man he'd known only as a parent and authority figure suddenly was transformed into a flying ace, tearing up the sky, then dodging German patrols and hiding in hay wagons. Dick Steele was captured only after a bit of bad luck when a soldier stabbed his bayonet into a hay bale and happened to catch him. He was hauled off to Stalag Luft One in Barth, Germany, where he survived by trusting in himself, fellow prisoners, and God.

No questions were allowed during his talk to the young Marty. After the day-long monologue—with barely a bathroom break—Dick Steele pushed back his chair and declared, "That's it." He was done. The book was closed on his war stories until another eighteenth birthday.

While Marty's stepfather instilled a deep patriotism and work ethic, his mother inspired a sense of compassion in her oldest son. Kitty Steele was a nurse who commanded respect through all social stratas of the college town, from day workers to professors' wives. She raised her children in the Roman Catholic faith, which was no easy task at a time when Catholics in the South were still considered outsiders, believed to be engaging in all manner of mystical nonsense and perhaps even taking orders from Rome against Protestants.

As America went to war in Vietnam, it was inevitable that Marty Steele, steeped in idealism and history, grew impatient sitting in the classroom at the University of Arkansas, listening to kids prattle on about the Beatles and the Beach Boys. Hairstyles, rock music, and fast cars seemed like foolish diversions to the young man with a boxer's build and a philosopher's keen eye. There was one exception to Steele's no-nonsense attitude toward life: Arkansas football. The fate of his hometown college team always stayed on a par with motherhood and country—and perhaps just a rung down from the Holy Trinity.

So in January 1965, before the start of his second semester of college, Marty Steele headed west to San Diego, where he, too, reported for recruit training. Later, he joined the 1st Marine Division, and before the year was out, everyone got word they were shipping out to Vietnam. Marty was in an outdoor theater at Camp Pendleton in southern California when the news came over the radio. Everyone tossed their hats into the air as if it were graduation day at the Naval Academy. By early 1966, he was running patrols near Chu Lai, and as his friends began to die around him, he realized this was nothing to cheer about.

Ray Smith and Marty Steele never crossed paths during boot camp, yet they were on parallel career paths. The Corps was on the lookout for quality young men, often college dropouts, who could be trained as platoon leaders in Quantico. "Everything had a frenetic pace to it," Smith recalled. "Everything was on a war footing." Short of drill instructors (D.I.) in San Diego, the Corps doled out extra duties to its top recruits, making Smith a de facto D.I. when he was just a private. His initial goal was to enroll in a flight school for enlisted men, but the program was cancelled because of the war buildup. Finally, a gunnery sergeant suggested in no uncertain terms that Private First Class Smith might want to apply to Officer Candidate School. Before he knew it, the raw-boned Oklahoman was catching a ride to Virginia, his first trip east of the Mississippi.

Marty Steele also was nudged eastward. After returning from Vietnam in late 1966, his leadership potential was recognized by sergeants, and now a meritoriously promoted corporal, he was sent to Quantico to help train lieutenants at Officer Candidate School. He served as an administrator and field instructor even though he was only nineteen years old.

Steele had considered returning to college and had been accepted by the U.S. Naval Academy. He probably would have gone to Annapolis but chose not to because they didn't allow midshipmen to have wives. His long time girlfriend, Cindy Bayliss, was the daughter of an Army colonel who had served as an artillery battalion commander in Patton's 3rd Army during World War II and later suffered a serious head wound during the Korean War. Cindy had been waiting patiently, but apprehensively, for Marty's return from Vietnam. They were only in their late teens but were deeply in love. Annapolis would have to wait: the couple decided to get married in early 1967.

He might have stayed in the enlisted ranks if not for a persistent staff sergeant named Karl G. Taylor. Taylor was an imposing man whose size and bulk reminded the young Steele of a biblical figure like Samson. He was so huge that he blocked the sun when he walked up one day after a field exercise. Taylor also had a speech defect caused by a cleft palate. Another man might have sounded like a weakling. Not Staff Sergeant Taylor.

"There's a calling for you, young man, and you've been rejecting it," he said intently. The veteran Marine could see this was a young man who was not meeting his potential.

He grasped Steele by the shoulders and chided him. "Listen to me, son. You could have played college football or professional baseball, but you didn't. Why? Do you think I'd be here if I could be practicing with the St. Louis Cardinals?"

Steele felt stung by the reproach, almost as if his own stepfather was upbraiding him.

"You turned down the Naval Academy!" Taylor said. "Now you're saying you want to be a good sergeant. But there's something more you should do!"

Steele took a deep breath, wondering what great feat he would have to perform to get out of Taylor's dog house. "You should quit turning down these opportunities," the staff sergeant said, "and seriously consider becoming an officer."

"But I'm proud to be an NCO," Steele protested. "I like being with Marines." He had rarely seen officers in Vietnam, so why would he want to become one now?

Taylor smiled inscrutably. "I'm not talking about what you like, Corporal Steele. I'm asking you to think about the Corps. We need men like you to lead our platoons into battle."

Still, Steele resisted, until the commander of Officer Candidate School urged him to take a college-level examination. After more prodding by Staff Sergeant Taylor, Steele took the test, passing with flying colors. This gained him admission to the twelve-week OCS program.

Staff Sergeant Taylor's only regret was that the young Marine wasn't placed in his training platoon. "I'll be watching you," he warned.

In March 1967, on a clear day in late winter, Marty Steele graduated near the head of his OCS class. As he left the ceremony in the base theater, he saw Taylor, grinning broadly and saluting him. By tradition, the Marine who gives a new lieutenant his first hand salute receives a silver dollar. Steele walked over to his mentor and handed him the silver coin.

"Do you have any guidance for me, Staff Sergeant Taylor?"

"Lieutenant," he said, "do your duty. That's all you need to know."

Marty took the advice to heart, determined to succeed at the next step in his training—The Basic School.

While Smith and Steele took blue-collar routes into the officer ranks, Jim Jones took a more traditional white-collar walk into the Corps. The soft-spoken graduate of Georgetown University held a degree in international relations and entertained vague notions of someday working for the State Department. One day, perhaps, he could become an ambassador. This was no pipe dream: He had grown up in Paris, the oldest son of an executive for International Harvester.

From an early age, Jones was fluent in French, adept at social graces, and steeped in Parisian art and culture. He was also rugged and athletic, excelling in baseball and basketball. A natural outdoorsman, he joined the Boy Scouts and took long marches and camping trips through the forests of France and Holland. He was a big, gregarious kid who by age twelve was taller than his father. Yet he always looked up to James L. Jones Sr., a bright, entrepreneurial man who not only read history, but lived it.

Growing up in postwar Europe, the Joneses saw the aftermath of two world wars: scorched ruins in Berlin, the endless cemetery at Normandy, the monuments to fallen Marines in Belleau Wood. Once a week, the young Jones's school day was interrupted by tests of air raid sirens—long, mournful wails that made everyone dread the possibility of more bombs and more wars.

Every July 14, on Bastille Day, his father took Jones and his siblings to the parade honoring the French Revolution. A detachment of Marine security guards from the American Embassy marched past, resplendent in dress blue uniforms. Young Jim came to look forward to this annual parade, and thought he glimpsed a tear in the eye of his normally unemotional father.

"There they are," James Jones Sr. proudly declared. "Here come the Marines." His father stood at attention and saluted the embassy guard passing on the Champs Èlysee. James Jones Jr. followed suit, snapping his first salute on the grandest boulevard of Paris.

Driving home, he would beg his father to tell him more about the Marines. Like Dick Steele and so many other war veterans, James Jones Sr. kept close counsel about his past. Over time, though, Jones managed to pry bits and pieces of memory from his father. He learned how, as a young officer, he led the 5th Marine Amphibious Reconnaissance Company in the South Pacific. His elite recon unit snuck up on Japanese positions on the Mariana and Marshall Islands, popping out of the ocean from submarines. The Force Recon Marines rode rubber rafts and made midnight raids to disarm mines strung along the beaches of Saipan, Tinian, and Okinawa. They prepared the way for the invasion of the regular Marine forces, which included Jim Sr.'s younger brother, Willie K. Jones.

The 1st Marine Division commander, Maj. Gen. Holland "Howling Mad" Smith, praised Capt. Jim Jones' leadership during the Marshall Islands campaign of early 1944. In a unit citation, Jones was cited for "annihilating all enemy resistance" and gathering valuable information about Japanese positions and fortifications. For his work, he received the Silver Star medal and other commendations.

Jim Jones Jr. also learned that his father's kid brother had fought in the same battles that bloodied the Pacific beaches. Uncle Bill was awarded a Navy Cross at Saipan, a Silver Star at Tarawa, and received a field promotion to lieutenant colonel at the tender age of twenty-seven.

After the war, James Jones Sr. left the regular Corps to return to his business career. He always spoke proudly of his younger brother Bill, who stayed in the Corps and became one of its rising stars. In 1961, Col. Bill Jones invited his nephew Jimmy to move from Paris to northern Virginia to attend his senior year of high school. As part of the transatlantic family transaction, he sent his oldest daughter, Carol, to spend her senior year in Paris. (Bill Jones would often say later that his brother definitely outfoxed him on the deal).

Jimmy Jones, as he was known then, jumped at the chance to live in America and be a regular teenager. He drove around in his Uncle Bill's 1956 Buick Special, danced at sock hops, devoured dozen upon dozen of Krispy Kreme donuts, played on a championship basketball team, and took long, hot showers, which he never got to take back in Paris.

More importantly, the string-bean young man with impeccable manners got to know his Uncle Bill and spent hours talking with him in front of the fireplace about the legendary island campaigns of World War II. Sitting in the living room of Bill and Charlotte Jones's new split-level home, the young Jim could look out on the Potomac River, where boats and barges passed by. He could see something else as well from his newly-adopted home: a future in the U.S. Marine Corps.

Jim Jones formed a special bond with his uncle and aunt, who laughed off the higher food and utility bills he generated and endured Jim's series of youthful follies, from wrecking the family Buick on the night of the Marine Corps Birthday Ball on November 10, 1961, to cutting through the carpet as he was wrapping Christmas gifts.

Five years later, in 1966, Jones graduated from Georgetown University and applied for an officer's commission in the Marine Corps. By then, his Uncle Bill was a major general and was deputy director of personnel at Headquarters Marine Corps. (In this post, he had the dubious distinction of signing the papers that would send Chuck Robb, the son-in-law of President Johnson, to South Vietnam.)

Jim Jones was proud of his uncle's continuing ascent in the Corps, but after enlisting, he learned that such family ties could be twisted into something of a knot for a new Leatherneck. After reporting for duty at Quantico, he managed to keep his uncle's identity under wraps until the very end of the ten-week Officer Candidate School. The jig was up, though, when each graduate had to list their guests at the OCS, and the new second lieutenant listed Maj. Gen. William K. Jones.

"My last week in OCS was unusually rough," Jones later recalled.

THREE

Obstacles

From the moment they walked into the Spartan classrooms of The Basic School on April 5, 1967, the class of 516 second lieutenants knew only geography mattered: Vietnam. The deepening conflict was integrated into most of the practical aspects of their training, including a mock village built in the woods to simulate a hamlet in Southeast Asia.

The Marine trainers donned the black pajama-like garb of the Viet Cong, while their students cautiously approached. From morning until night, the instructors crammed as much information into the lieutenants as they could—from small unit tactics, to the care and feeding of weapons, to platoon and company organization. (Anything above the company level was outside the lieutenant's domain.) They read a variety of texts, including the Marine Corps' *Small Wars Manual*, a classic primer from the 1940s that drew on the Corps' experience in "low-intensity" conflicts from Nicaragua to Haiti. Parts of the manual were outdated, such as its advice on handling pack mules and horses: "in desperate situations, it may be necessary to shoot these animals to prevent them from bolting into the enemy positions."[1]

Yet much of the manual's hard-won lessons still rang true, such as a cautionary note on ambushes. "The closeness and suddenness of the attack is supposed to disorganize and demoralize the enemy. A necessary protection against complete disorganization, and possible demoralization, is to prepare the troops mentally for the shock of ambush. They must be steeled to withstand a sudden blast of fire at close quarters and to react to it in a manner that will unnerve the enemy. To accomplish this, the troops must have a thorough understanding of what is likely to happen if they are ambushed."[2]

The lieutenants studied more modern texts about the use of tanks and other weapons. With supplies and ammunition being diverted to Vietnam, they had to make do with classroom training or field exercises. For example, when they were given a demonstration of light antitank assault weapons, they were told the rockets cost too much for each man to actually fire one. The same rule applied to calling in offshore naval gunfire, directing air strikes, or ordering indirect artillery fire. So even though they practiced such tactics during field problems, their final exams would not come until they reached Vietnam.

The student-warriors did get time on the firing range with the M-14 rifle, M-60 machine gun, M-79 grenade launcher, and the officer's sidearm—the .45 caliber pistol. In those days before global positioning systems, they also mastered the art of navigating in the bush with nothing but a map and compass.

Physical training was also paramount. The 516 graduates of the Basic School class of April 5, 1967, had many former college athletes or high school sports stars. Les Palm, a slim, taciturn kid from California farm country, played safety for the University of Oregon football team. Clebe McClary, a lanky South Carolina boy, was a track phenom who had become a high school coach before deciding to join the Marines in his mid-twenties. Burly Ron Oyer played in the same backfield as All-American Floyd Little at Syracuse University.

They were young thoroughbreds who jockeyed for position in the pecking order of their class. They nervously watched their class rankings and always strived to gain a few extra points on written tests or shave a few seconds off their times on the obstacle course. Few pushed themselves harder than Marty Steele, who was determined to break the record for the double-running of the obstacle course.

Carved out of the thick Virginia woods just past The Basic School complex, the O-course was the linchpin of the ongoing physical tests the lieutenants had to pass every few weeks. As summer approached, and the heat and humidity turned the forest into a natural sauna, it could be a grueling challenge to get past the series of barriers on the course—long wooden logs, eight-foot-high bars, six-foot-high walls, and, at the end, a twenty-five-foot-high rope. To pass the physical fitness test, the lieutenants had to run this not once, but twice, and get it done in less than three minutes. The physical challenge followed a three-mile run with a sixty-pound pack.

Ray Smith first became aware of Steele's O-course obsession one night in June, midway through the twenty-one-week-long training course. It was a hot, muggy night, and the air was thick with sweet honeysuckle. A crackling chorus of katydids in the woods reminded Smith of how far he had strayed from his old terrain out west.

Only a year ago, he was a carefree mountain man, hiking the Rockies among hawks and eagles and enjoying clear views of Montana's infinite possibilities. Now he was stuck on a southern military base with precious little time for himself. Smith longed to get back to the fresh air of the Rockies, far from Quantico's poison ivy and muddy trenches with barbed wire only inches above your nose.

He was lost in thought about Montana when he noticed something move behind O'Bannon Hall. Someone, or something, was scurrying about the field outside the dormitory. It appeared to be a gung-ho grunt out for some extra calisthenics. Sometimes he wished his fellow lieutenants would lighten up once in a while. Even during free time, this nut was trying to shave a few precious seconds off his O-course time.

Ray could see how the proud work ethic of the Marine Corps could drive men to such extremes, though. It was how the organization got rid of all but the most willing—or stubborn—players.

The class of 5-67, as it was known, began with 542 men, but over the first couple of months, two dozen had dropped out. This left 516 hormonally-charged guys fighting to prove themselves at every turn.

Smith peered into the darkness, where fireflies flitted in and out of the night. He noticed something familiar about the figure running in and out the shadows.

It was his roommate, Martin R. Steele, the outspoken and irascible native of Fayetteville, Arkansas, who had dropped out of college to join the Marines when Vietnam started heating up. Perhaps because they both started as enlisted men, they had become fast friends—even though they were as different as hot, humid Virginia and cold, clear Montana.

Steele was the passionate perfectionist who was never happy with himself and always ready to pull all-nighters with the books. Smith was no less determined to succeed, but he had that rare knack for keeping his reading to a minimum while managing to coolly ace most tests. Smith also was a gifted athlete, but one who enjoyed competition rather than painful exercise. He sometimes appeared at Steele's off-campus apartment with a couple of baseball mitts and, tossing a ball up and down, asked his friend if he wanted to play catch. Smith's off-handed ability to do well without working too hard drove Marty Steele crazy.

The sight of his relentless roommate was too tempting to resist. Smith zigzagged over to the field, and when Steele was close by, he jumped up and shouted in a command voice, "Lieutenant, atten-hut!"

Steele skidded to a stop and stood stock still. He looked around in the darkness, searching for the officer who had issued the command. Smith jumped out of the shadow, guffawing.

"Jesus, Smith, are you nuts?" Steele screamed, kicking the grass. "I could have sprained my ankle from stopping so fast."

Smith laughed. "*What* are you doing down here at this time of night?"

Steele was drenched in sweat. He wore faded gold gym shorts, a red T-shirt, and white high tops. At five foot nine, he had a compact build with muscular arms and legs that were like coiled springs ready to pump iron.

"I'm practicing," he replied.

"Practicing?" Smith scoffed. "For what? Hasn't the Corps gotten its pound of flesh out of you today?"

Steele ignored the wisecrack and shook his calves to keep them loose. "I'm practicing for the double running of the O-course race. I aim to smash the record."

Smith laughed again. That was just like Marty Steele. It was hard enough running the O-course twice, but Quantico's stifling heat and humidity provided another obstacle. It wasn't unusual for men to collapse in the summer sun and get thrown into tubs of ice to stave off heatstroke.

"Isn't it bad enough they make us run it twice without trying to kill yourself getting ready for it?"

Steele thought that over with a furrowed brow and the conscientious look of a penitent. Since becoming roommates in The Basic School dormitory at O'Bannon Hall, Smith had realized that Steele was the most intense and idealistic man he'd ever met. At twenty years of age, Marty Steele was the youngest officer at the school. Yet he was one of the few who had actually been in combat, two years earlier while serving with a tank battalion near Danang. In this school of warrior monks, Steele already had a leg up on the competition. Smith wondered if Steele's time in combat was what fueled his intensity. He seemed to already know the answers to the nagging questions lurking in the back of every lieutenant's mind: *How will I do under fire? How will I react when my life is on the line? Will I prove myself worthy to be a Marine?*

Steele kept to himself about Vietnam, making veiled allusions to nighttime ops against the VC and one tough mission to find the body of a dead buddy. And yet you could ask Steele anything else about the military trade and he might deliver a dissertation worthy of Clausewitz, the nineteenth-century Prussian military strategist on their reading list.

"You're wondering why I'm out here getting ready for the double run of the O-course?" Steele said. "Let me ask you something. Do you think the enemy goes beddy-bye every night, and lets the Marines stay tucked in, all nice and cozy?"

Smith protested. "I didn't mean that, Steele."

"And," Steele went on, "do you think that when you are in combat, you are somehow going to know exactly when and how your body will respond to the stress of being under fire?"

This got Smith's attention. Like every other lieutenant-in-training, Ray Smith wondered how he would respond to being in real combat. Would he wilt under pressure as a few men always did, or would he rise to the occasion? And how far could he rise?

Steele continued, "We need to do all we can to condition our bodies to endure the highest levels of stress and pain. You know what they say: Pain is just your body's way of getting rid of weakness."

Smith chuckled. "You are a piece of work, Steele. You've managed to make your crazy work ethic into some kind of new training dictum for the Marine Corps."

Steele accepted the backhanded compliment, then got back to work, doing wind sprints on the grass with the quick, mincing steps of a running back. Every twenty yards of so, he dropped to the ground and did thirty pushups followed by fifty sit-ups. He turned at the end of the field and dashed back in the darkness. Pulling up in front of his roommate, Steele said, "I'm practicing some new footwork. You want me to demonstrate?"

Smith declined the offer. "It's been a long day, and Colleen's probably worried because I'm late for dinner."

They strode into O'Bannon Hall, a three-story tan cinderblock building with all the elegance of a minimum security prison. It was named for Presley O'Bannon, an early Marine sent to North Africa to protect American merchant vessels against the Barbary pirates. President Thomas Jefferson dispatched the troops aboard a squadron to the Mediterranean in 1804. In this clash of Christian and Islamic cultures, O'Bannon helped defeat a much larger Arab force and sign a peace treaty in the Libyan city of Tripoli. After peace was restored, an allied Arab leader presented O'Bannon with a Mameluke scimitar, a curved sword that became part of the Marine officer's accoutrements. The victory was immortalized in the first line of the Marine Hymn: "From the halls of Montezuma, to the shores of Tripoli."[3]

That battle in North Africa had many of the elements that help define the role of the Marine Corps in America's defense: a small band of men faces off against a much larger force in an exotic locale that is deemed vital to America's strategic interests—in the North African case, protecting shipping lanes from pirates. Working with whatever Arab allies they could find, O'Bannon's tiny squad—only one sergeant and six privates from the ship *Argus*—charged through Tripoli, seized a fort on the harbor, and took over the palace. Such audacity and guts stamped the Marines as America's elite military force, one that could rightly adopt the motto stamped on the brass plates of their early uniforms: *Fortitudine*—"with fortitude."[4]

Fortitude, yes, but leavened with a sense of humor and sometimes even rebellion. For if they were putting their lives on the line, the lieutenants were determined to enjoy themselves in what little time they had left.

Opening the door of their room, Steele and Smith caught a whiff of their crimes against good housekeeping. "Our room is a pit," Smith said, switching on the ceiling light. "But I'll be damned if I'll clean it."

Steele shook his head and laughed. "Me neither."

Their messy room had become their own conspiracy against the Corps and particularly one obnoxious major who liked to bust lieutenants during Saturday morning inspections. Smith and Steele made a pact to defy the major's prissy standards. Now they looked around at the results of their defiance: dirty T-shirts hung off the bunk beds like ancient stalactites; old socks gave the floor a mossy look; dust balls skittered across the linoleum floor. This violated every tenet of military decorum, but they loved it. Stepping on a dust ball, Steele declared, "Lieutenant Smith, under the code of military justice, I hereby convict you of felonious housekeeping. This place is a pig sty, even for a razorback like me."

Smith pulled up a chair and looked about with a raised eyebrow. "It is pretty damn ugly. How long do you think we can keep this up?"

With the help of a sympathetic captain, they had gotten their room designated as a "supply closet." Somehow the hard-ass major had accepted this explanation, and bypassed them during his Saturday inspections. It had worked for several weeks now, but as Steele slipped out of his gym clothes and sniffed the air, he said, "Who knows? I guess we're safe until the odor seeps under the door and out into the hall. Of course, our room could be considered a top secret experiment."

Smith leaned forward, wondering what Steele was driving at. "How so?"

Steele sprayed on some deodorant. "Germ warfare, obviously. Some of your socks could be lethal if put under the noses of the enemy. If we mass produced them and shipped them over to 'Nam, Ho Chi Minh might surrender."

Smith laughed and wondered if this was a good time to pump Marty for more information about what it was really like to fight in a war. He tried to respect his roommate's privacy, but he still wanted to know what it was Steele wasn't saying. Why did he fall quiet sometimes when the subject came up?

Steele seemed in a hurry and only in the mood for light banter about the room. Smith hoped they would find time later to talk about it.

☆ ☆ ☆

When Ray Smith got home that night, his wife had dinner waiting in their small apartment in Woodbridge. He had met Colleen at a mixer in Washington and married her two months later. She was pretty and outspoken and had the kind of spunk that he admired in a woman. Moving near the Quantico Marine Base, Colleen had cheerfully accepted the modest living conditions of the military wife. She hauled down her own furniture from Washington to live in the one-bedroom apartment. Her mother had lived through World War II and managed to raise a family by herself. Colleen was glad she and her husband didn't have any kids yet and could enjoy the good times with other lieutenants and their ladies who liked to "party hearty," drinking and dancing late into the night. Among them was Marty Steele's wife, Cindy, who led the line dancing when "Long Tall Texan" was put on the record player.

The partying ended, though, as the military wives made do on their husbands' monthly paychecks of $300. Signs of this economic struggle were evident in the *Quantico Sentry*, the base newspaper, which ran ads such as this one for Liberty Loan: "Whether you want a $50 loan 'til payday . . . or a larger amount to $600, you can depend on Liberty's quick money service for military men and women."

There were some bargains around town. Peerless Cleaners in the town of Quantico offered dry-cleaning specials for plain dresses for 89 cents. And a 1962 Rambler station wagon, listed in excellent condition, sold for $350.

The wives stuck together. Each was a daughter of the military—Cindy's father was an Army colonel, and Colleen's a chief warrant officer—so they knew how to use the post exchange and commissary. Still, it was challenging buying groceries and other supplies on the shoestring budget of a lieutenant. Colleen and Cindy sometimes rubbed elbows with senior officers but rarely talked to them. There was an invisible caste system on the base and they knew better than to start chatting with anyone over the rank of lieutenant.

Colleen Smith, who supplemented their income with a job in Washington, took pride in sticking to an austere food budget of $14 a week—a tight rein that wasn't always easy to keep with a husband who ate like a horse. All she asked in return was some conversation. Her father had always told amusing stories about his day, so she was expecting the same from her husband.

As Ray Smith sat down to consume the large meal she had prepared after getting home from work, Colleen pulled up a chair beside him and said eagerly, "Well, honey, what did you do today?"

"Not much," Smith replied, between crunches of fried chicken.

"C'mon, Ray!" his wife protested. "That's not acceptable. If you expect me to slave over a hot stove to fix you dinner, you're going to have to tell me what's going on in your life!"

He realized his tactical mistake and tried to tell her about that day's "problem"—the hypothetical battle the lieutenants fought in a mock Vietnamese village out in the woods. The enlisted instructors wore the black pajamas of the Viet Cong and played the role of guerillas, surprising the lieutenants with smoke bombs and non-lethal booby traps. No shots were fired in these war games, and the only "kills" were numbers recorded in a grade book.

Colleen listened intently. She loved everything about the Marines—their planning, their intensity, their commitment to winning every battle they were called to fight. But she'd watched enough TV to know that Vietnam was a dangerous place that was taking a mounting toll on young soldiers and Marines.

☆ ☆ ☆

The summer of 1967 became known as "the Summer of Love" as LSD-laced punch became all the rage around San Francisco, and college students and various adult pied pipers traded their books for bongs, leaving the old straight life behind for . . . well, whatever turned them on. The world of love beads and peace signs might as well have been happening on Mars for all it mattered to the clean-cut lieutenants who were staring straight into the unblinking eyes of their own mortality. The uncertain future helped draw their wives together as everyone tried to get a bead on their lives after Basic School. Since Marty Steele was training to be a tank commander, he'd be one of the lucky few who wouldn't be shipped off immediately to lead a rifle platoon in Vietnam. He and his wife, Cindy, prepared to move to Camp Lejeune for more artillery training.

"What about Ray?" Cindy asked her friend Colleen Smith, "Has he told you what's going on?"

Colleen shook her head in disgust. "You know how hard it is to get a word out of him."

They laughed about their husbands' unlikely friendship. Marty was so intense, always pulling all-nighters to cram for his exams, while Ray was easygoing and tried to get home every night to relax. By morning, he would return to their dorm room and find Marty bug-eyed from hours of reading. Ray liked to play dumb, but he usually managed to score as high on the tests as his workaholic roommate.

"That drives Marty crazy!" Cindy confided.

They loved analyzing their hard-driven men who could still act like boys. For Colleen, it was a way to avoid thinking about the inevitable. She knew her husband's orders were coming and couldn't bear the thought of him leaving for the mess that unfolded on the evening news each night.

To blow off steam, she wrote a letter to President Johnson to express her disapproval of the strategy of fighting "a war of containment" against the communists. She told the president to let the Marines and Army troops cross the seventeenth parallel into North Vietnam and let them fight the war to win it, not to avoid losing it. And she posed a question to the president, who had two daughters: "If you had a son, would you send him?" (Johnson soon had a son-in-law, Chuck Robb, a Marine officer who was sent to Vietnam.)

Before Colleen could get her appeal sent off to the White House, her husband saw it and ripped it up. "What are you thinking, Colleen?" he said. "If any higher-ups read this, I'll get my ass chewed out. And it won't make a damn bit of difference."

He hugged her and tried to reassure her. "But please," he said, "don't cry." She was only allowed to cry when the orders came— and in this, she wasn't alone.

Each married lieutenant had a moment of truth with his spouse. Jim Jones, for his part, already had scrapped an earlier plan to move Diane to Florida for flight training school. This change of heart came months ago, before he even came to Quantico. After he enlisted in the Corps in the summer of 1966, he talked with his recruiting officer, Ron Beckwith, about his interest in flying.

"Want to go for a spin?" Beckwith asked.

Never one to turn down a challenge, Jones accepted. The next thing he knew he was jamming his six-foot-five frame into the back of a small training plane, sweating bullets in the 110-degree heat at Andrews Air Force Base in Washington.

"Ready for some fun?" Beckwith called over the noise of the airplane engine.

Ready or not, the pilot eased forward on the throttle and took off over the Potomac. Once they had gained some altitude, he executed a series of barrel rolls. The midair fun quickly dispelled any fantasy Jones had of becoming a flying ace. As he turned green and peered upside down at the pencil-shaped Washington Monument, he had little doubt that his future lay solidly on the ground.

Later, his desire to become an infantry officer heated up after a talk by a captain just back from Vietnam. The Marine in his green combat fatigues had a slightly world-weary air about him. He was every inch the warrior.

The captain spoke earnestly about the need for young leaders willing to fight, and maybe even die, in Vietnam. After the talk, Jones marched into his company's office and signed up for his Military Occupational Speciality, or MOS. He chose the gold standard for a Marine officer—O-3, infantry.

That night, driving back up Interstate 95 toward his apartment in Washington, he realized he'd failed to discuss his career choice with Diane. Not only were they not going to Florida—his early dream—but he'd soon be shipping out to Vietnam.

It was the first of many snap decisions Diane Jones would learn after the fact—a trend that would continue for years to come.

★ ★ ★

Before graduation on August 30, 1967, each of the 516 lieutenants received an official letter with an MOS. There were few surprises, as nearly the entire class was O-3, a free ticket to Vietnam.

The letters arrived before a final reception in the Hawkins Room, otherwise known as the Hawk. With pool tables and pinball machines, the Hawk's décor mixes a college frat house with a military museum. A wild boar's head juts menacingly from the brick wall over a mantle, right above a glass case. The case contains the elegantly curved Mameluke sword presented by the grateful Arab warlord to the pioneering Marine, Lt. Presley O'Bannon. Every year, O'Bannon's sword is used to honor the top lieutenant.

The juke box was playing "If You're Going to San Francisco," with its alluring invitation to come out west and escape reality: "wear some flowers in your hair."

The women swirling into the darkened club knew their men faced a far different fate, one that had nothing to do with flowers and peace and love. They would have to put helmets over their hair and hope they came back with their skulls intact.

Colleen Smith looked around the reception and saw some long faces among some men in Ray's Lima Company. They asked her if she knew Ray's MOS.

"Of course," she said. "Ray has never wanted anything but O-3 and Vietnam."

Not all of the Marines were so eager to go, though. Colleen could see that in their eyes. This group of reluctant warriors included a wiry lieutenant from Alexandria named Barry Kowalski. He had grown up around the corner from the Jones house overlooking the Potomac and had befriended young Jim after he arrived from Paris for his senior year in high school.

After graduating from Brown University, where antiwar sentiment was brewing, Barry Kowalski became deeply opposed to the war. Barry had joined the Marines anyway, as a way to lend credibility to his opposition. What better way to gain credibility, he figured, than to actually serve in Vietnam?

Technically, Barry should never have been allowed to enlist in the Marines. He was a quarter inch below the minimum height of five foot six. He met a recruiter in downtown Washington, Capt. Tony Studds, who was eager to find a way for him to get into the Corps. As he measured Kowalski, Studds ordered, "Stretch, son!"

Kowalski lifted his head, threw back his shoulders, and gave every inch of himself for Corps and country.

Studds shook his hand. "Congratulations," he said. "You're now tall enough to be a U.S. Marine."

The captain also ignored the fact that Barry Kowalski was legally blind, with 20/600 vision, and had to wear his thick glasses to have any chance of seeing the enemy. His vision problem was more than physical, though. As the time neared to ship out for Vietnam, he could not see himself killing another human being. At least not in this war, which he believed was an anticommunist crusade waged by Johnson for purely political reasons to prove he wasn't "soft" on communism.

Kowalski stifled his doubts for months at OCS and Basic School. Finally, he felt like he had to talk to somebody, and he asked Jim Jones to stop by his room in O'Bannon Hall. Closing the door behind him, Barry said nervously, "Sit down, Jim, I've got something to tell you."

Then he promptly spilled his doubts about the war, and Johnson, and the whole frigging mess. He told Jones he'd been mulling over an escape plan with his father, a retired congressman from Connecticut.

"My dad says he knows people who could help me get across the border to Canada."

Jones tried to laugh it off. "Canada? You planning on playing hockey, Barry?"

Jones was always the kidder, but Kowalski had to make him see this was serious business. "Goddammit, Jim, listen to me! I'm dead serious. I can't go to Vietnam. Not only will I get my ass shot up, but my men could get killed if my heart's not in it."

This got Jones's attention. "I don't know, Barry," he said, shifting uncomfortably. "Wouldn't that be . . ."

"Desertion?" Kowalski said, completing his thought. "Yeah, that's what I mean, that's why I can't do it—even though I think it would be the right thing to do under the circumstances. It's a bad war, Jim, being fought for all the wrong reasons. Politics, not national security. It's all to feed Johnson's ego and the Democrats' desire for reelection."

Kowalski had worked for the Democratic Party in Washington and knew a good deal about politics. Even Johnson's vice president, Hubert Humphrey, secretly harbored doubts about the morass of Vietnam.

"Aw, I don't know, Barry," Jones said, spreading his hands. As much as he liked his old high school pal, he secretly wished they'd never crossed paths in Quantico. What could he say? He felt compelled to state the obvious. "We're just lieutenants," he said, "sworn to follow the orders of our commander in chief."

Kowalski cut in. "Even if those orders are immoral?"

Jones got up. "Barry, I'm sorry, I really am. But I just don't agree with you."

He shook Kowalski's hand and left. Kowalski sat alone in his room, knowing he was bound for Vietnam, not Canada, and with only himself to blame.

☆ ☆ ☆

They were as ready to face combat as they would ever be. Jim Jones felt comfortable that he knew his trade as an infantry leader, from shooting rifles and machine guns, to executing small-unit tactics. Ray Smith and Marty Steele also were itching to test their new skills in real combat. Each man's leadership potential was reflected in the final class rankings posted outside the instructors' offices in Heywood Hall: Out of 516 men who completed Basic School, Jim Jones graduated nineteenth, with a final cumulative score of nearly 92 percent; Marty Steele placed eighty-third; and Ray Smith took the 119th position, both with a final score in the high eighties.

Yet before leaving Quantico, Steele was determined to make his mark one more time with the double running of the obstacle course. Breaking the record by finishing in less than two minutes wouldn't improve his class standing, nor was it likely to gain him much recognition. It was simply a personal feat he wanted to achieve—despite Smith's ribbing about his nighttime training exercises.

One sauna-like day in August, as the heat and humidity made Quantico feel like a waffle iron, Steele lined up for the final running of the course. He wore his utilities, without a cap or blouse, and combat boots. While his colleagues approached the running of the O-course as another day's work, Steele was different. His jaw was clenched with tension and his eyes were locked on the course with laserlike intensity. His extra practice was about to pay off.

The men took off in pairs at thirty-second intervals.

"Go!" a sergeant barked, starting the stopwatch.

Steele broke from the starting line and raced over the first log on the course like a tiger pursuing an antelope. He dashed to the next obstacle—an eight-foot-pole—and launched himself over it like it wasn't there. He landed and leaped over another log. He left his classmates in the dust as he scaled a six-foot-high wooden wall like Spiderman. He made short shrift of the other poles and logs and reached the last hurdle: a twenty-five-foot-high rope. He shimmied to the top, tapped the wooden bar, and slid to the ground. Then he ran down the middle of the course back to the starting line and got ready to do it again.

The sergeant with the stopwatch smiled grudgingly. Steele led the pack with a wicked pace of under forty seconds. He seemed assured of shattering the record.

Steele started his second lap, but by now his body was drenched in sweat, and he was starting to gasp for air. Still, he forged ahead and at long last reached the final obstacle again. Somehow he found the strength to start pulling himself up the twenty-five-foot-high rope.

A group of sergeants gathered around the timekeeper, marveling at Steele's performance—only in the middle of his last climb, the lieutenant stopped cold and was stuck in midair. A jolt of pain shot from his ankle to his thigh. At first, he dismissed it as a cramp—a familiar feeling from his football playing days. Yet this was something else, a bad sensation beyond comprehension. All he could do was hang on like a paralyzed monkey.

"Just touch the top, Steele!" the timekeeper hollered. "You've already broken the record."

Steele tried to reply, but nothing came out of his mouth. It seemed to be sealed shut. His head was spinning, and he had no idea how long he could hang on.

More men gathered below. Steele had hit the wall and may have had heatstroke. The timekeeper had seen enough and yelled, "Corpsman!"

Finally, after clinging for what seemed like hours, Steele managed to loosen his grip and slide down to the ground. He was carried to a waiting ambulance, where he was gently put into a bucket full of ice.

Steele stared at the white ceiling of the ambulance as it drove away from the course. He could hear its siren, but it seemed to come from a mile away. His teeth started chattering, reminding him of the last time he had been this cold. It was in Vietnam on his first tour of duty. He had never told his friend Ray Smith about that horrible experience, when he had to find a buddy's corpse in a frozen storage refrigerator.

Was he dying now? He winced from the pain of the cold piercing his skin like a thousand needles.

"You're going to be okay, lieutenant," the corpsman reassured him. "You just got a little carried away out there. It's early stage heatstroke."

Marty tried to reply but could only grunt in affirmation. His mind cleared, and he felt like he was watching himself in a movie. He pictured Cindy getting a call at home to meet him at the base hospital. She would be worried sick, and probably pissed. She was always telling him not to overdo things, but somehow her advice never sunk in. He had that record in his sights and had come within a couple of feet of breaking it before his body simply shut down.

As he cooled off and his teeth chattered, he sensed this was not his day to die. Vietnam was calling him to duty, and he damn well wasn't going to let a little heatstroke get in the way.

FOUR

Under the Enemy's Guns

The Marine Corps was assigned to patrol and defend the northern tier of South Vietnam, a rugged, mountainous region whose caves, jungles, and river valleys provided ideal cover for the enemy. By late 1967, as the rains of the winter monsoon fell, the hardened troops of Ho Chi Minh's North Vietnamese army were flooding across the border, with an estimated 200,000 in country— a number that nearly equaled the American forces of Ho's nemesis, President Lyndon B. Johnson.

The broader geopolitical picture was not easily grasped by the lieutenants reporting for duty from Quantico. They had more immediate concerns, such as keeping their men fed, clothed, and equipped. Among the new arrivals were platoon leaders Ray Smith and Jim Jones. They soon realized that Vietnam's realities were going to be much messier and disorganized than the war games they had been playing back home.

Jones was dismayed to find his men in the 2nd Battalion, 3rd Marines, suffering from severe shortages of supplies, ammunition, and rations. Even their backpacks and boots were tattered and worn, with some equipment dating back to the Korean War. It was shocking to see the state of disrepair, especially compared to the Army. Plus, around this time the Marines were making the transition from the M-14 to the M-16 rifle. The M-16 was a lightweight weapon, capable of single shots, short bursts of semiautomatic fire, and automatic fire. It worked well under clean conditions; unfortunately, Vietnam was a messy, mud-caked place.

In the muck and mire, the M-16 could be a nightmare. It sometimes jammed in the heat of battle, becoming notorious for malfunctioning just when the Marines needed it the most.

After frontline Marines began complaining in 1967, the Corps investigated the problem and found three out of every four of the rifles had structural flaws—pits in their firing chambers that could block bullets or prevent any possibility of hitting a target. The Corps' leadership scrambled to replace the pitted rifles, but only after an untold number of Marines died defenseless in the jungle.[1]

When Jones's platoon wasn't patrolling the countryside, the soldiers took time to find supplies—often courtesy of the U.S. Army. "We found ways to liberate Army supplies, which is an old Marine tradition going back many wars," he recalled.

Even the Army didn't have good rain gear, though, and the poncho was pitifully short to keep a big man like Jones dry. He wrote his wife, complaining about how soggy he was getting in the monsoon rains. So Diane Jones drove to the nearest Sears and bought a fisherman's rain suit, complete with trousers and a zippered jacket. Thanks to timely mail service, the tall lieutenant was soon marching about in his Ted Williams custom garb. Wearing a jacket bearing the Williams stamp was fitting, though: The Boston Red Sox slugger had left his record-setting career behind to serve as a Marine aviator during World War II and the Korean War.

For the newly arrived lieutenants in Vietnam, foraging for supplies or covers was relatively easy compared to following the complex, and sometimes questionable, orders they would get from their battalion commanders. As platoon leaders, the lieutenants were the advance guard for large-scale operations that often had dubious, even nonexistent, strategic ends. Too often, they were put in confusing and risky positions in the rocky countryside near the border with North Vietnam. Their experiences in these early battles would leave indelible marks on their hearts and minds, forever reshaping their thinking about life, death, and the importance of trusting one's instincts in combat.

On this score, Jim Jones and Ray Smith were catching up to their classmate Marty Steele, who had already learned the ropes during his first tour of duty in 1965. As a lance corporal and corporal with the 1st Tank Battalion of the 1st Marine Division, Steele had seen how vulnerable the Americans were when they left the safety of their compounds. Steele had served on many combat missions, patrolling treacherous terrain that had been expertly booby-trapped by the Viet Cong. He managed to dismantle huge wooden "Malayan gates," traps designed to drop down on unwitting interlopers, impaling them into the dank jungle floor.

One day in 1965, Marty Steele made an important discovery near Chu Lai, an American base on the South China Sea. It was a huge oasis with enough fresh water to supply an entire division. Its strategic value was evident by the number of traps the Viet Cong had put in place, including hand grenades on trip wires and enough Malayan gates to trap a herd of elephants. Steele led a squad that defused the explosives and took over the water supply. In recognition for his work, he received a meritorious battlefield promotion to corporal.

During this first tour of duty, Steele, barely twenty years old, witnessed the randomness of war. One of his friends, a kid named Eddie, was shot and killed on a routine patrol outside the barbedwire confines of Chu Lai. If only Eddie had been in a tank, Steele thought, he wouldn't have been so vulnerable. Steele made a personal vow to make the tank more of a part of the Marines' arsenal, shielding the good guys with as much armor as possible.

His friend's death became an even more pivotal event for Steele when he learned that the body had never been properly tagged over at an Army medical evacuation center. Without proper identification, Eddie, a street kid from south Philadelphia, would never get home for a proper burial.

After his performance in finding the Viet Cong's water supply, Steele was chosen by his battalion commander to find the dead

Marine and put a toe tag on the corpse. He had only the foggiest notion of where to find the body, but before he knew it, a jeep arrived from headquarters, and he was being whisked over to Chu Lai's medical compound. It was a shocking sight, like an old painting he used to see in his mother's religious literature— scenes of pain and suffering, with faces frozen in agony in the lower rungs of hell. Only this modern Hades used Huey helicopters to ferry the dead and badly wounded into medical stations along this "River Styx." The doctors used triage, operating only on those Marines and Army troops who seemed to have some chance of survival. The unlucky ones were carted out and stored in a makeshift morgue set up inside refrigerated storage boxes.

Steele warily approached an Army sergeant sitting out front. "I'm looking for a Marine," he said uncertainly. "Do you have any kind of . . ." He searched for the right word. ". . . list?" He started to explain his mission but was cut off. The sergeant looked dazed and depressed.

"In there," he said, waving impatiently behind him. "See for yourself."

Steele trudged over to the refrigerated units, which looked like some kind of converted containers from ocean-going ships. They had once carried pineapples or grapefruits picked from tropical plantations. Now they carried a much more precious cargo.

Steele swung open the door and stepped inside. He gasped at the underworld sight in the dim light. Bodies were stacked like cord wood—fifty, maybe seventy-five corpses in various states of undoing. Some had lost legs, others lacked arms, and a few were headless. The faces that remained seemed to stare right past Steele into a bottomless pit of time and suffering.

Though he was on a mission, Steele felt guilty being in this cold storage bin of the dead. He felt he was somehow disturbing their hard-won peace. He didn't want to look into their frozen faces, but he had no choice. Eddie was in here somewhere, and he had to find him. Marines did not leave their brothers behind.

He stepped gingerly between the bodies and tried to picture Eddie. He was a brown-eyed, black-haired, wiry youth who fit the classic enlisted Marine profile—struggled in school, had some scrapes with the law, but had plenty of street smarts that could be channeled in boot camp. Eddie would have made a fine tank driver, with his boldness and experience at hot-wiring cars and driving them on the back streets to Philly's chop shops.

But now the car thief-turned-Marine was in this strange human chop shop, where the rank smell of death was unmistakable despite the attempts to keep it on ice. Steele paced the aisle, gently lifting bodies and looking for his friend's noble Italian-American face. After an hour of searching this mass of humanity—white, black, and brown—he began to despair of ever finding him.

Then the cold set in and his teeth started to chatter. He knew he couldn't stay much longer and felt overwhelmed by the elements and the tough assignment. Finally, he broke down in tears and cried out, "Please, God, let me find him. Not for me, but for his family—and for the Marines. Please!"

After his quick prayer, Marty felt strangely calm. Rubbing his hands to stay warm, he decided to make one last try, searching a far corner that seemed to have escaped his notice. In the pale light, his eyes were drawn to one particular body with its back to him. The corpse wore the green camouflaged uniform of a Marine, with a red stain showing through the back. The fatal wound, Steele thought. The body was drawn up into a fetal position. Marty turned it over and saw his prayer was answered: Eddie.

His face was clear and appeared unscathed. Steele half-expected him to speak. After watching him for a while, Steele said, "Man, am I glad it's you. I didn't think I'd ever find you."

Steele was so moved that he hugged the body and thanked God for helping him. He shed a few tears on the kid's frozen face.

Then he went outside to warm up.

"I found him," Steele told the grumpy gatekeeper by the door.

"Who?" the sergeant said. The river of death seemed to have drowned the man's emotions.

"Never mind," Steele said. There was no point in explaining. He asked for an identification tag, went back inside, and set to work completing his task. He untied a boot and removed a decaying sock. He carefully printed his name, rank, serial number, and hometown—Philadelphia, Pa., USA—on the tag. Then he gently tied it around the big toe of his right foot. Maybe now Eddie would get a decent burial.

Steele hated to leave him alone like this. He wondered whether anyone back in Philly would actually take care of a former juvenile delinquent. So before leaving, he kneeled beside him and said the Lord's Prayer.

"May you rest in peace," he said, making the sign of the cross on his forehead. This might be the only service his friend would get.

★ ★ ★

Ray Smith's first brush with death came in late November 1967, about a month after he joined the 1st Battalion, 1st Marine Division. They were operating in a dangerous area known as Leatherneck Square, the four-sided region of Marine outposts spread over hundreds of square miles near the border of North Vietnam. This put them in easy shooting distance of the enemy artillery batteries dug in across from the euphemistically named "demilitarized zone," or DMZ. They also were near enemy infiltration routes from North to South Vietnam.

Only two months earlier, the Marines lost nearly 1,000 dead and wounded around Leatherneck Square—a number that would swell five-fold by year's end.[2] Disgusted by the heavy losses, the Marine leadership wanted to get their troops out of this dug-in, defensive posture and take the fight to the enemy. But the theater commander, Army general William Westmoreland, insisted that the Marines stay and defend their line of exposed bases.

One of the most galling orders came directly from Secretary of Defense Robert McNamara. The former Ford executive, a true believer in modern technology, insisted that the Marine Corps erect a thirty-four-kilometer-long line of forts, mines, and electronic sensors. It was the latest in a string of gimmicky projects that started in 1962, when the Kennedy administration ordered the construction of "strategic hamlets" in South Vietnam. The rural relief project was meant to win the hearts and minds of peasants laboring in rubber plantations north of Saigon.[3] But the effort was undone by the effective propaganda of the Viet Cong, along with abuses of power by the pro-American leadership in Saigon. It was hard to sell the Vietnamese people on the power of democracy when all they got in return was another corrupt regime.

Yet McNamara pushed ahead with the high-tech equivalent of the Maginot Line, which had failed to protect France from Hitler's invasion in World War II. It fell to the Marines, under intense shelling and ground fire, to try to build what came to be known as the McNamara Line.[4] Marine lieutenant general Victor "Brute" Krulak, who led the Pacific command, urged Westmoreland to face "the brutal facts" that the Marines were "under the enemy's guns." Krulak wrote that Ho Chi Minh's goal was "to get us as near to his weapons and to his forces as possible, drench us with high-angle fire weapons, engage us in close and violent combat, accept willingly a substantial loss of life for the opportunity to kill a lesser number of our men, and to withdraw into his North Vietnam sanctuary to refurbish."[5]

Backing this position, Lt. Gen. Lewis W. Walt said any defenses "should *free* Marine forces for operations elsewhere, not *freeze* such forces in a barrier-watching defensive role."[6]

Another Marine general caustically observed that one American base resembled a wagon train deployed in concentric circles to fend off an Indian attack. He compared one compound on the McNamara Line to an octagonal fort—an allusion to Dienbienphu, site of France's last stand against communist forces in 1954.[7] After that bloody defeat, the French pulled out of Vietnam, ending decades of colonial presence and creating a power vacuum that ultimately sucked in the United States a decade later.

★ ★ ★

As he set out on his first foot patrols, 2nd Lt. Ray Smith could have known little about the debates over military strategy and foreign policy raging in Saigon and Washington. He just knew that this was some pretty rough terrain, certainly much worse than anything he'd experienced around Quantico. When he started out,

Smith figured he would do his duty, his superiors would do their part, and everything would work out for the best.

On November 26, 1967, Lieutenant Smith was ordered to take his platoon on a probing mission outside the hilltop compound at Con Thienh. Months of shelling by the North Vietnamese had scraped much of the mountainous terrain down to bare red rock. Yet the hillside still had plenty of underbrush, fruit trees, and bamboo, the vestiges of an experimental farm left behind by the French. Bananas and pears still dangled above the sloping fields. This abandoned Eden was being exploited by the North Vietnamese, who were steeped in the attack-and-retreat tactics of the guru of modern guerilla warfare, Mao Tse Tung. The rotting orchard was a textbook setting for putting Chairman Mao's ideas into practice.

The Vietnamese called Con Thienh "the Hill of Angels," but the Marines had another name for it: "the Graveyard."[8] In early 1967, the North inflicted heavy casualties when four battalions of Marines ventured out of the barbed-wire confines of the compound. An entire company of men—160 Marines—was killed or wounded.

Now Lieutenant Smith had orders to repeat the same kind of search-and-destroy mission. Only this time, the Marines were risking fewer men with less firepower—one company, compared to the four battalions that tangled with the NVA in the last major skirmish. The intelligence was poor, with no solid estimate of the enemy's troop strength. As luck would have it, Smith's thirty-eight-man platoon was leading the mission.

Before leaving the compound, Smith expressed his concerns about getting ambushed to his battalion commander. Lt. Col. Marcus Gravel shook his head and admitted his own misgivings. But orders were orders. Someone at division headquarters thought it was time to probe the area.

Smith smelled trouble but had to ignore his instincts. He told his squad leaders to have the men check their ammunition. "I got a feeling we'll need it," he said.

Then he tried to explain their orders to corporals and sergeants who already had plenty of combat under their belts. The platoon would leave the compound at the head of a wedge formation. "We'll march in a kind of box around the hilltop, starting by heading west through the bush," he said. "We're supposed to blow up any enemy bunkers we find along the way."

With that, they left their armed camp, opening the gate onto the Hill of Angels. His men set to work destroying bunkers hidden in the orchard, throwing grenades into caves above the path. A drum roll of explosions echoed across the mountain and into the valley below. The Marines were just following orders, but damn, Smith thought, we sure are loud.

The enemy wasted no time in responding. Starting with staccato bursts from Russian-made AK-47 assault rifles, the North Vietnamese orchestrated a near-perfect ambush. Their rifle fire was augmented by the deep-throated roar of machine guns, punctuated by the crack of Chinese-made hand grenades. Saving the worst for last, they started lobbing in mortar shells that first toppled apple trees, then took out point men.

"Hit the deck!" Smith yelled. But it was too late, and his entire platoon was either pinned down or hit. Taking it on the chin was his nine-man point squad led by Garry Lynn Ihrig, a twenty-year-old corporal from Parkville, Missouri.

"Give me some tanks!" Smith shouted over the radio. "We're taking heavy fire."

The tanks were only a few hundred yards away. But because of the earlier massacre at Con Thienh, Smith's company commander balked at sending in reinforcements.

That fucking asshole, Smith thought. He's hanging us out to dry. It wasn't a cowardly decision, and it may have even been a prudent one, like what they taught back at The Basic School. But this was a long way from the classroom, and Ray sensed that this by-the-book captain was going to get them all killed.

Corporal Ihrig was shot in the throat and died where he fell. Other men were going down, including one with a leg wound that was bleeding badly. Corpsman Michael John Thirkettle spotted the wounded man pinned down in front of a machine-gun bunker.

Thirkettle was a big, blond surfer from southern California. At age twenty, he was seen by the younger men as a seasoned veteran, a Beach Boy with guts and Silver Star and Bronze Star medals to prove it.

Now the surfer-corpsman disdained any thoughts about his own life and ran through a hail of bullets to reach the side of his fallen comrade. Despite the withering fire, he reached the wounded Marine and covered him with his body to stop the bleeding. Thirkettle was riddled with bullets, sacrificing his life for the downed man, who survived.

Smith gave up hope of reinforcements and took his only other option, realigning his three remaining squads into a defensive position. If the North Vietnamese were going to wipe them out, they would have to pay for it. Smith ordered a counterattack and his men opened up with everything they had—M-16s, M-60 machine guns, and grenade launchers.

The enemy ambush let up, and Lieutenant Smith realized he had experienced a bit of luck despite this day of misfortune. The North Vietnamese ambush was set so near to the orchard path that they couldn't fire their mortars for fear of hitting themselves. Without the mortar fire, the Marines managed to regroup and started using their superior marksmanship to pick off the snipers who had been shooting from up in the banana trees. As evening fell on Con Thienh, the battle became a standoff.

Smith had a glimmer of hope. If his platoon could hold out until nightfall, they might escape their deadly predicament. Then his reluctant commander called with some good news: He was finally sending some reinforcements.

Lieutenant Smith resisted the urge to cuss him out. Any help now was coming way too late for Thirkettle and the others who had been left to die. But he kept his thoughts to himself, since his men needed encouragement, not whining. He urged his men on, hollering, "Looks like we're getting some help."

As the sun began to set in a pink and gold line above the orchard, the rest of the battalion cautiously moved out of the compound and began firing tracers into the caves and trees staked out by the communists. The North Vietnamese, in their inimitable way, nimbly avoided the counterattack by disappearing

like ghosts. It was a classic guerilla tactic, drawn from Mao Tse
Tung: "When the enemy advances, we retreat."

Smith scrambled around his platoon to take stock of the carnage: six dead and five wounded. He fought back tears at the
awful sight. Then, as the dead and wounded were loaded onto
amtracs, he saw something strange. One of the wounded men,
despite the loss of a lot of blood, seemed like he could have lived.
But when the Marine turned on his side, he saw a buddy lying
motionless beside him and started crying. His tears wouldn't stop,
and he started shivering and went into shock, passing out. A
corpsman tried to revive him, but nothing worked. The young
Marine, who appeared to have a good chance of surviving his
wounds and going home, died within minutes.

Thinking it over later, Smith felt sure the man would have
lived if he had not been so affected by the sight of his lifeless
buddy. His emotions seemed to have killed him, plunging him
into shock and then into a fatal coma.

Then and there, Smith made a pact with himself. Death has
its own way of sucking your life away, so it's better just to check
your emotions before going into combat. He made a mental note
to advise his men to do the same.

The next day, he wrote Colleen about the ambush:

> Well, I got my initiation into real war yesterday and it
> wasn't very pretty. The company went on a patrol around
> Con Thienh to the north. My platoon ran into real trou-
> ble.
> We were on the left flank. The company was hit hard
> from our left. One squad was pinned down and the rest
> of the platoon was pinned trying to get them. It took me
> about four and a half hours to get out of there, and it
> cost me six dead and five wounded doing it. It was a bad
> blow to take . . .
> I lost some really good boys and men yesterday. I lost
> three squad leaders, one corpsman, and two fire team
> leaders. I'm putting [Thirkettle] up for the Navy Cross.

One man got hit in the leg and was right in front of one of their machine gun bunkers, and the Doc ran out and covered him with his own body. He was killed doing it.

... My body is completely worn out, I guess from the tension. I feel like I've been beaten all over with a big stick.

Smith dropped his pen and fell back on his cot. He stared at the log top of his bunker and wondered how the other lieutenants from his class were doing. War was testing his very being. Leadership, he was finding, wasn't just about making the right decisions on where to position your platoon or bringing superior firepower to bear against enemy forces. There were other enemies on the battlefield, invisible forces lurking like booby traps inside your mind. Thinking back on his instructors in Quantico, he now understood the troubled looks that crossed the faces of combat veterans whenever students asked them to describe what it was really like to see men fight and die, or to kill someone. Some things about war simply didn't lend themselves to easy explanation.

Ray Smith was fortunate to survive the ambush at Con Thienh. Such early skirmishes in Vietnam took their toll on new lieutenants. Out of the 516 graduates of his Basic School class, eleven died during their first three months in country between October and December of 1967.

The war was about to enter a new and even more dangerous phase. The North Vietnamese were waiting for a national holiday—the Buddhist lunar celebration known as Tet—to launch a new offensive in early 1968. It was a brilliant, though sinister plan since it violated a longstanding cease-fire agreement recognized by both sides for years, though without a formal document. The annual truce allowed soldiers from both sides to return home to visit their families during the religious holiday. Despite alarming intelligence reports about an increasingly large flow of arms and men across the border, the South Vietnamese leadership chose to trust their gentleman's agreement with Ho Chi Minh and his military leader, General Giap. The communists may have been without religion, but they seemed to recognize the need for their own men to be able to move freely about the country to visit homes and families. So there was no reason to think they would not honor the Buddhist observance for 1968, the Year of the Monkey.

But cracks in the fragile truce began to show in the days leading up to the start of the Tet holiday on January 30, 1968. The rumblings began at the Marines' firebase in the hills a few miles away from Con Thienh. One of Ray Smith's Basic School classmates, artillery specialist Les Palm, had arrived to take what seemed at first like a routine assignment with the 1st Battalion, 13th Marines.

The base at Khe Sanh was near the DMZ and had been taken from the North Vietnamese in some hard fighting while Palm was in Basic School. When he arrived on the scene, the slim, soft-spoken Palm wrote his parents that the rugged hills had been quiet for the past six months. A senior officer had reassured him that he'd been assigned there because he was married and it was a "nice and quiet" place, away from more dangerous hotspots.

In his letter home, Palm made it a point to include the officer's reassuring words because he could see that trouble was brewing. The Marines at Khe Sanh were dug in deeply in hills marked with bomb craters.

Before leaving for the war zone, Palm was jolted to learn that one of his closest friends from Quantico, 2nd Lt. M. J. "Mo" Crary, had been killed in action. They had become close at Quantico despite the fact that Crary played baseball for Oregon State, the archrival of Palm's University of Oregon. Their wives also had become friends, teaching swimming at the officers' pool and taking shopping trips to New York.

Mo Crary's death hit all the harder because of its timing—one day before Crary's wife gave birth to their first child.

Palm was assigned to the 1/13's fire direction center, where he could put his Army training to good use, working with the first generation of computerized artillery. The FADAC—Field Artillery Digitally Automated Computer—allowed the Marines to compute firing data for 155 and 105 millimeter shells up to 13 miles away.

"By hitting the books hard, I'm finally getting snapped in at the Fire Direction Center," he wrote his parents.

He bragged about the strides the Marines had made in creating one of the military's first computerized firing systems for its big guns. The FADAC cost millions of dollars to develop, but looked like a window air conditioner, and seemed a little delicate to hold up in battle. Yet Les tried to focus on the positives as he told his dad, a former Army artillery officer, "Nowadays there isn't much work involved. . . . All you do is put the grid coordinates into it and select the battery you want to fire the mission."

If he punched in the right coordinates, with the shell's time of flight and the charge needed to propel it, "It will give you a first round hit every time." With that, he closed his letter and wished his folks a Merry Christmas.

Even in December, Khe Sanh was a warm, muggy place, with morning fog that rolled up from the river valley. It was easy to get lulled into thinking this was a safe haven in the clouds, a kind of Oriental Magic Mountain. The lull ended on January 19, 1968.

Les Palm had joined three howitzers of Charlie 1/13 on one of the hills surrounding the main fire base—Hill 881 South. The hill was heavily fortified, using the bunkers left by the Viet Cong, which had held up even under heavy American aerial bombardments in recent months.

On the morning of the nineteenth, a platoon-sized patrol from India 3/26 was sent out to enemy-infested Hill 881 North. Led by a Basic School classmate, 2nd Lt. Mike Thomas, the platoon ran into a dug-in NVA company. Palm's three Charlie battery howitzers provided direct fire for Thomas's platoon. After a fierce battle, with the support of the 105s, infantry 106-millimeter recoilless rifles, and mortars, the Marine platoon was able to break contact and withdraw back to Hill 881 South.

When they came back through the perimeter, though, one of the casualties was Lieutenant Thomas. It was a sobering moment for Palm as he saw a classmate being dragged back through the wire with a bullet hole between his eyes.

The Marines on Hill 881 South were in the fight of their lives as enemy gunners aimed for the howitzers and for infantry mortars. They didn't knock out any of the weapons, but all three howitzers wound up with flat tires. Palm's eyes and nose stung from the sulfur smell of exploding mortar rounds. He survived the first barrage, but several Marines and corpsmen in his vicinity had perished.

Death was all around, but there was no time to waste thinking about it. If it was his time to go, he figured, it was his time. He kept working, calling in fire missions to suppress or knock out the NVA mortars, which were exacting a stiff toll on the Marines. As they grew accustomed to the incoming mortar fire, Palm and his platoon mates learned to recognize the sound of rounds leaving the enemy tubes. They had twenty seconds to take cover; "incoming" was a cry they came to dread.

Yet like a forensics specialist, Palm took time to analyze the craters from the explosions. He used those calculations to fix the direction of his howitzers to return fire on the NVA artillery.

During a break in the fighting, an enemy soldier appeared at Khe Sanh's northeastern perimeter, waving the white flag of surrender. He was brought back inside the compound and interrogated. La Thanh Tonc headed the 14th Antiaircraft Company attached to the 325C Division of the Army of North Vietnam. He approached the Americans as a "rallier," a term for enemy soldiers who defected under South Vietnam's "chieu hoi," or open arms, program.[9]

Tonc answered questions freely and gave valuable, if alarming, intelligence about plans to annihilate the Marine base. The North's goal, he explained, was to drive out the American forces by squeezing the life out of every U.S. base along the DMZ. He detailed the methodical infiltration of troops, supplies, and weapons. Four seasoned divisions of General Giap's army—40,000 men strong—were bearing down on Khe Sanh, supported by two artillery regiments and armored units.[10]

The Marines, by contrast, had less than 6,000 men in the area. Though the Americans had superior firepower, the North had the advantage of surprise, stealth, and decades of experience in fighting foreigners on their home turf. After the ground skirmishes of January 19 and 20, the North Vietnamese artillery opened fire, backed by rockets and mortars shot from hidden caves across the border in Laos. The Battle of Khe Sanh was on.

One of the early casualties was the 1/13 battalion Fire Direction Center, which took a direct hit from NVA artillery fire. Les Palm witnessed the smoldering damage after he was ordered down from Hill 881 South to take over as the battalion fire direction officer, replacing a wounded Marine. The FDC had been moved to the east end of the combat base. Palm also found that the officer hooch he'd first slept in had taken a direct hit. His cot and Val pack, which had been stowed there, were blown away. So much for fresh utilities, he thought.

The FADAC managed to survive the carnage. Palm and other artillery specialists used the computer and manual gunnery to compute the firing data to fire over 40,000 rounds a month at the NVA positions around Khe Sanh during the period from February through April. The enemy artillery and rockets scored many direct hits, including a spectacular one on the Marines' ammo dump. Some 1,500 rounds of ammunition exploded, causing major damage around the combat base.

Khe Sanh was an inferno. The steel-plated airstrip on the mountaintop was torn to shreds. Helicopters exploded like popcorn. Tear gas grenades were hit in storage sites, sending eye-stinging, throat-choking clouds of chemicals into trenches and bunkers. The Marines had to flee into the open air, which exposed them to enemy fire.

Adding to the chaos, a large cache of C-4 plastic explosives erupted with a cataclysmic blast that rocked the base and cracked the timbers of the command post of the 26th Marines. The staff fell to the ground, wondering if the roof would hold. After settling by about a foot, the beams held fast.[11]

As the battle for Khe Sanh raged on, it became the subject of intense debate in Saigon and Washington. When General Westmoreland learned of the all-out assault, he countered by ordering B-52 air strikes and unleashed the largest payload ever dropped on a tactical target in the history of warfare—seventy-five thousand tons of explosives over a period of nine weeks.[12]

Westmoreland even ordered a feasibility study of using tactical nuclear weapons on the enemy troops crossing the DMZ. But he was blocked by Johnson's White House, which knew that any press leaks about such doomsday thinking would fuel a groundswell of antiwar sentiment.[13]

LBJ became obsessed by the siege of Khe Sanh, as the North blocked the resupply of the Marines' food, water, and equipment. The president feared it was spiraling into a defeat on the order of the French downfall at Dienbienphu, the infamous base whose surrender led to France's exit from Vietnam. Johnson ordered sand-table models of the Marine base constructed in the basement situation room at the White House. Dressed in a bathrobe, he prowled the chamber during the night and read the latest teletype reports from the field, studied aerial photos, and ordered casualty figures.

Fearful of history repeating itself, Johnson angrily told the chairman of the Joint Chiefs of Staff: "I don't want any damn Dinbinphoo."[14]

FIVE

The Rocket Dodger

On January 30, 1968, Ray Smith's battalion was ordered to move out on the coastal highway as part of the U.S. strategy to shift more men and materiel to support the Marines under siege at Khe Sanh. He'd heard about the approaching truce for the Buddhist New Year, but as a lowly lieutenant trying to keep his men alive from day to day, Smith didn't know Tet from tat.

That morning, the commander of South Vietnam's 1st Army Division held a flag-raising ceremony in the historic Citadel at Hue. He happily celebrated the start of the Year of the Monkey and sent most of his men home for the week.

Perhaps the general was lulled by Hue's hypnotic beauty. The Citadel was built in the 1800s, part of a fairy-tale town of temples and palaces built by the French military and the emperor Gia Long to copy the seat of his Chinese patron in Beijing.[1]

Hue was South Vietnam's third-largest city, but even more important, it served as the nation's cultural and spiritual center. It was an Oriental Oz, with an Imperial Palace, a Forbidden River, a Perfume River, and a Palace of Perfect Peace. In Buddhist myth, Hue was "the lotus flower growing from the mud" with "the serenity and beauty of a city at peace in a nation of war."[2] Surely, the conventional thinking went, nobody would damage such a national treasure.

These were not conventional times, though. Even as the ceremonial flag was being raised, a massive invasion force of Viet Cong and North Vietnamese was poised to tear the city apart one lotus leaf at a time. They struck that night as part of a broader thrust of 70,000 troops in surprise attacks across South Vietnam in what became known as the Tet Offensive.

Down south in Saigon, 4,000 Viet Cong tried to seize the ultimate prize: the American Embassy. They were beaten back after six hours, but the bold stroke was a public relations coup for Ho Chi Minh. Millions of Americans watched on TV as a war that once seemed winnable seemed to be spiraling out of control. After years of promises from President Johnson, the U.S. effort to stop communism in Southeast Asia began to look like a war without end.

On the ground, though, the beleaguered soldiers, sailors and Marines had no time to consider the public relations or political fallout of the bold attack. They were fighting for their lives. Ray Smith, acting as company executive officer, was separated from his unit that was diverted to Hue to try to retake the city. Along the way, he was caught in a massive traffic jam on Highway One, the country's major north-south route.

The highway, known as "the street without joy," was choked with refugees and fleeing South Vietnamese soldiers, along with American troops desperately trying to redeploy. Initially, Smith was told there was only a small enemy force inside of Hue. He soon learned the estimate was ridiculously low. A North Vietnamese brigade of 7,500 soldiers had surrounded several thousand South Vietnamese troops and a few hundred Marines. It had the makings of a massacre.

The next morning, as Smith kept pushing toward the city, the rest of his company—the lead element of the Marine relief force—

arrived at Hue City as the cold and fog lingered over the Perfume River. Alpha Company of the 1st Battalion, 1st Marines, marched warily into the city's outskirts. Capt. Gordon D. Batcheller, a rugged Princeton graduate, had orders to rendezvous with South Vietnamese reinforcements. When no allied support arrived, Batcheller's unit hooked up with four M-48 tanks and rolled toward the American military compound on the south side of the river.[3] Sniper fire greeted them, wounding several Marines.

Smelling an ambush, Batcheller ordered his men out of their trucks and told them to mount the M-48s for protection. They roared down the empty streets, and the captain's wariness proved to be more than warranted. The North Vietnamese launched a barrage of rocket and machine-gun fire from behind the windows and roofs of the city's ornate churches, temples, and schools. Batcheller was sliced by shrapnel as other men were cut down by this opening volley. The 1/1 pushed on, led by their wounded commander. Batcheller was hit again and tumbled off the tank. Though he was torn open, he had the presence of mind to order everyone else to stay back, away from the ambush.[4]

Gunnery Sgt. J. L. Canley, a veteran NCO, reorganized the company and pushed on. The 1/1 was supported by a lumbering, tank-like weapon—the Ontos—fitted with rows of .50-caliber machine guns and 106mm recoilless rifles. Canley ordered the Ontos and some rocket launchers to lay down a crushing line of fire that smashed the walls of the ancient buildings that were providing cover for the enemy gunners. Once their cover was blown, they ran for their lives.

So began the Battle of Hue City, a fight that would quickly join Tarawa, Guadalcanal, and the Chosin Reservoir in the annals of Marine Corps history. And Ray Smith was heading for center stage of the epic battle. When he finally made it to the city after a two-day-long trek, he took Batcheller's place as Alpha Company commander.

Though the infantry company had taken some hits, Gunnery Sergeant Canley ably kept it moving deeper into the Imperial City. Smith was impressed by the tall, unflappable NCO who briefed

him about a foe that was smart, resourceful, and unpredictable.
The communists were skilled urban fighters, wraithlike in the way
they moved from alley to alley and building to building, shooting
and moving before the Americans could pin them down.

Soon after Smith arrived, the 1/1 received orders to attack
a large contingent of soldiers inside the St. Joan of Arc School
and Church. The Roman Catholic complex had two buildings
that faced one another like half squares, with a schoolyard in the
middle.

The company's point men fought their way into the complex.
They were led by Sgt. Alfred Gonzalez, a quiet twenty-one-year-old
Texan, who two days before shrugged off shrapnel wounds to drag
other Marines to safety. Gonzales was acting third platoon commander and had been a heroic figure in the company's hard fight
into the city.

Smith ordered Gonzales to take his platoon into the school
side of the St. Joan complex and try to take out the enemy gunners
blasting away from the church. Gonzalez and his men ascended
the school's stairs to the second floor. He kicked in a door and ran
across a classroom. B-40 rockets, launched by enemy gunners
across the schoolyard, shattered the windows and punched holes
in the walls.[5] Smoke and dust filled the room, and wooden support
beams crashed to the floor.

Undaunted, Gonzalez scrambled to the window with his shoul-
der-fired light antiarmor weapon. Just as he took aim with his
LAAW, an enemy gunner beat him to the punch. A rocket crashed
through the plaster wall and pinned Gonzales to the floor, killing
him immediately.[6]

On the street below, Smith learned of the sergeant's fate.
Sweet Jesus, he thought, starting to fill with regret at sending Gonzales to his death. He had to put a lid on his emotions, though,
and try to get even.

"Get me Colonel Gravel," he said somberly to his radioman as
they crouched behind a wall. More rocket propelled grenades and
machine-gun fire were raining down from the church, stopping
the Marines in their tracks.

"Sir," he told Gravel, "I think our mortars and recoilless rifles can suppress their fire. But with the church and all, we need your approval."

Gravel was under orders to minimize damage to the historic buildings of the Imperial City. However, he refused to lose men in the name of historic preservation. The battalion commander gave Smith the green light, and the Marines opened up with 81-millimeter and 106-millimeter rifles, coupled with mortars. The suppressing fire peeled back the protective cover of the church wall by wall and beam by beam. Once again, they sent the communists packing.

When he walked into the smoky church, Lieutenant Colonel Gravel surveyed the damage as sunlight streamed through the gaping holes punched into the church by the Marine gunners. He marveled to see that a large bronze crucifix remained standing on a wall behind the altar.

Two priests—one French, the other Belgian—rushed from their hiding place inside the sanctuary to survey the damage. This was no welcome party by the Catholic clerics. They were livid, waving their arms and calling out, "Mon Dieu! Mon Dieu!"

Gravel walked across the plaster-strewn floor and tried to reassure them that the Marines had no choice. He spoke no French but could see they were upset. He kept apologizing for the damage, but when they persisted in wagging their fingers at him, the battalion commander turned away to avoid making a scene. Though they appeared to be scolding him in French, the truth was the priests were lucky to be alive. In their dark tunics, they easily could have been mistaken for Viet Cong.[7]

The Marines secured St. Joan of Arc Church and School, but at a steep price—eleven dead, thirty-four wounded. Nearly everyone, including Ray Smith, was cut by flying rock and gravel. Yet they pushed on because Hue City was far from secure. Cpl. John Ligato, another tough kid from south Philadelphia, suffered his third shrapnel wound as Alpha Company conducted house-to-house searches.

While a corpsman treated him, Ligato looked up to see Lieutenant Smith watching. The lieutenant admired Ligato's spunk and didn't want to lose him as a squad leader. It wasn't a man's size or brawn that made him a warrior. Smith had learned to spot an indefinable quality about his Marines—call it courage or selflessness or street smarts—that made the fiercest fighters. Call it what you will, but Corporal Ligato had it in spades.

Ligato could see the lieutenant keeping a close eye on him, like the street vendors in Philly used to do when he'd get too close to their soda pop, ready to snatch a bottle and run. Ligato tried to read the lieutenant's inscrutable face and felt an almost subliminal message. Don't go now, he seemed to be saying. This fight is just getting interesting, and I can sure use you. Stick around—we've got a long way to go.

The corpsman finished patching him up. "So you want me to ship you out?" he casually asked Ligato. "I can have you evacuated."

His shrapnel wound could be a free ticket out of this deadly city. Ligato pictured the hospital ship floating offshore like a mirage. He would be flown in a medevac helicopter out of Hue, over the jungle and across the blue waters of the South China Sea. Then he would land on the ship, where young Navy nurses would flutter around him like swans, tenderly taking him on a gurney to his room. They would brush against him with their full hips and gaze down at him with blue eyes filled with saintly concern. As Ligato looked up at the battered church above him, he thought St. Joan herself couldn't conjure a sweeter vision.

When he returned to reality and saw the Marines still running and shooting at the entrenched enemy, Ligato remembered all they'd endured the past couple of weeks. He was proud to be a squad leader, one of Ray Smith's wingmen. He felt as attached to him as a squire to a knight. Smith was still watching him to see what he'd do.

"You know what?" Ligato said to the corpsman. "I'm OK."

Smith nodded and walked away with the slightest smile.

Later, Ligato was back at the lieutenant's side, providing covering fire as he led Alpha Company on its search to root out the enemy, house by treacherous house. Along one wide boulevard,

Ligato watched with a mixture of horror and amazement when his leader's luck seemed to run out: a North Vietnamese soldier crouched behind a wall about 150 yards away caught Smith in his crosshairs as the lieutenant crossed the street. Ligato heard the distinctive pop of a rocket-propelled grenade.

The B-40 RPG was a gawky-looking weapon resembling a broomstick with a rocket stuck on its end. It was often compared to an old German potato masher grenade, yet it was bigger than the World War II–era weapons and had enough firepower to pierce tank armor. The B-40 had a little space-age toughness, as well—tiny fins that popped out once it was launched, helping stabilize its flight.

Smith didn't hear the RPG's firing, though he did glimpse a puff of smoke out of the corner of his eye. The rocket seemed to float toward him, and when he realized he was caught dead to rights, all he could do was keep running like Marty Steele churning his legs back on the obstacle course. Smith thought this was it—he'd crossed one street too many and it was his time to go. He'd never see Colleen again. He would be pierced by this sizzling rocket just like Sergeant Gonzales up in the school room. Who would have thought his life would end in this exotic place, amid temples and churches built to inspire love and peace?

He kept running, even when he felt his right leg burning. He was hit, but his momentum kept him moving toward a doorway on the far side of the boulevard.

Lieutenant Colonel Gravel was right on his heels, shouting, "Stay down, Ray! Get in that door." They scrambled into the entrance of an abandoned house, then Gravel threw himself over him like a human shield.

"Are you okay?" Gravel asked, out of breath.

"I think so," Smith said doubtfully. He feared his right leg had been blown off, but he couldn't bring himself to check. He felt like throwing up. The burning sensation seemed to say it all. The RPG had hit him, and he had somehow survived the wound. He would have to face facts: He had lost a leg and would live as an amputee. What did the Corps do with cripples? Probably muster him out and send him home—another hotshot Marine struck down in his prime. He wondered how Colleen would take the news.

As this grim future crossed his mind, Smith finally asked Gravel, "How is it?"

His commander cast a cold eye on his leg. Time seemed to stop until Gravel said, "You look okay. It may have just grazed you."

Only then could Smith assess the damage and glance down to see that, though his leg was bleeding, it was only a graze wound. He had somehow dodged the rocket. He sagged in the doorway, grateful that he had been spared to fight another day.

Ligato, who watched Smith's close brush with death, also saw the end of the story. The RPG grazed Smith and then hit a wall at the end of the street. A Vietnamese peasant woman, who had ducked behind the wall for refuge, was killed on the spot.

☆ ☆ ☆

The Marines took back Hue City block by bloody block, mounting a counterattack that made headlines back home. CBS anchorman Walter Cronkite was in Vietnam during the Tet Offensive and wanted to file a report from the Imperial City. Lieutenant Colonel Gravel was given the task of handling the newsman, and he mulled over which unit to visit. He chose Lieutenant Smith's 3rd Platoon, led by Al Courtney, a stud of a Marine if there ever was one. A big, brash, and bold Texan, Lt. Allen W. Courtney Jr. was one of Smith's best friends in the 1/1. Like Smith, he'd been wounded—hit in the calf by a machine-gun round—but was patched up and kept fighting.

"He'll be perfect for Cronkite," Gravel told Smith. "Courtney's a fine young Marine."

When Gravel and Smith stopped by the lieutenant's position, they were met by a gruesome sight: an enemy corpse was lashed by a rope to a chair in the middle of a bridge over the Perfume River. The dead North Vietnamese soldier was perched in an upright position, with one leg crossed over the other and a *Playboy* magazine in his lap. A cigar was stuck in a corner of his mouth, though part of his face was blown away.

Courtney could see his commanding officer was upset by his handiwork, so he tried to explain. The seated corpse was meant to serve as a warning to the North Vietnamese, he said, to keep them from trying to attack his Marines. Gesturing to the body, Courtney grinned and said, "I think he's a Chinaman. He's too fat to be North Vietnamese."

Smith turned away, trying not to laugh at Courtney's prank, which seemed innocent enough. Only the timing was terrible. What if Cronkite were here with his camera crew? Courtney's practical joke could be portrayed as a battlefield atrocity and not a simple lapse in judgment. The Marines would look like barbarians.

Lieutenant Colonel Gravel was livid. "Take it down!" he snapped. Turning to Smith, he pointed at Courtney and said, "I want charges brought against him." Desecrating a corpse not only violated the Geneva Convention and the military code of justice, Gravel thundered, but it was a truly revolting and immoral act.

Courtney spread his hands and kept trying to plead his case. Gravel cut him off. "Not a word more, lieutenant, or I'll have you hauled out of here right now." He ordered Smith to collect the corpse and give it a proper burial.

Gravel then radioed division headquarters. "Hold off on that visit by Cronkite," he barked. "We'll have to hook him up with someone else."

Smith thought his boss was overreacting. After all the fighting, he'd come to believe that when someone died, they were simply gone. A corpse—any corpse—was nothing special, really, just the remains of a lost life. He was quite sure that Al Courtney never meant to desecrate the fat soldier of unknown origin. He simply had seen so much death and carnage that he'd gotten kind of callous, too. Al was only in his early twenties, the same brash age as the college seniors back in the States who were out drinking and partying and chasing girls. It was, in many ways, a frat boy's prank.

Smith could see that Lieutenant Colonel Gravel was dead serious about disciplining his playful lieutenant. Smith surmised there was only one way out of this mess. Drawing Courtney aside, he said, "Al, you're medevaced out immediately. Your leg needs immediate medical attention."

Courtney protested, "Aw, Ray, my leg's not that bad. I can't leave now. My men have been through too much. I'm sorry about my stunt, but you know how it goes."

Smith shook his head. Gravel's decision was final, and he was seriously considering ordering a general court martial. "If you're not careful," Smith said, "you'll be placed under arrest. So listen to me: you are out of here, now!"

Al Courtney reluctantly heeded his friend's advice and was flown out of Hue for medical treatment. Smith's strategy worked, as Gravel eventually cooled off and had to focus on the ongoing battle. A few weeks later, Courtney returned to his platoon, not much older but a lot wiser. He remained a popular officer until late 1968 when he stepped on a land mine and died near Khe Sanh. Smith's third son bears his name.

☆ ☆ ☆

After nine days of fighting, Ray Smith's Alpha Company swung over to the east side of the city, where they came under attack from a nearby soccer stadium. A Marine was wounded and went down in the street when the one tank attached to his company dashed forward to cover him. Hit by a recoilless rifle, the tank caught fire. Smith needed supporting fire, but the Americans remained under orders to minimize property damage. He tried to radio the nearest South Vietnamese command post but couldn't find anyone with the authority to give him the green light to attack.

An unarmed civilian approached with his hands up. He introduced himself in English as a South Vietnamese major who had been trapped in his home since the NVA attack. He said an enemy battalion headquarters was stationed in his home. Smith decided he was legit. Then the major got on Smith's radio and found the local commander, who gave the Marines the go-ahead to use artillery and air support.

Smith made another call for help to 1st Battalion headquarters. He provided the coordinates of the major's home and requested all the firepower at his disposal—eight-inch howitzers, 155-millimeter cannons, and mortars. Within five minutes, the Marines delivered a barrage that roared overhead and landed inside the stadium with deadly accuracy. Game over.

"Let's go in," Smith said to Canley and Ligato, "but watch yourselves." They fanned out through the block, driving the now-retreating NVA before them. Smith felt a grudging respect for these young soldiers. In another time and place, they would be going to college or getting married or starting families. Instead, they were caught like his Marines in a war started by their elders for reasons that were about as clear as the smoke rising from the grass field. Sure, these defeated soldiers were communists, and he was glad they would not be shooting at him any more. But he gave them credit for being a tough and implacable foe. The Marines had simply been tougher.

The Americans won the Battle of Hue City and repulsed the other attacks across the country. Years later, North Vietnamese and Viet Cong officials admitted they had suffered huge losses by launching the Tet Offensive: up to 50,000 men killed, compared to 4,000 South Vietnamese and 2,000 Americans dead.[8] However, news of the house-to-house combat in Hue and the bold assaults in Saigon scored a major psychological blow back in the States. Many Americans began to question their complacent acceptance of President Johnson's regular calls for more men and money to stop the spread of communism in Southeast Asia. Middle America, which had mostly ignored the political dissent on college campuses, now began to consider the unpleasant possibility that the North Vietnamese and their Viet Cong counterparts could take years to defeat. It didn't help matters that the South Vietnamese Army often let the Americans bear the brunt of the fighting.

Walter Cronkite returned from Vietnam to report his own dim view of the war. At the end of his February 27, 1968, broadcast of the *CBS Evening News*, the avuncular anchorman departed from his normal script to deliver a somber assessment challenging the Johnson administration's promise of ultimate victory. After witnessing the bloodshed in Hue and Saigon, Cronkite said it seemed "more certain than ever that the bloody experience of Vietnam is to end in stalemate."[9]

For the Marines on the ground, though, his pronouncement might as well have come from the moon. They were locked in combat and missions that may not have made sense but still had to be completed. After the nearly two-month-long siege of Khe Sanh, the Marines drove off the larger North Vietnamese force, only to be told to abandon the base. It was a bittersweet ending for Les Palm, who spent forty-five straight days locked in artillery combat with the North Vietnamese. It was mid-February before he finally came down off his hill and took his first shower of 1968. Khe Sanh had been renamed "the duck farm" by Marines who felt like sitting ducks.

Despite the politically-charged comparisons between the battles of Khe Sanh and Dienbienphu, historian Stanley Karnow would later note the differences of the pivotal clashes. "About eight thousand Vietminh and two thousand French army soldiers died at Dienbienphu. But the struggle for Khe Sanh cost the Communists at least ten thousand lives in exchange for fewer than five hundred U.S. Marines killed in action." A Communist veteran later "recalled the carnage inflicted on his comrades" as "some North Vietnamese and Vietcong units suffered as much as 90 percent losses under the relentless downpour of American bombs, napalm and artillery shells."[10]

The Marines won the shooting match, but a decision was made to dismantle the base because, as the now-departing General Westmoreland wrote, it had "outlived its usefulness."[11] By late June, rugged Route 9 between Ca Lu and Khe Sanh was choked with trucks and other heavy equipment on a mission to retrieve any weapons, radios, and other goods left behind. Also on hand were men from the 3rd and 11th Engineer Battalions and the 3rd Shore Party Battalion, who set to work dismantling the battered base.

"Even burned out vehicle hulks and damaged equipment were cut apart into smaller pieces, moved to secure areas, and buried to prevent their use in enemy propaganda," the Marines said in their official account. "The same Navy Seabee unit which had toiled to repair and upgrade the airstrip months before now returned to rip up the steel matting runway."[12]

They crushed more than 800 bunkers and untangled three miles of concertina wire, "throwing the wire into the trenches and filling them with soil. They slit open the countless sandbags and emptied them, wrecked standing structures, and burned what remained to the ground. As a final step to discourage the North Vietnamese from attempting to dig through the ruins for useful material, the Marines sprinkled the area with CS powder, an irritant chemical agent."[13]

It was a dangerous mission, and soon NVA guns started to lob harassing fire at the Marines. First Lt. Ray Smith already was at Khe Sanh with the 1/1, which had been sent in May to replace the 26th Marines. He recalled heavy losses in his battalion around the time of the pullout from the base. A July 7, 1968, clash was detailed by Lt. General H. W. Buse Jr. in a citation awarding Smith his second Silver Star of the war:

> Company A was assigned to assist in repulsing two North Vietnamese Army companies that had penetrated the Khe Sanh Combat Base. Observing the intense enemy mortar and antitank rocket fire and realizing the seriousness of the situation, First Lieutenant Smith unhesitatingly led his men across 100 meters of fire-swept terrain to the beleaguered unit's positions. Ignoring the hostile rounds impacting near him, he skillfully deployed his platoons on the line behind the containing forces and continued his attack against the enemy.

Smith, who received cuts over his hands and arms, "fearlessly moved about the hazardous area shouting words of encouragement to his men and skillfully directing their fire against the

North Vietnamese soldiers. With complete disregard for his own safety, he calmly coordinated the evacuation of casualties while resolutely leading his Marines in driving the enemy from the perimeter and subsequently reestablishing the battalion's defensive integrity."

Lieutenant Smith's "bold initiative and heroic actions inspired all who served with him," upholding "the highest traditions of the Marine Corps and the United States Naval Service."

☆ ☆ ☆

Before the closing of the base in July, one of Smith's former classmates from Basic School Class 5-67 arrived in time to witness the extent of the carnage. Second Lt. Ron Chambers, a baby-faced transport officer from Indiana, was part of the convoy on the recovery mission.

The entrance road was pockmarked from months of shelling. The terrain smoldered with the detritus of destruction—helicopters, planes, trucks, all pounded into oblivion. Even the steel-plated airfield—once an engineering marvel that allowed the Marines to fly in supplies—resembled a moonscape.

Chambers held his nose against the stench of rotting bodies. In the distance, he heard the rumble of bulldozers as engineers dug mass graves for hundreds of enemy left on the rocky battlefield.

The scene reminded Chambers, a history major in college, of the epic standoff at Carthage during the Punic Wars. The Roman army lay siege on its pesky enemy on the coast of North Africa for three years, then invaded and wiped out their homes and crops in 146 B.C.

Two millennia later at Khe Sanh, with so much ruin on both sides, Chambers found it difficult to say who had played the role of the Romans and who played the Carthaginians. In many ways, it seemed like a standoff. The ancient and modern fortresses did share one thing: each had erected front gates that provided little help against enemy marauders.

After his troops had picked up anything of value, Chambers sent his trucks out through the front gate of Khe Sanh. When he noticed it was still ajar, he wondered if he should close it or leave it open.

Either way, it could send the wrong message. Leaving it open would signal an intent to return, which he had been told was not likely. Yet closing the gate could send a message that the Leathernecks were forgetting those who had made the ultimate sacrifice.

Finally, Chambers decided to drag the big wooden gate shut. It seemed like the right thing to do, if only out of respect for the dead of both nations. For whatever its place in history's final register, the abandoned fort at Khe Sanh was now little more than a cemetery, where any declaration of victory was as fleeting as the mountain mist.

SIX

Green for Go, Red for Stop

After the Tet Offensive, 2nd Lt. Jim Jones was a company commander with the 2nd Battalion, 3rd Marines, patrolling the dangerous hills in the northwestern corner of Vietnam. The Marines had liberated Khe Sanh, and the 3rd Division under Gen. Raymond G. Davis was running Operation Pegasus to keep open the main highway—Route 9—and to keep knocking the North Vietnamese back on their heels.

The 2/3 was known as a "rent-a-battalion" that was used as a troubleshooting force whenever the fighting got heavy and additional troops were needed. Leading his forty-man platoon, Jones got used to taking on the much larger elements of the North Vietnamese Army that had poured into the country across the DMZ or across the borders from Cambodia and nearby Laos.

Jones knew he could call on the Marines' superior training, firepower, and technology. One of his favorite new toys was a battery-powered device called the Starlight Scope, which absorbed starlight to enhance vision. The scope was an early version of night-vision goggles that would later become standard issue for American ground forces and aviators.

Lieutenant Jones had come to appreciate the value of superior technology earlier in the year, during a January operation in the rice paddies outside of Danang. One night his radio operator shook him awake. There was something the lieutenant had to see to believe. He pulled on his boots and helmet and shuffled over to the observation post. He picked up a forward observer's rifle fitted with a Starlight Scope and gazed into the distance: a line of up to 2,000 enemy soldiers was marching along the tree line about a mile away on the horizon, away from the Marines. Viewing their ghostly figures in the scope's pale green light, Jones assumed this was the same battalion-sized unit they had clashed with earlier in the day. He had called in a series of artillery and air strikes, which appeared to have beaten them up enough to send them packing.

Jones patted his young radioman on the shoulder and said, "Good work. Now let's give them a going away present."

He calculated their location on the grid map, then radioed for artillery fire. A few minutes passed before the battalion's 105 millimeter guns launched a barrage that rocked the ground and lit up the sky. The lieutenant peered through the scope at the furious movements of the NVA vainly trying to flee in the water and mud of the rice paddy. It was too late, though. They were caught out in the open, and Jones's men spent much of the night picking them off, with the aid of the Starlight Scopes on their M-14 sniper rifles.

Although Jones had surprised the enemy this time, he knew he'd been lucky. He spent a sleepless night thinking of the resiliency of the NVA. They were hardened fighters who knew how to sneak through a network of intricately carved tunnels and trails that spread like a spider's nest on and below the Vietnamese heartland. The tunnels were dug by hand during the decades of civil war against the French and now the Americans. Now they were deep and hardened enough to withstand even some of the biggest bombs dropped from high-altitude B-52s. Still, Lieutenant Jones remained supremely confident in himself, both as a leader of men and as a battlefield tactician. By his peers, he was nicknamed "The Hawk," because of his thin, almost emaciated frame and his resemblance to the bird of prey.

In mid May 1968, he was ordered to leave Golf Company, where he was the executive officer, to become acting commander of Foxtrot Company while its regular leader took a well deserved rest and relaxation (R & R) break in Hawaii.

His new company was undermanned because of dysentery and the other occupational hazards associated with fighting in the 100-degree-plus weather. There was nothing pleasant about spring in Vietnam, and Foxtrot Company was down to about ninety men—almost half of its normal size.

On May 25, Lieutenant Jones' former company was operating in the hills west of Route 9 when they came under withering fire from the NVA. Lt. Col. "Black Jack" Davis radioed Jones and ordered him to move out to help Golf Company. Jones moved his men up to a ridge line to gain a flanking position on the NVA, helping repel the enemy assault.

As night fell, the lieutenant ordered his men to set up a defense on the rocky ridge, which had a good view of the mountains to the west, including Co Roc, a well-known mountain in Laos where the NVA had lobbed artillery shells toward Khe Sanh. He radioed battalion that they were dug in for the night.

The ridge line ran from north to south, with a depressed area—or saddle—in the middle. It had a high point on the south end that Jones dubbed the "crow's nest" because it resembled a lookout post near the top of a ship's mast. This gave them an even better view of the tree-lined hills, which were known to be a major infiltration route from Laos.

PFC Harold Blunk, one of the scouts, shoveled through the elephant grass to carve out an observation post ringed by sandbags. When the OP was completed, Bunk climbed in and marveled at the view. Looking west toward Laos, the battered earth resembled a sprawling golf course with too many sand traps—craters from carpet-bombing B-52s. A couple miles to the east, he could make out the Marine outpost at Khe Sanh.

The next day, Blunk saw something stirring in the bush below: steel helmets glinting in the tall grass. He called for an artillery strike on what appeared to be a small enemy force trying to sneak up on the Marines. The howitzer shells exploded around them, and must have killed some of the invaders. Still more shiny helmets could be seen bobbing along like buoys on a sea of grass. Blunk promptly called in an air strike by two F-4 Phantom jets. After the bombing, an American spotter plane reported a number of dead North Vietnamese soldiers, but also reported continued enemy activity, including fortified bunkers dug into neighboring hills.[1]

That evening, the Marines of F Company used their night-vision technology to direct mortar fire on the invading force. As close as they were to the Laotian border—about fifteen miles to the west—Jones realized his company had become a thorn in the side of the North Vietnamese Army.[2] He couldn't be sure of the size of the force massing below, but fresh intelligence reports indicated the presence of a large enemy force within three miles of the ridge. He moved his depleted ranks into defensive positions and tried to get some sleep.

For three uneasy days, they stayed dug in and observed through their binoculars and night scopes as enemy troops moved with mounting impunity across the rolling terrain. On the morning of May 27, Lieutenant Jones decided he'd seen enough, and it was time to move off the ridge. By now, he was sure his forward observers and scouts had been spotted, and it was just a matter of time before the NVA attacked.

He radioed his battalion headquarters down at the firebase called LZ Hawk. Lieutenant Colonel Davis was a competent leader but was known for sharp mood swings, hence the nickname "Black Jack." From the start of their conversation, Jones knew he'd hit his boss on one of his bad days.

"Sir," he said, "I'm not feeling real good about our position up here. We've been here too long, there are too many places for the enemy move in on us, we're too exposed, and we're too undermanned to send out patrols." The lieutenant knew he was pushing his luck but forged ahead for his men's sake. "Sir, I want to move to a better position. Something about this ridge just doesn't feel right."

Davis barked through the radio, "Goddamnit Jones, if I wanted to know how you *feel* about your position, don't you think I would have asked?"

"Yessir, but I just thought . . ."

Davis cut him off. "I know what you thought, lieutenant, and I don't give a damn. You will stay put. Understand?"

"Roger, Six . . . loud and clear," Jones replied, gingerly replacing the radio's hand set. "Black Jack" was living up to his nickname. Live with it, his commanding officer said. It was a Marine's occupational hazard. Along with "Semper Fidelis," it could be the flip side of the Marine Corps' motto: *Live with it, and die with it.*

Dig in, Jones ordered, stay alert; we aren't moving. His trepidation continued as he received more intelligence reports based on the electronic sensors between Foxtrot Ridge and the Laotian border. An attack seemed imminent. Such reports were fairly common, Jones recalled, and "you didn't go to battle stations every time. This one proved to be true."

He sent extra ammo and weapons up to Blunk and the other men in the crow's nest, and took a number of other protective measures, including making sure the artillery battery (Bravo 1/12) had 360-degree preregistered defensive fire. He also changed his observation and listening posts, since he was sure they were marked on some NVA commander's map.

One of the Marines bracing for battle was a newly arrived gunnery sergeant, Ralph Larsen. In his mid-thirties, Gunny Larsen was a full decade older than Jones, and he quickly became a father figure for F Company. He was an old-school grunt in the proud tradition of Chesty Puller. Larsen had joined the Marines at the start of the Korean War at the tender age of seventeen. By his nineteenth year, he was battling Chinese Communists, shooting a machine gun and sometimes engaging in hand-to-hand combat. Only a bad knee would force him into early retirement with a medical discharge in his early thirties.

Larsen decided to reenlist, though, after reading that President Johnson was sending the Marines to Vietnam. He was still thin and physically fit, but his reentry would take some sleight-of-hand: five years earlier, he'd suffered a serious knee injury in a parachuting accident. This left him on a retired-with-disability list, which meant he would flunk any honest physical exam. Walking around Bethesda Naval Hospital, though, he found a sympathetic orthopedic surgeon who agreed to sign his medical papers, authorizing his reenlistment.

So it was that Larsen—secretly wearing a knee brace under his jungle utilities—shipped out to 'Nam. He kept his condition to himself, despite the sharp pain he suffered, especially marching downhill.[3] Now, as he saw how vulnerable they were to attack, the gimpy gunny wondered whether he'd be able to backpedal to Saigon. The ridge top was a ridiculous place to be. He took small comfort in knowing he'd been in worse spots in Korea.

It was a clear night, and shortly after midnight on May 28, the enemy launched a small diversionary attack on the eastern slope of Foxtrot Company's perimeter. All OPs and LPs were ordered inside the lines. Lieutenant Jones ordered fire from his 60-millimeter mortars to avoid muzzle flashes that would give away his fighting positions. The small group of invaders dispersed, but everyone knew the night was still young.

The elephant grass snapped from the sound of men dragging machine guns and satchel charges up the hill. The North Vietnamese were so close that they could be heard breathing hard from the exertion.[4]

Jones called his listening posts on the western side of the ridge, but to no avail. They'd been silenced by the stealthy NVA hitting their fighting holes with satchel charges. Around 1 A.M., three green flares flashed overhead, followed by whistles and bugles. An entire battalion of NVA regulars—more than 500 men strong—was attacking the ninety Marines.

The Marines fired back with rifles, machine guns, grenades, and mortars. Lieutenant Jones radioed the battalion, requesting artillery support from LZ Hawk and Khe Sanh. Nine batteries of artillery responded with a lethal shelling that stifled the NVA advance. "They hadn't retreated, though," Jones recalled later. "They had gone to ground for cover, and as soon as the barrage stopped, they attacked again."

Most of the Marines wisely dove for cover in their fighting holes, but adrenalin got the better of a few men who raced across the ridge, firing wildly. Gunny Larsen thought, *Fools, stay in your holes! Don't move around, or you'll be shooting at each other.* He knew from Korea that friendly fire casualties usually happen at the start of a battle, when emotions are running high.

Up in the crow's nest, Private Blunk was having his own problems as the NVA started to overrun his position. The young forward observer remembered the claymore mines set out earlier as a defensive measure.

"Blow the claymores!" he hollered. The Marines attempted to do so. When nothing happened, Blunk realized the NVA must have spotted them laying the mines and defused them before hitting the high ground.

A green flare burst overhead, signaling another NVA thrust. Firing AK-47s, the soldiers shouted in frenetic, often high-pitched voices. Some sounded slightly wigged out, as though they were on drugs. Even if some were stoned, the NVA outnumbered the Marines by a four-to-one margin. And they had suicide bombers—known as "sappers"—armed with explosive satchels willing to sacrifice themselves to kill an American.

Gunny Larsen hugged the dirt in the saddle of the ridge, thinking of Custer's Last Stand. Only now the commanding officer was named Jones. Would they die together, and if they did, would anyone remember?

No matter how bad things got, though, Jim Jones knew he had to keep his wits about him. Otherwise all was lost. The twenty-four-year-old had an idea. He reached inside his shirt pocket for his pencil-sized flare. He inserted a red flare and fired it high into the sky, thinking that if green was the signal to attack, then red, perhaps, was their signal to pull back. The ploy worked, and the NVA ended their attack.

Gunny Larsen joined in, popping off some of his red flares, too.

The trick bought some time as Foxtrot Company reloaded and repositioned itself for whatever was next. They were low on ammunition, so the Marines "borrowed" large numbers of AK-47s, ammunition, and hand grenades from the growing ranks of enemy dead.

Unfortunately, the NVA's commanders quickly saw through Jones's and Larsen's ruse and reorganized. Some reported that enemy leaders began shooting at their own men to halt the retreat. After they were forced to turn around, the now-reluctant attackers gamely headed back up the hill, once again, toward their entrenched foe.

This time, they were successful in overrunning a portion of the 1st Platoon on the northern end of the ridge. Jones grabbed the radio and ordered the platoon to pull back and reestablish the perimeter higher up on the ridge. In this new formation, Foxtrot Company proved to be an even more effective fighting force, able to pick off the NVA from several different directions.

The young lieutenant called for more artillery fire, which wound up exploding on his front doorstep. The Marine gunners' aim was true, though, and they killed scores of NVA, whose screams filled the night.

The communists were a determined lot, shooting and throwing grenades into the Marine fighting holes. The "ChiComs," as the Chinese weapons were known, had fuses that sent sparks into the night. They landed with a thump on the ground, and if the fuses were still hissing, the Marines threw them back.[5]

Lieutenant Jones knew his men were tough and resourceful, but how long could they hold out? Ammo was running low, but Jones believed that if they could just hold out until dawn, he could call in air support and survive this bloody night. But they would have to keep cool and conserve bullets. "Hold your fire as much as possible," he told his squad leaders over the radio.

Jones exuded calm, but he pleaded with battalion HQ for immediate air support. Wait until daybreak, he was told, but "Spooky's coming" now. This was a reference to the highly armed AC-47—known as Spooky—filled with enough weapons to provide a truly battle-altering amount of fire. As his Marines held their ground through the night, Jones reflected upon the fact that this plane was built back in Los Angeles in the Douglas aircraft plant, where his Uncle Vernon had worked in the 1940s. That was when his father and Uncle Bill were fighting the Japanese in the South Pacific.

Time seemed to stand still. One war bled into another. Jones strained to listen for anything flying his way. Finally, he heard one of the sweetest sounds of his young life—the droning of Spooky's propellers.

The Douglas AC-47 was a World War II–era transport converted into a plodding but highly lethal gunship. Armed with rapid-fire machine guns, rocket launchers, and a state-of-the-art night vision capability, the twin-engine airplane performed well at night.

The plane circled overhead in the pale sky. An accompanying craft dropped illumination flares that lit up Foxtrot Ridge. Then the gunship erupted with machine-gun fire—18,000 rounds per minute—that shredded the enemy forces. Many enemy soldiers died on the spot or as they tried to escape the conflagration. Foxtrot Ridge had become a shooting gallery.

Jones wasn't taking any chances and called for a napalm strike the next morning, as the enemy still refused to break contact. The skies cleared, and two F-4 Phantoms screamed over the ridge line. As they made a practice pass, one fighter was so close to the ground that the Marines could see the pilot's mask. They came around for the real thing.

No one needed any prompting to hit the deck as the silver canisters tumbled slowly toward them, glinting in the morning sun. The bombs were filled with flammable jelly made from naphthene and palmitate: napalm. Back home, napalm had become a symbol of the brutality and indiscriminate use of force in Vietnam, torching jungles and frying villagers. After Jones's near-death experience, though, the silver canisters were a welcome sight—until they ignited.

Exploding as close as 100 feet away, the napalm immediately turned the ridge into an inferno. A wall of fire sucked up the oxygen and raced toward the men of F Company, burning everything in its path. Spontaneous combustion in living (and dying) color for the Marines of Foxtrot Company was everywhere.

"Get the hell out of here!" Jones hollered. His men already were double-timing it down the east side of the hill, leaving everything behind, except their weapons. Fanned by an early morning breeze, the fire consumed backpacks, equipment, and everything else the men carried, including Jones's pictures and letters from Diane.

The fire quickly burned itself out on the rocky terrain, and the Marines hustled back up the hill to regain their defensive position. The NVA was retreating, although some were still shooting. But the battalion was decimated, and the assault was burning out like the napalm. The few surviving NVA fled back toward the safety of the Laotian border.

That afternoon, an American observation plane buzzed overhead and saw a hilltop littered with bodies.[6] An estimated 230 North Vietnamese died on Foxtrot Ridge, with 200 or more wounded. Lieutenant Jones lost thirteen men, with forty-four wounded.

Only after they had evacuated the dead and tended to the wounded did Jones find time to reflect on this trial by fire. Before the fight, he had a somewhat foolhardy view of combat as a kind of sporting event, not all that different from playing basketball back in Virginia.

"I had good instincts, I studied my trade. I could look at a map and it felt three dimensional to me," he said, thinking back on the defining battle of his early career. "After Foxtrot Ridge, I realized that my confidence was not particularly intelligently rooted. It was more emotionally rooted. I walked away from it no longer feeling impervious to being killed. I was in contact with my own mortality."

He also learned never to underestimate an enemy, especially implacable foes like the North Vietnamese and Viet Cong fighting on their home, or allied, turf. The old tactics of conventional warfare were as outdated as an M-1 rifle or a swagger stick. "The first thing I jettisoned over there were Basic School tactics of frontal assaults and things like that," Jones recalled. "I quickly became a believer that maneuver was much more important than the attrition warfare business that we were still teaching in our schools."

He never lost his respect for the courage of his father and uncle in their head-on attacks against entrenched Japanese pillboxes. Only now the young Marine was forming his own theories of what it took to win on a modern battlefield. The first thing to go was the idea of storming enemy beachheads, no matter the cost in American lives. "I came to a philosophy very quickly that you don't send a Marine to do what a bullet can do."

His other insight was similar to the lessons learned by Ray Smith and Marty Steele after their first brushes with death. "Almost intuitively," Jones said, "I figured out the only thing worth dying for over there was another Marine."

About 10:00 A.M. that morning, a sister company, Echo, arrived to relieve him. His ordeal was over. Lt. Jim Jones had acquitted himself well. So had his men.

"When we left Foxtrot Ridge," he recalled, "every Marine in the company had an AK-47" taken from a dead enemy soldier.

Over the next few days, Jones worked to resupply his men, ordering much-needed stores of food, water, clothing, and ammo. As his company licked its wounds, Black Jack Davis brought in fresh officers, including a second lieutenant named Jerry Martin.

The acrid smell of scorched earth and flesh still hung in the air. Martin, who had followed Jones's Basic School class at Quantico, tried to hide his shock at the sight of a large pile of packs and helmets, as he realized the gear was spattered with the blood of dead and wounded Marines.[7]

"Where's the skipper?" he asked, wondering how he would ever fit in with such a seasoned bunch of fighters. The men all looked gaunt, and some appeared shell-shocked. Yet to a man, their faces lit up when he asked to see their boss.

"Over there," a private said, pointing toward a scantily clad man in boxer shorts with tiger stripes. The rangy lieutenant wore unlaced combat boots and was as emaciated as everyone else. Like the rest of his men, he was waiting to get a new uniform.

"That's Lieutenant Jones," a Marine said.

Jones shook the hand of the green lieutenant in his crisp new uniform and shiny boots. He sent Martin over to a platoon sergeant, who told him to get a field pack. The only packs, though, had been stained with the blood of fallen Marines.

F Company was now down to about sixty men—a third less than before the battle and less than half its optimum size. Yet its morale remained high. Perhaps it was the exhilaration of surviving what could have been their last night on earth. Martin also sensed something special about the confidence exuded by the skinny guy in tiger-striped shorts.

On May 29, Foxtrot Company returned to LZ Hawk and marched up to the battalion commander's post. One by one, the Marines proudly delivered the captured AK-47s, creating a large stockpile of enemy weapons outside Black Jack Davis's tent. Then Jones led them off to get their new uniforms and other supplies.

That day, the division commander, Maj. Gen. Ray Davis, flew into LZ Hawk and talked to Black Jack about the battle. He told him about Jones's gutsy performance, and the general nodded.

"Oh yeah, I've known Lieutenant Jones a long time," he said.

A few days later, Black Jack called Jim with a message from the general. "He wants you to be his aide. It's a good opportunity, and I'm not going to stand in your way."

Jones would have to give this some serious thought. General Davis was a Corps legend and old family friend. He'd served in Paris in the 1950s and knew Jim through his father, who was then in the Marine Reserves.

Ray Davis was a hero of the Pacific island campaigns of World War II and won a Medal of Honor for valor at the Chosin Reservoir in Korea. His many other commendations—the Navy Cross, two Silver Star medals, and four Bronze Stars—made him one of the most highly decorated men in the Corps. Jones knew him simply as a quiet guy who coached baseball in Paris, where he served as assistant coach on Davis's American Little League team.

It was tempting to rejoin him under very different circumstances. He could learn a great deal, and it might help advance his fledgling career. And yet after all he'd been through with his guys, he felt torn about leaving. He couldn't decide, so he asked Lieutenant Colonel Davis to make the call. When Jones put down the radio, he wondered if he was a fool for not accepting on the spot.

Black Jack called back a few minutes later. "Jim," he said, "my advice is to join General Davis. It'll be good for both of you." He had been a tough boss, but on this day, the battalion commander sounded downright avuncular.

Lieutenant Jones was ordered to return to his old company, since Foxtrot's commander, Bo Dishman, was back from his R & R. He was upset about missing the fierce firefight. "Bo Dishman was a real warrior," according to Jones

Jones could have taken his own R & R in Hawaii but didn't because the battalion had a shortage of officers. He also had an intuitive sense about what might happen if he returned to civilization. Taking off might mean he'd lose his fighting edge. He'd seen it happen to other guys, some of whom got killed. So the lieutenant stayed with his old unit, Golf Company, for a few weeks before reporting for his aide duty.

The outside world managed to intrude in the war zone, though. On June 6, 1968, he was awakened in the middle of the night during another driving monsoon. Rain sprayed into his tent. "Sir," a radioman said, "sorry to bother you, but the battalion operations officer is calling. He says it's urgent."

Jones sprang up. Were they being overrun again? Ever since the battle for Foxtrot Ridge, he was a little on edge. He pulled on his boots and scrambled into the stormy night, getting soaked within seconds. His Ted Williams rain suit had been toasted by the napalm blast.

He was shivering by the time he reached his command post. He took the radio headset and heard Capt. Bill Throckmorton, the battalion operations officer.

"Morning, Jim," he said calmly. "We've got a telegram of an urgent nature from Washington, D.C."

Washington, D.C.? Jim's mind raced for answers. "So what is it, sir?"

"Just hold your horses," Throckmorton said. "We'll get to that. Just let me read the whole thing." He cleared his throat.

"'From: U.S. Naval Hospital.'"

Diane?

"Subject . . ."

"Sir, would you mind reading a little faster," Jim said. "It's raining like hell."

"Now, now," the captain chided. "Subject: birth announcement. Paragraph one: delivered from Mrs. James L. Jones, a six-pound, eleven-ounce boy."

Dripping wet and cold, Jim felt a warm glow enveloping him. After all the death and destruction, it was hard to believe that he could be blessed by the birth of a baby boy, James Logan Jones III.

"Congratulations, Jim!" Throckmorton said, chuckling over the radio.

It was good his face was already wet from the rain. No one could see his reaction as he went back to his tent and tried to grasp the fact that he was now not only a Marine, but a father, too.

SEVEN

Positions of Authority

In peacetime, serving as a general's aide could be a cushy job, chock full of rich food, cigars, cocktails, and embassy parties. Aides were seen as rear-echelon dandies who tended to their grizzled old bosses as they planned the next parade or dinner party. The position once had a certain Victorian quality described by an old British military manual: "An aide-de-camp is to his general what Mercury was to Jupiter."

Any grandiose notions Jim Jones may have held about being an aide didn't last long in the pressure cooker of Vietnam in the summer of 1968. It was all he could do to keep up with his boss as Maj. Gen. Ray Davis shook the 3rd Marine Division out of its fighting doldrums. After the Tet Offensive, Davis felt the 17,000 Marines under his command suffered from a defensive mindset that was unacceptable for the offensive-minded Corps.

Davis shifted his troops into overdrive by taking the fight to the North Vietnamese and leading from the front. He shunned the second guessing coming from the brass in Saigon and applied the hard lessons learned in hand-to-hand combat with the North

Koreans, Chinese Communists, and Japanese. After Jones became his aide, Davis told him, "My theory is to have an overpowering force, so when the enemy comes, you not only stop him, you destroy him."

In one of his first moves, Davis quietly broke the official American rules of engagement for clashes with the North Vietnamese along the demilitarized zone. Officially, the Marines were limited to squad-sized patrols near the DMZ. Davis circumvented this policy by building up the Corps' troop strength to stand by just outside the neutral zone. That way, when the North attacked, the 3rd Division was ready to beat them back.

Davis ordered a series of mobile air and ground attacks through the summer that started to shift the strategic equation, putting the North Vietnamese on the defensive. "He was sick and tired of the Marines waiting for the enemy to engage us," Jones said later.

Davis's warrior mentality was all the more heartening after Jones' harrowing night on Foxtrot Ridge, when his company had been so badly outnumbered. He watched with an apprentice's awe as Davis, the master tactician, kept the enemy off-balance and positioned his forces to block escape routes into the mountain enclaves of neighboring Laos.

Davis was determined to attack the enemy's supply lines, strangling the ammo, food, and supplies the NVA snuck across the DMZ and from Laos. "He choked off their ability to exist in the northern I Corps," Jones said. "Once he got the division turned around, the number of attacks almost disappeared to nothing. General Davis always felt that should have been part and parcel of defeating the North, including invading Laos, Cambodia, and the DMZ."

The general from Georgia taught Jones another valuable lesson: senior leaders should be seen by their troops. Early each morning, he left his command base at Dong Ha and boarded a Huey helicopter to visit as many units as he could across the many hundreds of miles of terrain under his command. The flights could be harrowing as they ran a gauntlet of gunfire from snipers lying in wait below. The command 'copter took plenty of hits but was never shot down.

Jones came to admire Davis not only for his courage but also his subtle leadership style. The division chief managed to get his point across with a few well-chosen words rather than resorting to invective. After more than a year in the Corps, Jones was used to getting chewed out by blustery, old-school Marines who seemed to relish abusing their juniors. Such verbal abuse might work on impressionable kids at Quantico or Parris Island, but on the stressful stage of Vietnam, it seemed shallow and stupid.

There was nothing shallow about Ray Davis, who showed Jones that a quiet man can be a strong leader. He rarely raised his voice. Indeed, some senior officers would pull Jones aside to complain that the general from Georgia was so low key that they couldn't figure out what he wanted them to do. Just listen carefully, Jones advised, and you'll see what the general wants. His suggestions were his orders. If you picked up the nuance, you'd be fine. "The guys who didn't figure that out were not around for long," Jones recalled.

Davis also had a fun-loving side and tried to make the best of life in a hot, miserable war zone. As the temperature topped 120 degrees, he often ended his day in the helicopter by landing on the beach for a cool dip in the South China Sea. This wasn't far from known enemy strongholds around the DMZ.

Davis and his staff would jump out of the helicopter, discard their sweat-soaked uniforms, and dash into the sea for a cooling swim in the buff. Sometimes regimental commanders would drop by in their own helicopters to swim and talk over the next day's plans.

During one such chat, geysers of water began shooting up from several hundred yards offshore. As the splashes started moving inland toward the Marines, the general and his entourage realized these were not whale sightings. Enemy mortars were walking the rounds toward them, closer and closer.

Everyone raced out of the water and double-timed it toward the helicopter. The Huey pilot had his whirlybird ready for a getaway. They jumped inside, and after everyone was aboard, Davis gave the thumbs-up for takeoff. The beach and the explosions were receding below them when Jones realized something of personal, if not tactical, importance. They'd left their uniforms on the sand.

"Sir," he told Davis, "We can't go back to the division CP like this."

Davis smiled at the prospect of landing in Dong Ha in the nude. However, he agreed that they should avoid such a cheeky display before the troops. *Stars and Stripes* would have a field day: *General Escapes Mortar Attack, Moons Men.* "OK, Jim," he said, "let's pay a visit to the 2nd Battalion and borrow some clothes."

After months of flying around the I Corps section of South Vietnam, Davis's chopper, Seaworthy 4-3, was a familiar sight. When it hovered over the alternate landing zone, 2nd Battalion commander, Lt. Col. Billy Duncan, dashed out to greet them. He was strapping on his pistol and adjusting his hat to be properly attired.

When Davis and his entourage jumped out of the helicopter in all of their glory, Duncan saluted and managed to say with a straight face, "Nice to see you again, sir!"

Jim Jones's three months as an aide was a seminal experience that helped him decide to stay in the Marine Corps once his three-year commitment ended the next year. He was in the minority among the 516 men of his Basic School class, however. After the harrowing experiences of Vietnam in 1967 and during the Tet Offensive of 1968, most of his classmates chose to return to civilian life. Some had no choice: thirty-nine of the lieutenants from Quantico were killed in action. Some, such as Clebe McClary, suffered near-fatal wounds and may have wished they had died.

McClary, the South Carolina track star, whose wife, Deanna, had charmed the officers at Quantico, suffered traumatic injuries when his Force Reconnaissance Platoon in the 1st Marine Division was attacked by a much larger force of North Vietnamese regulars in March 1968. Like Jim Jones, he'd been ordered to occupy a hill of little strategic value. Yet he had not escaped unscathed. A suicide bomber, or "sapper," leaped into his fighting hole bearing a satchel of explosives. McClary was blown out of his hole and fell back to earth like a rag doll. His left hand was torn off, an eye was gone, and he was almost left for dead.

His recovery was long and painful, and would continue for the rest of his life. Despite dozens of surgeries, his body remained riddled with shrapnel that constantly shifted around his interior. Yet with the help of his dedicated wife, Clebe McClary endured.

In the summer of 1968, was sent to the Bethesda Naval Hospital. As he began trundling about the fourteenth floor recovery unit, he took an interest in a lieutenant next door whose condition was even worse than his own. The patient had a private room and a personal corpsman, which seemed odd. Yet when McClary learned his identity, he understood.

The badly injured man was Lewis B. Puller Jr., son of Gen. Lewis B. "Chesty" Puller. Chesty Puller was a Corps legend, winner of five Navy Cross medals and the epitome of a U.S. Marine.

Lew Puller was critically wounded by a booby-trapped artillery round on the day Jones was leaving Vietnam. Everyone at the air base at Danang heard that General Puller's son had stepped on a booby trap.

One day, McClary stopped by and tried to strike up a conversation. Young Puller ignored him, though, acting glum and unresponsive. Word spread around the ward of an impending visit by Chesty Puller himself. McClary was mortified, since he hadn't cleaned up and didn't feel squared away. Since Deanna wasn't around, he called out for help. "I need a shave! Corpsman!"

A civilian with a bulldog face appeared in the doorway.

"What's wrong with you, Marine?"

McClary recognized Chesty Puller from his photographs and sat up in bed. It was as close to standing at attention as he could manage.

"Oh, sir, I heard you were coming," McClary sputtered. "I was hoping to get a shave before—"

Waving aside McClary's objections, he marched over to his bed. "Aw, hell, Marine, I can shave you."

With that, Chesty Puller found a razor, filled a bowl with warm water, and set to work. McClary felt honored to be shaved by a living legend. His sense of pride helped him endure the pain as Puller—no doubt distracted by his own grief over his son's condition—dragged the razor blade along McClary's jaw and unwittingly pulled out some stitches.

Over the days and weeks in Bethesda, McClary and his wife could see that General Puller was hurting as he tried to accept the plight of his only son. Not only was Lt. Lew Puller in bad physical shape, he was also deeply depressed. McClary couldn't help wondering whether the general's son had been brought back to the States too soon because of his special status. It was hard enough dealing with the loss of limbs, but the added burden of being Chesty Puller's son seemed to make things worse.

The crusty general fought to hide his feelings, sometimes by slipping into McClary's room just to have a good cry. McClary would leave him alone, and after a few minutes, Puller rubbed his eyes with a handkerchief and put his bulldog face back on. Nothing more was said.

During his own recovery, McClary experienced a religious awakening and decided to evangelize in the recovery ward. He hobbled over to Puller's room with some Christian music tapes and a small recorder. "Hey, Lew, how about playing these?"

Puller shrugged and didn't comment, which McClary, in his newfound fervor, took as a yes. He put the recorder by the bed and turned on the gospel music of Ray Hildebrand, a former pop singer known for his hit, "Hey Paula." Puller listened but showed little interest. McClary took the hint and turned it off, returning to his room.

The next day, Puller's corpsman came over and said, "Sir, the lieutenant asks if he could hear that music again." McClary was happy to do anything he could to try to lift his neighbor's spirits.

Clebe McClary went on to become a motivational speaker and evangelist, appearing with the likes of Billy Graham and former New York Yankee great Bobby Richardson. They were voices in the wilderness during this period of national turmoil. The America that the Marines left in 1967 was hardly recognizable a year later. The Vietnam War had divided the country, sparking street protests and a deep distrust, even hatred, of authority—especially the military. Meanwhile, the Civil Rights movement had spiraled into violent protests, sweeping up groups like the Black Panthers, who mixed community service in the inner city with target practice on police.

The kaleidoscopic events put the Marine Corps in the uncomfortable position of fighting a war on two fronts: the continuing battle in Southeast Asia and the domestic rebellion in the States. Starting in 1969, the Nixon administration started using Marine, Army, and National Guard troops to protect the government against the threat—real or imagined—of rioters and latter-day anarchists. The White House's growing paranoia put young officers like Jim Jones and Marty Steele into positions of authority that forced them to make life-and-death decisions about civil unrest. One wrong move—a thrust of the bayonet, a squeeze of the trigger—could light the very short fuse on the streets of the nation. Out on the ramparts, the lieutenants found that every bit of their training, experience, and good judgment was put to the test. The domestic tensions also put their commitment to the Corps to a new kind of test that often hit very close to home, even threatening their families.

Throughout 1968, Marty Steele was itching to get back to Vietnam. He was tired of sitting on the sidelines in the States when so many of his Quantico colleagues were in the thick of the fighting. He was learning his chosen trade within the Corps, working with tanks and naval artillery. He had come to believe that the Marines needed to upgrade their mechanized armor if they were going to be a part of the defense of Western Europe. A war with the Russians was a doomsday scenario that, God willing, would never get beyond the stage of war games and NATO exercises. Steele had seen how outdated and outgunned the Marines were in both tactics and heavy armor. As a young officer, he realized he could make a difference in catching up with the dominant player when it came to heavy-metal fighting—the U.S. Army.

His urge to upgrade the Corps' tank prowess often had to take a back seat to more immediate concerns, such as the riots in the streets. In August 1968, after the violent clashes in Chicago at the Democratic National Convention, Marty received an alarming order: he was to organize 17 tanks and more than 100 Marines at Camp Lejeune, North Carolina, and get them aboard a freight train bound for Washington, D.C., as part of the Marine Corps' preparations for antiwar protests.

Federal authorities were on edge in the wake of events in Chicago, where Mayor Richard Daley had called out 20,000 police, National Guardsman, and soldiers. To the horror of millions of Americans watching on TV at home, the police and protesters clashed. Flower power was easily crushed by police power, but the strong-armed tactics helped generate sympathy for the war protesters.

Watching this travesty unfold on a flickering TV screen at Camp Lejeune, Steele couldn't help wondering whether this was the start of a new Civil War. This was a bleak prospect for a man who, only a few years ago, had helped defend the rights of black friends in Fayetteville, Arkansas. Now, armed with canister rounds and machine-gun ammunition, Steele's company was ordered to ship out to Washington to set up a defensive ring around the nation's capital.

Marty winced as he watched college students and radical Yippies rioting in Chicago, calling police "pigs," burning flags, and shouting obscenities. Yet he was equally troubled by the sight of Chicago's cops clubbing demonstrators and dragging them off to paddy wagons.

He followed orders, though, and got his tanks and men aboard a train waiting at a rail siding at Jacksonville, North Carolina, home of Camp Lejeune. As the C&O train rumbled through the dark pine forests of eastern Carolina, Steele wondered how he could order his 110 men to fire on fellow Americans—mostly young people who had managed to avoid the draft and were expressing pent-up frustrations about the war. Now the war was coming to them in the form of a highly lethal U.S. Marine tank company.

As they neared the Virginia border, word came down the line that the orders were rescinded. No tanks would be sent into Washington, at least not this day. Steele felt his pulse go down and awaited some official explanation about the sudden change of plans. None ever came. The C&O diesel locomotive chugged into a rail siding and stopped to switch engines for the trip back to the base.

Steele hopped off the train and breathed in the fresh air, a fragrant mix of pine and honeysuckle. Though he was usually pumped up for any assignment, he was relieved to be turning back to the home base at Lejeune. The Marines weren't meant to serve as riot police, and besides, he'd already had to face down one angry crowd.

That had taken place four months earlier on the night of April 4, 1968, when Dr. Martin Luther King Jr. was assassinated in Memphis. Steele was the duty officer at the U.S. Naval Base in Guantanamo Bay. The death of the civil rights leader struck a deep chord of anger and despair even at this remote, twelve-mile-long outpost in Cuba. Upon hearing the news, hundreds of workers from the Dominican Republic formed a mob and marched into the base stadium to vent their outrage. As duty officer, Steele moved to cordon off the area to protect the people on the base, Americans and Dominicans alike.

First, he ordered a line of M-103 tanks into place outside the stadium. Then he strapped on his .45-caliber pistol, grabbed a bullhorn, and marched down a tunnel to the soccer field. Walking out into the warm spring night, he looked around at the milling crowd, taking stock of the situation and watching the faces of the Dominicans, most of whom didn't speak English. Tears streamed down their cheeks and wails of anguish rose over the field like a siren. They didn't appear to be violent, just hurt and confused by the news of King's violent death.

Picking up his bullhorn, he announced, "Please return to your homes!"

To his amazement, this got their attention. The shouting subsided and they were listening. He hoped enough of the crowd understood English to pass the word on to the others.

"Friends, we grieve with you about Dr. King's death," Steele told them. "Now let's leave here in a way that pays respect to his memory."

Something in Steele's voice or manner must have struck a chord because the Dominicans soon dispersed and went home. That night, as he filled out a report on the incident, he reflected on how he was uniquely prepared for dealing with the near riot.

As a young man, he had been thrust into a number of tense and sometimes dangerous situations in the racially divided South. His hometown of Fayetteville, Arkansas, was a university town with factions of moderate-to-liberal thinkers. It became known for having one of the first integrated school systems south of the Mason-Dixon. For Steele, it had been no big deal to have black friends as classmates and teammates in baseball, football, and track.

While they could study and play together in their hometown, the world beyond was not as welcoming, to put it mildly. Trouble followed the integrated teams of Fayetteville whenever they ventured outside their city limits. As captain of what was known as Fayetteville High's "mixed" football team, Steele became the lightning rod for racists from Arkansas to Texas. One game night, his team pulled into the high school parking lot at Springdale, Arkansas, only to find a player's effigy hanging on a tree. The effigy had been burned and hung with a sign around its neck that said, "Nigger lover." The charred jersey had Steele's number on it, 44. The boys of Fayetteville played the game anyway, with Marty scoring a touchdown to tie it as time ran out.

Another incident from high school seared itself into Steele's consciousness and helped shape his behavior as a Marine and as a man. During track season, he happened into a Little Rock restaurant with a group of teammates taking a break from Arkansas' 1964 all-star track meet. As they waited to be served, the laughing and joking boys were approached by the restaurant owner. The man squinted down at the table, then pulled out a .38-caliber revolver and stuck it in Steele's ear.

"White boy," he sputtered, "if you don't get these niggers out of here, I'm going to blow your fucking head off."

The pistol made Steele's ear bleed. Yet he had the presence of mind not to make any quick moves. Instead, he calmly looked around the table and said to his friends, "You didn't want to eat here anyway, did you?"

He headed toward the door, and the other boys followed. It was not the last time Steele would show grace under pressure.

In Cuba four years later, Steele found it strange to think that he somehow had been placed in the role of an authority figure trying to quell a brewing race riot. God truly worked in mysterious ways, he thought, and so did the Marine Corps. Where else would a lowly twenty-two-year-old lieutenant have to assume that much authority?

Cuba was an eye-opener in other ways, providing vivid reminders of the continuing struggle between democracy and dictatorship, as well as the price of freedom. Steele witnessed the lengths people would go to flee Castro's police state to reach American soil—or as close as they could get without going out to sea. The Guantanamo naval base dates back to 1741 when British Marines invaded the island to secure a port for the British fleet.[1] It had become an American stronghold after the United States defeated Spain in the Spanish-American War of 1898. By the 1960s, it had become a thorn in the side for the Soviet Union and its leading ally, Fidel Castro, helping to serve as a continuing reminder of the military response that would come with any threat against the American mainland. As such, it became a beacon of hope for Cubans trying to escape Castro's police state.

On Easter Sunday, 1968, Steele was officer-of-the-day when he received a report that a family had hijacked a train and was heading toward Guantanamo Bay seeking political asylum.

The desperate Cubans—about a dozen men, women, and children—nearly wrecked the train by hitting its air brakes and screeching to a halt. They leaped off and ran for their lives. A squad of Cuban soldiers gave hot pursuit, shooting wildly from jeeps. They wounded a few of the asylum-seekers, and some gave up their run for freedom. A few reached the barbed-wire fence of the base, though, forcing the Marine guards to decide what to do:

help them, which would be a serious breach of the treaty with Cuba, or let them be arrested and, likely, killed. The Marines helped, and Steele was glad. The looks of relief and joy on the faces of the fleeing Cubans were worth any questions he would face from his superiors about the guards' actions.

The Cuban soldiers quietly collected the wounded outside the fence and left without a fight or much of a protest. They seemed embarrassed and wanted to forget the whole affair, lest word of it get back to Fidel, who was known to fly into rages over such incidents.

As the Marines found food and shelter for the survivors, Steele reflected on the Cubans' courage and that of people around the world seeking freedom and democracy. He was itching to get back to Vietnam, where the major struggle for freedom was underway.

He finally got his wish in the spring of 1969 as the tenor of the war was changing. A new president, Richard Nixon, was pursuing an exit strategy of "Vietnamization," a euphemism for a gradual pullout that would allow the South Vietnamese to sink or swim. The hope was that by 1972 they'd be ready to defend themselves.

As far as Steele was concerned, though, the war was still in full swing. He was happy to put his skills to work as a forward aerial observer for the USS *St. Paul.* The heavy cruiser was steaming up and down the coast of South Vietnam, providing fire support for ground troops of the Marines and Army fighting inland. It earned the distinction of shooting more rounds than any other ship during the near decade of fighting in Vietnam.

The ship needed its own eyes to guide its heavy guns, which was where Steele, now a first lieutenant, came in. He regularly helicoptered to shore to an Army airfield, where he boarded a single-engine 01 Bird Dog. This lightly-armed observation plane skimmed over the tree line at only 100 miles per hour. The creeping plane was a tempting target for enemy sharpshooters, but its slow going let Steele scrutinize the mountains and jungle for troop movements or hidden fortifications. When he spotted something, it was his job to call for air or naval bombardments.

On one such flight over the Central Highlands, Steele scanned the sharp ridge that seemed to stretch from north to south like the spine of a slumbering dragon. It was a crystal clear day with visibility of ten miles or more. Steele was enjoying the spectacular view when something caught his eye—a flicker of light.

"Did you see that?" he asked the pilot, Captain Brown.

"See what?"

Brown was a high-strung aviator who had given off strange vibes from the moment they met at the airfield.

"Something shining down below," Steele said, narrowing his eyes and pointing. "Right there! Take me down."

"Aw, lieutenant, are you sure?"

Steele was entranced by the sighting and ignored Brown's hesitation. "Take me down," he ordered.

Brown finally took the single-engine plane on a downward arc as Steele studied the sleeping dragon, searching for the light source. Was it a signal of some sort—someone flashing a mirror, perhaps even a downed American pilot? He pressed his forehead against the cockpit, straining to see, and to solve the mystery. The mountaintop was choked with elephant grass that camouflaged the troops and supplies steadily sneaking into the country on the Ho Chi Minh trail.

The Bird Dog leveled off about 500 feet above the grassy ridge. The plane bore 2.75-inch Zuni rockets on each wing, but the rockets wouldn't help much against any strong antiaircraft fire. The longer they hugged the mountain, the more agitated Brown became. Although Steele did not outrank the Army captain, his firm voice and manner gave him the upper hand in the cockpit. Steele was as determined as Captain Ahab stalking Moby Dick.

"There!" Steele shouted, pointing below. "Someone just slipped into a cave! Did you see?"

Brown said he hadn't seen a thing.

"Well, I did," Steele said, his mind racing. What *was* it? Then he had his own flash: the sun had reflected off a Soviet-style metal helmet. The North Vietnamese soldier must have been ducking into a cave, which led . . . where? To a tunnel perhaps, or a supply complex, or an ammo dump! The possibilities were endless. Steele's adrenalin was pumping like a Texas oil well. This could be something big.

Reaching for the radio, he hailed the Marine commander on board the *St. Paul.*

"We've got some enemy activity below," Steele told Capt. John Fanning. "Request for fire."

Fanning, his senior colleague aboard the *St. Paul,* said he would consult the ship's captain. A minute later, Fanning was back on the radio, requesting the firing coordinates. The ship's firing battery was ready.

Lieutenant Steele calculated the position, knowing that the more precise the map coordinates, the more likely the *St. Paul's* 8-inch guns would hit the target. The cruiser was nearly fifteen miles away, out in the South China Sea, so his best hope was to strike within about 100 meters of the cave—from that distance, the equivalent of a bullseye. He requested a delayed fuse; that way, the shells could pierce the mountaintop before exploding.

Fanning took note of the coordinates and the fuse order. "Hang tight, Marty," he said. A few seconds later Fanning reported, "Shot over."

A strand of smoke rose like a genie on the eastern horizon, and Steele reported the sighting: "Shot out."

Steele held his breath for what seemed like an eternity. Yet it took only a few seconds before the shell hit the ground, so near that Steele felt he could touch it. The *St. Paul* was dead on target, scoring a bullseye from the sea. And that was only the start. The single shell with a delayed fuse set off a string of secondary explosions which Steele counted from his aerial perch. The entire mountain seemed to shudder as a dozen underground blasts rippled across an area the size of seven football fields. The Bird Dog shook in the air above, rocked by the explosive updraft.

As Steele stared in awe at the mountain, it brought to mind something of biblical proportions, of trembling earth and belching smoke. It had been his lucky day. By spotting one helmet, he'd helped destroy what appeared to be a major North Vietnamese ammunition dump. He savored the results and radioed them back to Fanning on the *St. Paul.* The Marines and sailors manning the guns cheered.

The Bird Dog pilot was in no mood to celebrate, though. He looked pale and shaky. "My God, Lieutenant Steele," Brown cried in a trembling voice, "let's get out of here!"

"No," Steele said. "I want to see if any troops try to get out."

"But . . ."

"Bank the Bird Dog back around," Steele said firmly. "I want to take another look." He touched the holster on his hip.

Brown reluctantly banked the plane above the inferno. Somehow an enemy soldier escaped the explosions and starting shooting at the airborne enemy that had wreaked such havoc. The bullets scored a few hits on the fuselage—*plink, plink, plink*—but missed the engine and fuel tank. God, those North Vietnamese are tough bastards, Steele thought. He could live with some bullet holes in the wings, but he dreaded taking a shot up his rear. Still, he was mesmerized by the roiling explosions of the mountain, as though the earth was vomiting the North Vietnamese from its very gut. After so many monotonous hours of buzzing over the mountains, this was like hitting the jackpot.

Brown continued to be shaky, and when another bullet pinged off the wing, he pleaded, "Lieutenant, please, can we please return to base? We're going to go down!"

Steele had heard enough. He pulled out his .45-caliber pistol, opened the window of the cockpit and started returning fire.

"We're not done with this mission yet," he hollered through the roar of the wind. "Fire your rockets."

Brown obediently turned the plane again and aimed the Zunis.

"Fire!" Steele hollered.

The rockets raced toward their assailant, but with all the smoke and dust, it was hard to tell if they hit anything or did any damage.

Brown kept pleading with Steele to turn back to the air base. "I've only got a week to go here, Lieutenant Steele," he said, breaking down. "I don't want to die!"

Steele didn't want to die either, but chickening out was not an option. Both of them were risking life and limb, and they had a mission to complete. It was time to impress this fact on the nervous pilot. He leaned forward and placed the cold barrel of his pistol against Brown's skull. "We *will* complete this mission," he said.

The message sunk in, and Brown glumly continued flying the Bird Dog despite sporadic gunfire and the distinctive *ping* of bullet on metal. Steele forgot his problems with the pilot while he savored the sight below. God, he loved the guns of the *St. Paul.* One true shot from the sea was all it took to destroy thousands, maybe millions, of the enemy's bullets, shells, and rockets. He enjoyed seeing it go up in smoke because he knew the ammo wouldn't be used against his fellow Marines and soldiers—guys like Eddie, who had died from a single shot in his back.

Finally, as the plane began running low on fuel, Steele allowed his miserable pilot to fly to the coastal airfield. Only after they landed did Steele realize his panicked pilot had soiled himself.

He gave Brown time to clean up before talking to him alone in the locker room. By then, Brown was sobbing and apologetic. "I've been over here for more than a year," he said, his face wet with tears. "I just want to make it home."

Steele was disgusted by what he viewed as cowardice on the pilot's part, and actions that deserved a court martial. Since Brown was a short-timer, though, he simply patted him on the back and told him he understood.

Before leaving the base, Steele found the commanding officer and informed him, "Don't let that pilot fly again. He's a danger to himself and everyone else."

That night, Steele caught a helicopter back out to the *St. Paul.* After climbing aboard the heavy cruiser, Fanning clapped him on the shoulder and said, "Well done!" They held a short celebration with their band of Marines and naval gunners. The *St. Paul* had destroyed the largest enemy ammunition dump ever found in the Central Highlands.

Amid the beer and the toasts, Steele thought of Cindy back home and wished he could call her about his memorable day. He also wished he could tell his mentor in Quantico, Staff Sgt. Karl Taylor.

Taylor was gone, though. He had distinguished himself during Operation Meade River on December 8, 1968. After learning his platoon leader was killed in an ambush, Taylor and another Marine crawled forward to their beleaguered unit through a hail of fire. He shouted encouragement to the men and deployed them to protected positions. Eventually, Taylor saw there was only one way to win this fight. He charged a machine-gun bunker, firing his grenade launcher as he ran. He squelched the attack but was mortally wounded in the process. Taylor was posthumously awarded the Medal of Honor.

Aboard the *St. Paul*, as the adrenalin rush of the day subsided, Marty Steele strolled on the deck for some fresh air. It was a clear, bracing night, and his thoughts drifted back to when Taylor had eclipsed the sun standing outside the auditorium in Quantico after Basic School graduation. He could still hear the sergeant's final advice to him. His speech was marred by a harelip, but his message was clear: "Lieutenant, do your duty."

EIGHT

May Day Malaise

Long before the Vietnam War, a senior officer named Victor H. Krulak eloquently expressed the paradox of the role of the Corps in the life of the nation. "The United States does not need a Marine Corps mainly because she has a fine modern Army and vigorous Air Force," Krulak wrote in a 1957 memo, as the Marines were trying to fend off one of the regular attempts to do away with the smallest of America's military services. (President Harry Truman had tried the same thing after World War II.) "Her Army fights on the ground—on any kind of ground—and does it well. Her Air Force fights in the air and does it well too. . . . The Marines claim to have a mystical competence in landing operations, but they really don't."[1]

No, Krulak concluded to then–Commandant General Randolph Pate: ". . . in terms of cold, mechanical logic, the United States does not *need* a Marine Corps. However, for good reasons which completely transcend cold logic, the United States *wants* a Marine Corps."[2]

And yet by the chaotic days of the late 1960s, one would have been hard pressed to discover a national desire for anyone in uniform—Marine, sailor, soldier, or cop. After years of protest and rebellion, nothing was sacred, unless one counted the high esteem given that wild weed, *cannabis sativa.* After the children of the Baby Boom inhaled marijuana, they saw life in a whole new strobe light. On college campuses—where the struggle for Civil Rights morphed into what historian Theodore Roszak called "the making of a counterculture"—students and many of their professors traded in the literature of Hemingway and Eliot for the Eastern meditations of Baba Ram Dass ("Be Here Now") or, if they spent any time on the past, tapped on the doors of perception of the English mystic, William Blake, who wrote during an earlier revolutionary period: "Rouse up, O Young Men of the New Age!"

Unlike Blake, who witnessed England's wars and birth pangs of democracy in the early 1800s, the modern rousings were often driven by drugs and loud music that—in that quintessential way of the Baby Boomers—could stimulate and depress the national psyche, often at the same time. After the Chicago riots of 1968, the Jefferson Airplane captured the rebellious spirit in "Volunteers of Amerika" (the "k" replicating the spelling of America by the absurdist novelist Franz Kafka): *Look what's happening out in the streets/Got a revolution/Got to revolution.*

Yippie leader Jerry Rubin advocated a "youth international revolution" staged by "tribes of long hairs, armed women, workers, peasants and students." The White House would become "one big commune," and the Pentagon would be "replaced with an LSD experimental farm."

Though Rubin, a former sportswriter, undoubtedly was trying to stick it to America's comfortable middle class, the growing violence in the streets and clashes with police were not games. And for that short-haired tribe of Marine warriors, the leftist politics and Baby Boomer bacchanalia sometimes pushed their patience to the limit.

Jim Jones returned from Vietnam in late 1968 to attend the Marine Corps Birthday Ball at the Washington Hilton. Jones in his dress blue uniform and Diane in her long, green satin dress looked like a young prince and princess, and a throwback to a simpler, more conventional time. Beneath his polished exterior, however, Jim was still adjusting to life in this strange new land, wondering what had happened to the America he'd left behind. Making matters worse, he sometimes felt edgy since his internal alarm system had not shut off after leaving the war zone. He thrashed in his sleep and sat up in bed wondering if his men were under attack. "Go back to sleep, Jim," Diane would say. "You're back home now." It took a long time to feel back at home.

In late 1968, he reported to Camp Pendleton for duty with the 2nd Battalion, 2nd Infantry Training Regiment, where he worked with recently minted Marines from boot camp at nearby San Diego. Things went well enough that the next year he earned a promotion to captain, and got new orders that took him back to Washington, D.C., and the historic Marine Barracks.

Normally, working at the history-rich facility near the Capitol was a plum assignment, reserved for the best, poster-perfect Marines. The gregarious captain—tough with troops but with impeccable manners—fit the role to a T. He could take the social graces and nuances of his new job. However, he never bargained on becoming a street cop.

That became his fate, though, in the spring of 1971, as thousands of college students hitchhiked, jammed into VW microbuses, and otherwise tumbled into town for an antiwar protest meant to tie up Washington's main traffic arteries, paralyze the government, and make President Nixon choose between continuing the war or face anarchy at home. "The aim of May Day actions," one militant group declared with a Marxist tone, "is to raise the social cost of the war to a level unacceptable to America's rulers."

The immediate cause of the protest was Nixon's decision to invade Cambodia. Thousands of disaffected veterans—part of the Vietnam Veterans against the War—camped on the Washington Mall to prepare for a march to shut down the government. Beyond Cambodia, though, was the sense that the end was in sight in Indochina, and what better time to come together than on a sunny spring day, just after the cherry blossoms bloomed on the Ellipse.

Reading the papers, Captain Jones was troubled by some of the protesters' actions, such as throwing medals over the fence of the White House. And he was disappointed to hear a bright former Navy lieutenant, John Kerry, testify before the Senate Foreign Relations Committee that he joined fellow veterans on "one last mission—to search out and destroy the last vestige of this barbaric war, to pacify our own hearts, to conquer the hate and fear that have driven this country these last ten years and more."

Jones knew his own heart, and it had not been filled with hate and fear. It had been filled with a sense of duty and, though he rarely talked about it, love for his Marines. Now Kerry and other disaffected vets were implying that he'd been duped by his government and should make amends.

"So when thirty years from now our brothers go down the street without a leg, without an arm, or a face," Kerry said, "and small boys ask why, we will be able to say 'Vietnam' and not mean a desert, not a filthy obscene memory, but mean instead the place where America finally turned and where soldiers like us helped it in the turning."

It was a time of soul-searching and self-criticism by the young men of the middle to late 1960s who had started with one set of assumptions about their country—that its leaders could be trusted—but wound up bitter and disillusioned. The atmosphere of doubt was understandable, especially after the release of the Pentagon Papers, top secret reports leaked to the *New York Times* in 1971 by a former high-level defense analyst named Daniel Ellsberg.

The forty-volume document showed, for the first time, the dubious and flawed assumptions made by the Pentagon and White House during the buildup in Vietnam. Added to mounting evidence of government blundering and cover-ups were disturbing reports of military atrocities, including the murder of twenty-two Vietnamese civilians at My Lai.

As returning veterans like Kerry tossed away their medals, Jones considered his own Silver Star for his actions on Foxtrot

Ridge. Was it a fraud? Was *he* a fraud? Had he been duped? Was he just a cog in the military-industrial machine?

He thought back on Barry Kowalski's own misgivings about going to Vietnam. He never agreed with his old high school buddy, and he didn't agree with this new batch of doubters either. For all of America's missteps, he still believed America was standing up for democracy in a region sorely in need of freedom. North Vietnam had turned on its Roman Catholic, West-leaning citizens and deprived them of property and often their lives. Sure, idiots like Army lieutenant William Calley had committed atrocities at My Lai, and other men lost their cool under fire. Yet this was not the true face of America. To Jones, the real patriots were guys like Ralph Larsen and Harold Bunk and all the other men who stayed at their posts and fought because they had taken an oath to do so. It was easy to sit around the States and smoke dope and listen to protest songs, but it should never be done at the expense of men still in the field. The grunts in Vietnam read the news in *Stars and Stripes*, and heard the news on the Armed Forces Radio. They couldn't help but be demoralized by the widespread rejection of all things military back home. And there were still POWs enduring torture and deprivation in Hanoi's prisons, including John McCain, the downed Navy pilot.

Jones's Uncle Bill had been promoted to three-star general and transferred to Hawaii, where he lived across the street at Pearl Harbor from McCain's father, Adm. Jack McCain, who was CINC-PAC, commander of all U.S. military forces in the Pacific. (Lt. Gen. William K. Jones commanded the Marine Corps' Fleet Marine Force Pacific.) McCain was a crusty, cigar-smoking former submarine skipper. Despite his tough exterior, he bore the burden of awaiting the return of his son from the hands of torturers.

Jim Jones didn't buy the underlying premise of the protesters—that the brave "people's" regime of North Vietnam wore the white hat in this shootout, while the United States was backing the bad guys in Saigon. This simplistic rhetoric fed Ho's propaganda machine and endangered the American POWs, something that the Jane Fondas and Jerry Rubins of the world never seemed to care about.

Yet as the May Day protest in Washington approached, Jim Jones had no beef with his peers who were taking to the streets. He respected their right to peacefully assemble and protest. At the same time, he was uneasy about the future, as the country seemed to be rupturing. He felt like he was straddling a kind of fault line and was in danger of falling into a historical abyss.

On a sunny day in spring, May 13, 1971, Capt. Jim Jones donned his helmet and strapped on his pistol. Then he marched his 140-man company several miles from Marine Barracks to the northern edge of the 14th Street Bridge. Joining D.C. police, the Marines helped keep traffic flowing on this key gateway into downtown Washington. It was a raucous scene, with long-haired collegians passing a few feet from his Marines, who stood at parade rest.

"One, two, three four," the protesters yelled, "we don't want your fucking war!" Jones kept a poker face and a close eye on his men, looking for signs of trigger happiness. They managed to stay cool, despite the F-bombs dropping all around and occasional taunts from the marchers. Jones passed the time by picturing the men in Foxtrot Company who died for their country—and for the rights of these kids to protest and holler obscenities. What would the dead Marines' wives and mothers say about the insults? Had the deaths been in vain, or was there something enduring about laying down one's life for the country?

Amid the throng of long-haired students, Jones noticed a cluster of older guys in tattered fatigue jackets covered with peace signs and service medals. Some looked like biblical characters—bearded, gaunt, John-the-Baptist figures who looked ready for sackcloths and a diet of locusts. One guy carried a bed sheet crudely painted with "Vietnam Vets against the War." Jim looked for the Navy lieutenant, John Kerry, but couldn't spot him in the throng.

There was another protester Jones didn't see that day: his old chum Barry Kowalski, who was in town along with his father, Frank. After returning from Vietnam, Kowalski had entered law school in Washington and helped organize a political group—GIs for McGovern—campaigning for George McGovern to beat Nixon in 1972.

The morning rush hour passed with no major problems, and Jones got orders to return to barracks. Attorney General John N. Mitchell held a press conference to declare, "The traffic is flowing. The government is functioning."

Over the next few days, however, Jones and his Guard Company Marine Barracks endured a number of challenges to their resolve and self-control as they protected the seat of government, including the Capitol. They encamped in the Rotunda, with orders "to repel by any means necessary" any interlopers. Jones hoped he would not have to use deadly force against the protesters. Nearby, the marble bust of Abraham Lincoln calmly gazed down, a timeless reminder of an earlier schism that the Republic managed to survive.

Fortunately, the demonstrators didn't try to break in, staying outside to chant and sing. By the end of the day, Jones gazed up at Lincoln's statue and wondered what the Great Emancipator would have thought about this clash of ideas and cultures. All Jones could say for sure was that his Marines had made it through another long day, with no blood shed.

"Let's go home," he told his men. With that, he led them out of the Capitol, and back to the Marine Barracks about a mile away. The fragrance of dogwoods and cherry blossoms filled the air. The sound of boots on pavement echoed against the old townhouses of southeast Washington.

The protest hadn't shut down the capital, but D.C. police arrested more than 7,000 people and thwarted the protesters' plans to shut down key bridges across the Potomac. As the city returned to normal, Jones hoped he'd never be asked to patrol its streets again.

There was one personal detail of the march that he didn't learn about until much later: His baby sister, Diane, was in the march. A student at Tufts University in Boston, Diane Jones was nine years younger and worlds apart from her brother in lifestyle and politics. Like Jim, she had grown up in Paris and experienced its anti-Americanism. She never attended high school in the States, though, and by the time she arrived in Boston in 1970 to attend college, she tended to agree with much of the criticism of her native land. The following spring, she joined thousands of other college students in Washington to voice her dissent.

She rarely talked with Jim and never told him about her participation in the May Day march. It was several years before their father, after one too many drinks, asked his Marine son, "Wasn't it funny that you were inside the Capitol guarding it, while Diane was outside protesting?"

Jim Jones was not amused by this revelation. He countered by posing a hypothetical situation involving his father's older brother, Vernon, who stayed home during World War II with a vital job in the defense industry.

"OK, Dad," Jones said, "how would you have liked it if Uncle Vernon had wrapped himself in a Japanese flag while the Marines were out in the Pacific, protesting the war because too many Marines died on Guadalcanal?"

The elder Jones, who could still picture the bloody battle, put down his martini and stopped laughing. His son had drained the vermouth out of his cleverness.

1971 was a dark year when the laughing stopped for lots of people. The country seemed stuck in a cycle of doubt and paranoia, fueled by drugs and psychotic cults. America seemed to have lost its grip on the old values of faith, flag, and family. Indeed, "family" itself took on a whole new, and insidious, meaning after Charles Manson and the three women in his California commune were sentenced to death for the brutal slaying of actress Sharon Tate and six others near Hollywood.

Further undercutting the military's credibility, Army lieutenant William Calley was found guilty of the murders at My Lai. And a group called the Weather Underground claimed responsibility for a bomb blast in the bathroom of the U.S. Senate.

America's presence in Southeast Asia was staggering toward a bitter, unsatisfying end. U.S. troops were being sent home in droves as the South Vietnamese were given responsibility for all ground fighting, whether they were ready or not.

Even as America was turning its back on South Vietnam, a cadre of diehard Marines was trying to return to a war they knew wasn't over. Ray Smith was part of this group known as the "advisor mafia."

Smith had all the tools to return to Vietnam and work with its military. He had been promoted to captain in late 1970 after a stint at Camp Pendleton as a platoon and company commander. He went off to Vietnamese Language School in Arlington and, by the fall of 1971, was ready to put his new linguistic skills to work. He had faced a major hurdle, though: He was supposed to put in some staff time either at Marine Headquarters in Arlington, or down the hill in the Pentagon. Though he knew he had to punch this career ticket—shuffling papers and doing administrative work was part of a captain's life—his heart was pulling him back to the conflict.

After all he'd endured in Hue City, Khe Sanh, and the subsequent action near the DMZ, the twenty-six-year-old war hero was ready for another crack at the communists. As the protesters and pundits squabbled about American foreign policy, Smith had his own view of the matter. It was perhaps best expressed when he went home to Oklahoma to attend a family funeral, and an old teacher asked, "How long are you staying in the Marines, Ray?"

"I'll stay," he said, "until I kill all the communists, or they kill me."

Now that he could speak the language, Captain Smith longed to return to the tough South Vietnamese Marine Corps to serve as a *covan*, the native word for "trusted advisor."

Finding a way back required more than foreign language skills. He tried to convince his monitor—the senior officer in charge of his assignments—to quietly circumvent the Corps' personnel policies and transfer him back to Vietnam. It was an uphill battle at Headquarters Marine Corps. His monitor, Capt. Jack Kelly, said in no uncertain terms that, despite Ray's laudable intentions, he must endure his staff job just like everyone else.

A Vietnam veteran himself, Kelly also itched for a return engagement, and respected junior officers like Smith who wanted to get back in the fray. The captain was under strict orders to keep up-and-coming Marines alive and well, ready to fight another day. The Corps already had seen a mass exodus of young officers after their three-year hitches ended, and it was important to protect those who remained.

Yet Smith sensed that older officers like Kelly agreed that the South Vietnamese, for all their faults, deserved a better fate than having America turn its back on them.

After trying the direct approach, Smith knew he'd have to be more sophisticated in his tactics. In the Marine brotherhood, there's no stronger moral force than the gunnery sergeant, the backbone of the Corps. They serve as the head coaches on the battlefield because, in Shakespeare's words, they know "the discipline of war."

Smith's gunny from Hue City, Gunnery Sgt. J. L. Canley, knew his old sidekick was itching to get back to the war. So he took it on himself to plead his case with Kelly, with whom he'd served in Vietnam, using the kind of authority that transcended mere rank or seniority.

When Gunny Canley arrived unannounced at Kelly's office in Arlington, the captain was surprised and delighted. He stood up from his desk and gave him a warm welcome, shaking his hand and clapping him on the back.

"Have a seat, Gunny Canley. To what do I owe this pleasure?"

"Sir," Canley said, "you can't keep Lieutenant Smith strapped to a desk. Not when he sees how things are shaking out in 'Nam. You know they need him."

Kelly's face dropped. He could see what the broad-shouldered sergeant—a decorated Navy Cross winner—was trying to pull, and he initially tried to resist Canley's moral suasion. He launched into an explanation of the Corps' personnel policy and the importance of protecting the small crop of future officers.

Canley heard him out, then looked him in the eye. "Sir," he said, "with all due respect, you know that's a load of BS. Captain Smith is a warrior, and this is the only war shaking right now."

Kelly felt his defenses crumbling. He might as well have been having a little chat with Chesty Puller himself.

"OK, gunny, you win," Kelly said, laughing and raising his hands. "I surrender. I'll find a way to send him." With a worried look, he added, "Let's just hope he comes back in one piece."

NINE

"You Sonuvabitching Americans"

By early 1972, President Nixon's "Vietnamization" plan to turn over all military responsibilities to the South Vietnamese appeared to be about as solid as a bamboo hut in a typhoon. American intelligence indicated a massive buildup by North Vietnam, with a large offensive expected by spring. The only question was when and where the heavily-armed divisions of General Giap would storm across the DMZ and attempt to score a deathblow in the long-running war. Only the South Vietnamese Marine Corps, along with a handful of their "trusted advisors," the American *covans*, stood in their way.

At noon on March 30, 1972, the main body of Giap's army ended the suspense by launching an infantry and artillery assault. It was Thursday in Holy Week, but there was nothing sacred about the cannon fire and rockets that exploded around Ray Smith and his colleagues in the 4th Vietnamese Marine Battalion.

Smith was a *covan* for two companies on a hilltop called Nui Ba Ho, near the DMZ. He could see a long line of North Vietnam's Soviet-made troop carriers driving with impunity along

Highway Nine, the key east-west route bordered by a lush green valley. Thousands of enemy troops—several divisions by the look of things—were coming right at him. Two South Vietnamese outposts fell in the first wave of the attack by 200 Russian-built tanks and long-range 130-millimeter guns.

As Nui Ba Ho was pounded by artillery, Smith dove into his bunker and radioed for close air support. The response from brigade in Mai Loc was not encouraging: too much cloud cover, they said. "Shit," Smith muttered to no one in particular, "the one time I ask for air support and they wimp out over the weather."

A battery of 155-millimeter howitzers back at Mai Loc also fell silent. It was starting to feel very lonely atop Nui Ba Ho. Some of his company's mortar platoons returned fire, but it was like using pop guns against a tank. If they were this outgunned now, it would be only a matter of time before everyone would be killed or captured. Smith knew his South Vietnamese Marines would not be taken alive. Unlike the softer, less reliable soldiers in the Army of the Republic of Vietnam (ARVN), these guys were hardened veterans—a worthy counterpart to the U.S. Marines. Many had been defending their country against the communist invaders and Viet Cong insurgents for more than a decade and had scores of battles under their belts. Ray, for his part, was proud to fight with them—even if it wound up being his last battle.

Now that he could speak Vietnamese, Smith felt he better understood the underlying reasons for their commitment to fighting for a democratic nation. Many were professionals—lawyers, doctors, and engineers—whose lives had been ripped apart by Ho Chi Minh's ruthless regime. As corrupt as the Saigon government could be, it was nowhere near as bad, they told Smith, as the rapacious police state that seized their homes and tried to brainwash them with communist dogma.

Many of the fighters fled south in the late 1950s, eager to fend off the Soviet-backed regime and confident of returning home someday. After America entered the war in 1964, they became even more certain of a final victory.

Things had not gone as planned, though. The Tet Offensive had turned the tide of American public opinion, and they could see their American allies were losing the will needed to win any war. By the time of the 1972 invasion by the North, most Americans had given up and gone home. The American Congress had cut off funding, leaving behind a skeleton crew of 6,000 men, including the Marine and Army *covans*.

The North smelled blood. General Vo Nguyen Giap, leader of the northern army, thought time was on his side, especially with the upcoming U.S. presidential election in 1972.[1]

For the past two years, Giap had been busy stockpiling supplies including SA-7 heat-seeking missiles to counter America's air superiority. The materiel was smuggled into South Vietnam by lone soldiers marching hundreds of miles along the Ho Chi Minh trail. One man might take three months lugging a rocket launcher, with another following with the rocket shell on his back. The Northern troops continued to show the same kind of resourcefulness and resilience that had marked their performance the last time Smith had been in country.

Though Smith and other *covans* despised everything about communism, the northern leaders drew on equally strong convictions of national pride. Giap later told historian Stanley Karnow, "Our profoundest ideology, the pervasive feeling of our people, is patriotism."[2]

This clash of ideologies backed by the world's two great superpowers became known as the Easter Offensive—a name that seemed to capture some of the sacrifice and loss both sides would suffer in the days ahead. As the artillery barrage continued through the afternoon of Holy Thursday. Smith radioed for B-52 strikes around Nui Ba Ho. It was a risky move, since the Air Force pilots flew at high altitudes and their bombs could easily fall on him. This time the strikes were dead on target and slowed the progress of the NVA battalions heading his way.

Smith was especially worried about the fate of his *covan* counterpart, Maj. Walt Boomer, whose company also had been hit by the artillery onslaught. He kept trying to raise Boomer on the radio, but heard only an eerie static.

A hard rain started to fall, turning Nui Ba Ho into a muddy, slippery fighting ground. Smith also lost touch with his longtime radio operator, a nineteen-year-old South Vietnamese Marine named Mat. Known as a "cowboy," or personal assistant, he cooked for Smith and looked after him on the battlefield. Mat was rangy for a Vietnamese, nearly six feet tall, and looked his *covan* straight in the eye. Over the past few months, Smith had grown fond of the big, skinny kid who dreamed of visiting America. Mat loved to page through shopping catalogues, imagining buying his own 8-track cassette tape deck or maybe even a color TV.

Now Smith was afraid his cowboy had bitten the dust. Already dozens of South Vietnamese Marines were sprawled in the mud, victims of the intense artillery barrage and increasingly close recoilless rifle and machine gun fire. Smith didn't know how long they could hold on.

Then he heard a banshee's cry in the sky overhead: two U.S. Air Force F-4 Phantoms swooped in and started strafing an enemy squad placing a cannon on the hillside. The howitzer was obliterated and about a dozen North Vietnamese perished. The Phantoms circled back for another attack, but more clouds rolled in, forcing them to abort their mission.[3]

The weather continued to make life miserable for the American pilots. That night, a Stinger C-119 gunship circled overhead, dropping parachute flares to find the friendly positions. More fog rolled in, though, and the gunship had to return to its base.

The gunship's flares illuminated the landscape, inadvertently providing the lighting on the deadly fate that was awaiting Smith and his band of South Vietnamese Marines. The north slope of Nui Ba Ho was being overrun.[4] The green-clad NVA were meticulously peeling back the concertina wire protecting the base. The wire was booby-trapped with hand-grenades, which exploded in some of the invaders' faces. That barely slowed their determined advance, though, and Ray and his men knew they needed to steal away through the night.

Holed up in a bunker, Smith heard a familiar voice. His cowboy, Mat, had been captured and was being interrogated only a few yards away. Smith translated to himself as an NVA barked, "Where is the major with the beard? And where is the tall American captain?"

The major with the beard was a reference to Major Hoa, the South Vietnamese Marine commander who was Smith's counterpart and friend. And "the tall American captain," Smith realized, was himself. The NVA must have been spying on them before the invasion, and had a hit list.

Mat refused to talk.

"Come on," the inquisitor said in an annoyed tone. "Where is the American captain and the major with the beard?"

Smith pressed himself against the cold earth, straining to catch every word. Mat practically spat as he said, "I don't know what you animals are talking about."

A shot rang out in the night. Mat was dead—a loyal cowboy to the end.

Major Hoa turned to Smith. "Captain Smith," he said in the formal way of the South Vietnamese, "we must get out of these bunkers and off this hill. We are being overrun, and our time is short."

"You're right, Hoa," Smith said, trying to sound as nonchalant as if they were deciding to drop by a local bar. He didn't want to spook any more of his men. "But let's wait for the right moment."

They couldn't have known it at the time, but another Marine was listening in and decided to try to help create the right moment for escape. Corporal An-Ngu found a peanut-sized light bulb that he attached to an old radio battery. After hooking up the light, he placed it outside Smith's empty bunker, where it cast a pale glow against the nearly-impenetrable darkness. An-Ngu took off before it drew the attention of the North Vietnamese, who moved to surround the "lighted" bunker.

The diversionary tactic worked.

"Let's get out of here," Hoa said.

Smith nodded, and radioed his boss, Maj. Jim Joy, back at Mai Loc. "We're getting out of here, sir. The NVA is in the wire."

Before they left, one young South Vietnamese, paralyzed by the constant shelling, stayed crouched in a corner of the bunker and refused to budge.

"Come on, Marine," Smith implored, "this is no time to freeze. They'll kill all of us."

The skinny youth, who barely filled his baggy uniform, was shaking. He hugged the ground like it was his mother. Smith wished he had time to talk the kid out of his confusion, but time was running out. "Let's go," he said sternly to the rest of the men, strapping the company radio on his back.

Smith peered out of the bunker into the rainy night, waiting for the right time to make a break. He could barely see four NVA soldiers squatting on their haunches nearby.

"Where did they go?" one said to another in Vietnamese.

"We didn't see them," another replied.

Then a voice called out, "Un Mi! Un Mi!" It was a warning cry: "American! American!"

Chills shot up Smith's spine. Had they been spotted? Were they dead meat? The enemy soldiers dashed toward the warning cry. Only then did Smith realize this was yet another ruse by An-Ngu, the creative corporal. It was the break they needed. Smith hustled out to the hilltop and beckoned everyone to follow. Someone was running after them, sloshing through the mud, and Smith feared the worst. He was relieved to see it was An-Ngu, who somehow had swung around to meet them.

"Captain Smith!" he said, snapping a salute.

Smith returned the salute. An-Ngu's diversion had given them time to escape and probably saved their lives. Yet there was no time to thank him now.

"Let's get the hell out of here!" Smith said, pointing downhill. With luck, they might make it back to the fire support base and headquarters at Mai Loc. Then they would sort things out with Major Joy and the rest of the brigade and try to counterattack.

First, they faced death traps of their own making: the entire hillside was surrounded by booby-trapped razor wire in two deadly rings around the base of Nui Ba Ho. When the Marines reached the first set of wire, Smith could see they were leery of testing the explosive barrier.

"Go! Go!" Smith shouted.

The men froze like deer staring into headlights. Since there was no time to hesitate, Smith grabbed one of the smaller Marines and heaved him over the wire. The man rolled over it and landed in the mud below. And nothing blew up. Now that everyone could see escape was possible, the men awoke from their collective trance and ran through the gap held open by Captain Smith and Major Hoa.

Yet enemy soldiers lurked above them in the darkness. A voice called out, then a shot that whistled close to Smith's ear. The NVA shot flares to illuminate the base of the hill and stop the escape. Fortunately for the Marines, Nui Ba Ho was too steep and slippery for anyone above them to get a clean shot. The rain began falling in sheets, providing more cover from the pursuers. Pausing for a moment, Smith felt his hands and legs stinging from razor-thin cuts of the barbed wire. Blood trickled from his skin, but this was no time for first aid. It was time for him and Major Hoa to get through the fence themselves.

"Go!" Smith said, pushing Hoa through the wire before he could resist. Then Smith stopped and listened in the dark. He held a weapon given to him by his brother, Joe, an Army sergeant first class who knew the value of extra firepower. The collapsible automatic rifle, or CAR, was not a standard issue weapon for Marines. He liked its small size and big punch.

He gripped his weapon with one hand and held the fence open with the other. Another NVA soldier's boots sloshed in the mud, making a sucking sound like a wound that wouldn't heal. The soldier stopped nearby, gasping for breath. His body reeked of too many nights out in the field. Suddenly the man opened fire, shooting over Smith's head and down the hill toward Hoa and the others. Smith sprang up and swung his rifle like a sword, driving it into the soldier's chest, knocking him down. It was just like the drills at Basic School, when they dueled with pugil sticks. Only now there were no pads, no helmets, and no sergeant to blow the whistle and end the hand-to-hand combat. This was the real thing.

Shocked and senseless, the NVA soldier stared up at his assailant. The dazed soldier's mouth started to move to shout a warning, but his words were cut short when Smith shot him once through the heart.

His sawed-off rifle sounded as loud as a mortar. Surely, Smith thought, he'd given himself away. When no one fired back, though, he calmly continued his escape through the hole in the razor wire. For all their superior numbers and firepower, the North Vietnamese seemed disorganized as hell. Smith hoped to capitalize on the confusion and lead everyone to the safe haven of Mai Loc. When he found Hoa and the other Marines at the bottom of the hill, they were frozen again. Smith could understand their reluctance to test the booby-trapped wire, with its razor-sharp teeth grinning like an angry god.

After a day and a half without sleep, most were at the end of their ropes. As Vince Lombardi said, "Fatigue makes cowards of us all." Some were weighing their own options—a bullet in the head from the NVA, or getting blown to bits by their own death trap.

Smith wasn't about to let the wire stop them in their muddy tracks. Somehow he managed to see past their fears. This was just one more obstacle to surmount—something he'd been doing since his earliest days at Quantico. They came with the territory, as Marty Steele had demonstrated with his double runs of the O-course. Nui Ba Ho was simply more complicated, like a graduate-level exam. Only here there were only two possible grades—A if you lived, F if you died.

Smith racked his brain for a way over the booby-trapped fence. It was no wonder these guys were scared. Those hand grenades tangled in the wire were nothing to take lightly. Then a strange thought crossed his mind: Maybe the radio pack on his back would protect him from an explosion and the surgically-sharp wire.

Before he could talk himself out of it, Captain Smith charged the barricade and launched himself like a human missile. He managed to turn in midair and hit the wire on his back. The booby-trapped fence sagged beneath the weight of his radio pack. Smith waited for the fence to blow. Some grenades did explode down the fence line, but hurt no one. He felt his fingers and face. All there. Though he was cut and scratched and his clothes were torn, he appeared to still be in one piece.

Major Hoa and the others stood transfixed by this act of heroism. Like Moses parting the Red Sea, Smith had created their
escape route, freeing them to fight another day. "Move out! Move
out!" he shouted in Vietnamese as he lay on his radio pack,
crunching the wire.

No one hesitated this time. In fact, they ran right over this
human bridge to freedom. Somehow, with the rush of adrenaline
and thrill of escape, Smith managed to endure the stampede.
After everyone had cleared the fence, he rolled back and let the
weight of the radio carry him to the other side.

The North Vietnamese finally made it down to the fence line
and started shooting at their fleeing prey. Bullets ripped through
the mud, but were off target as Smith kept exhorting, "Go, Go!"
Soon they were into trees and thickets along a narrow stream that
gave them a modicum of cover.

Smith ducked in a stand of trees and tried out his radio. He
was amazed when it worked. He radioed Mai Loc and, again to his
surprise, reached a fire control officer.

After the pummeling they'd taken all weekend, Smith didn't
expect much in the way of artillery support. However, he called in
the coordinates of Nui Ba Ho and within minutes heard the sweet
sound of friendly artillery. The barrage bought them a little time
and gave Smith time to take stock of his wounds. The palms of his
hands were slashed and bleeding; his shirt and trousers were
ripped to shreds, exposing his rear end to the night air. Otherwise, he seemed to be all right.

He felt a bit like Tarzan, dressed in ragged clothes, and racing
through the jungle. They could hear the pursuing NVA on either
side of them, calling to each other. The sound of a barking dog
stopped them in their tracks. "They might have attack dogs,"
Major Hoa whispered.

After what seemed like an eternity, they were able to locate
the source of the sound: a tree frog. Everyone had a good laugh.

Smith took stock of his equipment, and was glad to see his
most valuable possessions had survived—flashlight, map, handset
to his radio, and his CAR. Touching his ammunition belt on his

near-bare waist, he felt four extra clips of ammo. He would have to conserve his bullets until they were resupplied.

They kept moving silently along the stream. Smith took count: only he and 28 survivors of the 250 men on Nui Bao Ho. Only now did he take time to think back on the harrowing escape, which defied any rational explanation. What had possessed him to fling himself into the razor wire, and then absorb the pounding of men running over his chest and guts? Remarkably, he didn't feel too worse for the wear. He did feel the sting of cuts on his face, arms, and legs, but that was about it. As he replayed the sequence of events, the captain had no idea how he made it out alive. He wasn't a particularly religious man, but did carry a St. Christopher's medal from Colleen. It had been blessed by the 1/1 chaplain at Con Thien in 1967. Father Lyons must have performed one heck of a blessing.

Still, they weren't out of the woods. Most of the men were exhausted and running out of steam. The first rays of sunlight shot through the jungle canopy—not a welcome sight since it would tear away the protective veil of night.

Smith knew they needed to push on as far as possible, but there was no way of knowing how far that would be. There was no intelligence available, since all of the South Vietnamese units along the DMZ were under attack. Their only choice was to press on through the bush to the brigade's base at Mai Loc, as he did his best by compass and his map.

Early Monday morning, An-Ngu, the resilient radioman, ran up beside him. "Captain Smith, we have a problem," he said. "It's Major Hoa, sir. He's falling behind."

Smith checked down the line of the Marines who were utterly exhausted from their trek through the bush. Major Hoa cramped up and fell heavily to the ground.

"Keep them moving, Corporal," Smith told An-Ngu.

Approaching Hoa, Captain Smith thought how they'd grown close over the past four months since he was assigned to the major's company. They ate together, feasting on crab and turnip soup, and drank beer together. Maj. Dang Hoa was something of a party animal and a noted singer. His thick, black beard reflected his artistic temperament and set him apart from his clean-shaven countrymen.

Even in war, Hoa managed to pursue a successful singing career, and was one of South Vietnam's best known entertainers. He had released several records and he fronted the band that played for battalion parties during lulls in the fighting. To pass the time out in the field, Smith and Hoa would sing duets, sometimes in English but more often in Vietnamese. Hoa taught Smith ballads in his native tongue, such as "Toi, Em di ve di" ("Sweetheart, you must go back").

Now Hoa felt that he should go back, or at least stay put. "Go on without me," he urged his American friend. "I have no more energy, but I must not slow you down."

Smith never considered leaving the company executive officer behind. "Major, it's time for you to rest."

Hoa shook his head sadly. "No rest, Captain Smith. No time."

"Nonsense," Smith said, taking off part of his bulky radio pack. He kneeled down, and before Hoa could object, he scooped his friend over his shoulder. "If we can just reach Mai Loc, we'll be safe." With that, the march continued.

After a while, Hoa shifted his weight and groaned.

"What is it, Major Hoa?"

Something was hurting him. "Damn radio antennae," Hoa said. "Jamming my balls."

Everyone laughed at his blunt complaint. They adjusted Smith's backpack, trying to make a better perch for the major.

The waters of the flooded Cam Lo River surged only a few feet below the jungle path. The river was swollen from the spring monsoon. The sounds of artillery fire rumbled down the valley. Smith wondered if the NVA was pounding their destination, Mai Loc. He realized that the notion of a safe haven could be an illusion.

Then Hoa started mumbling again. At first, Smith figured the antenna was poking him, then realized it was something else.

"What's that, major?" Smith asked.

"You sonuvabitching Americans," Hoa replied.

Smith apologized and said he move his pack again.

"No, no, it's not that," Hoa said. "I mean, you come over here and fight for us, then you carry us, too. You sonuvabitching Americans."

You sonuvabitching Americans! It was the highest praise Ray Smith ever hoped to hear—higher than his medals from Hue City, higher than his promotion to captain. *You sonuvabitching Americans!* Hoa mumbled some more, then drifted off to sleep.

Tromping through the jungle, Smith couldn't help thinking Hoa could just as easily have said, *You sons of bitches! You come to my country, encourage us to take on the communists, even train us as Marines. But now your countrymen no longer care about us, and your politicians in Washington have cut off the funding to fight the war, so here we are, running from the invaders, fleeing like deer from the mouth of the tiger.*

You sonuvabitching Americans, indeed.

On Monday afternoon, they reached a hill above Mai Loc. Capt. Ray Smith could see his sinking feeling was right. This was no sanctuary from the Northern offensive. Hiding in the bush, he could barely make out the command post for all the smoke and dirt snaking into the blue sky. It was still under attack, and a shell whooshed overhead and smashed into the base like a giant's fist. He could hear shouts from the men still inside. Smith was now at the end of his rope, desperately in need of rest.

He backtracked through the jungle and let the men into what appeared to be a safe haven—at least for the night. After three days of steady fighting, with hand-to-hand combat and serving as a human bridge, the young captain needed some rest. Finding an empty hut, he fell into a sleep as deep as the South China Sea.

Upon awakening, he was lost in time and space. He was on a cot in a thatched hut with a dirt floor, but where was he and how had he gotten there? At first, he thought he was dreaming. His trousers, so badly torn by the razor wire, were patched up and almost as good as new. His shirt was stitched together, too. He sat up and rubbed his eyes.

He was astounded to find his boots were clean and polished. As he shook out the cobwebs, the events of the past few days started rushing back to him. He vaguely recalled stumbling into a village and finding this hut. Had he passed out? Rising from the cot, he felt every muscle and bone in his body, like he'd just gone fifteen rounds with Muhammad Ali. Feeling his cuts, he could see someone had rubbed healing balm on his body. Clearly, he had stumbled into the right place for a battered and bruised fighting man. His trousers' seat, torn by the concertina wire, had been sewn up.

Smith pulled on his repaired trousers and shirt and went outside. He found a village woman doing chores for some of the other men. She was middle aged, with graying hair and a plump, prosperous look about her. She wore black pajama bottoms and a faded white top.

Smith bowed and said, "Cam un, chi." ("Thank you, big sister.")

The woman smiled and replied, "Cam co chi." ("You're welcome.")

Looking around the poor farming village, where only a few families remained, he thought: These people are worth fighting for. They are clean and kind and caring. They just need help to get out of this cycle of war and brutality. Smith hated to think what would happen to this peasant woman if the communists ever learned about her act of kindness to an American.

Cannon fire clapped like thunder up and down the river valley. Only now, with some sleep under his belt, did Smith stop to think about his own home, and his wife and three young sons. Did they know of his fate? He should have returned to the States over Easter to see Colleen, but he postponed the trip after she fell ill. She had insisted Smith stay put until she got better. Now he wondered if she was worried sick back in Virginia.

Before that Easter weekend, Colleen Smith had taken her boys back to her childhood home in Silver Spring, Maryland. The two-story brick home was on an oak-lined street in the suburbs of Washington, D.C. With its tiny living room and kitchen, the 1940s-era house provided a refuge for the returning daughter and Marine wife. Her boys—ages three, two, and one—loved visiting their grandpa with his magic tricks and their grandma who let them frolic in the kitchen. After her husband's months-long absence, Colleen needed a break from single-parenting.

Yet she wasn't expecting to get much sympathy from her parents about her plight. A few years earlier, Colleen made the mistake of complaining about what she viewed as a stupid assignment from the Marines. Her father, an Army veteran of World War II, got upset and shouted, "I never raised my daughter to question orders."

She tried to heed her father's advice and remain strong during her husband's second tour in Vietnam. It had turned into an ordeal, with three sons under three years of age to care for by herself. Though she kept in touch with friends, the Marine Corps of the 1960s didn't reach out to young women living off base with husbands deployed abroad. The wives were on their own—for better or worse.

That Saturday morning, Colleen stepped outside and inhaled the fragrance of Maryland's cherry trees and dogwoods. She felt melancholy, thinking how Ray would have been home now on leave if she hadn't come down with double pneumonia. Days before, they had debated his trip through telegrams and phone calls. When Ray heard she was sick, he called over the military's ham radio network.

"Colleen," he said through the static, "Let me come back. I'll take care of you."

It was hard to turn him down. She longed to hold him and longed for him to see their boys. Yet as bad as she was feeling, she figured it would have been a miserable time for everyone. Ray finally agreed and canceled his leave.

Colleen quickly recovered from the pneumonia and wondered if she should have let him return. Picking up the Saturday morning paper, she wished he were with her, ready to snatch the sports page and read about the start of the Washington Senators' season.

She opened up the *Washington Post* and idly scanned the headlines until she saw the front page: SOUTH VIETS IN RETREAT NEAR DMZ.

The headline hit her like a Frank Howard line drive. DMZ! Ray was there, close to Maj. Walt Boomer. "Fighting raged across the northern and eastern parts of Quangtri Province," the *Post* story said. "Military analysts here said the North Vietnamese artillery barrages were the heaviest since the siege of Khe Sanh four years ago."[5]

Khe Sanh? That sounded bad. Colleen scanned the story for any sign of Ray in the list of bases that had fallen in the invasion. Then she saw it: *Nui Ba Ho.* Her eyes raced across the paper, searching for specifics—who was alive, how many dead, where were the survivors? And what about the American advisors, including the other Marine *covan*, Maj. Walt Boomer?

The article lacked those details, though. It was couched in broad generalities about troop movements and the North Vietnamese strategy of mounting an Easter Offensive to overwhelm the South and wreck America's efforts to give up military control in an orderly fashion.

Then she dropped the *Post* and sagged against the doorway. The Marine Corps probably would be calling soon, trying to break the bad news about Ray, if it had any. She dreaded seeing the officers at the door, ready for the bad news . . .

No! Something inside of Colleen refused to believe he was dead. Ray was too strong and resourceful for that. If there was any way to escape the invasion, he'd find it. She knew of his exploits in Hue City and his Houdini-like talents for getting out of trouble.

Now Colleen felt she had to find her own way out of this bizarre situation. Her mind went into survival mode as she hatched a scheme to avoid hearing any bad news from the Marine Corps. Since she was not at home near Quantico, they wouldn't know how to find her. If she just stayed here, no one could deliver the dreaded message.

She picked up the paper and wandered back inside, thinking back to other times she'd dealt with war's gut-wrenching uncertainty. She had been glued to the tube during the Battle of Hue City, wondering if she'd see her husband on TV running across the street with other Marines in the house-to-house combat. Things were different now. For one thing, the American networks weren't covering the war the way they used to, and nobody was reporting from the front. For another, they were four years older, raising a family, and the stakes seemed higher. If Ray died now, she would be left to raise their three sons alone.

Her worst fear wasn't being a single parent or a widow. Her deepest dread was the thought of facing the rest of her life without her husband.

Walking into the kitchen, she saw her mother sipping tea. Colleen tried to act normal, and pretended to read the paper. Helen Hendry couldn't miss the pain etched on her daughter's face.

"What is it?" she said. "What's wrong?"

Colleen shook her head, trying not to talk. She couldn't do it, though, bursting into tears. Her mother hugged her as Colleen poured out her plan to hide from the bad news from Vietnam.

Helen patted her but eventually made her face reality. She calmed down enough to phone Col. Archie Van Winkle, who commanded the 1/1 in Hue City.

"Oh, Archie," Colleen cried, "he's gone, isn't he?"

Van Winkle tried to reassure and comfort her. "Ray can take of himself," he said. "I'll find out what I can and get back to you. In the meantime, you go have a Scotch and water and settle down."

"All right, Archie," she said. "I'll try."

Colleen hung up the phone and relayed the colonel's suggestion. Her mother frowned. "What kind of a person would tell you to have a Scotch at ten in the morning?"

Colleen didn't answer, but she was thinking, *A Marine, that's who.*

An hour later, Colonel Van Winkle called back to say that one American Marine was reported killed in action, but he had come off a ship. Colleen felt relieved for a moment, then was plagued by guilt because somewhere the wife and parents of a young Marine were getting a visit from a duty officer bearing grim news.

During the Easter Offensive of 1972, the line of firebases meant to protect South Vietnam from invasion collapsed like a house of cards. Among them was a major base, Camp Carroll, that caved in early with barely a fight. In the face of withering artillery and tank fire, the regimental chief for South Vietnam's army, Lt. Col. Pham Van Dinh, surrendered, taking his 1,800-man battalion with him. He was adamantly opposed by the American *covans*, Army lieutenant colonel William Camper and Maj. Joseph Brown, who resisted capitulation. Van Dinh's mind was made up, though. He said the attack was too formidable and any resistance would be a waste of life. The *covans* could sneak out or, if they wanted to maintain their honor, commit suicide.

"That's not what Americans do," Camper replied.[6]

The Americans, refusing to surrender, barely escaped when a U.S. Army helicopter pilot, Capt. James C. Avery, endured heavy ground fire and airlifted them to safety. It was just one of many heroic acts by the handful of Americans who stayed to fight alongside their South Vietnamese brothers-in-arms in an epic battle that barely registered back in the States. The American media, with a few exceptions, sat out the end of a war that had consumed it for the past decade. Now the U.S. fighters were on their own, and it would take years before their exploits became known—and even then, it was often within the narrow confines of the professional military.

Perhaps the most legendary drama unfolded on the morning of April 2, when Ray Smith and Walt Boomer began their long march to safety. It happened on a bridge over the Cua Viet River, near the American base at Dong Ha. Marine captain John Ripley and Army major James E. Smock found themselves trapped under a bridge as they tried to stop the juggernaut of two North Vietnamese armored divisions with 30,000 soldiers and 200 tanks.

The intrepid pair found a cache of TNT that had been stashed under the bridge as a kind of last resort should they ever find themselves in such dire straits. "In order to reposition approximately 500 pounds of explosives," the Navy Secretary later wrote in Ripley's citation for a Navy Cross, "Captain Ripley was obliged to reach up and hand-walk along the beams while his body dangled from the bridge. On five separate occasions, in the face of constant enemy fire, he moved to points along the bridge and, with the aid of (Smock) who pushed the explosives to him, securely emplaced them. He then detonated the charges and destroyed the bridge, thereby stopping the enemy assault."

Ripley also attempted to rescue a young girl after the bridge blew. The blast sent Ripley and the girl "flying as if a powerful hand had slapped them from behind," wrote John Grider Miller. "Then the noise arrived, growing louder and louder in a series of explosions that soon merged into a steady roar. . . . They tumbled into ditch, their fall cushioned by the bodies of the dead."[7]

The bridge at Dong Ha was in flames, sending plumes of gray smoke into the sky. The destruction was photographed by an American reconnaissance plane, and became a front page photo across the world—the first visible sign that the North Vietnamese advance had been slowed.

Smith and Boomer, for their part, never found refuge at Mai Loc. The regimental headquarters was pounded into submission, and by the night of Easter Monday, it was evacuated. "Canteens were filled and each advisor was directed to eat as much as possible to provide for needed energy after nearly seventy-two hours with minimal sleep," Marine Maj. Jim Joy wrote in his after-action report. The American *covans* opened their C-rations and wolfed down food and candy to get needed calories for the long trek ahead.

Before they left, they burned classified documents and used incendiary grenades to blow up sensitive decoding equipment, search beacons, and radios. They also slid incendiary grenades down the barrels of four 155-millimeter guns to keep them out of enemy hands.

Under Joy's leadership, more than 1,000 South Vietnamese Marines and a handful of *covans* fought their way out of the camp and slipped into the bush. They made their way through the jungle until they hooked up with Smith, Boomer, and the remnants of the 4th Battalion, South Vietnamese Marine Corps. It was now five days since the start of the Easter Offensive.

For now, Boomer and Smith could only tend to their wounds and let the American command in Saigon know their location. Some warm food would be a nice change of pace as well.

Boomer was a tall, rangy man who usually looked every bit as tough as his name. Dehydration and continuous combat had taken their toll on him. Like Major Hoa, he was on the verge of collapse. Boomer was too heavy a load to bear, so Smith came up with another solution. He took a piece of parachute cord hanging from his radio and tied it around his friend's waist. With that, he steadied Boomer and helped him walk thirty kilometers toward Quang Tri.

When the engines of an American AC-130 gunship hummed overhead, Smith tried to reach it on his radio.

"Spooky, Spooky, this is Mike," Smith said, using his code name.

The pilot replied in a skeptical voice. "Unknown station," he said, questioning Smith's call sign. "Authenticate Alpha Charlie."

The pilot wanted to hear more exact code words, ones that Ray could find only with the aid of a deciphering device. Only now did he realize he'd lost his "wiz wheel" during his escape from Nui Ba Ho.

"Spooky," he said, "am unable to authenticate. I lost wiz wheel two days ago. Need your help relaying to uniform," or division command.

The pilot sounded unconvinced, and the plane began to fly away. "You must authenticate."

Smith grew exasperated and cut through the code-speak. "Look buddy," he said, "I'm no NVA. I'm Capt. Ray Smith, U.S. Marine Corps. I grew up in Oklahoma and my current address is 3813 North Findley Road, Dale City, Virginia."

After a pause, the pilot asked, "Which Dale is that in?"

Dale City, a bedroom community off Interstate 95 south of Washington, had several subdivisions ending in "Dale."

Ray controlled his anger long enough to say, "Forest Dale."

"OK, Marine," the pilot said. "I'll accept that authentication. My home is in Darbydale." He radioed Quang Tri and reported the location of Capt. Ray Smith and Maj. Walt Boomer. Their long march was over, at least for now.

☆ ☆ ☆

Back home, Colleen Smith returned to Dale City and awaited word of her husband's fate. The radio news reports on WTOP weren't encouraging. Most of the American-backed combat bases had fallen into enemy hands. Several thousand South Vietnamese Marines and soldiers were dead. The location and condition of the American advisors was unknown.

Then the phone rang in the kitchen. Colleen turned down the radio.

"Hello?"

"Mrs. Smith," said a woman whose name she didn't catch, "I just heard from my husband in Saigon. He says your husband and Maj. Walter Boomer have been heard from and are alive."

Colleen felt like her heart might pound straight through her chest. The woman was part of the ham radio network that connected service families around the world. It was a strange way to get such news, but Colleen knew it was probably legitimate.

She wanted to reach through the phone and hug the woman, but all she could manage was a whispered, "Thank you."

After composing herself, Colleen called Walt Boomer's wife, Adele. They'd talked earlier in the week, and Adele had not been willing to accept the bad news from Vietnam.

"You know the newspapers," she said, "they're always wrong."

Now Colleen got her old friend back on the phone and said, "Adele, are you sitting down?"

"I will sit down, Colleen," she said, bracing for the worst.

"Walt and Ray have been heard from," Colleen said. "They've alive."

"*Thank God.*"

The line fell silent. Adele exclaimed, "Oh, my God, they could have been killed!"

Colleen laughed through her tears, choosing not to point out the obvious. Their husband's lives had been in danger for months while they were stationed near the DMZ. They're warriors, Colleen thought, they fight, sometimes they kill. And when things go badly, they might die. It was a hard truth, but she knew she better get used to it.

Night came, and Colleen was reasonably sure that her husband was OK. Then again, he would avoid reporting any injury that might get him sent home.

Colleen tucked her boys into bed, but knew she couldn't sleep. Around 1:00 A.M., she went downstairs to the tiny kitchen and stared at the telephone on the wall.

Ring, phone. Ring and be Ray.

To her amazement, the phone rang.

"Honey?" her husband said through the static, "Are you all right?"

Colleen laughed and cried and laughed again. Am *I* all right? That was so typical of him. She sank to the floor, weak with relief.

"Of *course*, I'm all right," she said. "I'm safe at home in Dale City. How are *you*?"

It was a question with no simple answer.

TEN

Soul of the New Corps

R ay Smith flew back to the States in November 1972 and tried to adjust to life after combat. It wasn't easy, though. The nearly decade-long war had taken a physical and mental toll on the Marine Corps, and put its much-vaunted spirit to the test. Staying gung ho was one thing when your country was behind you, but it took a special sense of mission to keep the faith during the doldrums of the 1970s. Smith, Jones, and Steele each found his way of coping with the dismal year of 1973, with the Watergate hearings in Congress and the Arab oil embargo. The low point for most Marines, though, came early in the year, on January 27, 1973, when the U.S. signed the cease-fire agreement with North Vietnam, finally ending America's military presence in the South.

While much of the country felt relief, most Marines agreed with Brig. Gen. Edwin H. Simmons's thoughts on seeing the country fall: "Much of the northernmost Quang Tri Province was now in Communist hands and heartsick U.S. Marines read in the newspapers that Khe Sanh and Dong Ha, scene of their hard-won victories, were now North Vietnamese airfields."[1]

So many lives lost or shattered—13,000 Marines killed and 88,000 wounded. And for what? So Henry Kissinger could win a Nobel Peace Prize with Le Duc Tho, the North Vietnamese negotiator in Paris? Such dark thoughts could make it hard to return to normalcy, but if you stayed in the Marines, you had to move on. There was too much work to do just to keep their heads above water as Congress kept cutting funding and the armed forces faced major downsizings. The Corps, always the smallest of the armed services, had hit peak strength at more than 317,000 during the Vietnam War. This was smaller than the 485,053 men and women who served in the Marines during World War II. Yet Vietnam was fought under peacetime personnel policies, so the Corps' total number of troops during the nearly decade-long Vietnam War— about 800,000—exceeded the 600,000 men and women who served during the four years of World War II.[2]

By the year of Watergate, the Corps had dwindled to a skeleton crew of 200,000. For the young officers who stayed in, it was a time for reflection, study, and professional growth—or at least attempts at it. Ray Smith was sent back to Quantico to attend the infantry officer's postgraduate training at Amphibious Warfare School. Marty Steele took a different tack, going home to Fayetteville to finish his undergraduate degree at the University of Arkansas. Jim Jones stayed at Marine Barracks in Washington, though for a couple of months he joined Ray in class at Quantico.

All three men were like thoroughbreds training for future races. Smith's fiery temperament made him feel more like a stallion bucking and kicking in his stall. He just didn't like to see much of what was happening to his beloved Corps. At twenty-six years of age, Smith already was one of the most decorated Marines of his generation. If Nui Ba Ho had been fought during a declared war, most of his peers felt, he would have been put up for a Medal of Honor. Instead, he received the next highest commendation, a Navy Cross medal from then–Navy Secretary John Warner, who cited Smith's heroics at the ring of barbed wire, sacrificing himself to forge a path to freedom. Copies of the citation circulated around Quantico as a new generation of officers learned about this new hero in their midst.

For extraordinary heroism during the period 30 March to 1 April 1972 while serving as advisor to 250 Vietnamese Marines located on a small hilltop outpost. . . . With the Command Group repulsing several savage enemy assaults, and subjected to a continuing hail of fire from an attacking force estimated to be of two-battalion strength, Captain Smith repeatedly exposed himself to the heavy fire while directing friendly air support.

When adverse weather conditions precluded further close air support, he attempted to lead the group, now reduced to only 28 Vietnamese Marines, to the safety of friendly lines. An enemy soldier opened fire upon the Marines at the precise moment they had balked when encountering an outer defensive ring of barbed wire.

Captain Smith returned accurate fire, disposing of the attacker, and threw himself backwards on top of the booby-trap-infested wire barrier. Swiftly, the remaining Marines moved over the crushed wire, stepping on Captain Smith's prostrate body, until all had passed safely through the barrier. Although suffering severe cuts and bruises, Captain Smith succeeded in leading the Marines to the safety of friendly lines. His great personal valor and unrelenting devotion to duty reflected the highest credit upon himself, the Marine Corps, and the United States Naval Service.

Despite all of the recognition, Ray Smith found himself down in the dumps now that the action was over. He let his hair grow out and sprouted a mustache. Leaning against the bar at the officers' club, he looked like an aviator, not an infantryman, but he didn't give a damn. Things weren't right inside the Corps and inside his country.

While attending AWS, Smith should have been getting professional training that he could apply to other wars in other lands. Instead, he grew weary, and sometimes testy, from being lectured by some staff instructors who knew less about combat than he did.

The majors and lieutenant colonels at the school prattled on about the Viet Cong's superior guerilla tactics, acting like this was ground-breaking information. They ignored the fact that the Marines actually had beaten the VC at their own game during the Tet Offensive. "Christ," he muttered to his fellow students, "we won that war three years ago."

When they talked about the invincibility of Soviet tanks, Smith shut his eyes and pictured the many Russian-built tanks he'd seen destroyed by the South Vietnamese Marines and *covans* like John Ripley in the counteroffensive of 1972. Ray had to stop himself from coughing into his hand like a schoolboy and muttering "bullshit."

After five months of classroom agony, Ray received his next assignment—an offer to become a company commander of the elite troops at the Marine Barracks in Washington. He would replace his old Basic School classmate, big Jim Jones. Since he had a choice in the matter, Ray wanted to talk to Jones about it. It seemed like a plum job, serving on the front lines of the Commandant's personal parade unit at 8th & I streets. He would march in summer parades, serenaded by the Marine Corps Band—the "president's own"—and the Drum and Bugle Corps. Colleen and the boys could sit in the grandstands and proudly watch the spectacle, as though he were playing centerfield for the New York Yankees. Indeed, the assignment was an honor, like being picked for the Marines' all-star team. There would be pressure to look and act as stoically as a Grenadier Guard at Buckingham Palace, with the parade deck stretching out like a royal carpet in front of the Commandant's nineteenth-century home. He could lead a company at Marine Barracks Washington, and have the feeling he'd made it to the top—even as a lowly captain.

Something was bugging him, though. Driving up I-95 to talk to Jones, he had a nagging feeling this wasn't the right fit—at least not in his current frame of mind. When Smith arrived at the cramped office at the barracks, Jones saw right away that all was not well with his old classmate. With his mustache and a scar on his cheek, Smith looked like one of the French Foreign Legion veterans Jones used to stare at during the Bastille Day parade in Paris.

They shook hands and caught up on the latest scuttlebutt, then got down to business.

"I know I should probably take this job for my career's sake," Smith admitted, "but . . ." He shook head. "I don't know, Jim. Maybe it's just a phase I'm going through. I'm definitely not feeling particularly fond of politicians in Washington, not after what they did to us while we were still trying to fight in Vietnam. I don't think I could stand to be in the same room as Hubert Humphrey. I know Colleen would kick him in the shins."

After his stint as LBJ's vice president, Humphrey was reelected to the Senate from Minnesota where he set to work shrink-wrapping the defense budget. Smith had plenty of time to mull over Humphrey's handiwork as he getting pounded by enemy artillery in 1972.

Jones tried to stay upbeat, but also felt compelled to give his friend a clear assessment of life as a Barracks Marine. Everything wasn't as neat and tidy as it appeared. It was a splendid place, with its towering Commandant's house on one end, surrounded by the brick barracks and postcard-perfect parade field. During the War of 1812, the British invaders who burned most of Washington to the ground in 1814 had driven out the Marines and taken over the mansion as their headquarters. But they "left the House and Barracks unmolested as a mark of their esteem for the stand the Marines had made at Bladensburg; or as professional officers, they would not burn married officers' quarters," writes historian Brig. Gen. Edwin H. Simmons.[3] Simmons observes, however, that there was no evidence to support either explanation, and the Marine Barracks may have been spared "simply because they escaped the incendiaries' attention."

Over time, it provided the perfect location for the Marines to show their best face to the world—and to their supporters in Congress, which met within marching distance of 8th & I. The Barracks Marines had other jobs, too, such as protecting buildings and guarding the presidential retreat at Camp David, Maryland.

Given the political sensitivity and security issues of their assignments, the Corps' leadership wanted only the best and most trustworthy men on the post. After Vietnam, though, the Marine Barracks was going through a hard time. "I had my share of troublemakers trying to get out," Jones said later. The spit-shined surface was scuffed up by combat veterans who were burned out and eager to exit the Corps before their tours of duty had ended. This caused a fair amount of heartburn because the Washington post was the one place where no Marine could get an early release from active duty.

The NCOs pulled lots of little stunts and miscues to get transferred elsewhere and still qualify for an honorable discharge. Junior officers like Captain Jones constantly had to write them up for petty offenses, even though many were war heroes. "It was pretty challenging," Jones admitted.

Ray Smith had his own problems with the vaunted outpost. Sitting in Jones's office, he confessed, "Driving up here I didn't feel real thrilled about the offer. What if I did get assigned to escort one of those liberals who opposed the war? I really don't know if I could hold my tongue, and get my ass in a sling."

They had a good laugh over that. Jones eyed the blue ribbon with a white stripe on his friend's chest—the Navy Cross. There was no doubt that Ray Smith was one of the Corps' best known fighters, a modern-day gunslinger. Yet he also knew that he could be a bull in the china closet of Washington, D.C.

Jones sensed their paths were diverging. He took pride in his own skills as a combat leader and considered himself a rifleman and ground pounder. He wanted to return to lead men in the Fleet. Somehow, though, he'd been blessed with a kind of amphibian quality that Smith lacked. He could breathe the rarified air of the nation's capital, while Smith choked on it.

Whether it was his upbringing in Paris, or simply his gregarious personality, Captain Jones could adapt to life in D.C. If Smith wanted to keep advancing his career, he would have to learn to control his impulses.

"I don't think you want to take this job," he told Smith, "at least not in your current state of mind."

They shook hands, and that was that. Smith decided to keep marching to the beat of his own drummer, not to the Marine

Corps Band. Eventually, he found a different job more to his liking: staying at Quantico and teaching tactics at the Basic School. That way, he would pass along some of the hard-won lessons of Vietnam to a new crop of leaders.

There was no doubt that Ray Smith got the lieutenants' attention. When he taught patrolling, they knew they were learning from a master. At the first sign of indecision, he was all over them, as one later recalled, "like stink on shit." It wasn't an act or a power trip, though. He simply wanted to keep them alive. Because when the shooting starts, any hesitation could get you and your men killed.

Yet, the flinty-eyed instructor knew when to let up and get to know the Basic School lieutenants, the first of the post-Vietnam era. After slogging through the tick-infested woods of Quantico, Smith made it a point to hang out at the Hawk lounge and hoist a few beers. It seemed like only yesterday when he and Steele were conspiring to get out of their room inspections and pull other stunts. As a captain, Smith tried not to be like the stuffed shirts they used to mock.

After he'd taught for a few weeks, he noticed that some of his students were ordering expensive fighting knives from a mail order house. The decorative weapons seemed to enamor this new generation, which, unlike his Basic School class, wasn't facing the immediate possibilities of war and death. For them war was still at arm's length, something to study and ponder. Smith surmised that buying the expensive knives was a reaction to this—a way to make a statement that, even though they weren't heading off to war, they, too, were warriors. It bothered Smith to see how overpriced the knives were, considering the paltry pay of a second lieutenant.

Finally, he admonished his class about the fad. "You might as well be using entrenching tools for all the good those fancy knives will do you in combat," he said. An entrenching tool—or e-tool— is the small, standard-issue shovel every Marine carries into battle.

"Captain Smith," a lieutenant asked, "did you ever use an e-tool as a weapon?"

Ray thought back and decided to share the story of his unit's escape from Nui Ba Ho. During that chaotic fight and flight, he seemed to recall using his e-tool to knock down one of his pursuers. He really couldn't be sure. He added, "But a rifle's as good a weapon as an e-tool."

Like eager kids at bedtime, the lieutenants pressed him for more details of the fighting. Captain Smith wasn't one to blow his own horn, but he could tell these guys needed to know the rest of the story of Vietnam—the part that had been largely ignored by the press, and in many ways, minimized by the Marine Corps itself. The cadre of *covans* was full of independent-minded guys like himself who didn't necessarily toe the line of authority, and certainly spoke their own minds about matters of war and peace.

So Ray Smith ditched his lecture for the day and told the story of the Easter Offensive. You could have heard a pin drop in the lecture hall as he explained how he had used his collapsible rifle to knock down one of the soldiers who made the fatal error of pursuing him off the side of Nui Ba Ho.

And when he told them how he shot the soldier through the heart, every one of the lieutenants in the room hoped deep in their hearts that if they were ever put in the same position, they could coolly pull the trigger just like Captain Smith.

And when they asked him more questions, Smith told them about his instinctive decision to throw himself back on the razor wire, and how he had knocked down the fence and became a human bridge to freedom. When they heard this, the lieutenants knew that here was a man they could follow anywhere—a true warrior who lived and breathed the Corps' credo, *Semper Fidelis*.

The lieutenants of 1973 felt cheated by missing the action in Vietnam. So the stories from the captain with the scar on his cheek spread among them, acquiring a near-mythical quality. Smith's off-handed remarks, which were simply meant as a kind of lesson on personal economics, quickly became part of the tribal lore at the Basic School.

Over time, the story morphed from Smith using his rifle to knock down his pursuer into a darker tale, one where Captain Smith *slit the soldier's throat with his entrenching tool*. The extent of the carnage grew with each retelling until the story was told of

Captain Smith decimating an entire tank crew using only his e-tool and his righteous anger. By now the simple shovel acquired the magical quality of King Arthur's sword, Excalibur.

Smith first became aware of the growing myth when, a few days after his first admonition about spending too much on knives, a lieutenant instructor came into class and approached the lectern with something in hand. "Captain Smith," he said respectfully, "you forgot your pointer." Smith looked down at the student's gift—a brand new entrenching tool. Everyone laughed, and he forgot about it for a while.

Yet, as surely as legends were born among the Celts, a new tale of courage was spawned in Quantico in 1973. Whether or not he had actually killed anyone with his shovel didn't matter anymore. His students knew that, whatever tools of the trade he actually used in Vietnam, the captain was a true warrior and henceforth would be called "E-Tool" Smith.

Considering the problems the Marines faced in the early 1970s, it was no wonder that its young officers were seeking heroes for inspiration. The Corps itself was a mess, reaping the harvest of bad seeds it planted in the Vietnam years. There were juvenile delinquents sent into the service by well-meaning judges who saw the Marines as a good alternative to prison. The Marine Corps was rocked by the same problems that were dragging down the rest of society: drugs, racial violence, and crime. Whether by destiny or chance, Smith's old roommate found himself at this nexus of the negative influences that seemed to be eating away at the soul of the Corps.

After he returned from Vietnam, Marty Steele was sent to Portsmouth, Virginia, as officer in charge of the Marine Sea School. Each year the school trained 800 young enlisted men to be deployed around the world as security guards aboard ships of the U.S. Navy.

The sea-board security dated back to the earliest days of the Corps. Indeed, the Marines' first written record comes from the pay roster of the USS *Enterprise* dated July 4, 1775. The payroll shows that Marine guards were posted aboard American warships four months before the Corps was officially formed by an act of the Continental Congress on November 10, 1775.

The Sea School was established in 1921 at the Portsmouth Naval Shipyard, near the Navy's huge base at Norfolk. Over time, the school trained Marines to provide security aboard all kinds of warships, from aircraft carriers to cruisers to submarines. Among their more delicate duties, they were charged with guarding nuclear weapons on aircraft carriers and subs. They also learned the ceremonial etiquette involved in escorting government dignitaries and royalty who visited American warships.

Reporting for duty in 1970, Capt. Marty Steele expected to find the cream of the Corps' enlisted ranks at Portsmouth. Instead, he found its dregs. Of 800 students in the program, he discovered that nearly every one of them actually had failed to meet its high academic and intellectual standards. He knew, however, that the Sea School wasn't alone: the entire U.S. military was dealing with flunkies.

The turmoil of the 1960s made it hard to find the kind of good kids who traditionally used the military as a stepping stone to achieve a brighter future. The inner cities and rural South had once been fertile recruiting grounds for such young men and women who wanted to escape poverty and better themselves.

Steele soon realized that the American Dream was as dated as old Elvis 45s or bobby socks. Even in Portsmouth, Virginia, a working class town of dockworkers and railroad brakemen, racial tensions were red hot. He decided he had to address the problem with his young Marines.

So when a melee broke out between black and white high school students, Captain Steele learned one of his men had a brother who was charged in the incident. Since riot control was one of the duties of the Sea School, Steele thought it prudent to have a chat with the young black Marine, and called him into his office.

"If you were posted to guard the base," the captain asked the young man, "what would you do if your brother came up to your bayonet?"

The private had a pained look as he pondered the question.

"Sir," he said softly, "I'd do my duty. I don't want to shoot my brother. I hope he doesn't taunt me. But I'd stay in control."

Steele was pleased with the answer, but he pushed a little more. "But if he does try to start trouble, it could become an international incident, with two brothers on opposite sides of the fence." Steele spread his hands and looked into his eyes. "You see what I mean, private? Are you sure you could handle it?"

The private gulped but kept his professional bearing even as the words poured out. "I'm going to pray that I have presence of mind, sir. I don't want to harm my brother, but I have a job to do, sir, and a responsibility, and I think I'm right and he's wrong."

Steele nodded and dismissed him. Good, he thought, at least one of my men is dependable. After the high school riot, Portsmouth quieted down for a while and no one had to choose between family and Corps. The chaos wasn't that easily quelled, though, and Steele kept his eye out for any signs of trouble.

Making matters worse, Steele was given a task of a completely different nature at Portsmouth, one with a ton of responsibility for a mere captain. Gen. Leonard F. Chapman Jr., the twenty-fourth Commandant of the Marine Corps, regularly stopped by the base because Portsmouth was in his wife's hometown. The base commander was afraid of slipping up around the Commandant and delegated the task to young Captain Steele.

So whenever General Chapman arrived in his staff car, Steele met him at the gate and escorted him around the base. The visits usually started with a stop at the barber shop. It was more than personal grooming. In this post-Woodstock era, he was trying to defend the Corps' traditional "high and tight" haircuts, and its rigorous ban on facial hair and sideburns. This wasn't easy, though, since the Navy was liberalizing its rules, allowing longer hair, sideburns, and trim beards.

Chapman spoke for the Old Corps when he told reporters, "We're not going to change our regulation. It requires neat and closely trimmed hair and prohibits beards and eccentric mustaches."

Hair was just one of many problems that left the generals scratching their heads as the military's need for order collided with the disorder of the day. Chapman, who had joined the Corps during the Depression, simply couldn't compute the changes sweeping through society like a marijuana-laced wind. Still, he was trying to understand the new generation, and liked using Steele as a sounding board as they strolled around the Sea School's campus.

Steele, for his part, didn't hesitate to speak his mind to the Commandant. "Sir," he told Chapman, "I've complained to Headquarters Marine Corps about some of the sorry excuses for Marines they're sending us."

Chapman, known for his cool, managerial style, nodded. "I know, Marty. I've heard the same thing at other bases. I want you to know that we're working on it, but it's not easy. It'll take time, but we'll get through this." He clapped him on the shoulder in a fatherly way.

As they came to know each other better, Chapman told Steele about other serious and disturbing issues he faced every day, including an alarming rate of drug-related offenses. The Army was setting up rehabilitation programs, but the Corps wasn't interested in going that route.

"We're not getting into the counseling business," Chapman said.

When they reached the barber shop, the Commandant thanked the young captain and said, "Hang in there, we'll get back to normal before too long. You've just got to deal with it."

On another visit, Steele decided to tell the general about something that had been bugging him ever since he arrived at the Sea School. The Marines' dress blue uniforms—key to their crisp appearance—were arriving from the manufacturer looking downright shabby. Steele showed the general the blue jackets, a traditional garb dating back to the Revolutionary War. Then, pointing at the front of the uniform, Steele said. "Look, sir. Army buttons!"

Chapman fingered the buttons and shook his head in disgust. They had no eagle, globe, and anchor, the emblem honoring the

Marines' naval history. It was a disgrace, the general agreed. Even our uniforms are losing their identities. Chapman promised to take care of it.

A few days later, Steele got an urgent call from Headquarters Marine Corps informing him that the matter had been investigated and the manufacturer in Philadelphia had confessed to making the switch to cut costs. The Portsmouth Marines would get their custom-made brass buttons.

Problems weren't always so easily solved, though. The challenges facing Captain Steele and other young officers of the early 1970s cut far deeper than buttons. The very fabric of the Corps seemed to be unraveling. How, Marty wondered, could the Marines remain the world's most elite fighting force if its recruits grew up in a country where nothing was sacred? The Corps always relied on reshaping young Americans—brainwashing them, really—at its boot camps in South Carolina and California. The indoctrination method worked with machine-like precision. To survive under fire, every Marine had to unflinchingly obey orders. Questioning authority was out of the question. Now, it seemed, young people did nothing but question authority, whether in school, on the job, at church, or in their homes.

Making matters worse, the recruits' mental abilities were sinking like a leaky ship. For whatever reason—looser education programs, social promotions in schools, divorce, drugs, Dr. Spock, TV—the new crop of high school graduates could barely read or write.

This meant that Steele faced the dual challenge of inspiring young people who had marginal mental ability, but chafed at anyone telling them what to do.

The Marines, for all of their colorful characters over the centuries, had limits to how many derelicts they could train. By the early 1970s, though, young officers like Steele felt like they were wardens at a reform school. Part of the problem was their own recruiters, who sent in too many bad apples because they were hard-pressed to meet enlistment quotas. Recruiters increasingly cut corners and even broke the law by signing up convicted felons.

This disturbing trend presented itself in stark terms one day when a student knocked on his office door. Captain Steele waved him in. The private, a strapping youth from Georgia, had distinguished himself by his hard work during the training program. Soon he would graduate with honors and qualify for high-level security work, perhaps guarding nuclear weapons on a carrier.

Something was bothering the private, though, and he blurted out, "Sir, I'm living a lie. I can't take it anymore."

Then he poured his heart out: He was a convicted rapist, who'd managed to escape from a Georgia prison but had nowhere to go. He'd heard that the Marine Corps builds men, and he wanted to be a true man. So he dropped by a recruiting office, and met an eager recruiter. He didn't tell the sergeant that he was an escaped convict, but that became evident after a records check showed he was on the lam from a Georgia prison. Instead of calling the police and having him picked up, the sergeant went ahead and signed him for a three-year hitch.

Captain Steele was stunned by all of the deceit and duplicity—not so much by the kid himself, who at least was owning up to his troubled past. What most disturbed Steele was knowing a Marine recruiter had brought him, even encouraged him, into the Corps in the first place. If the kid hadn't confessed, Steele quite likely would have sent an escaped convict to guard the nation's most potent weapons. He could have been in a top-secret post where he could have been blackmailed or recruited as a Soviet spy. And all because a Marine recruiter wanted to make his quota.

"What did he tell you to do?" Steele asked about the recruiter. "He must have known you would be caught someday."

"He told me to lie forever," the Marine replied.

Thank God the kid had a conscience. He would rather be court-martialed and return to prison than keep living a lie.

Steele thanked him for his honesty, shook his hand, and called the MPs. The kid was placed under arrest and taken to the brig.

The rapist's confession was only one of many horror stories for Marty Steele during those dark days. It was bad enough that so many felons and malcontents had wiggled their way into the

Corps. The errors were exacerbated by the behavior of older, staff-level officers, including some at the Sea School. These career officers thought that if they just kept their heads buried in the sand and ignored what was going on, it would all go away. Many of these ostrich-like officers were in their late thirties or early forties, trying to hang on until they had twenty years of military service and could retire with full benefits. It didn't help matters that many were lushes, too, following Bismarck's credo: "Red wine for children, champagne for men, and brandy for soldiers."[4]

Every day, right at 5:00 P.M., base commander Maj. John Lisbon left his office for a round of drinks at the officers' club. Most nights, Major Lisbon stumbled out of the club as drunk as a sailor on leave. Things would get worse when he felt under duress, as he did when the Inspector General planned a visit. Lisbon was cowed by the reputation of the head of the inspection team, a no-nonsense colonel known for leaving no stone unturned and no file unread.

As inspection day approached, Lisbon called Captain Steele into his office. He avoided looking at the junior officer as he confessed his deep dread of the badgerlike colonel. Lisbon knew the base was not as ship-shape as it should be, but he seemed incapable of doing anything about it. He was, Steele knew, a very poor example of an officer.

His forebodings only got worse when Major Lisbon peered up with bloodshot eyes and asked, "Will you do the pre-inspection drill, Marty? Will you get the men ready?"

It was a huge request, one that fell far outside Steele's normal duties as the officer in charge of the Sea School. But he could see the fear and loathing eating up the major, who clearly was not up to the task. Steele agreed to do it, but on one condition: The preparations would be done his way, with no interference from any senior officers.

"You're in charge," Lisbon said, heaving a sigh of relief.

Steele set to work getting the barracks' 150 Marines to clean their rooms, press their uniforms, spit-shine their shoes, and clean their rifles—things they should have been doing every day. Once they were squared away, he ordered the men to don gym clothes and report to the parade field. Then he spent several hours a day working their tails off.

After a week of preparation, Steele thought he had them whipped into fairly decent shape. It was a good thing, too. For when the notorious colonel arrived with his entourage, he did not disappoint: He was a big bull of a man, with an intense bearing and a fierce gaze that seemed to bore right through you. No wonder Lisbon made an excuse that day, saying he was sick and staying in his office. The inspector obviously didn't suffer fools gladly. He was a man on a mission, like a detective searching for stolen loot.

After shaking hands, he dispensed with the formal inspection and made a beeline to the old armory. Captain Steele trailed behind, with a mixture of awe and dread. What did this wily colonel have up his sleeve?

Built before the Civil War, the Portsmouth armory contained M-16s, ammunition and other weapons used both for the Barracks' and for the Sea School's training. The high-ceilinged, brick building was a locked-down, high-security area. Flinging open its gray wooden doors, the colonel glanced at the weapons neatly arranged in cases along the faded brick walls. The rifles were padlocked in place. So far so good, Steele thought.

The colonel continued his hunt for some unseen prey. A certain gun, Steele wondered, or maybe some unsecured ammo? He was a human bloodhound, doggedly following his own instincts. Then he stopped and stared at the armory's old windows, which had black metal bars across them. His footsteps echoed off the concrete floor as he approached the long wall, where slivers of light snuck through the antebellum interior. The colonel stood in front of the windows for a moment, his face trellised with light. He surprised everyone by reaching up to grab the black bars. Then, with a loud grunt, he yanked them with all his might.

Much to Steele's amazement, the bars came right off their hinges, falling to the floor with an iron clang. The Herculean colonel turned around in a cloud of plaster and dust and growled at his stunned audience, "You failed!" With that, he stomped out of the armory, followed by his note-taking entourage.

The inspection was over. The colonel and his crew got back in their staff car and drove back to Washington. The report would be filed by morning. The Portsmouth Marine Barracks had failed miserably to maintain security in its armory—a major infraction.

Steele hardly knew what to do, so he hurried over to Major Lisbon's office to report the dramatic inspection—the colonel's search for the one weak point in the armory, his grunt and pull, and the iron bars snapping off their hinges. "It was an amazing sight, sir," Steele said.

Lisbon sank down in his chair and muttered, "I'm doomed."

"Oh, no, sir!" Captain Steele said hopefully. "We can get the bars fixed."

"No, Marty, you don't understand," Lisbon said. "That colonel is notorious for busting officers like me. I'm done. Finished. Kaput! When he pulled off those bars, he was sending a message that the Corps has ways of getting rid of old warhorses like me."

Steele tried bucking up Major Lisbon, but he was already plotting an early exit to the club. He would rather drink himself into oblivion than face reality.

There was nothing else for Steele to do. He had his own life to attend to, including a full load of night classes at nearby Old Dominion University in Norfolk. He was working to finish the undergraduate degree that he'd cut short when he enlisted in the Marines and went to Vietnam.

That night, Steele was taking a test when his professor gave him an urgent note from the base. He rushed to a phone and called the duty sergeant. "Sir," he said, "a Marine's been shot dead and we need an officer to identify him at the morgue at Portsmouth Naval Hospital."

Steele was stunned. "But where's Major Lisbon, or one of the other staff officers? Why can't they handle this?"

The sergeant hemmed and hawed until he finally said, "Well, sir, frankly—they're all drunk."

Steele said he would go to the Portsmouth hospital right away to visit the morgue. Putting down the phone, his mind raced as he tried to grasp this latest crisis. A Marine shot dead? How had it come to this? And the base commander was too blitzed to even realize it. How had the proud Corps gotten so screwed up?

Only as he pulled up to the Portsmouth Naval Hospital did Steele realize that history was repeating itself. Once again, he had been given the hard task of identifying a dead Marine. After his experience finding Eddie in Vietnam, Steele had hoped to avoid ever playing undertaker again.

He followed a young doctor down a line of stainless steel drawers until he stopped and pulled one open. He recognized the face inside: Lance Corp. Bobby Baldwin, a quiet kid who was supposed to get special honors at the upcoming graduation. Instead he'd gotten a bullet through his chest.

"What killed him, doc?"

The physician shook his head. "He took a single 45-caliber bullet through the heart. There was nothing the emergency room could do for him." He pushed the drawer shut.

Steele's mind was racing. The base guards carry .45 revolvers. Baldwin must have been shot in some kind of altercation with a fellow Marine. But how?

When he got back to the barracks, the duty sergeant explained what happened. That afternoon, after the inspection from hell, the Marines at the front gate were changing the guard. It was a routine process, but one with a strict protocol as one Marine replaced another and turned over authority to guard the base.

Baldwin was starting to leave the post when his replacement grabbed his sidearm and yelled, "Freeze! If anyone moves I'll blow their brains out!"

Everyone froze, though the duty sergeant thought it was just horseplay by a wiry private named Atkins. He called out to him from inside the guard shack, "C'mon, Atkins, knock it off! Quit playing around, and I'll pretend this didn't happen."

"This is not a joke," Atkins said, pressing the gun against Baldwin's temple. "I'm dead serious," the rogue Marine repeated. "You move, and I'm going to kill him."

Baldwin trembled, but didn't resist. He knew Atkins was an idiot. Anything was possible.

The standoff lasted for some time. Finally, as quickly as he'd started, Atkins pushed away his hostage and snickered, "I'm just shitting you. Let's go on."

Everyone was so relieved that they all agreed to ignore the outrageous, and highly illegal, stunt. Baldwin got his pistol back and walked away, simply glad to be alive. Atkins was obviously disturbed, but if the duty sergeant wasn't going to discipline him, there was nothing he could do about it. Atkins took his post, guarding the front gate.

Baldwin drove into town to drown his sorrows. That night when he came back to the base, he obviously was driving drunk. And his tormentor, Atkins, was still on duty.

"Out of the car," he barked.

"Aww, man," Baldwin said. "Leave me alone."

"Get out! Now!"

Baldwin warily obeyed. Atkins ordered him to stand spread-eagled against his car for a pat-down search.

"Back off, man," Baldwin said, his words slurred. "Just leave me fucking alone!"

"Don't talk to me like that, Marine," Atkins said, whacking him with his nightstick. The drunken kid instinctively reached for the stick. Atkins reacted by drawing his pistol and firing a single bullet that tore through the heart of the hapless Marine.

The next morning, Captain Steele found Major Lisbon dozing at his desk, hung over and miserable as usual. When Steele told him about the shooting death, Lisbon put his head down and cried out, "Oh my God! We've got to keep this quiet. We can't let the papers know. Maybe it'll blow over."

Steele curtly informed him that the shooting death already had made the local papers and TV news. An investigative team from the judge advocate's office in Washington was on its way. Lisbon trembled at the prospect of seeing the cold-hearted colonel again.

"It won't blow over, sir," Steele said gently. "You know it won't."

He was right. Atkins was court-martialed and sent to prison for manslaughter, while Major Lisbon was transferred and forced into early retirement.

Despite his anger at the burned-out major, Steele knew his was not an isolated case. Lisbon was simply hampered by years of bad habits fueled by some of the outdated traditions of the Marine Corps brotherhood. Far too often the Corps embodied what the Roman satirist Juvenal observed of first century Rome: "Now we suffer the ills of a long peace." With too much time on their hands while they trained at remote bases, some of the Corps' officers spent more time than they should have at government-subsidized clubs. Alcoholism was commonplace, though it would take years for anyone to acknowledge the problem—much less do anything about it.

Indeed, it was known at bases like Quantico in the 1950s that senior officers and their ladies formed drinking clubs that prided themselves in the amount of liquor they could hold during binges that ran from Saturday night well into Sunday morning.

So Major Lisbon was only one of many Marines who stumbled about in a drunken haze. When a crisis happened—whether an inspection or a shooting—he was immobilized by self-doubt and self-pity.

Captain Steele found this out on the job. And since he didn't have a drinking problem himself, he found the inner resolve to help Lisbon and other Marines of this period try to escape the dark decade of the 1970s. He'd gotten to know many of the old salts from Korea and World War II, and knew their strengths and their weaknesses. He knew the Corps would survive this dip in its fortunes. Inspired by the likes of Sgt. Karl Taylor, and classmates like Ray Smith and Jim Jones, he knew they had the kind of men who could lead them back to their former glory. They just needed to remember the rubrics of the brotherhood—and never forget the precious blood shed from Tripoli to Tarawa to Tet.

So Steele continued to serve at the Sea School and kept working to shape up his young, sometimes clueless charges. He hung tough because he felt too many Marines had died to do anything but give it his best shot.

"I realized that I got it, I understood it," he said years later of the struggles. "I loved doing it."

For Marty Steele, "it" was the art and science of being a Marine leader. Yet it wasn't for everyone. As their three-year hitches expired by 1970, most members of his Basic School class chose not to reenlist. Some, like Ron Chambers and Barry Kowalski, went back to school, searching for themselves in civilian life. Chambers, who had witnessed the carnage at Khe Sanh, went to Mexico and contemplated a career in writing. He also sought refuge from the antiwar protests back in the States, and the implied accusations of people his age who wondered whether he was the next ticking time bomb, the next William Calley.

Kowalski, after his time in the peace movement, went to law school and became a star attorney in the civil rights division of the Justice Department.

Clebe McClary got back on his feet and embarked on a speaking tour as a Christian evangelist and motivational speaker. His story of survival struck a chord with his listeners, especially those Vietnam veterans struggling to adjust to life in a country that had mostly forgotten them.

Yet even McClary wasn't immune to the antimilitary sentiment of the early 1970s. While passing through the New Orleans airport, a young man noticed him struggling with bags. The youth offered to help and asked McClary how he'd lost much of his left arm. "Were you in a car wreck?"

"No," McClary explained, "I was a Marine who was hit in Vietnam."

"Well, fuck you!" the youth said, dropping McClary's baggage and walking away.

There's no record of how many members of the Basic School class 5-67 continued to serve, but it appears to have been no more than a few dozen. And to a man, they had to deal with the follies of the day. Les Palm, the artillery officer from Khe Sanh, once discovered a young officer in his unit at Quantico was injecting heroin under his tongue and his foreskin to hide needle marks. Most of his enlisted men were smoking pot.

Out of a company of 100 men, it wasn't unusual to have fifteen go "UA," unauthorized absence. Things became so unruly that duty officers dared not enter barracks alone. Race riots became commonplace in Okinawa, and Palm had to walk the streets like a beat cop, along with his first sergeant.

The Marines had met the enemy, and in the words of Pogo, it was themselves.

ELEVEN

Drawing the Line

By the mid-1970s, the Corps hit bottom on race, drugs, and lawlessness, a mockery of its proud claim to being "the few, the proud." Among some Marines, the only pride that seemed to matter was black. This, in turn, brought out white supremacists who staged cross-burnings and other KKK activities.

Marty Steele had seen it coming. As early as 1968, he'd witnessed the early stirring of the Black Power movement within the Corps. He'd known a black sergeant at Camp Lejeune who was a fine leader with a promising career ahead of him, but he was living a double life as a secret organizer for the Black Panthers, the radical group seeking the violent overthrow of the U.S. government. It was an impossible conflict—trying to overthrow the government as a Marine who had sworn to protect and uphold the United States.

Whenever a black Marine checked into Steele's 2nd Tank Battalion, a strange, forbidden ritual would play out. This sergeant's cronies would escort the newcomer into a well-guarded storage room. It was set up like a courtroom, with the sergeant behind a desk acting as a judge, and other black Marines sitting off to the side like a jury. With a hard stare, the sergeant would ask each new arrival point blank, "Are you a black man or are you an Uncle Tom?" Depending on the answer, the Marine would either be accepted into the brotherhood or shunned as an outcast.

The Black Panthers started instigating violence around the base, including severe beatings of white Marines. Out of twenty sergeants in Steele's company, nearly all sustained injuries—often from beatings with axe handles stolen from his tanks.

Only a stroke of luck broke up the dissident cell. One day a Marine arrived from Chicago with experience in law enforcement—he had been a narcotics agent. When he was escorted into the kangaroo court, the savvy newcomer played along to see what was going on. After agreeing to join the Panthers, he went undercover and provided information that led to the sergeant's arrest and court martial.

Unfortunately, such shenanigans weren't isolated to Camp Lejeune. They occurred from the East Coast to the West, and beyond to the Marines' training bases at Okinawa and other foreign camps. By 1975, the Corps had the unenviable distinction of having the highest rate of courts-martials, AWOLs and desertions among the four major armed services.

Marty Steele kept plunging ahead, though, working toward his dream of commanding a tank battalion. After his stint at the Sea School and completing his degree at Arkansas, he was transferred in 1974 to the Marine Corps' western training base at Camp Pendleton, where he joined Company A of the 1st Tank Battalion. The picturesque beach in southern California had bleachers for generals and other senior officers to observe amphibious landing exercises. Steele found happiness hunkering down in his tank, ready to roar onto the beach from his landing craft.

During one set of maneuvers, Steele was called on his radio to report to the bleachers to see the division commander.

"Now?" Steele asked, disappointed.

"Now," his battalion commander barked.

Steele was intent on moving his tanks toward the objective—a group of Marines playing Soviet soldiers occupying the high ground with antitank weapons. Now he had to stop everything, peel off his headset, and see what his boss wanted. He sighed, thinking there was only one issue that would have drawn the brass' attention, and it had nothing to do with military tactics or Russians or driving a tank. It had to do with a troublemaker named Sidney White.

Climbing out of his M-48 tank, Steele thought back on the last few weeks and all the time he spent on the case of the malcontent private. White was articulate, with a beautiful wife, and in another time and place, he could have had a fruitful tour in the Marines. Alas, he was one bad apple.

Before the field exercise, everyone in the 1st Tank Battalion was supposed to sharpen their skills at running the tank—its maintenance, weaponry, and all the little details that could gum up the works. Private First Class White's problem was that he *wanted* to gum up the works to get out of the field exercise. So before they boarded the landing craft, he'd drained all of the oil out of his tank's engine. The engine locked up from lack of lubrication, causing thousands of dollars of damage.

Steele considered this an act of sabotage, but also knew it would be hard to prove. White could claim there was a leak in the oil pan or come up with some other excuse, which undoubtedly would include an allegation of racial discrimination. So Steele wrote him up for refusing to participate and punished him with a two-week restriction and extra clean-up duty. White *would* come on the field exercise, though. Any more missteps, Steele told him, would bring a court-martial and dishonorable discharge.

Rather than accept his punishment—fairly light considering the expense of the damage—Sidney White challenged Steele's edict. Under the code of military justice, he could request a legal proceeding with the commanding general, known as a request mast. Steele could see what the private was up to: by requesting the proceeding, White would get to stay behind and miss the landing exercise. He'd give the seditious SOB credit for one thing: White never missed a trick.

Such were Steele's thoughts at he tromped across the beach toward the 1st Division commander, Brig. Gen. William McCullough, who was up in the grandstands. Surely, the general was ready to chew him out for not handling White's case better. With so many screw-ups in the Corps lately, many senior officers liked to blame their juniors for any lapses of discipline. *Don't bother me with your problems,* they seemed to say. *Make them go away.*

Steele's pulse quickened as he neared the general and the inevitable tongue-lashing. He just hoped he could keep a lid on his strong feelings about a derelict like White. General McCullough rose to meet him, looking serious and reserved. *This is it,* Marty thought. *My career as a Marine officer is over.*

Steele's life flashed before his eyes in the bright California sun. How would he break the news to Cindy, and how would he support his young family? Maybe he could find work back in Arkansas, going to work for the university or maybe entering the construction business.

McCullough stepped down to shake hands with Steele, discreetly leading him behind the bleachers. It was worse than he imagined. The general was actually taking him out to the woodshed.

As they walked side by side, the general surprised Steele by putting his hand on his shoulder and saying, "On behalf of the Commandant of the Marine Corps and all general officers and senior leaders, I want to apologize to you for having to put up with Marines like Sidney White."

Steele was stunned, and he felt a heavy burden lifted from his shoulders.

"What happened, sir?"

McCullough's eyes burned. "Captain Steele," he said, "there are two times in my Marine Corps career that I have been so angry with a Marine that I wanted to strike him. The second time was with your Sidney White. After he came in to see me at the mast, all I wanted to do was take him over my knee and spank him because he's such a bad Marine. And I pledge to you that we will do something about this, and we'll rid you of the responsibilities of trying to make that guy a Marine when he obviously is not one."

For once in his life, Marty Steele was speechless. The general dismissed him, wished him well on the rest of the training exercise, and promised to keep him informed about the case.

Over the next few weeks, military investigators learned that Sidney White had been convicted of arson for burning down his junior high school in the Midwest. He'd served a brief prison term and entered the Marine Corps when a recruiter ignored the felony conviction. White discovered he could use the Corps as a kind of government sinecure, a place to draw a paycheck and, perhaps, even continue his life of crime. If not for his hard-headed commanding officer, White's scam might have worked. He could have cut a swath of destruction wherever he went, destroying valuable equipment and hurting fellow Marines.

Even facing a court martial, though, Sidney White would not go gently into the California night.

Before the trial, Steele was working in his office on base at Camp Pendleton when he heard a fracas outside. "You can't go in there!" the first sergeant shouted. Sidney White and his wife stomped into his office. The private pointed at Captain Steele and said in a cool, detached way: "You're dead." As his wife nodded approvingly, White continued, "Your wife is dead. Your two kids— they live at 205 Skipjack Lane—are dead." Then the couple turned and left the building.

Steele thought of calling the MPs but changed his mind. Arresting White would just create another incident, perhaps adding to his long list of grievances against Steele, the Marine Corps, and the United States of America. When General McCullough learned of the threats, he ordered round-the-clock protection for the Steele clan.

Private First Class White's case was taken up by the local NAACP, which tried to portray him as a victim of the insensitive Marine Corps. Even as the case was picked up by the local media, Steele had to keep his mouth shut even though he was dying to tell everyone about the sabotage of the tank and the threats against his life and his loved ones. In the end, military justice did prevail and Sidney White was court-martialed and kicked out of the Corps with a less-than-honorable discharge. And he never made good on his threats.

Later, Steele learned that the Commandant himself, Gen. Louis H. Wilson, had been kept apprised of the case. Wilson eventually developed a new disciplinary policy in which any Marine found guilty of three violations of the uniform code of military justice was summarily discharged.

✯ ✯ ✯

It was time to clean up the Corps, and like it or not, Capt. Marty Steele realized he was part of the clean-up crew. He became aware of his small role in helping with Wilson's reforms when he received a call within a month of White's exit. It was Maj. Gen. Charles Mize, who was succeeding McCullough as division commander.

"Do you want to be my aide?" Mize asked.

Steele was taken aback at first but didn't hesitate to give an honest answer. "No, sir, I don't," he said. He was now the tank battalion's operations officer—the S-3—and was as happy in that job as a cowboy on a cattle drive. The S-3 was usually an assignment for a major, but Steele had been given the position as a lowly captain.

"Well, I want you to think about it and come back," Mize said.

Steele had no choice but to ponder the general's invitation. He racked his brain, trying to think of ways to turn down the job without offending a general and his division commander. As a Roman Catholic, Steele felt like a lowly parish priest being called to serve his bishop. Only instead of a diocese, Mize led an 18,000-man division. Despite the call to duty, Steele wanted to stay in his personal parish—his tank battalion—and serve his fellow parishioners, the men who operated M-48 tanks. His mission was to spread the good news of advanced tactics.

It wasn't that he didn't admire Mize. As a young officer, he'd fought courageously in Korea, winning the Navy Cross, and raised the flag over Seoul after the American landing at Inchon. Marty was duly impressed, but even if Chesty Puller himself had called he was in no mood to become anyone's aide. Let someone else open the car door for the general and draw up dinner party seating arrangements with his wife.

The next morning, Captain Steele reported to division headquarters at Camp Pendleton and was brought into the general's office. After exchanging pleasantries, Mize asked if Steele had thought over his offer.

Yes sir, he said, but with all due respect, he still didn't want the job. Steele explained that he was happy to be training with the Marines of the Pacific fleet.

"I believe tanks are the future of the Corps, sir, as we improve combined arms operations with the Army," Steele added, hoping he wasn't speaking out of turn.

Mize studied this captain who spoke so evenly and honestly, but in a respectful tone. McCullough had spotted a good young officer who possessed a special blend of integrity and intelligence. He also had the guts to speak his mind.

"This may not be your choice, Marty," Mize said, smiling slightly. "Sometimes aides who don't ask for the job wind up becoming the best ones." Ultimately, Mize chose Steele to assist him, and his prediction proved to be prescient. He hit it off with the young captain and used him to continue the clean-up work that began with the expulsion of the ex-felon White. Mize was determined to put the Commandant's edict into action, purging the Corps of its bad apples. There was no more important task for the generals than to extract these human worms who were gnawing at the Corps standards and identity. Between 1975 and 1976, Mize discharged thousands of Marines from his 18,000-man division for everything from inciting riots to dealing drugs.

Steele served as a kind of deputy sheriff as the general cleaned up his sprawling camp in the foothills of the Pacific. Early each morning, Steele carried hundreds of record books out to the general's green staff car. Then they set out across Pendleton, with its sandy hills and ravines, visiting each and every unit. They started by meeting with commanders about recent disciplinary problems, and whenever something significant was reported, Mize immediately signed papers booting out the troublemaker.

It was critical work, but it could take its toll on the general. At the end of one long day, Mize's shoulders sagged, and he asked Steele somberly, "What's going on with our Marine Corps?"

"It's not just the Corps, sir," Steele replied. "The whole country needs cleaning up. We're just getting some of the refuse."

Mize nodded and they drove on to the next unit. For despite the endless array of losers with bad attitudes, Mize managed to maintain a fundamental optimism about human nature. He always tried to talk to the Marines in trouble, like the father in the parable reaching out to his prodigal son. Of course, the disgruntled enlisted men usually didn't appreciate his advice, and some even lashed out at him. Many complained about the military's injustice and refused to take responsibility for their mistakes—whether it was drug possession, insubordination, theft, or going AWOL. In simpler times, such behavior would have landed men in the brig. In what had been dubbed the "Me Decade," though, these derelicts were counseled by a kindly general. Some miscreants returned the favor by cursing Mize to his face.

After one such incident, Steele stopped the interview and intervened. "General, get in the car."

"But I'm not finished yet, captain," he protested.

Steele had heard enough. "Sir, I need you to get in the car." After ushering out the general, the captain stepped back into the office where the offending Marine was waiting and got in his face. "Who do you think you are, talking to the general like that?" Marty roared. "He's a true hero, a man who put his life on the line so that punks like you could live in freedom. Now go get your gear and check out of here before I lose my temper. You're a disgrace to the Marine Corps!"

Despite all they'd been through, Marty Steele still didn't know exactly why Mize had picked him to be his aide. This wasn't revealed until they stopped by the recruit training depot at nearby San Diego and met with the commander, Brig. Gen. Joe Fegan. The two men had forged a lifelong bond during the Korean War. Fegan was a big man—more than six foot six—while Mize was nearly a foot shorter and a hundred pounds lighter. Nonetheless, after Fegan was wounded in combat, Mize found the strength to hoist him over his shoulder and carry him over rough terrain to get medical attention. This act of strength and courage saved Fegan from dying on the battlefield.

When they arrived in San Diego, Fegan gave his old friend a warm greeting, but Steele was surprised when he asked General

Mize to leave his office. Once they were alone, he turned to the captain and said, "You know why I want to talk to you alone?"

"No, sir, I don't."

"I want you to know that's the finest Marine who ever put the uniform on," Fegan said, nodding toward his anteroom. "Listen to him. You'll learn a lot. And I'm sure he'll listen to you because that's why he hired you."

"Well, sir, that's an interesting thing," Steele said, relaxing a bit. "I still don't know why he hired me."

Fegan laughed. "Everyone knows the story, captain. How you took on Sidney White, and it got the Commandant's attention and helped his effort to clean up the Corps."

Captain Steele was speechless. During weeks of working elbow to elbow, Mize had never uttered another word about the White episode. Somehow, though, the case had made the rounds among the Marine brass as an object lesson on why it was important to deal sternly and immediately with serious troublemakers. It was important to be fair and honest, but if men were being destructive, it was equally important to send them home. Such men were a pox on the Corps. There could be no compromise and no moral relativism trying to justify poor behavior if the Marines were to regain their focus on being the nation's premier fighting force.

Gen. Lou Wilson's zero-tolerance policy helped lift the Corps' morale around the globe. Finally, officers could stop worrying about whether they were somehow at fault or had shortcomings because they couldn't inspire deadbeat drug addicts. The guilt trips were over, and the Corps was moving on. It would rebuild itself one man, and one Marine, at a time.

It would take years to accomplish, Fegan told Steele, but the effort was worth it for the good of the Corps and for unsung heroes like Charles Mize. Leading Steele to his door, Fegan confided, "This is a tough time, so your opinion's going to be sought on very, very difficult issues. He knows you're going to give him thoughtful and honest answers. *That's* why he hired you."

Serving at the general's side gave Steele an inside look on how a leader must deal with a steady stream of issues, some large but many small. And it showed him the importance of trying to turn off the faucet of demands on one's time. One day Mize might have to prepare a routine speech to the Oceanside Chamber of Commerce, the next he might have to make arrangements for a visit by the president.

In this post-Watergate period, the commanding general at Camp Pendleton was given the thankless task of handling visits by recently resigned President Richard Nixon. After leaving the White House under the shadow of impeachment in the summer of 1974, the controversial chief executive flew back to his compound in San Clemente, California, just a few miles up the coast from Pendleton. Though he was suffering from phlebitis, Nixon was an avid golfer who liked to play the links at the Marine base. It was military protocol for a senior officer to accompany any former president, but, under the circumstances, the Marine hierarchy chose to handle Nixon's base visits with care, avoiding public appearances and the press. So it fell to Captain Steele to join Nixon for his golf games during his early days of exile.

Steele expected to meet a broken man on the verge of suicide. Instead, he found a bright, energetic warhorse who, despite his limp from the phlebitis, liked to chat about everything from foreign policy to college football. The icebreaker in their first meeting was Nixon's recollection of what had been called college football's "game of the century," the 1969 clash between top-ranked Texas and number-two Arkansas. After they got to know each other, Nixon regaled Steele with tales of his historic trip to China and his efforts to normalize relations. He found Nixon to be a complex but engaging man who hoped his foreign policy successes would one day restore some of his lost reputation. The ex-president seemed to cope with his downfall by rationalizing his mistakes and focusing on his successes.

Accompanying Nixon was just one of the many challenging assignments Marty Steele had in his nearly two years as a general's aide. There were comic moments as well, such as a trip to view a promotional film meant to honor the Corps' bicentennial on November 10, 1975. Hollywood has always been enamored by the Marines, from *The Sands of Iwo Jima* with John Wayne to TV shows like *The Lieutenant*, whose creator, Gene Roddenberry, best known for launching *Star Trek*, was a former Marine.

General Wilson had commissioned a short film to be shown as a surprise feature at Marine Corps balls around the world on November 10—the bicentennial of when the Continental Congress raised two battalions of Marines in 1775. The movie's plot was simple: A motley crew of past and present Marines was driving across country on Route 66 on the Corps' anniversary. Along the way, they encounter a storm and get stuck together in a motel at Flagstaff, Arizona. To pass the time, the old Leathernecks start sharing their experiences, with a World War II vet talking with one from Vietnam, and a Korean War survivor chatting with an old codger who fought at Belleau Wood in World War I. Over its thirty-minute span, the film was meant to convey a sense of the Marines' legendary esprit de corps, but in a contemporary way— *The Mod Squad* meets *The Lieutenant*.

Before driving to the preview, General Mize read the plot précis. For some reason, Wilson wanted his frank opinion of the finished product before giving the green lights for its premier. Mize knew this was not a routine matter, since the birthday balls are an important annual celebration of the Corps' origins. Innovation at such storied events could backfire, especially a film like this that tried to span so much history. A good production would likely be remembered for years; a bad one would be a black eye for the Commandant.

Steele tried to avoid the trip. "I'm no film critic, he said."

The general insisted that they both meet the producer, a colonel in the Marine reserves. With his polyester leisure suit and long sideburns, he looked like he'd just left a disco. He was eager to show the film and led Mize into his screening room. The general sat in the front, while Marty stayed in the back.

The film credits began rolling and the bicentennial movie was under way. The first scene showed a modern-day Marine with long, mutton-chop sideburns. Steele grimaced, and the film just kept getting worse. The Marine meant to represent Vietnam vets had shoulder-length hair and looked like he'd probably chucked his medals over the White House fence. This 1960s Marine was now a rock star. And so on down the line, until the film showed a World War I vet, an old codger who sounded like Walter Brennan from *The Real McCoys*. Steele could see that every one of the characters was a cardboard cutout, probably created over martinis around the producer's swimming pool.

Faced with this disaster, Steele slouched down in his seat, thinking, *Sweet Jesus, they can't show this at the 200th anniversary. We'll look like idiots. What has this guy been smoking?*

He couldn't see General Mize at the front of the screening room, but was dying to know what he thought. What could he possibly say to this producer? How would he break the news to him that this film was the biggest bomb since Hiroshima? At times like this, Steele was happy to be a junior officer, a mere aide of no importance.

Finally, after the longest thirty minutes of his life, the surreal ode to the Corps ended and the lights came up. Mize stood and stretched, acting like he didn't have a care in the world. Steele stayed glued to his seat, covering his face and hoping not to draw attention to himself. Through his fingers he could see the producer, who finally blurted out, "So what did you think, sir?

Mize managed to look as inscrutable as Dirty Harry. "I'm not saying a word," he said. "I'm going to defer to my aide." Turning to Steele, he said, "Captain Steele. What did you think?"

Steele gulped and sat up. This was a dirty trick worthy of Richard Nixon. "Sir, you really want me to express my views about this movie?"

Mize nodded, then turned his back on him.

Steele searched for a way to politely express his opinion. It was an impossible task. What could he do but tell the blunt truth? He stood up, faced the producer, and said, "With all due respect to you, sir, there is no way I would show this movie to anyone in the United States Marine Corps at this time. It's a horrible movie. It doesn't accurately portray Marines either past or present, and it's an embarrassment. I had a hard time sitting here watching it."

The producer/colonel was unfazed, though. "Well, it's not your decision to make," he snapped.

Mize wheeled around and raised his hand for silence. "I just told you, colonel. It *is* my aide's decision."

"What?" the producer said, crestfallen.

"I told you I was deferring to my aide."

"Surely you're not serious, General Mize," the colonel protested. "We put thousands of dollars into this thing, and you're not going to—"

Mize cut him off. "I just did it. General Wilson asked me and I'll give him Captain Steele's opinion. If he wants to show it over our objections, then that's his call. The Commandant asked me to review this movie, and I'm going to give him my aide's verbatim response."

Later that day, Mize called the Commandant and delivered Steele's critique—as tough as anything from Pauline Kael. Wilson said he appreciated the candor, since it confirmed his own judgment. The bicentennial film was a good idea, but poorly executed. Wilson promptly canceled its premier at all of the birthday balls.

Riding back to the office, Steele asked the general why he'd put him on the spot.

Mize grinned. "I knew you'd tell the truth, Marty. That movie stunk. It was better for him to hear that from you than from me."

☆ ☆ ☆

In a strange way, though, the movie simply reflected the mediocrity of the entire Me Decade—for the Corps and the country. It was a messy and confused time, and a period when many people and organizations struggled to find solid ground to move into the future. The Marine Corps, for all of its efforts to remain above the fray, couldn't help but reflect the pros and the cons of its native ground.

Marty, Ray, and Jim all turned thirty during this time and moved on in their professional and personal lives. They raised families and managed to maintain their marriages despite the Corps' relentless demands on their time and energy.

There were a few respites along the way. In the fall of 1972, Marty returned to his hometown of Fayetteville, where he spent the next fifteen months finishing his bachelor's degree at the University of Arkansas. He majored in history and managed to get a near-perfect 3.9 grade point average by reading late every weeknight and playing every weekend. "I'll close the library every night, but never open a book on the weekends," he told Cindy.

Steele even let his hair grow a little and sprouted sideburns. He engaged in lively debates with his professors, including those with long hair and beards. He learned to overcome his own prejudices about academics and hoped that, by knowing him, they could get over their own stereotypes of Marines as knuckle-dragging troglodytes.

During the Easter Offensive, as Ray Smith was fighting for his life, Steele debated his professors about the need to halt the spread of communism. And later, after Smith returned to the States, Steele got him to come out to Arkansas with Colleen. They partied at the Steeles' rented house in the country, a bucolic setting with a pond where the two old roommates sat and drank and debated tank tactics.

When Steele finished his studies in early 1974, Dr. James S. Chase, the chairman of the University of Arkansas history department, wrote the Commandant commending the captain as "one of the very best students I have known in my thirteen years in the profession. . . . For whatever it may be worth, you may be assured that Captain Steele made friends for the Marine Corps, some of it in unlikely places."

Ray Smith also spent time close to the civilian world, with a two-year assignment in Chicago as secretary of the general staff at the U.S. Military Enlistment Processing Command. He later returned to college through the Corps' "bootstrap program" for officers, receiving a bachelor's degree in Asian studies in 1979.

While at Oklahoma State University, Smith studied with an expert in Soviet affairs and was given the assignment of studying an island he had never heard of—Grenada. He didn't keep the paper but often thought about it later when he was sent on a special assignment to the Caribbean.

The lieutenants of the 1960s rose through the ranks in the 1970s, and by decade's end, each had been promoted to major. They now had put in a full decade as officers, paying their dues in staff jobs that lacked the glamour of fighting on the front lines. Marty Steele in particular had to work far from the oceans that usually defined a Marine's life. He was sent to the nation's industrial heart—Detroit, Michigan—to monitor the quality of tanks rolling off the assembly line at Chrysler.

Wherever they landed, though, they always looked for ways to return to the Fleet Marine Force, either in the Atlantic of Pacific. Of course, it wasn't always glamorous duty, as Jim Jones discovered in 1975 when he started a thirteen-month-long unaccompanied tour on Okinawa. The 454-square-mile island northeast of Taiwan became an American base after the Army and Marines defeated the Japanese in World War II. The last great battle of the Pacific war exacted a steep toll before it concluded on June 21, 1945: 36 U.S. Navy ships sunk and 368 damaged—more than at Pearl Harbor—and 4,907 sailors slain. The Marines lost 2,899 men, with nearly 12,000 wounded, some of whom later perished from their wounds. The largest amphibious operation in the Pacific war cut an even wider swath through the fabric of the Rising Sun: 107,539 Japanese and Okinawans died, with a stunning number of Japanese airplanes lost—7,830, nearly half of them shot down by Navy and Marine pilots.[1]

Reporting as company commander with the 2nd Battalion, 9th Marine Regiment, 3rd Marine Division, on Okinawa, Japan, Jim Jones found it hard to reconcile the level of sacrifice of his father's generation with the degree of incompetence shown by the Pepsi generation.

Years later, he wryly recalled the words of Lt. Col. Gene Deegan, who commanded 2/9 at Camp Schwab and later became a major general: "I'm going to give you the worst rifle company in the United States Marine Corps."

Jones soon realized this was no exaggeration. "It was the longest year of my life. I've always said that when I was in Okinawa

I wasn't sure if I was in the Marine Corps or in the French Foreign Legion."

At other times, he felt like he a social worker trying to help a bunch of outcasts and misfits who bumbled their way into the Marine Corps. In one case, a young private from Iowa, Tommy Underhill, declared that he must depart from Okinawa immediately to get home to help with the fall wheat harvest.

"Private Underhill," Jim replied, "there are only two ways you can get off this island. The first is to pay about $2,500 to buy a plane ticket, but you might have some problems getting out of the country since you don't have a visa or passport. Or you could go to the beach and start swimming home. Now go back to your barracks and think it over."

Jones figured that was that—until a half hour later when his first sergeant threw open the door of his office. "Captain, I think you better come down to the beach!"

Sure enough, Private First Class Underhill had gone down to the water, stripped down to his skivvies, and was now swimming about 200 yards offshore. He had taken Jones literally and was dog-paddling toward Iowa.

Jones hopped into a motorboat and raced alongside the private. "How's it going, Underhill?"

"Pretty good, sir!" the private replied between strokes. "I think I can make it."

Jones waited for a moment, then posed a question. "Before you get going too far, Underhill, did anyone tell you about the sea snakes?"

The private's eyes got as wide as clam shells. "Sea snakes, sir?"

Jones acted nonchalant. "I wouldn't worry too much about them, though. The only time they might bite you is when they come up for air . . . but their bite isn't poisonous . . . good luck, Underhill!"

With that, Jones turned the boat back toward shore. He would have let the farm boy keep swimming, too, except that he called out, "Hold on, sir! I'm coming in!"

After the trying year on Okinawa, Jim was happy to be reunited with his family back in Washington in 1976, ready to begin a three-year hitch in the officer assignments section at Headquarters Marine Corps. The staff job was a career ticket to punch, and he got to rub elbows with his contemporaries such as Peter Pace, who later would serve with him in the Pentagon and become the first Marine Chairman of the Joint Chiefs of Staff.

Still, the Me Decade remained a trying time for Marines who had the thankless task of trying to assign—and encourage—officers who were tempted to get out of an organization whose pay wasn't keeping pace with inflation and whose morale was just starting to rekindle itself.

In mid-1979, Jones had been promoted to major and was grateful to receive orders to leave his staff job and attend Command and Staff College at Quantico.

Before departing headquarters, though, Major Jones was asked to visit the head of the Manpower Management Division, his boss, Maj. Gen. Bob Haebel. There, he was shocked to learn that his orders to Quantico had been changed. The Corps needed someone to work as the Marine Corps Liaison Officer in the U.S. Senate, working in legislative affairs. He'd report to the Legislative Assistant to the Commandant of the Marine Corps and represent the Marines to such powerful senators as John Tower, Sam Nunn, and John Glenn.

Jones balked. "I can't *not* attend Command and Staff College," he protested.

Haebel said he understood, but the Corps needed Jones more across the Potomac. "I want you over there," Haebel said. "We'll pull you out within two years."

"Two?" Jim said doubtfully.

"Two years," the general said, nodding solemnly.

It was 1979. Jimmy Carter was near the end of his troubled presidency, the core of the Three Mile Island nuclear reactor had a partial meltdown, and the Shah of Iran was ousted by Islamic radicals.

In a strange way, Maj. Jim Jones, eager to keep pace with his contemporaries, sensed his career was taking its own kind of radical turn. Only he wasn't quite sure where—or how—this leg of the journey would end.

TWELVE

Star Quality

On his first day on the job at the Senate's Russell Office Building, Jim Jones felt out of place. On the one hand, he was honored to be working in the shadows of such respected senators as John Tower, Barry Goldwater, Sam Nunn, John Glenn, and newcomer William Cohen. Yet the normally self-confident major experienced a rare moment of self-doubt as he tried to remember the last time he studied government affairs—some fifteen years ago at Georgetown, when he posted what was generously called a "gentleman's C." Now that he was the legislative face of the Corps, he knew he'd have to take an on-the-job crash course in the making of laws and budgets and building political alliances.

His mood wasn't helped by the new clothes he had to wear—a dark business suit and striped tie. He was adhering to the policy for all of the military's legislative affairs officers to not wear uniforms to work on Capitol Hill. He wasn't quite sure why, but someone high in the Carter Administration had deemed it better for the military to keep a low profile and try to blend into the congressional landscape.

Yet wearing anything but his uniform made Jones feel out of character, almost an impostor—an IBM manager, maybe, or a stockbroker, but certainly not a proud Leatherneck. He was mulling over his identity problem when he finally reached his office in the basement of the Russell Building, where he met a Navy captain who had a gnomish grin and iron handshake.

"Welcome aboard, Major Jones," he said. "I'm John McCain."

Jones's doubts about the assignment quickly dissipated in the presence of the straight-talking former POW. McCain took him on as a kind of apprentice, showing him the ways and means of working on what everyone simply called "the Hill."

Jones was struck by McCain's direct, no-BS manner and willingness to question authority. McCain, for his part, was impressed by this big Marine who looked like he'd stepped right off a recruiting poster. He showed Jones around and introduced him to the friends, and the enemies, of the Navy and Marine Corps. The key to their jobs, McCain explained, was knowing who really had their hands on the controls of power and learning to work with them.

Besides meeting the old warhorses in the Senate, McCain introduced him to the new class of reform-minded leaders elected in the wake of the Watergate scandals, including Gary Hart of Colorado and Maine's Cohen.

Before long, they formed quite a team, as McCain could see the Marine major helped draw even more senators and staff members into the joint office of the Navy and Marine Corps, outperforming the liaisons of the Army and Air Force.

It was a more collegial time in the Senate, when character and personality mattered. It was the last hurrah for bipartisan collaboration in Congress, before focus groups, push polls, and PACs poisoned the waters of civil governance. "Party" was not a word that drove people apart or made them worry about drinking too much. So at the close of business on many weekdays, the Navy/Marine Corps Senate liaison office opened for business. Amid the beer, wine, and bad jokes about Billy Carter, many lifelong friendships were formed.

When Monday morning rolled back around, McCain and Jones knew their calls were more likely than others to get answered. This lasted about a year, until McCain retired from the Navy and decided to apply some of his on-the-job training. The famous POW launched his own political career in Arizona, starting as a congressman and then senator. Before leaving his liaison post, though, he gave Jim Jones a priceless gift: his Senate business—his list of contacts and his endorsement as a go-to guy. "I'm very grateful to him because he was such a powerful figure in uniform," Jones said later. "He was easily the dominant figure of all the people in the liaison business."

Senator McCain, for his part, said his most vivid memory of Major Jones was his deadpan sense of humor. "He used to jog every afternoon by the Capitol," McCain said. "One day, two French tourists were coming down the steps. The woman said in French to her husband, 'The Capitol sure is ugly architecture.' Jim ran by and said in perfect French, 'It's a hell of a lot nicer than anything you've got in Paris.'"

There was more to the job than straightening out French tourists. Up in the Senate gallery, Jones struggled to stay awake through day-long committee hearings as senators droned on about troop levels or base closings. It had all the appeal of an 8:00 A.M. history class. Still, he managed to stay awake long enough to realize he was gradually taking in enough knowledge to qualify for an on-the-job degree in political science. "You learn the other piece of how a government works, and the separation of powers comes into focus," Jones reflected. "You learn the difference between the authorization process and the appropriations process, how those two entities interrelate. You learn about your own service and how it works, from a distant view." Most importantly, though, "You learn what the framers of the Constitution had in mind when they wrote the words that the Congress shall raise armies and maintain navies."

He also had a front row seat when the service chiefs sat in the hot seat before the Senate Armed Services Committee. He started putting himself in their shoes, wondering how he would argue for more funding or advocate the need for new weapons or spar with senators about America's defense needs. "When you get to sit in the cheap seats for five years listening to the leaders of every branch of service," he said, "you can't help but absorb a lot of knowledge."

Working in Washington also put Jones face-to-face with America's hangover from the 1960s, with the antipathy toward the military. "When I first got over there, I was told you don't wear uniforms on a daily basis," he said. "They wore all-civilian clothes. We were still coming out of the Carter years when there was definitely a de-emphasis on wearing uniforms." Even inside the Pentagon, members of the armed forces could only be in uniform two days out of the work week.

After mulling it over, Jones decided to stage his own quiet rebellion. After all, it had not been that long ago that he was marching with his company from the Marine Barracks to guard the 14th Street Bridge and the Capitol against antiwar demonstrators. He found it ridiculous to require a Marine officer to report for duty in Congress in civilian garb.

He vowed to wear his uniform at least once a day—a fashion statement that was noticed right away by some of the Senate heavyweights, including Arizona's Barry Goldwater. "What are you doing here?" he asked Jim one day as he passed him in the Russell building.

Jim explained he was the new Senate liaison officer for the Marine Corps.

"You are?" Goldwater replied. "Good to see that uniform! You ought to wear it more often."

Encouraged by Goldwater's thumbs-up, Jones extended his experiment and started wearing his uniform all day long. He soon realized that nobody was going to stop him. The ban was being forgotten in the twilight days of the Carter administration. Finally, the ban was ended when Ronald Reagan was elected in 1980. By then, Jones's quiet rebellion already had helped set him apart as a straight shooter and independent thinker.

William Cohen, a freshman senator from Maine, increasingly relied on Jones's advice. As a member of the Armed Services Committee, Cohen soon became weary of the bickering and in-fighting between the different branches of the military. He was also leery of the spin that each service branch gave on every issue, trying to funnel more money their way.

Jim Jones managed to represent the Corps' interests without sounding preachy or parochial. "The general perception was that Jim Jones was a Marine, but he will give you the straight scoop," Cohen said many years later. "If he thinks it's good for the Marines, he'll tell you. If he thinks it's good for the other services, he'll tell you."

For new senators with no military experience themselves, such candor was highly prized. Over time, Jim Jones attained a kind of "most favored officer" status, meaning he was often the first name that came to mind when senators were looking for military escorts for international trips made by congressional delegations, known as "codels."

Between 1979 and 1984, Jones escorted fifty codels—about ten per year. The work increased his exposure to congressional leaders, as well as members of the press; moreover, it helped the Marine Corps stay on the front burner of policy and funding decisions.

The duty did have some pitfalls since, in the post-Watergate era, the codels were easily branded "junkets"—frivolous trips made by congressmen and their wives. Jones became something of an expert on the handling of everything from travel money to media relations, and even wrote a research paper on the topic while attending the National War College. "Television crews are regularly at Andrews Air Force Base, filming departures and arrivals of delegations, reporting operating costs of dedicated aircraft, number of passengers traveling, itinerary, and estimated cost to the taxpayer."

Under such a media microscope, he wrote, there is "no tolerance for error."

His theory was based on painful experience. During a visit to one of the finest hotels in Madrid, Jones was entrusted with a briefcase containing senators' passports, travel documents, and $2,300 in cash. He walked into a hotel lobby with Arnold Punaro, senior aide to Sen. Sam Nunn of Georgia and staff director of the Senate Armed Service Committee.

After checking in, Jones put the bag down and turned his back for a few seconds. Turning around, he looked down for the bag and realized it was gone. The hotel had a professional thief who snatched it from under his nose.

"Fan out!" he shouted.

Punaro broke to one side of the lobby, while Jones went to the other. The bag was gone, though, seemingly into the thin air of Spain. The theft proved to be a major embarrassment for Jones, who had to scurry to replace the passports, papers, and money. When the codel returned to Washington, he was called on the carpet by a Navy admiral who supervised the military liaison office. He'd been waiting for a chance to bring Jones down a few pegs, since Jones had refused to run errands for the admiral and even make coffee for him. He hinted that Jones could face disciplinary action that could become part of his permanent record.

Punaro saw it as a clear case of professional jealousy, and one that could cause lasting damage for Jones's professional standing. "There were people in the Navy who thought Jim lived a charmed life. They were out to teach him a little bit of a lesson."

A Vietnam vet who became a Marine Corps reserve officer, Punaro saw a way of short-circuiting the admiral's nasty scheme. He wrote a note informing him that there had been a Navy aide in the lobby of the Madrid hotel. Since that officer had done nothing to try to apprehend the thief, Punaro suggested, perhaps he too deserved some form of reprimand. That way, the Navy and Marines could be embarrassed by the incident in Madrid.

"If you persist," he wrote, "I'll give this to my boss"—that is, Senator Nunn, not someone the admiral wanted to cross.

In the end, Navy Secretary John Lehman intervened and ordered the case against Jones to be dropped.

Punaro had first seen Jim Jones around 1978 during one of Senator Nunn's subcommittee hearings about the effectiveness of the new all-volunteer military, and in an unusual move, Commandant Louis Wilson called on a junior officer to represent the Corps. Capt. Jim Jones was called on to testify.

"Most services wouldn't dream of a letting anyone with less than two or three stars testify," Punaro noted later.

Jones managed to state a clear and concise case for switching to an all-volunteer military. By the early 1980s, his star was soon rising, at least in congressional circles. "We all said he's going to be Commandant some day," Punaro said. "He was so head and shoulders above everyone else."

Jones knew better than to get cocky, since the odds were clearly stacked against him. About 75 percent of captains are promoted to major, 66 percent of majors make lieutenant colonel, and only 50 percent of the light colonels are promoted to full colonel. The biggest hurdle comes with promotion to general: only about 7 percent of all colonels get a star.[1]

The longer Jones worked in the power corridors—keeping him out of important assignments in the Fleet Marine Force—the less he thought he would overcome the odds and get promoted by the Corps' officer selection boards. He also faced the complications of his personal life, as Diane was diagnosed with breast cancer in 1983, and their daughter, Jennifer, suffered from a variety of health problems and required constant care. They also had three boys to raise. So even though Jones was itching to escape D.C., his superiors delayed his transfers to give him time to settle his family issues.

It looked like Jim Jones was teetering on the verge of failure— all because he was too good of an advocate for the Marine Corps for anyone to transfer him from Washington. He feared getting branded as a "political Marine," someone whose warrior days were now just the stuff of legend, and who might be getting soft around the middle from too many cocktail parties.

Not that he was alone. Basic School brethren Marty Steele and Ray Smith found themselves facing other kinds of controversies— ones that imperiled their own climb up the Corps' career ladder.

THIRTEEN

Combat at Chrysler

The Soviet Union invaded Afghanistan in late 1979, and the United States reacted by halting shipments of 17 million tons of grain and suspending sales of high-tech equipment to the Russians. President Jimmy Carter also ordered the U.S. Olympic team to boycott the 1980 summer games in Moscow.

Those were a few of the high-stakes foreign relations games played out in public. The start of the 1980s was marked by various forms of saber, and silo, rattling between the two superpowers. Yet in what turned out to be the twilight of the Cold War, other dangers lurked in the shadows of the most unlikely places—even in America's car capital, Detroit. Marty Steele, who seemed to have a natural affinity for internal conflicts, was stuck in the middle again. Instead of dealing with delinquent Marines, though, he found himself walking a fine line between the civilian and military worlds, all in an effort to make sure the Marine tankers got a fair chance to hit their targets.

It began in 1978 when Steele accepted an assignment that, on the face of it, looked about as sexy as becoming an accountant: liaison officer to the project manager of the M-60/M-1 Tank programs at the U.S. Army Tank–Automotive command. Steele's job was to ensure that the Marines' tanks coming off the assembly line at the Chrysler plant in Warren, Michigan, were in good working order.

Not a glamorous job, but an important one. Steele knew from his two tours in Vietnam, and his subsequent training with Marine tankers, that improving the quality of the Corps' tanks and other heavy armor was critical. The Marines were playing catch up with the Army when it came to armored weaponry. The Army, as the larger ground force, bought the most advanced tanks—like the M60A3, which was equipped with the latest in night-vision technology and computer-based guidance systems. The Marines' standard issue M60A1 was an older model that was less computerized and lacked the night vision capability of the Army version.

Soon after arriving at the sprawling Chrysler factory, Steele got the feeling that all was not well on the assembly line. The Big Three automakers were bleeding red ink as they lost business to Japan, which was sucking in American car buyers with sturdier and more fuel-efficient Hondas and Toyotas. Even though the global marketplace was hard on the American auto oligarchy, Chrysler always knew it could count on Uncle Sam as a deep-pocketed customer for tanks.

Like Jim Jones in Congress, Marty Steele soon learned the value of wearing his uniform in public. He realized that the workers tended to talk to him more, and even confide in him, when they saw he was a Marine. Watching the increasingly automated production lines, which were as long as several football fields, Steele began to see that some of the workers wanted to speak to him in private. They were rugged men and women, and some were ex-Marines. When he'd talk to them, though, Steele often got shooed away by nervous supervisors, mumbling about union rules or making other excuses. These managers seemed tense, which made Steele, with his nose for fraud, even more interested. Eventually, he found out why everyone wanted him to keep moving.

It took ninety days to make an M60A1 tank. This involved three eight-hour shifts a day for three months straight. Steele quickly surmised the problem wasn't the workers, who were honestly performing their jobs. The heart of the problem was the stream of badly-made components coming to Chrysler from outside vendors, all in an effort to cut costs and increase the profit margin on each tank, whose engines alone cost $100,000. Each tank took three months to build and test, and had thousands of parts.

Some officials and allied contractors had been cutting corners by purchasing cheap and unreliable parts. This allowed them to lower production costs, and increase Chrysler's profit margin on each tank. They could get their bonuses for helping the bottom line, and no one would be the wiser—not even the U.S. Marine Corps.

Steele slipped in during mid-shift to get out on the production floor, where he heard from disgusted workers. Holding up the flawed engine parts, they flatly declared, "This is a piece of shit, major. It will prematurely fail."

Steele took his concerns to the weekly engineering board meeting, where company and government engineers hashed out production issues. He was the lone military representative.

He told them what he'd found and declared, "I don't want my son or my Marines riding in a substandard tank."

"Don't get emotional," one Chrysler manager said dismissively. "This is a business decision, Major Steele." Other board members nodded. In the safe confines of an executive office, the lives of soldiers and Marines out on the field or in combat simply didn't seem to matter. The company men were blinded by budget targets and bonus payments.

Steele would not back down. "This is not a business decision," he said, pounding the table. "This is a life and death decision about young men defending your sorry asses as they sweat out the start of combat with the Soviets or some other enemy. Our Marines and soldiers are defending our way life, and I'll be damned if I won't get emotional about it!"

So Maj. Martin R. Steele became persona non grata among the Chrysler managers as he launched his own investigation of the quality controls of the tanks' production. He forced his way down to the factory floor, where he knew he'd get the straight scoop from patriotic auto workers. They were veterans themselves, or had relatives in the Marines, and took pride in their work.

Steele found he made the biggest impression when he wore his green uniform. He sometimes got up to go to the graveyard shift in the middle of the night. Then he'd really get an earful about managers' orders to take shortcuts and use shoddy parts. On the plus side, though, he learned the workers were creating their own internal quality controls for the tanks, painting big white "M's" on the turret, marking them as the Marines'—and Marty Steele's—own.

And yet too many tanks were still rolling off the line with major defects, including air filtration systems that choked up with water and mud when they driven out into the field. The defective equipment would slam to a halt, the engines wrecked as if a Soviet antitank missile had scored a direct hit. Steele did find a willing partner in Teledyne, the engine maker, to pressure Chrysler to fix the flawed filters.

Ultimately, all of these defects and internal investigations slowed the production schedule of the Marines' tanks—more than 700 in all during Steele's three-year stint in Michigan.

The most contentious issue, though, was the quality of the tank's periscopes. The scopes, made by two major outside vendors, required precision-made optical equipment. This was one tank part where corners absolutely could not be cut. Otherwise, they would render useless thousands of Army and Marine Corps weapons stationed in the most strategic spots in the world, including the front line forces against the Soviets in West Germany.

Much to his alarm, Steele learned that the scopes had "slop" in them, causing the reticles (crosshairs) to flop up and down. Bad scopes meant the tanks' aim was not true. When he communicated this delicate information to superiors in the Pentagon, he was met with a skeptical reaction, especially from Army tankers. Train your crews better, they told Steele's bosses. Teach them to hit the damn targets.

It would have been easy just to drop the whole thing, but that wasn't Steele's way. It would have been a dereliction of duty. The flap wasn't the first time he'd gone turret to turret with tank experts. Before moving to Michigan, he underwent extensive training at the Army's armor school in Fort Knox, Kentucky. Though he was one of a handful of Marines, Steele managed to make quite an impression when he was chosen the school's distinguished graduate in 1977. During a ceremony at the Patton Outdoor Museum, an Army major general shook his hand—but seemed to do it grudgingly. As he handed Marty a cavalry sword and silver bowl, the general grumbled, "This is a disgrace to the United States Army that a Marine is a distinguished graduate of this school." At first, Steele was shaken by the insult. Then he was just downright mad. When the general shook his hand in front of his applauding classmates, Steele pressed harder and pulled him closer.

"General, I'm sorry you feel that way," Steele said, as the two men moved across the stage side by side, apparently in deep conversation while the Army tankers cheered the Marine for his unique accomplishment.

Steele waved with his other hand but still kept the general close by and scolded him. "This is a very proud day for all the people in the class," he said. "If you'll look, they're all standing there cheering. I had a great bond with these soldiers. I'd go to war and die with them. And yet you chose to ruin this day with your comment."

The general tried to pull away. "Captain, let go of my hand."

"I'm not going to do it, sir," Steele said.

"I'm ordering you to let go of my hand."

"Sir, I'm not going to do it. I'm not going to let you ruin this day."

The impasse continued for several minutes, as Steele braced his legs and refused to release the general, who outweighed him by about fifty pounds. "I've been in the Marine Corps for eleven years," Marty continued. "I've been an aide to two generals. I'm not intimidated by you or what you just said. I'm disappointed. My winning this honor is not a disappointment for the U.S. Army. This is a great day for all of us. We're comrades in arms and will be on battlefields together in the future, and it's not an embarrassment."

Finally, the general gave in and offered a half-hearted apology.

The Fort Knox flap came to mind as Steele found himself running up against the same kind of tired old warhorses as the insulting general. Their guiding philosophy, he found, could be summarized by three letters: CYA, that is, "cover your ass."

Marty Steele could have adopted the same status quo mentality, except for one thing: he loved his fellow Marines too much. He knew that sending them into combat in such questionable equipment quite likely would endanger their lives, and possibly even endanger the United States if it ever entered a large-scale conflict. So it was that he decided to mount an experiment of his own to test drive—and shoot—the Chrysler-made tanks in the unforgiving terrain of 29 Palms, California, home of the Marine Corps' Mojave Desert training base.

He flew, along with a technical expert, from Detroit to Palm Springs, where they got a car and drove up the windy roads into the high desert. Once on the base, they were taken out into rocky, snake-infested terrain where they found a top gunnery sergeant conducting field exercises with the M60A1s.

The midsummer sun beat down on them and the temperature topped 115 degrees. Stepping inside a field tent, Steele briefed the tankers on the problem with the periscopes. "Have you noticed any slop?" he asked them directly.

"There's nothing wrong, sir," the gunny said in a flat voice. He appeared to be avoiding looking Steele in the eye, though.

"Are you sure?" Steele said. "Because I've chosen your scope to inspect and we believe there's slop in it. You're telling me there's nothing wrong."

He paused for effect. These were good Marines, that much was clear. They were sweating their brains out in the desert sun to improve their gunnery skills, and were clearly dedicated military men.

Yet Steele could tell that they were afraid of stepping on someone's toes, or getting involved in something bigger that might give them, or their unit, a black eye. So as sweat dripped off his temples, he decided to give it to them straight. "You know, I can see that you are honest men, and damn good Marines. But your moment in history is right now. Now, if you tell me nothing is wrong, I'll change course and might even end my investigation of these tanks here and now. But if there's something wrong, you need to tell me. It's the only way I can get these fixed, and maybe, just maybe, we can save some other Marine's life by not sending him out into combat with defective equipment."

The corporal glanced at his gunny and asked, "Do you want to tell him?"

"Naw, you tell him," the gunny said.

"Good," Steele said. "Let's get it out in the open."

The corporal spread his hands and said with a crooked smile, "Sir, we couldn't hit a McDonald's from across the street with these pieces of shit. We've been using Sergeant York windage and guessing where the round could go, and where the sight should be. We haven't used this fucking thing in over eight months because it's so bad, and we can't figure out what's wrong with it."

They talked some more about their frustrations with the tanks' periscopes, then Steele patted each of the good Marines on the back. "You've done the right thing. Now let's go out to the range." They fired some test rounds, and just as the corporal predicted, they missed a six-foot-wide panel from 1,200 meters—the minimum standard of marksmanship. The periscope had too much play, or "slop," to do any better.

The more he dug into the problem, the madder Steele got. Out of fifty-three tanks in the high desert training ground, forty-eight were deficient. This was only the tip of the iceberg, though. The Army was upgrading its tanks with more sophisticated thermal sights and could solve the problem. Until those were replaced, however, about 10,000 tanks in the Army's inventory had the same faulty periscopes as the Marine tanks at 29 Palms. What if they were called on to actually fight the long-dreaded land war against the Soviets, Steele asked. Would they get outgunned by the superior Russian tanks and lose the opening round of World War III— all because some pencil-pushers in Detroit cut corners?

The Marines in the field had not blown the whistle, though, because they had gotten used to dealing with bad equipment— from the M-16s in Vietnam that failed when they got dirty to the aging helicopters they still flew that leaked more oil than a Texas tycoon. They were so used to "work arounds"—that is, making the best of bad equipment—that they figured this was just one more problem to solve on their own.

For his part, Steele knew he would be seen as a lone crusader, trying to get the brass's attention on a matter of national security that nobody wanted to address because it involved millions of dollars to fix. He pressed on, though, and sought out other officers who began to admit their own deep concerns about the tanks. At one conference at Fort Knox, an Army commander confessed, "I have a brigade in Europe, and we can't hit the target at all with any of our tanks. But we've been lying. We've lied extensively all the way up and down the chain of command. I have taken the scores from qualifications where they didn't hit the target and said they did hit the target."

Known as "pencil licking" the target, Steele learned this practice had become widespread. This was not only an ethical failing, but had serious national security ramifications. If the Soviets knew the American tank force in Europe had been compromised, they might take advantage of the situation—either in Germany or, perhaps more likely, on some other Cold War battleground.

While respecting the sensitive nature of his discovery, Steele quietly moved the issue up the chain of command. His report was labeled top secret, and very quietly, the Defense Department established a $15 million fund for the recall and replacement of the sloppy periscopes.

"We kept it out of the national papers," Steele said later. "It was a scandal of huge proportions."

For his trouble, Marty and Cindy Steele started getting life-threatening telephone calls at their Michigan home. He'd dug too deep into the inner workings of the auto industry and had dared to speak openly at meetings about his suspicions of collusion between contractors and government inspectors.

At one meeting, Steele flatly declared, "Someone is driving a Mercedes-Benz as a payoff." Suddenly, one of the government inspectors at the table dashed off to the bathroom and started throwing up. Later, Steele learned that the inspector really was driving a brand new Mercedes—and the Marine major's comment had struck a bullseye.

The periscope affair was played out behind the scenes, and it earned Steele no medals or extra pay. Instead, he endured months of criticism, heartburn, and the loss of a good friend. A quiet engineer in the automotive tank command, Elmer Wesela, became increasingly stressed-out as he joined Steele's crusade. "What if the Soviets come tomorrow?" Wesela said on one trip. And as they traveled to 29 Palms, the tank engineer keeled over and died of a heart attack in the airport terminal at Palm Springs.

Because it was handled quietly, and was a classified matter, the internal affair surrounding the Marine and Army tanks has never been publicly scrutinized. One key survivor from the tank command, while confirming there were some problems at Chrysler, did not agree about the scope of the problem. Retired Army major general Oscar Decker confirmed that some tanks did have play in the periscopes. However, in a telephone interview, Decker characterized that as just one of many issues he dealt with in Detroit.

"But there was no scandal involved in that," Decker said.

For his part, Marty Steele walked away from his assignment at Chrysler with faith in the essential decency of Detroit's autoworkers. Despite the collusion he found in some management ranks, the assembly line employees "would do the right thing if they had a reason to do the right thing," he said. Without their honesty, Steele said, he never would have spotted the scam taking place right before his eyes.

Detroit might not have been a particularly glamorous assignment, but it was, in Marty's words, a "transforming tour of duty"— one that showed the good and the bad of his fellow countrymen.

During this period, Ray Smith was training at Camp Lejeune, where he was executive officer of the 2nd Battalion, Eighth

Marines. The 2/8 was getting ready to ship out to Beirut, Lebanon, a routine "float" to the Mediterranean. Nothing could have prepared Ray and his men for what lay ahead on their journey to the east. The Marine Corps was about to enter one of the most trying—and fatal—stretches in its history, with assignments to save American lives caught in the crossfire of two civil wars, two oceans and thousands of miles apart.

FOURTEEN

Mid-Course Correction

Aboard ship, eastern Caribbean

By the fall of 1983, Ray Smith was a lieutenant colonel in command of a 1,200-man battalion landing team (BLT). He had been training for this deployment, or "float," with the 2/8 to Beirut for many months, running with his men through the pine forests of eastern North Carolina and conducting amphibious landing exercises along the coastline. After spending so much time in the field, Smith was confident that from the lowliest private to his highest-ranking field grade officer, these were top-flight Marines.

Gone were the tumultuous 1970s, with its drug busts, race riots, and law enforcement duties. The all-volunteer force had brought in more motivated and educated men and women willing to follow orders and, with a few exceptions, stay out of trouble.

The Marine Corps was back on its feet and doing the right things to maintain force readiness. The gospel at Camp Lejeune was maneuver warfare—winning battles through surprise and stealth rather than attacking the enemy head on. There was no more zealous proponent of "maneuverism" than Smith's commanding general, division commander Maj. Gen. Al Gray. The gruff general was a rare bundle of intellectual and emotional energy. He encouraged his Marines to read the ancient Chinese classic by Sun Tzu, *The Art of War*, along with more modern books about coping with change in the business world by consultants such as Tom Peters.

After a hot day out on the field, Gray liked to huddle with his leadership team in the base movie theater for a debriefing. Like a football coach, he dissected their plays during war games. Thoughtfully chewing tobacco, Gray would quote maneuverists like military theorist William Lind, who said the secret was "to avoid the enemy's strength and hurl your strength against his weaknesses. You want to use judo, not fight a boxing match."[1]

Gray, who started as a private in the Korean War, was determined to teach his men the lessons of Vietnam and get back to being smart, no-nonsense warriors. He was also a proponent of technological innovations, and wanted every Marine to be a "high-tech samurai," mastering the growing arsenal of digitally-driven "smart" weapons.

Under Gray's leadership, Ray Smith felt a renewed vigor the likes of which he hadn't experienced since going tête-à-tête against the North Vietnamese. His new sense of optimism in the military was fueled in large part by President Reagan's fundamental toughness against the "Evil Empire" of the Soviet Union. God, he loved the Gipper. Damn right, we've got to stop the communists, he thought. And it was only a matter of time before we had to fight them again.

He could never have known he would be thrust into the center of the international boxing ring.

On October 18, 1983, Battalion Landing Team 2/8 shipped out from Morehead City, North Carolina, in a five-ship Navy convoy. Their orders were to relieve their counterparts in the 1st Battalion serving as part of a multinational peacekeeping force in Beirut. It was a thankless task in the thick of a civil war that had been raging in Lebanon for the past seven years with no end in sight. Making matters worse, the American forces had to watch out for a growing number of car bombers and other terrorists who received training and materiel from Syria and Iran. Terrorists had blown up the U.S. embassy in Beirut in April of that year, killing sixty-three people, including eighteen Americans. Lurking in the smoke and shadows was the Soviet Union, which was busy funding and equipping the foes of the United States. It was Russia's way of foiling America's attempts to broker any kind of peace agreement in Lebanon, making Beirut the epicenter of the latest proxy war between the world's two superpowers. Israel played for the American team (albeit on its own terms) and Yasser Arafat's Palestinian Liberation Organization sided with the Soviets.

The Navy-Marine convoy started out by sailing east for two days toward Beirut. Then, somewhere around Bermuda, the ships plotted a new course. One of the first Marines to notice the diversion was one of Ray Smith's platoon sergeants, Staff Sgt. Mike Leiphart. Whenever he was out at sea, Leiphart liked to test his men's navigational skills. "What direction are we sailing in?" he would ask.

By checking the time on their watches against the sun's position on the horizon, most of the troops could make an educated guess about which way the ship was heading.

In the early hours of their third day at sea, Leiphart, a tough farm boy from Pennsylvania, was surprised when he started playing his own navigational game. The early morning sun should have been dead ahead, but instead it was rising off the port side of the USS *Manitowoc*. They were steaming south.

Leiphart was a careful man who liked to know where he was going, so he felt a bit disoriented about this sudden diversion. Why weren't they going straight to Spain, and then east to Lebanon? The ships had been loaded to disembark on the beach at Beirut, once a crown jewel of the eastern Mediterranean. It used to be a great place to visit, with bars and beautiful local scenery and exotic women.

Leiphart had already pulled one tour of duty there, but amid reports of car bombings and shootings at the 1/8 Marines, this promised to be a much tougher assignment. The country had been racked by civil war since 1975 as its ancient feuds had fueled superpowers' struggles for dominance in the Middle East.

"If a government wanted to make a point without itself going to war, it commissioned a battle in Beirut or hired an assassin to knock off one of its enemies there," wrote CBS News correspondent Larry Pintak.[2]

Former Marine and author James Webb had cautioned President Reagan to "never get involved in a five-sided argument that's been going on for 2,000 years."[3] And yet Webb, a decorated veteran of Vietnam, knew the Marines traditionally were sent into foreign combat zones with complicated, often impenetrable, history and geography.

Among the goods stored in the holds of the troop transports were three-by-three-foot maps to help the Marines navigate Beirut's labyrinthine streets. The ships also bore food, medical supplies, and weapons that would be unloaded as soon as they reached their destination in the eastern Mediterranean.

When the convoy made its mid-course correction near Bermuda, 2nd Lt. John Watts, the battalion logistics officer, got a queasy feeling about how he'd packed the gear. From prepackaged meals to first-aid kits to replacement generators, everything the Marines needed to fight was packed neatly into the ships to be unloaded on the sandy beaches of Beirut. Watts worried about this side trip, and whether his packing job would work out now.

The rumors flitted across the tropical waters like so many flying fish. Leiphart gathered his men below decks around a shortwave radio to listen to a BBC report of trouble on the tiny island of Grenada. They only could make out bits and pieces, but what they heard sounded like something lifted from a James Bond movie.

A Marxist military strongman staged a coup, overthrowing the island's socialist government and killing its president. The coup leader, Gen. Hudson Austin, imposed a round-the-clock curfew as his troops terrorized the mild-mannered citizens of Grenada and its capital, St. George's.

The Reagan White House was most concerned about the fate of several hundred American students at St. George's Medical

School. The students, and a few other foreign nationals, were thought to be held hostage, but their fate was unknown.

Adding spice to the plot was the presence of Cuban engineers building a long-range airfield. Cuba had an unknown number of soldiers and arms on Grenada.

Leiphart listened carefully to a spokesman for the People's Revolutionary Army warning about any U.S. intervention, vowing that "the beaches would run red with American blood."

Leiphart thought, *We'll see about that.*

At 3:20 A.M. on October 22, Ray Smith was awakened and handed a top-secret message from the Navy's Atlantic Fleet headquarters.

The task force had been ordered to steer south and take station about 500 miles northeast of Grenada in the lower reaches of the Caribbean.[4] The coded message imposed radio silence—or "emissions control"—to avoid detection by Soviet satellites. This meant the ships could not radio for more information about the precise nature of the secret mission.

Smith rolled out of his rack and went to find his boss, Col. James P. Faulkner, commander of the 22nd Marine Amphibious Unit. Piecing together reports from the BBC and Voice of America, they realized that within the next forty-eight hours they would be attacking a well-guarded, hostile, and basically unknown island. But Secretary of State George P. Shultz, a former Marine, said the nation must act to avoid the loss of American lives in Grenada's civil war.

Combined with other elements of the task force, including a helicopter squadron and support elements, the Marines were ready to send 1,200 men from sea to shore. They could expect support from the Army's 82nd Airborne Division, along with Navy SEALS who were busy conducting special operations on the island.

Grenada is the southernmost of the Windward Islands, south of the Virgin Islands and Barbados. With only 110,000 inhabitants, its 1980s economy relied largely on bananas, nutmeg and tourism. The former British colony generally escaped the attention of the State Department or military planners.[5] It gained notoriety in 1979 when a charismatic leader, Maurice Bishop, staged a coup overthrowing the country's democratically elected government. Bishop led the Marxist-inspired New Joint Effort for Welfare, Education, and Liberation, or New JEWEL Movement. He quickly established ties with Cuba and the Soviet Union, and by 1980, 100 Cuban military advisors were crisscrossing the island's rugged terrain.

Grenada is strategically located off the coast of Venezuela and its deep oil reserves. Fidel Castro, sensing a chance to expand his military power near this key sea lane, proposed building an airport at Port Salines on the southern tip of Grenada. Bishop accepted the offer, and before you could say Che Guevara, the Cubans were erecting two battle-ready camps with barracks, headquarters, communications, and weapons storage. As a payoff, Bishop's regime received military and economic aid from Cuba and the Soviet Union.

This new stepping stone for Cuban-Soviet influence set off major alarms in the fledgling administration of Ronald Reagan. The conservative Republican was a veteran Cold Warrior and outspoken critic of the Soviet Union, which he branded in a 1982 speech as the "Evil Empire." Faced with Reagan's tough stand, Bishop started hedging his bets in this high-stakes game. By 1983, the Marxist maverick started softening his anti-American rhetoric with plans to hold free elections and enter into talks with the United States.

Bishop never got to play this hand, however. On October 13, 1983, hardliners in his party, led by General Hudson, staged a coup and established a Revolutionary Military Council. Within a week, Grenadans staged a counterrevolution and freed Bishop. But it was a brief uprising, though, and was quashed when the People's Revolutionary Army (PRA) opened fire on a crowd of Bishop's backers.[6] Bishop was summarily executed on October 19.

Four days later, in the wake of this bloodshed, the Navy-Marine convoy arrived at its station 500 miles to the northeast.

The Organization of Eastern Caribbean States requested American assistance to deal with "current anarchic conditions, the serious violations of human rights and bloodshed, and the . . . unprecedented threat to the peace and security of the region by the vacuum of authority in Grenada."[7]

Despite the series of developments, some of the officers aboard ship doubted Reagan was serious about intervening in the island anarchy. Ray Smith was not among the doubters. While avoiding taking sides in politics, he found himself drawn to Reagan's in-your-face rhetoric toward the Soviets. It struck a chord with Smith, who still saw his primary mission as fighting communism. If it took a diversion to an obscure atoll, so be it.

"From the very beginning, when we got that divert order, I felt certain that we were going to do it," he said later. "I just felt it in my bones."

Smith wasn't the only Vietnam-era officer itching for a fight. Grenada promised to be the first major U.S. military action since the last helicopter lifted off the roof of the U.S. Embassy in Saigon during the ignominious exit in 1975.

"Precisely because Grenada was the first sustained American military action in a decade, each of the four services was hungry for a piece of the action," Rick Atkinson wrote in *The Long Gray Line*. "'It doesn't matter which war you were in,' according to a military truism, 'as long as it was the last one.' No one wanted to be left behind."[8]

Yet the military's eagerness to prove itself in battle was tempered by recent debacles, such as the failed rescue attempt in 1980 of the U.S. Embassy hostages in Tehran. That operation was aborted after a collision of a helicopter and a C-130 fuel tanker that left eight American servicemen dead in the middle of the Iranian desert.

"One of the catastrophe's lasting effects was an overkill mentality," Atkinson wrote.

This sense of caution led Pentagon planners to reject a limited strike using Army Special Forces to extricate the American medical students. Instead, they cobbled together a large, complicated operational plan reminiscent of the legendary landings of World War II and Korea.

"Most amphibious operations, from Guadacanal to Inchon, required months of detailed planning," Atkinson wrote. "In Grenada the military had only a few days to prepare, and Reagan did not sign the final invasion order until 6:00 P.M. on October 24, less than twelve hours before the operation was to commence."[9]

The rushed planning for a huge, multifaceted invasion of Grenada sparked near-pandemonium in the board room of the *Guam*, the convoy's command ship. Ray Smith and Colonel Faulkner hurriedly organized the Marine Corps' part of the invasion, dubbed Operation Urgent Fury.

The Marines would seize an airstrip at Pearls Airport and the adjacent town of Grenville on the island's northeast coast. The Army would secure the Cuban-built air base at Point Salines on the southern tip.

The Marines and Army, which constantly fought for dollars and prestige back in Washington, would act in unison for a change. Or at least that was the plan.

For the Marines forming below decks, it soon became evident that Operation Urgent Fury had a frenzied quality about it. The snafus started with the maps: There weren't any, or at least none that were reliable. The Navy did have a full set of nautical charts, but they were based on British naval drawings from 1936, before most of the men were born.[10]

Fortunately, the amphibious group's chief staff officer, Commander Richard A. Butler, was an amateur yachtsman who had navigated the waters around Grenada a few years earlier. His recollection of the coast, tides, surf, and beach proved invaluable.

Ray Smith had his own special knowledge of Grenada. After returning to Oklahoma State in the late 1970s, he was assigned a faculty advisor of Eastern European history who often traveled through the Soviet Union and allied countries. One of the more intriguing discoveries the professor shared with Smith was the growing Soviet presence in the southern reaches of the Caribbean, on the tiny island of Grenada.

As a result, Ray wrote a paper about the seizure and occupation of Grenada as a live-fire training exercise for a Marine amphibious brigade. He could never have imagined that his academic exercise would one day be put to the test, and he would be in thick of it.

As the last-minute planning for the invasion bumped along, a parade of brass flew in by helicopter. This group included a stocky, outspoken general who soon began to grate on the nerves of the Marine and Navy planners: Maj. Gen. Norman Schwarzkopf.

The joint command structure—who reported to whom—became as twisted as an old sail. Schwarzkopf, the top ranking Army general aboard ship, appeared to have the Pentagon's blessings and started giving orders to any officer in sight. Lieutenant Colonel Smith bit his tongue and drew aside Vice Adm. Joseph Metcalf III, the highest-ranking flag officer aboard ship. Explaining his confusion, and the apparent interference of Schwarzkopf, Smith bluntly declared, "Frankly, sir, we don't have time for this bullshit."

Metcalf confessed that he wasn't quite sure why the Army had sent in Schwarzkopf, but advised Smith simply to steer clear of him. The admiral knew that anytime you put Marines in the same room with Army commanders, it was a volatile mix.

"This was nothing new," Metcalf said later. "I discounted all this crap." Work together, he told everyone. We're supposed to be on the same team.

Adding to the preinvasion stress was a shocking news report over short-wave radios on the morning of October 23: the Marine barracks in Beirut had been destroyed by the massive explosion of a truck laden with TNT. At least two hundred Americans were dead, mostly members of the 1st Battalion, 8th Marines. When the last body was dragged from the ruins, the death toll stood at 241 Americans, including 220 Marines. It marked the worst single day for the Corps since D-Day at Iwo Jima in 1945.[11]

Across the convoy, the 2/8 Marines were in shock. After all, they had been on their way to replace their brothers-in-arms who were now dead in the rubble of Beirut.

Aboard the *Manitowoc*, Staff Sergeant Leiphart wondered why the U.S. government had put the Marines in such a vulnerable spot. Leiphart knew Beirut was a dangerous place from a tour of duty in the summer of 1982, when the Marines were sent in to help evacuate soldiers of Arafat's PLO to avoid a slaughter by the advancing Israeli army. In one of the strangest episodes in the Corps' more than 200-year history, the Marines stood guard between the two armies, providing a human buffer zone. The assignment strained the patience and fighting instincts of the Marines, who kept their unloaded M-16s by their sides.

Leiphart watched as some 6,000 PLO fighters roared in by the truckload to Beirut and boarded cruise ships bound for Cyprus. The staff sergeant gritted his teeth and gripped his rifle as the Palestinian fighters screamed wild epithets and curses against Israel and fired AK-47s into the air. The Marines were in a "peace-keeping" role, but there was nothing peaceful about the PLO's earlier exit from Lebanon.

Matt Collins, a weapons specialist from Lexington, Kentucky, heard one of his gunnys predict, "We're going to take them to Cyprus, and they're going to come right back."

Spent bullets from the wild shooting fell back to earth, creating a lethal rainfall. The Marines kept their helmets on as the stray bullets shattered windows, pinged off cars, and, occasionally, killed the PLO evacuees.

Capt. Robert K. "Bob" Dobson had his own Beirut memories. During his 1982 tour of duty, the tall, terse Californian drew the task of finding a barracks and headquarters for the returning Marines. Dobson began scouring the terrain around Beirut International Airport, looking for a defensible place to house the American garrison. Hiking across the undulating land between the coastal road and the airport, he noticed a battered building near the terminal.

The blocky structure once housed Lebanon's federal aviation administration. Now it was a bombed-out shell, with shards of glass everywhere in its halls and lobby. But Dobson could see that if it were cleaned up, the concrete building had potential as a barracks and headquarters. It had plenty of space, limited access, and enough thickness in its walls and roof to provide protection against indirect fire—artillery, mortars, and rockets launched from a distance—and any direct fire from tanks, machine guns, rifles, or rocket-propelled grenades. It was also centrally located and on what Dobson viewed as defensible terrain since, at that point, the main road to the airport was closed. It was only later, after the road to the city was reopened, that its defenses were compromised and terrorists found a way in with their bomb-laden truck.

After news of the bombing, Dobson stifled his emotions and focused on the readiness of the infantry company under his command. He had driven Golf Company hard back at Camp Lejeune. Before he assumed command, the 150 men in the unit were known for fighting well in the field, but acting like yahoos once they returned to base—fighting, drinking, missing roll call, sometimes getting arrested.

Ray Smith had known Dobson from Quantico, where he been one of the lieutenant's mentors at The Basic School. Dobson was thrilled to find himself serving with Smith in the 2/8, helping shape up Golf Company.

Dobson's elite crew included a Cuban-born Marine, Sgt. Manuel A. "Manny" Cox. Cox was five foot ten, with dark brown eyes and a steady gaze. His intense, no-nonsense demeanor intimidated anyone who was dogging it or playing any games with him.

At age twenty, Cox was about the same age as many of the men in his squad. But his hardscrabble life had given him the insights and bearing of an old salt. His father had once been a respected geologist and professor at the University of Havana in the early 1960s, but like thousands of other intellectuals caught in the persecutions of Fidel Castro, Guillermo Cox was lined up against a wall and executed by a firing squad.

Cox's mother, Maria, fled with her baby boy to the United States. What they lacked in income, the Coxes made up for in work ethic and self-respect. The young Cox became a good student and gifted violinist with dreams of attending the Julliard School of Music.[12]

His dream was deferred, though, when his mother died of brain cancer. At age fourteen, Cox was left to fend for himself in Union City, New Jersey. Sometimes he slept on park benches and worked odd jobs to feed himself. By age seventeen, he was a year shy of the legal age to enlist in the military. But a Marine recruiter forged his grandmother's signature, and Cox left for boot camp at Parris Island.

After spending years as a street urchin, Manny Cox soaked in the discipline and order of the Corps, and soon became a star performer. Like his battalion boss, "E-Tool" Smith, Manny Cox was determined to battle communists. And he dreamed of one day returning to Cuba and liberating it from Castro and his blood-thirsty communists.

Cox's letters home to his pregnant wife, Evi, during the "float" to Beirut revealed a gentler side to the sergeant's personality. "Darling, we are all very sad today here on the ship," he wrote after the Beirut barracks bombing. "This is terrible, and we all had friends there. But you, my darling, must not worry. All this that happens makes us stronger.

"We are still on our way to Grenada," he continued. "We'll arrive there sometime tomorrow evening, and do the evacuation that next morning. . . . I really thought that with all of this going on all over the world my squad would begin to get nerves, and jumpy, but they haven't. In fact, it's the opposite. They have taken this like true professional Marines, like true men. I'm proud to be their squad leader, but more than anything, I'm prouder to be your husband."

As news of the carnage spread across the convoy in the Caribbean, Ray Smith started worrying about how the 2/8 might react once they hit Grenada. Would their frustration boil over to the civilian populace?

After all, this was supposed to be a rescue mission and any mistakes—particularly any civilian deaths—could turn into an international incident.

So he gathered his company commanders in the board room of the *Trenton*. Studying the faces of Dobson and other young officers, no one appeared too cocky. That was good. Smith had gone into combat dozens of times and knew it could be hard to find the right balance between aggression and reason. As George Patton said, "No sane man is unafraid in battle."

Smith told everyone to sit down, then pulled out a plug of Red Man tobacco and passed around the bag. He chewed thoughtfully and explained why he had called the meeting.

"I want you to think about how you brief your NCOs and squad leaders about this mission. I want you to say, 'Hey guys, these are friendly people. These are not people who have blown up our brothers in Lebanon.' I want you to tell your men, 'Don't take it out on them. Don't kill anybody who doesn't need to be killed.'"

Dobson nodded. *Don't kill anybody who doesn't need to be killed.* After eight years as a Marine, this would be his first time in combat. Across the battalion, many men had that same sensation of finally being put to the test. Like the old salts of World War II, Dobson reflected, we're ready to hit the beach.

Indeed, the night before he'd shown *The Sands of Iwo Jima* to get his men in the right frame of mind. Unlike the Marines in the John Wayne classic, though, Dobson's men probably wouldn't go up against fortified machine gun bunkers. Instead, they would face Soviet-made antiaircraft guns the Grenadan rebels were known to possess. But the biggest concern was the Cubans—how many soldiers did they have on the island, dug in to battle the Americans to the death?

Despite the perils, Smith stressed the importance of using restraint even as they applied all of the weapons at their disposal—from attack helicopters to new infrared antitank weapons. "We're there to eliminate the PRA resistance and to evacuate Americans," he said. "We don't want to kill anybody on the island, except for the Cubans or enemy soldiers. So when you meet civilians on the roads or in the towns along the way, tell them to just go on about their business. Tell them not to gather in any large groups, and not to take any hostile actions toward us. Some of these militias may just be kids or old men, you know. We need to get the word out to the population that if they take any potshots at us, they're probably going to get killed."

D-DAY, OCTOBER 25, 1983, 1:00 A.M.

"Reveille, reveille!" The wake-up order, as old as Napoleon, barked over the PA system. "All hands heave out and trice up." The men of Golf Company rolled out of their cots on the *Manitowoc*. Some rubbed sleep from their eyes, while others rose stiffly after a restless few hours on their backs.

Staff Sergeant Leiphart had been one of the sleepless ones as he went down his mental checklist, from making sure his men were issued the right amount of ammunition to reminding them to fill their canteens with fresh water.

The ship's quarters were hot and crowded. The men squared away packs, cleaned M-16s, and scrawled final notes to wives, sweethearts, and friends.

At 2:00 A.M., they were called up to the chow hall for a rich breakfast of scrambled eggs, biscuits, and pancakes. It was a Navy tradition to feed the Marines well before entering combat—a ritual that combined the Last Supper and a meal fit for King Arthur's Knights of the Round Table.

Marty Steele runs past defenders during a Fayetteville High School victory on November 1, 1963. PHOTO COURTESY OF MARTY STEELE.

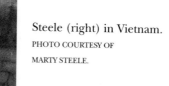

Steele (right) in Vietnam.
PHOTO COURTESY OF
MARTY STEELE.

Ray Smith with a shotgun in a sandbagged bunker in Vietnam, 1968. PHOTO COURTESY OF RAY SMITH.

Smith receives a Silver Star medal at Hill 861 in Khe Sanh. The commendation was for heroic actions during the Tet Offensive at Hue City. PHOTO COURTESY OF RAY SMITH.

Jim Jones at mail call in the vicinity of Da Nang, Republic of Vietnam, 1967. His I.D. bracelet is that worn by his uncle, William K. Jones, during World War II. PHOTO COURTESY OF JIM JONES.

2nd Lt. Jim Jones (left) with Lance Cpl. Dave Regal in Vietnam, 1967. PHOTO COURTESY OF JIM JONES.

Lt. Les Palm in front of 1st Battalion, 13th Marines, FDC bunker at Khe Sanh, March 1968. PHOTO COURTESY OF LES PALM.

Hill 881S being resupplied with water in used fifty-five-gallon barrels, February 1968. The water had a diesel taste to it, but it was all they had. PHOTO COURTESY OF LES PALM.

Picture taken from the top of Hill 881S looking toward 881N (held by the NVA) at Khe Sanh, January 1968. 3/26 had sent a patrol to 881N and engaged an NVA unit. The fire is napalm being dropped on the enemy positions. PHOTO COURTESY OF LES PALM.

2nd Lieutenant Marty Steele (far right) stands with his reinforced tank platoon from Company C, 2nd Tank Battalion, in Guantanamo Bay, Cuba, in March 1968. PHOTO COURTESY OF MARTY STEELE.

Lt. Col. Ray Smith in Beirut, November 1983, soon after arriving from Grenada. His battalion relieved the Marines decimated by the terrorist attack on the American headquarters. PHOTO COURTESY OF RAY SMITH.

Marines debrief in Grenada after taking Fort Frederick. PHOTO COURTESY OF ROBERT DOBSON.

Marines dig in, Beirut, November 1983. PHOTO COURTESY OF ROBERT DOBSON.

Marines of 2/8's Golf Company fortify positions in Beirut, 1983.
PHOTO COURTESY OF ROBERT DOBSON.

Manny Cox (right) with close friend B. J. Trump on 1982 "float" to eastern Mediterranean and Beirut. Cox returned to Lebanon in 1983 and got caught in the crossfire of warring factions. PHOTO COURTESY OF EVI COX-JORDAN.

A Marine standing guard on the outskirts of Beirut in 1983. His weapon is an M-16 with an M-203 40-millimeter grenade launcher attached. A low-velocity, high trajectory weapon, the M-203 provided Marine squads with their own "mini-artillery." PHOTO COURTESY OF ROBERT DOBSON.

Lt. Col. Marty Steele (right) briefs Marine Corps Commandant Gen. Al Gray on desert sand table during a 1st Marine Division exercise at 29 Palms, California, in 1987. PHOTO COURTESY OF MARTY STEELE.

A view of the elaborate sand table at 29 Palms. PHOTO COURTESY OF MARTY STEELE.

Ray Smith and John Ligato at a ceremony at FBI Headquarters in Washington, D.C., 1999. Ligato, who served under Smith in Vietnam and later became an FBI agent, has just received the Director's Award, one of law enforcement's top honors. PHOTO COURTESY OF RAY SMITH.

Marty Steele and his son David. PHOTO COURTESY OF MARTY STEELE.

Gen. Jim Jones accepts the colors of the Corps from outgoing Commandant Gen. Chuck Krulak, 1999. PHOTO BY THE ASSOCIATED PRESS.

David Steele in Iraq beside his Cobra attack helicopter. PHOTO COURTESY OF MARTY STEELE.

General Jones and his wife, Diane, aboard an Osprey in California, summer 2002. PHOTO BY THE ASSOCIATED PRESS.

Then-Lt. Gen. Jim Jones meeting President Bill Clinton, 1998.
PHOTO COURTESY OF JIM JONES.

General Jones with Gen.
Peter Pace (currently
Chairman of the Joint
Chiefs of Staff) at the
Marine Barracks,
Washington, D.C., 2001.
PHOTO COURTESY OF JIM JONES.

General Jones throws out the first pitch at a Padres game in San Diego, 2002. PHOTO COURTESY OF JIM JONES.

General and Mrs. Jones with President George W. Bush and First Lady
Laura Bush, 2002. PHOTO COURTESY OF JIM JONES.

Gen. Jim Jones meets with Afghan President Hamid Karzai in the
Presidential Palace in Kabul on August 30, 2005. PHOTO BY DAN R. WILSON.

Iraqi Prime Minister Jalal Talabani and NATO Secretary General Jaap de Hoop Scheffer cut the ribbon at the opening ceremony of the Iraqi Joint Staff College in Baghdad on September 27, 2005. Gen. Jim Jones, Supreme Allied Commander, looks on. PHOTO BY DAN R. WILSON.

Around 3:00 A.M., they marched down to the tank deck, four floors below. The launch of their amphibious assault vehicles was now one hour away. They started checking weapons and supplies. True to Leiphart's midnight anxieties, he discovered some ammunition already missing for the M-16s. There were other shortages of machine-gun ammo and blasting caps for C-4 explosives. Great, thought Leiphart, somebody's already hoarding bullets and explosives. He decided not to say anything about it, but kept a close eye on his men.

Logistics officer John Watts had his own worries. Several amphibious tractors—amtracs—failed to start because their engines were sluggish from the salt air. If they were landing in Lebanon, this wouldn't have mattered. The Marines simply would have grabbed some replacement generators in Beirut and no one would be the wiser.

This was a whole different scenario, and the entire U.S. military command—indeed, the president himself—was waiting for the Marines to get off the Navy ships and mount the invasion. It was like starting out playing a routine football game against a crosstown rival and winding up playing for the national championship in the Rose Bowl. And Watts was the team's equipment manager.

Lieutenant Colonel Smith was counting on him to get the game off to a good start, and he couldn't even get the amtracs' engines started. He would probably be court-martialed. Watts scurried through the dark hold of the ship searching for spare parts. The tightly-packed supplies and equipment reminded him of the wooden puzzles he'd done as a kid, with pieces that had to be moved together to get everything to fit.

Finally, Watts found the replacement generators. He had them hauled out, and the Marine mechanics managed to install them in less than an hour. They switched on the engines, and the sluggish amtracs started. Watts, who was drenched in sweat, never heard a sweeter sound.

By 4:00 A.M., the assault vehicles were lined up in pairs, seven rows deep. Dobson's 150 men, loaded with heavy packs, started shuffling on board.

The ship's long, narrow exit trough was several feet above sea level. When the order came to launch the amtracs, they would drive down the ramp at the rear of the ship and slide into the ocean off Grenada's northeast coast.

If things went well, the airtight amtracs would splash into the sea like diesel-powered sea turtles. As the men settled in, 2nd Lt. Matt Aylward realized something was missing: talk. The men were somberly shaking hands and bidding each other farewell instead of kidding around. It was a kind of graduation, the culmination of months of training as amphibious warriors. Now they were ready to test their mettle as Marines, roaring from sea to shore and liberating a troubled tropical island.

"See you, Cox," someone said to Sgt. Manny Cox. "I'll buy you a beer when we get back."

Cox wished the man good luck, adding, "God is with you."

Aylward, who commanded Leiphart's 2nd Platoon in Golf Company, was glad they were close to launch. But as L-Hour neared, he thought it would have been nice to know their exact mission, not to mention *where* they were. There were no maps, and no written orders. And where was Lieutenant Colonel Smith?

As the 4:00 A.M. launch neared, Ray Smith was aboard the command ship *Trenton*, listening in on a classified radio frequency to see how things were going in the first hours of Operation Urgent Fury. A small group of Navy SEALs, dispatched to rescue Grenada's governor, was in trouble because it was surrounded by a well-armed unit of the Peoples' Revolutionary Army.[13] Machine-gun fire crackled in the background. "This is a trap," one SEAL called out. "This is another Desert One."

It was a reference to America's joint rescue attempt in Iran—the desert debacle no one wanted to repeat.

Admiral Metcalf had heard enough. He ordered an airborne force of 2/8 Marines to fly in to help the stranded soldiers. Echo

Company of the Marines would seize the Pearls Airport and the nearby town of Grenville on the island's northeast coast. Then Metcalf ordered the other contingent, Bob Dobson's Golf Company, to switch its landing site to north of the capital city, St. George's.

But then the "fog of war" rolled in: radio problems prevented Smith from briefing Dobson before he splashed into the sea.

It was not the only hitch in the early hours of the invasion. Marine Cobra helicopter pilots flying in support of the 82nd Airborne's assault weren't given the proper radio frequencies to contact the Army units. This created some dicey moments as the Marine helicopter pilots relied on ground spotters to avoid shooting American soldiers.

Still, the Marine aviators fought through the confusion as they attacked enemy targets in the hills above St. George's that normally would be prime targets for naval gunfire. But to protect civilians, the Navy's firepower was held in abeyance, and the Marine and Army aviators swooped in low, firing rockets and machine guns as they battled to knock out the PRA antiaircraft guns. They flew into a wall of fire, though, and three Marine pilots perished.

Offshore, Echo Company of the 2/8 took off on CH-46 helicopters to secure the northeastern coast. The chopper pilots flew in total darkness using new night-vision goggles, a relatively untested technology.[14] Nonetheless, the pilots led by Lt. Col. Granville "Granny" Amos landed and the Marines hit the ground running. They quickly repulsed the PRA soldiers, who dropped their weapons and fled into the hills.

Smith ordered his Marines to continue in hot pursuit, which was easier said than done in the steep terrain and tropical climate. His men were in top shape, but they also were weighed down by packs, flak jackets, and rifles. In the heat of the morning, they couldn't catch the unencumbered islanders fleeing in T-shirts, shorts, and sandals.[15]

Aboard the *Manitowoc*, a one-hour delay stretched into an interminable wait throughout the day. Some men managed to lean back on their packs and doze off. But others couldn't sleep through all the racket and rumors: *The beaches are mined and we're being taken to a new landing zone. The Army Airborne is in hand-to-hand combat with the Cubans. North Korean soldiers are being flown in.*

Capt. Bob Dobson became increasingly frustrated as his orders kept changing. At one point, he was told to get his company up to the ship's deck and prepare to board helicopters for an airborne assault. His men dutifully squeezed through the ship's narrow corridors and, loaded down with heavy packs and weapons, climbed up four flights of stairs to the flight deck. The salt air and drizzle felt bracing after all the time down below. They were told they'd be boarding CH-46 helicopters to join Echo Company's assault.

Finally, Dobson thought, *we're going in.*

But it was a false alarm. The ship's captain received new orders to change course to the western side of the island, then stand by offshore. *We'll never get to fight,* Dobson thought, as his men shuffled back below decks, grumbling all the way. He was certain their part in the joint operation would be delayed until the next morning.

"Go pack the gear for the night," he told his platoon leaders. "Let's go have chow."

But as soon as they had stowed their gear and were sitting down to dinner, an order blared through the PA that a troop launch was imminent: "L-Hour is 30 minutes! L-Hour is 30 minutes!"

A mad scramble ensued as the men of Golf Company rushed back to their quarters to retrieve their packs and rifles. Then they dashed down to the tank deck and climbed into the amtracs.

Dobson looked at his watch: It was 1730—5:30 P.M. On this late October evening, it was getting dark early and the moon wouldn't rise until midnight.

They would deploy in pitch blackness, heading for an unknown shore on an ill-defined mission. It was a long way from the tightly orchestrated "maneuver warfare" they'd practiced with General Gray back in Camp Lejeune. No matter how much they prepared, Dobson mused, some things about being a Marine would never change. Out on the ocean, you truly had to go with the flow.

It was time to leave the *Manitowoc* and conduct an amphibious landing in combat conditions. The stern gate at the rear of the ship began lowering like a creaky drawbridge. It opened to the gray light and whitecaps of the Atlantic, with Grenada waiting over the horizon.

The loud clang of metal on metal filled the well deck as the steel treads of the assault vehicles rolled down the steel ramp. Then they splashed into the sea, bobbing underwater for a few tantalizing seconds.

Lt. Matt Aylward peered through the vision blocks in the front of the amtrac. He followed the trail of bubbles toward the surface, evidence that they were heading in the right direction. The water jets kicked in, and the assault vehicle started churning through the waves toward Grenada.

With a Navy guide boat leading them toward shore, the formation moved roughly in line to hit the beach together. The Navy boat should have accompanied them all the way in, but, for some reason, it veered off early, about 200 yards from land.

The Marines of Golf Company were on their own, searching for a safe haven on the dark island. Semiautomatic and antiaircraft fire crackled in the distance—the first sign of combat on Grenada. An Air Force AC-130 gunship was pouring bright tracer rounds that arced across the sky like dragon fire.

The Marines bounced through waves toward land, but instead of finding a beach, they hit a rock wall at Grand Mal Bay. As a result, the amtracs started stacking up. Dobson glanced warily at the hills surrounding the bay. There was no telling who or what was up there, including any American forces that might mistake them for the enemy. This was the Army's initial area of responsibility and, given all the snafus so far, Dobson suspected no one had communicated with them that the Marines were landing. They were sitting ducks for enemy and friendly fire alike.

So Dobson found a better place to land with room to maneuver the amtracs. Once they hit dirt, he ordered reconnaissance teams to fan out across a 1,000-meter-wide beach. Within minutes, a patrol returned and reported they were on a stretch of muddy beach, surrounded by chain-link fence. The squad leader pointed up to some looming shapes that Dobson could barely make out in the darkness.

Those are fuel tanks, sir, the Marine said, probably containing thousands of gallons of gasoline. One good shot and they'd be toast, he said. The beach would be a barbeque pit, and the Marines would be dead meat.

Dobson ordered heavy machine guns and tanks to set up on either end of the beach, blocking anyone who might try to attack from the nearby coast road.

Golf Company had secured the beach, but, now, all it could do was wait for further orders. They could radio each other but, because of the radio problems, could not contact Lieutenant Colonel Smith on the battalion landing team's ship.

Although the Marines had landed, as Dobson ruefully reflected, they were completely in the dark.

☆ ☆ ☆

Meanwhile, on the other side of Grenada, Ray Smith was mad as hell. He'd spent most of D-Day coordinating the successful helicopter assault on Pearls Airport. But along the way, he'd lost communications with Dobson's unit as the ships steamed off shore beyond radio range.

Walking near the Pearls airport that afternoon, Ray had sized up the island's steep mountains filled with banana and palm trees. Some islanders appeared to live nearby in small villages. The landscape jutted skyward from the beach, or sank into wet, soggy bogs. It reminded him of the coastal areas of Vietnam, only without North Vietnamese artillery raining down.

Once the airfield was secure, Smith hopped on a Huey and flew back to the *Guam*. So far, the invasion plan was on course. The Marine Amphibious Unit's operations officer, Maj. Ernie Van Huss, told him about the new plans to land Golf Company on the

other side of the island at Grand Mal Bay. That seemed reasonable enough. Van Huss outlined a plan to hook up the 2/8's two
other companies with Dobson's men. The three prongs of the battalion would move together to free key facilities, such as the governor's mansion. They also could support Army units and Navy
SEALs that seemed to be under heavy fire.

Everything seemed to be perking along until an aide to Admiral Metcalf burst in the board room.

"The damned thing didn't get turned off!" he yelled.

Van Huss jumped up. "What do you mean it didn't get turned
off?"

Smith didn't know what they were talking about. *What* didn't
get turned off?

"Will you guys knock it off and tell me what you're talking
about?"

They explained that the landing hour for Dobson's troops
had been set for 1600, or 4:00 P.M. But a decision had been made
to move it back, or "turn it off," for two hours later. That way Dobson could be briefed on the mission. But no one had gotten
through to the *Manitowoc* to delay the mission.

Smith checked his watch. It was 3:40 P.M.—twenty minutes
before Golf's new launch time. He could picture Dobson's men
down in the well deck, grasping their M-16s, their stomachs churning with fear and anxiety. Making a daylight landing exposed them
to antiaircraft guns along the coastline.

Lieutenant Colonel Smith ran to the bridge and ordered a
sailor to radio the *Manitowoc* and delay the launch. Much to his
relief, he managed to contact the captain and tell him to move it
back to 6:30 P.M. That would give him two hours to reach Dobson
and brief him about the mission.

Then things got even more topsy-turvy. First, Smith was
bumped off the first helicopter he was supposed to take, creating
a half-hour delay. He finally secured another helicopter, but the
pilot flew the wrong way.

"What in the hell is going on?" Smith shouted when he realized they were heading south toward Point Salines. That screw-up

burned up another hour. It was now past 6:00 P.M. The helicopter was low on fuel and was forced to land. There were only twenty minutes left to reach Dobson. Smith tried raising the *Manitowoc*, but once again, the radio frequencies were messed up. Communications definitely was not a strong point of Operation Urgent Fury. He radioed back to Van Huss too see if he could reach Dobson's men and stop their launch.

It was too late. By then, Golf Company was already in the water. Smith landed at Pearls, grabbed a couple of radio operators, and formed a small command element. They flew off in his third helicopter of the day.

As they lifted off, the lieutenant colonel joked with the young pilot, "I really doubt anyone knows where the *Manitowoc* is." It was no joke, though. To his amazement, they flew for several more hours over the dark ocean, but no one on the Navy ships seemed able to give the pilot the right coordinates to reach the ship or his Marines at Grand Mal Bay.

Then the pilot said with a slight tremor in voice, "Sir?"

Smith braced himself for more bad news. "What is it?"

"I've lost communications with the *Trenton*."

"Sweet Jesus."

"And sir?"

"Yes?" Smith replied.

"We're running out of fuel."

"Just fly back to the nearest ship, okay?"

Smith had been flitting around Grenada for six hours and was no closer to reaching Dobson's company than when he started. It was one of the most frustrating episodes of his life.

★ ★ ★

Back at Grand Mal Bay, the 2nd Platoon of Lt. Matt Aylward and Staff Sgt. Mike Leiphart patrolled the rugged ground around the fuel depot. It was hard to see on this moonless night, but so far no Cubans or PRA soldiers appeared to be lying in wait in this coastal area north of Grenada's capital. The enemy had missed a chance for an ambush. Most islanders appeared to be sitting out the fighting. Some took their goats, sheep and chickens inside their homes for protection.

As they patrolled, a white figure appeared out of the darkness and approached the Marines. Leiphart raised his M-16 and released the safety. If it wasn't a soldier, it might be one of the rabid dogs that had been growling at them along the road.

Before he fired, though, Leiphart stopped himself when he heard a loud *baaah*. It was a goat on the loose.

"Damn," Leiphart muttered to himself. "We've got to get out of this place."

Lieutenant Aylward was thinking along the same lines. It was crazy to be so near the fuel tanks, with no apparent military objective. So after several hours of tense patrols, he was relieved when he heard a *whup whup whup* reverberating over Grand Mal Bay.

The CH-46 helicopter circled overhead, looking for a place to land. But the incoming tide had rolled over the beach. Finally, the pilot, wearing night-vision goggles, decided to touch down in shallow water. A rear exit ramp dropped, and some figures ran out— E-Tool Smith among them.

Dobson and his lieutenants gathered around him, but Smith didn't waste any time on chitchat.

"Do any of you know where you are?" he asked, spreading a map out on the sand. He illuminated it with a red flashlight to avoid becoming an easy target.

Dobson knew their location because he had the jury-rigged map. But his junior officers were hesitant to confess their ignorance.

Finally, a lieutenant spoke up. "Sir, I have no idea where we are," said Mitch Eskew, the 3rd Platoon commander.

"It's okay," Smith said, reflecting on his night-long Keystone Cops escapade around the island. "You've landed between a battalion and regiment of the PRA."

The battalion was north in the town of Victoria, he told them, and the regiment was thought to be located in the hills at Fort

Frederick to the south. Intelligence reports indicated the presence of Soviet-made tanks. The Marines had managed to get ashore a few M60 tanks of their own. But they weren't prepared for a large armor duel. Instead, the Marines would apply the principles of maneuver warfare they had worked on all year, where speed and deception would trump brute force.

He briefed Dobson and his lieutenants on what had transpired over the past twenty-four hours. He explained the rescue operation of American medical students and the effort to restore order after Grenada's military coup.

Then he pulled out his four-page-long written orders and began reading. The Marines would "conduct military operations to protect U.S. and designated foreign nations in Grenada, neutralize Grenadan forces, and stabilize the internal situation— restoring civil order and maintaining peace."

The 2nd Battalion, 8th Marines, would "move ashore as rapidly as possible and expand its area of control as quickly as possible commensurate with troop safety in order to prevent Grenadian forces or civilian population from reacting to our presence before we have established control."

Looking around at the eager faces of his officers, he said, "We've done well so far, taking the area around Pearls Airport. We're starting to get cooperation from the civilians. They've been more than happy to point out the leaders of the People's Revolutionary Army."

By the second day of Urgent Fury, the PRA seemed to be crumbling. But Smith informed them that the Marines' helicopter squadron suffered some losses. Capt. Jeb F. Seagle, a Cobra helicopter co-pilot, was shot down as he supported the Army Rangers attacking Fort Frederick. He survived the crash but was later killed as he sought help for a badly wounded comrade.

Two other Marine pilots, Capt. John P. Giguere and 1st Lt. Jeffrey R. Scharver, died when antiaircraft fire knocked their Cobra gunship into the harbor.

"Remember what I said earlier," Smith said. "We're here to liberate the place, not blow the shit out of it. That doesn't mean I don't want you going after the bad guys. I do. If they fire at you, take them out."

He outlined their mission: to rescue the governor general, Sir Paul Godwin Scoon, along with thirteen Navy SEALs who were holed up, reportedly surrounded by enemy troops. They would also secure the house of the slain prime minister, Maurice Bishop. Intelligence about troop movements in the mountainous interior was lacking, the island's nineteenth-century mansions, forts, and prisons providing ample cover for anyone who still wanted to fight.

"We don't know how many Cubans or PRA might be around the place," Smith said. "There's been some sporadic fire from above the governor's mansion. You're going to have to be plenty careful. Looks like they've got some Russian-made 23-millimeter antiaircraft guns up there."

Lieutenant Colonel Smith took a pinch of Red Man chewing tobacco and chose his words carefully. "There are reports that the coup leader, Gen. Hudson Austin, may be inside. Colonel Faulkner said that if he's there, let's care take of him. If there's any question about him escaping, we ought to kill the son-of-a-bitch and run him up on the flagpole."

Pausing, Smith added, "But it would be better to bring him back alive."

It was pitch dark. Captain Dobson ordered his amtracs to start up and carry the Marines along a coast road. He had his M60 tanks bring up the rear. Dobson remembered E-Tool's warning about heavily armed Cubans. Would his five tanks and a few machine guns be enough to take them?

The first light of dawn shot its pale arrows over the dark green landscape, and Grenada quickly became a hot, humid place. The first stop for the 150-man force was a horse-racing track, where they got water and left their backpacks. Finally, they had to get out of their amtracs and start climbing the vine-choked path up the mountain.

It was a long trek up to the governor's mansion and prison. As they humped up a steep trail, they could hear explosions in the distance. An Air Force AC-130 gunship fired in long bursts, *BRRRRT*, that made Leiphart think of dragon farts.

They passed islanders who looked tired and scared, but happy to see them. Some Grenadans carried machetes, which Leiphart eyed warily. But he learned that the short swords served a utilitarian purpose for the natives: slicing open coconuts. The blades could pierce the hard shells to the milk inside. Drinking coconut milk was apparently hazardous to one's health, since many older men were missing fingers from misaimed machetes.

By 8:00 A.M., the Marines reached the bottom of a long set of stairs leading up to the governor's mansion. Dobson sent a recon team to scout the area. He was relieved that, so far, they had not encountered any enemy fire.

No PRA or Cubans were spotted, so Golf Company kept marching up the vine-tangled steps. When they reached the top, one squad secured the empty home of the prime minister, while the rest of the Marines hustled over to Governor Scoon's house. Along the way, they found several Soviet-style trucks brimming with AK-47s, ammo, and other gear. It looked like the PRA had fled. Dobson ordered his men to destroy the trucks with shoulder-launched rockets, and the explosions reverberated across the mountains.

Walking inside the Victorian estate, Sgt. Manny Cox gazed in awe at its posh interior, including paintings of what appeared to be British royalty. The dining room table was set with silver plates and fine crystal. Cox laughed to himself: did they expect 150 grunts for dinner?

They found Governor Scoon and his wife, exhausted but unharmed. The SEALs were okay, too. The Marines promptly escorted everyone back down the mountain on what they now called "the thousand steps of liberation."

Back at the Queens Park racetrack in St. George's, Dobson reported the successful rescue. Smith complimented Dobson on the smooth operation, then gave him another mission: take Fort Frederick.

"What's the objective, sir?"

"To evict any remaining enemy soldiers—PRA or Cuban—and secure the fort." Reports indicated it was a regimental headquarters, possibly holding some Grenadan resisters.

Dobson wiped his brow and considered the biggest problem of marching back up into the hills—water. Smith nodded, knowing water was as vital as ammunition to winning any battle. "Without supplies," said Clearchus of Sparta in 401 B.C., "neither a general nor a soldier was good for anything."[16]

Though they were surrounded by water on all sides of Grenada, the Marines struggled to keep their canteens full. It was the same with food and ammo. As full as the ships were for Beirut, it had been hard to unpack them and transport supplies on short notice. Plus, many of Grenada's bridges couldn't support the Marines' trucks that otherwise would have delivered supplies.

Smith managed to get the company restocked with water and food, and by noon, Golf Company started its second mountain trek of the day. This time, they followed switchback roads into the hills. Each turn, it seemed, could provide cover for an ambush. At one point, Aylward spotted an abandoned armored car down the road, with its gun barrel aimed their way. Nicknamed "Bam Bam" after the *Flintstones* character, the twenty-three-year-old Naval Academy graduate decided to blow up the Soviet-made vehicle himself. He ran up, pulled the pin of a grenade, tossed it inside, and took off.

Running along, he couldn't remember if he had pulled the grenade's thumb clip.

He started to turn back toward the blocky car—then *BOOM!* It went up in black smoke, and its ammunition started popping like firecrackers. Aylward had a ringing his ears, which he hoped would always remind him to never double back on a live grenade again.

Drenched in sweat and shaking his head, he reached his platoon. He shook his head at Staff Sergeant Leiphart, with an expression that seemed to say, *Am I a dumbass, or what?* Leiphart, for his part, was simply glad Bam Bam hadn't been turned into pebbles.

Farther along the road to Fort Frederick, the 2nd Platoon saw more signs that the PRA members had abandoned their posts, including another armored car. This one was still running, with its cannon cocked toward them.

After the close call with his first hand grenade, Aylward decided to radio Captain Dobson for orders.

"Can I take out this vehicle?"

"No," the captain said flatly. "Go investigate it."

"Investigate it?" Aylward said, trying to mask his surprise. "Yes, sir. Right away."

Putting down the radio, Aylward glanced at his 1st Squad leader, Sgt. Kenny Goss, and shrugged. Investigate it? By now, they'd gone nearly two days without sleep, and Matt was feeling fuzzy-headed. He tried to understand why his stern commanding officer wanted an investigation, one that could easily get him killed. Why not just toss another grenade inside and be done with it?

But Dobson was the boss. Perhaps there were enemy battle plans inside the abandoned vehicle. Maybe it carried coup leaders. In his sleep-deprived state, it didn't matter why he was doing it. The captain said to check it out, so he had no choice.

The BTR 60-PD armored vehicle was about 100 yards away. His men were watching, ready to cover his back.

But they couldn't do much if the Soviet cannon started firing. It was the longest walk of his young life. When he was about thirty feet away, Aylward stopped and sized things up. The car's engine was idling, its hatch open. There was no sign of life inside.

He crossed the final ten yards, then hopped on the armored vehicle. With no driver inside, Aylward simply turned off the engine and hollered, "All clear!"

Leiphart and the rest of the men of the platoon heaved another collective sigh of relief.

Farther west on the ridge line near Fort Frederick, Dobson's Marines were witnessing a strange sight: A group of eight to ten soldiers was high-tailing it down the other side of the mountain. Were they really abandoning the fort, or was this a trap?

Dobson sensed the enemy's resistance was folding. "Let's go in!" he shouted. The Marines double-timed it to the fort's thick door. They shoved it open and gazed at something out of a story-book.

The eighteenth-century fortress had brick and mortar walls, with a balcony around the inner courtyard. It had a small lawn with a flagpole planted in the middle. Soldiers' tents were pitched on the grass, but judging from the clothes and dishes strewn across the ground, the PRA seemed to have made a quick get-away. The Marines seemed to have ruined their dinner plans.

Dobson toured the compound and was amazed by the size and scope of the weapons cache his men were finding. The fort's armory had AK-47s, light and heavy machine guns, and enough ammo to fight for a week.

Opening one bunch of boxes, he found brand new scopes for machine guns in packages stamped with the hammer and sickle of the Soviet Union.

Descending a stone staircase, the Marines entered a labyrinth of tunnels, where they found more clues about the depth of Grenada's ties with Russia, Cuba, and other communist allies.

A corporal found a leather briefcase and brought it to Dobson. They popped it open with a K-bar knife. Rifling through the papers, Dobson saw a binder that contained a number of official papers, including an arms agreement between Cuba, Grenada, and Nicaragua and the Soviet Union. There was also the passport of Gen. Hudson Austin. It was the coup leader's personal briefcase.

Dobson understood the significance of the find and slammed the briefcase shut.

"Take this to battalion headquarters down at the racetrack," Dobson said to a runner. "Tell Lieutenant Colonel Smith it contains classified material."

He noted that the arms pact in Hudson's papers called for large shipments of weapons over the next two years. The Marines had landed not a minute too soon.

Dobson wanted to call his officers to tell them about his find, but it was getting late. His platoon commanders were starting to post men on radio watch and telling everyone to bed down. They had performed well over the past two days—coming from sea to shore, conducting a rescue mission, and seizing a key government facility without firing a shot or suffering a casualty.

Not that the men of Golf Company were perfect. In the middle of the night, as water seeped through fissures in the stone walls, Aylward felt water dripping on his head. He woke up and heard a voice calling out on the radio. It was Dobson's command post, and the company was making a routine check of each platoon.

But his guard had fallen asleep. It wasn't the first time this man had dozed off at his post, so Aylward was furious. The 240-pound lieutenant stomped down the steps and picked up the slumbering guard. Shaking him like a ragdoll, he screamed in his face, "Are you sleeping again?"

The commotion awoke Leiphart, who thought about joining in the chewing out. But when he saw the startled Marine dangling eight inches off the ground, Leiphart rolled over on the hard floor and went back to sleep. Bam Bam had the situation well in hand.

FIFTEEN

The Mayor of St. George's

The next day, a young man kept walking by Ray Smith's command post near the Queen's Park Race Course on the northwestern edge of St. George's. The bayside city had an Old World feel with crowded streets, shops, and foot traffic. By setting up camp in plain view of the public, Smith hoped to gain more information about PRA leaders who started slipping away during the early hours of the invasion.

The curious youth wore a stocking cap of green, orange and black—the colors of African liberation. After nervously passing the Marines' outpost, he finally stopped and talked to a guard. The guard listened and nodded, then came over to Smith's command tent.

"Sir," he said, "this kid says he want to talk to 'the mon.'"

Smith grinned. Back home, he remembered student protesters and black activists deriding police as "the man." Now he seemed to have achieved this dubious distinction himself.

Bring him over, Smith said. As the youth stepped into his tent, the lieutenant colonel stood and introduced himself as commanding officer of the Marines. "And who are you?" he said with a smile.

The youth furtively glanced about. "First, sir, I must ask you a question," he said in an accent mixed with Caribbean and British flavors.

"Shoot."

"Sir, are you going to leave here soon?" the eager youth asked, tugging on his cap. "Because if you leave without arresting the brutal killers, they will punish us. They still have weapons. They will simply stay and kill us when you leave."

Smith looked the lad in the eye. "This battalion isn't going to be staying very long," he said, "but the American forces, and our allies from the Caribbean nations, they will stay as long as it takes to restore order and democracy."

This seemed to satisfy his visitor, who smiled and extended his hand. "That's what I needed to hear, sir. My name is Beeko Renwick."

Smith listened intently to his story: Beeko's family had been terrorized for months by the PRA, and some of his friends and relatives had been killed for not cooperating. Houses had been seized, women had been raped. Now these thugs had taken off their uniforms, hidden their guns, and were freely roaming the streets around them. The Americans would never be the wiser.

"It's happening right here, sir!" he said excitedly. "Even as we speak they are driving by and laughing at how easy it has been to fool you. You must put a stop to that."

Smith thought it over. His orders were to neutralize the PRA and help evacuate the American medical students. After one day, despite the snafus, they had accomplished that. Going beyond that first mission and trying to rout out the insurgents was quite another matter—one Ray wasn't sure they were equipped to handle.

"We're really not here to do police work, Beeko," he replied.

But the youth, who looked about eighteen years old, was adamant. "You *must* do something about it, sir. These men cannot be allowed to go free. They'll come back at night and start doing the same things. They are evil, sir."

Ray was stirred by the plea for freedom from tyranny. It reminded him of the flags the Marines waved in the early days of the Republic—*Sic Semper Tyrannis*, they said. Thus ever to tyrants. Now here was a kid hardly older than his sons who was appealing for freedom from modern-day tyrants on his island—and communists at that. Beeko Renwick had risked his life to let the Americans know that things were not what they seemed. Tyranny still lurked in the shadows of St. George's.

Smith needed time to decide what to do, so he asked Beeko to return the next day.

"I will be back, sir," he said with a determined nod and a quick shake of the Marine's hand.

That night, Lieutenant Colonel Smith sat back and thought about the events that had unfolded over the past few days. Along with his friend "Granny" Amos, the helicopter squadron leader commander, and the tough MAU commander Colonel Faulkner, the Marine commanders created two pincers on the island that helped the Army snuff out the PRA resistance and rescue the American medical students. The Marines also rescued Grenada's leaders and bailed out the surrounded Navy SEALs. Except for the tragic loss of the helicopter pilots, it had all been done without significant casualties.

Indeed, Smith was hearing that their speed and efficiency were drawing rave, if somewhat anguished, reviews in some high-level military circles back in Washington. The chairman of the Joint Chiefs of Staff, Army general John Vessey, fumed to the head of the Army 82nd Airborne, "We have two companies of Marines running all over the island and thousands of Army troops doing nothing. What the hell is going on?"[1]

Still, it was hardly a flawless operation. Urgent Fury was marred by intelligence lapses on all sides, including the rescue and evacuation of the American medical students. The biggest gaffe was the revelation of a second campus of the medical college. After Army Rangers rescued students at the True Blue campus in St. George's, the students had informed them that most of their colleagues were at another campus, two miles away in a beachfront hotel at Grand Anse beach.[2]

The Army Rangers and Marines regrouped and managed to extract all 595 students, without suffering any more casualties—unless one counted the bruised egos of the Army command.

Despite Admiral Metcalf's orders to the contrary, the old Army-Marine Corps rivalry boiled over at times during Operation Urgent Fury. Ray witnessed some of the in-fighting aboard the *Guam* as Colonel Faulkner tried to run his show without interference from the Army's Schwarzkopf. The Marine commanders felt the pugnacious general was trying to micromanage them, suggesting when to attack, shoot, and move around the island. But since these suggestions didn't come in the form of direct orders, they simply ignored the bossy general.

Tempers flared, though, when Schwarzkopf ordered the Marines to send their CH-46 helicopters in to support the Rangers' rescue operation at the Grand Anse medical school campus.

"Like hell we are!" Faulkner replied. The palm trees near the landing zone will put my pilots at risk, he said. They could clip their rotor blades. Why not land a little farther out?

(Schwarzkopf provided a different account of the confrontation aboard the *Guam*. Without naming Faulkner, he wrote in his autobiography that "the Marine colonel in command of the entire battalion . . . listened impassively as I sketched out the plan. Finally, he said, 'I'm not going to do that.'" According to Schwarzkopf, the Marine commander told him, "We don't fly Army soldiers in Marine helicopters," and offered a time-consuming alternate plan that never would have worked.)

Faulkner sticks to his version of the events, saying his sole concern was the safety of the Marine pilots, who already had suffered some losses in the early hours of Urgent Fury.

Smith, for his part, offers a third account. He says the nose-to-nose argument on the bridge of the *Guam* became physical, with cursing, shoving, and threats of reprisals.

Metcalf provides a fourth side to the story. "They never had an argument in my presence," adding, "I would not have stood for it for more than thirty-five seconds."

Metcalf did recall interceding in the debate over using Marine helicopters to ferry the Rangers for the beachfront rescue. He never saw fisticuffs. "As far as I was concerned," he said, "they worked it out."

For all the sound in Urgent Fury, the second rescue mission was a success, with the swift evacuation of 200 American medical students. But Faulkner's concern about the narrow landing area proved to be warranted. One of the helicopters had to land close to overhanging trees, clipping its blade in the process. The pilot was forced to abandon the damaged helicopter.[3]

True to his word, Beeko Renwick returned the next morning to the Marine command post. He listed all of the PRA officials the Marines should arrest. These thugs, he said, had ordered soldiers to fire into crowds of unarmed citizens and killed many Grenadans before the Americans landed.

Smith asked where he could find them.

"Up there!" Beeko cried, pointing to a nearby street. The lieutenant colonel dispatched some Marines to accompany his informant, who quickly arrested a group of PRA leaders. As word spread of the capture, a line began to form at Smith's command post. The aggrieved citizens were more than happy now to name names.

When a car passed by, Beeko became agitated. "Stop him! Stop him!"

The Marines then made the biggest arrest of the day. Major Gehagan, the PRA's operations officer, was wearing civilian clothes and, along with some cronies, appeared to be driving around town with baskets of oranges to give to the Americans—all in an apparent show of support for the liberators.

There was more than fruit in the car, though, as the Marines found a cache of 9-millimeter pistols and bullets. Gehagan and his gang were arrested and marched to a makeshift holding pen inside a lumber yard.

Lieutenant Colonel Smith decided to chat with this PRA leader himself. At first, Gehagan was cocky, bragging about his travels in the Soviet Union and Cuba. Gehagan's tales were interesting for a while, but then he began to insist, "I demand my rights under the Geneva Convention. I have the right to see a legal representative, and a representative of the International Red Cross, and . . ."

Ray tuned him out. After all he had seen on the island— including evidence of executions up at Richmond Hill prison— Gehagan's grievances had a hollow ring.

Nodding to a guard, Smith said, "Put him over in the ditch by the fence."

"No, no!" Gehagan said, shaking his head. "You can't put me over there. That would violate the terms of the Geneva Convention. I could be shot from the street."

"Do it," Smith said, and the guard led Gehagan away, along with his cronies. One of them protested, "You must separate me from him." Gehagan's fear of reprisals appeared to have some merit.

Smith had the crony put at one end of the ditch, and Gehagan in the other.

The arrest was not lost on the neighborhood residents, who had gathered to watch how the Marines handled their former tormentors. They laughed at Gehagan's objections, and applauded the treatment of prisoners who, only hours before, had ruled the streets like Mafia dons.

A nearby merchant nodded in approval from her storefront. Known simply as "Mama," the large woman in a flowered dress walked over and asked to talk to "the mon." Smith agreed, and offered her a seat. He was starting to feel like the mayor of St. George's.

"How can I help you?" he asked.

"Mon," she said with a furrowed brow, "some of these people you have in the cage, they aren't communist. Some of them are just people that Beeko and others don't like. They aren't PRA. They are just enemies of *some* of the people, but not all."

Ray paid close attention. He'd noticed Mama calming the crowds around her store and helping maintain order. She seemed to wield the influence of a veteran city councilwoman who commanded the respect of her constituents.

"Okay, Mama," he said, "do *you* know who the communists are?"

"I know everyone," she said as a broad smile spread across her ebony face. Smith could see that this shopkeeper's only agenda seemed to be to restore order, not exact revenge.

"Okay then," he said, "when we bring men in here, you tell me whether we should put them in the pen, or turn them loose. You be the judge."

"I will do that, mon," she said, "if it will keep innocent people out of trouble."

So it was that Mama's Court was put in session. Smith knew it was a form of frontier justice and definitely was not on the curriculum back at the Basic School. The Marine lawyers—the JAG boys—would have a fit, not to mention members of the press corps, if they ever got wind of it. But there was little press coverage in the early days of Urgent Fury, since Admiral Metcalf managed to restrict media access on the island.

Mama lived up to her promise and started sorting out the good guys from the bad. She spent several days identifying those prisoners who were truly guilty of violent crimes or theft. She also fingered those PRA leaders who were still at large. The Marines, meanwhile, were scoring points with the populace by distributing spare rations, and by working with local clerics and Red Cross workers.[4]

Smith kept working on his prime suspect, Major Gehagan. He left him holed up near the street as people passed by and shouted "killer!" and "murderer!"

The PRA, for all its socialist rhetoric, had devolved into a group of thugs armed to the teeth by Fidel Castro. The angry citizens gave Smith an idea. Calling over a guard, he said, "Tell Major

Gehagan he's right about the Geneva Convention. I have no right to hold him. I'm going to turn him loose."

The guard delivered Smith's message of release, then hustled back to say the prisoner would like to talk to Lieutenant Colonel Smith. Ray sauntered over to the ditch.

"Hello, major," he said casually, "you ready to be released? Time to join your fellow countrymen and get back to work?"

Gehagan was agitated. "No, sir, no, sir! You cannot release me! I am a prisoner of war."

Smith pulled out a plug of Red Man, offering the major a chew. The major shook his head and shuddered.

"But Major Gehagan," Smith said, his voice dripping with sarcasm, "you told me earlier that I was holding you in violation of international law. Now that I'm ready to comply, you don't want to be freed. Why is that?"

Gehagan glanced through the fence, where a crowd was forming. "You have to protect me," he said, adding, "please."

Smith nodded his approval. Gehagan remained in custody and became a valuable informant. The PRA leader drew an elaborate chart of his entire military organization, filling in names, ranks, and duties of each individual. It was quite a chart, showing some 1,200 positions, with at least half the names filled in, including most of the officers. It became a vital intelligence tool in rounding up the rest of the PRA's ringleaders.

But Smith had little time to revel in his intelligence coup. He received an emergency order from Admiral Metcalf to seize the only two towns of any size not yet in American hands—Gouyave and Victoria on the northwest coast.

☆ ☆ ☆

The lieutenant colonel wasn't worried about taking the towns, but he was concerned about the timing. Metcalf wanted it done in *two hours*. That seemed nearly impossible considering the rough terrain of the coast and the impending nightfall.

Smith choppered out to the *Trenton* and learned why the clock was ticking. General Vessey, the joint chiefs' chairman, was flying back to Washington after a quick tour of the island. Within hours, Vessey would brief President Reagan and his senior advisors. The general wanted to report that the entire island was in American hands.

Smith knew Vessey from his brief time in St. George's. He had taken the opportunity to tell him about the Marines' successful use of Gen. Al Gray's maneuver warfare tactics and—the sugar-coating as far as Smith was concerned—the successful intelligence-gathering about the Soviet and Cuban influence on the island. He also bluntly told the general that, in his view, the Army had used way too much firepower near civilians. The Grenadans, who initially welcomed the American as liberators, were starting to complain about the toll of the Army's bombing.

Smith knew it was risky for a lieutenant colonel to talk frankly to the nation's top military commander. He wanted him to know that civilians were fleeing some of the Army's area of operation and appeared to be holding the Americans to blame about collateral damage to homes, farms, and hospitals.

Vessey had been taken aback by Smith's revelations and didn't seem all that happy to hear the blunt assessment. But after Vessey left, Ray noticed the Army's bombing campaign seemed to be letting up.

Now it looked like the general was asking the Marines for a payback. He expected them to take two more coastal towns and close the loop on Grenada before he had to brief President Reagan.

Golf Company swung into high gear. Dobson's men hustled into their amtracs and roared up the coastal road. Smith worried they would present an easy target for any holdouts still up in the hills. Ideally, the Navy could provide fire support. But that would take hours to plan and execute.

So Lieutenant Colonel Smith took matters into his own hands by rolling an M48 tank onto a landing craft that cruised alongside the battalion—his own offshore battery. As it followed protectively alongside the Marines, Smith told the tanker to be prepared to fire on his order if anyone started taking potshots at them.

As an added precaution, Smith climbed aboard a chopper and flew overhead, serving as an aerial observer. It was a tactical tour de force that combined the three triads of the Marines' tools: air, sea, and land power. When Matt Aylward saw the tank on the landing craft and heard the chopper overhead, he felt reassured and impressed. At the Naval Academy, he had studied the use of supporting arms aboard transport ships, and recalled some instances when tanks could be adapted for such purposes. But only one tank could be used, and the ploy required the right kind of landing craft, known as a "mike eight" boat.

Now he was seeing a textbook case of that little-used maneuver being employed in an actual combat situation. He doubted many other officers would know about this gambit, and felt proud to be serving under the protective wings of E-Tool Smith.

As it happened, the tank didn't have to fire from the sea. But the maneuver freed the Marines from sending out recon teams, and helped speed their push up the coast to meet Vessey's approaching deadline. It also taught Aylward a lesson he never forgot: Think creatively to accomplish the mission with the tools you have, rather than puzzle over it.

Ray Smith, for his part, marveled at his Marines' own variety of talents and skills. Along the road to Gouyave, Golf Company was stopped by a ditch with a big Caterpillar bulldozer padlocked in place—a roadblock left by the PRA.

One of Dobson's streetwise engineers made short shrift of the obstacle by knocking off the padlock and hot-wiring the Caterpillar's engine—the old trick used by car thieves. The enterprising engineer also was handy with the bulldozer and soon had the ditch filled in with dirt so the convoy could pass.

The 2/8 made the deadline, sweeping into the last two towns at sunset. That night, Vessey reported to the White House, and proudly informed President Reagan that Grenada was completely in American hands. Minutes later, Reagan went on television to inform the nation that America was helping the island nation restore democracy.

On November 1, six days after their first landing, the 2nd Battalion, 8th Marines, launched yet another amphibious assault on Grenada's sister island, Carriacou. They had received reports that members of the PRA were seeking refuge there, along with some North Korean troops. But Smith had his own intelligence from Major Gehagan. The talkative turncoat assured him there was at most one platoon of soldiers left on Carriacou, and no North Koreans. This gave the lieutenant colonel confidence to land without delay.

As they lumbered off their amtracs yet again, the Marines were greeted by islanders bearing sacks full of grapefruit, oranges, lemons, and coconuts, shouting, "God bless you and Ronald Reagan!"

The Marines did find another cache of ammunition and equipment at an abandoned PRA headquarters on a mountainside. But Carriacou's several thousand people were even more pro-American than most Grenadans. Many of them had already worked or studied in the United States.[5] Some suggested that Smith run up the Stars and Stripes and annex the island.

It was a once-in-a-lifetime experience for a Marine commander and reminded Lieutenant Colonel Smith of being a sheriff out in the Wild West. "It was like a bunch of thugs had taken over a couple of counties in southeastern Oklahoma and we went in and threw them out."

Only nineteen members of the PRA remained, and after interviewing them, Smith decided they posed no serious threat to the populace or the Marines. So he let them go if they agreed to check in the next morning. He gave his Marines liberty, and a party started across the island. Excited boys and girls began climbing over the helicopters as though it was Independence Day.[6] The Marines and sailors chose up sides to play soccer against some of Carriacou's finest players.

The next morning, elements of the 82nd Airborne arrived to relieve the Marines and deal with the remaining PRA soldiers, who kept their promise and dutifully reported back to the Americans.

After all the hassles with the Army high command, the ease of the turnover with the 82nd Airborne was a relief to Smith. He was glad to receive orders to return to the Navy convoy and continue the transatlantic voyage to Lebanon.

A week later, the Marines assembled on the decks of the ships on November 10, the Marine Corps' birthday. The men of the 2/8 were far from the pomp and circumstance of the birthday balls the Corps and its retirees conducted with near-religious fervor around the world.

But this floating celebration had its own special flavor. After they wolfed down some sheet cake, the Marines had the honor of hearing directly from their commander in chief:

> To the 22nd MAU: Although you have scarcely cleaned off the sand of Grenada where you were magnificent, you now will shortly relieve the 24th MAU in Beirut. Once there you will assume the key role in our efforts to bring peace to Lebanon. You have proven without doubt that you are up to the task as our very best. Godspeed and a happy 208th. Semper Fidelis.

It was signed by President Ronald Reagan.

SIXTEEN

Bunkering Down in Beirut

While his men celebrated the Corps' birthday out at sea, Ray Smith and a cadre of officers flew on ahead to prepare for the 2/8's arrival in Beirut. The advanced party stopped for the night at the naval base in Sigonella, Italy, on November 10, 1983. The birthday celebration was already cooking in the officer's club with toasts, speeches, and songs.

Normally, Smith would have been in the thick of the revelry, but he was bushed after a long flight from Rota, Spain. Some of his young staff, including logistics chief John Watts, headed over to the officers' club for a beer. They'd been so busy getting here that they had lost track of time and forgot it was the Corps' anniversary.

Entering the club in dirty utilities, they were surprised to see all the Marines in their formal dress blues and even some ladies in elegant evening gowns. It was like walking into a storybook. Everyone turned to look at the interlopers who appeared, at first glance, to have forgotten their manners.

But when the Marines of Sigonella realized that Watts and his colleagues were the advanced guard of the 2/8, fresh from liberating Grenada, they started cheering wildly, "Oo-rah! Long live the United States Marine Corps! Oo-rah, 2/8!" The startled lieutenants received a standing ovation.

When the cheering stopped, Watts thanked everyone but raised his hand. "You need to hear from Lieutenant Colonel Smith and his operations officer, Major Anderson. They are who you should be applauding."

With that, he raced off to rouse Smith and Anderson, who reluctantly agreed to get up and dress. When they gingerly entered the club, the Marines stood again to applaud and shook the rafters with their primal chant: "Oo-rah, oo-rah!"

It was no night for sleeping. When word spread that E-Tool Smith was on base, Marines gathered like football fans around the winning quarterback. It was a night to celebrate the Corps' first clear-cut victory in years. After a few beers, Smith was urged to tell more stories about his career, the ones filled with more death and drama—his battles in the streets and jungles of Vietnam.

By the end of the night, his travel fatigue forgotten and his spirits high, Smith let down his guard and toasted the win in Grenada.

"We won one for the Gipper!" Then he added, "And the maneuver warfare was for Al Gray."

For the Battalion Landing Team's performance had confirmed the rightness and practicality of General Gray's doctrine of maneuver warfare. To be different from their Army brethren, the Marines had to be quick, wily, and deceptive. Grenada, though a small target, had been a good practice field.

The party lasted until dawn. The young officers gathered around E-Tool like worshipful students at The Basic School. He began to quiz them about the Gospel of Al Gray. Had they done their reading in the classics of maneuver warfare? Were they studying Clausewitz and Sun Tzu? The eager acolytes nodded yes and, even if they weren't actually doing the reading, vowed to themselves to procure the sacred texts.

Smith went back to bed for a brief nap before pushing on to Beirut. When he awoke later that morning, he was slightly hung over but happy to know the Marines' esprit de corps was flourishing.

Smith's new boss had already arrived in Beirut, a shattered city with little cause for celebration. Brig. Gen. Jim Joy had been hand-picked by Commandant P. X. Kelley to return and try to pick up the pieces after the cataclysmic bombing of the Marine Barracks.

Joy had extensive experience in the region, serving as the Marines' liaison officer with the 6th Fleet during the 1982 evacuation of Yasser Arafat's army. He understood the shifting sands of Lebanese politics—as much as anyone could—and why the Americans had drawn the tough assignment guarding Beirut International Airport.

After the PLO's chaotic exit the year before, France, Italy, and the United States divvied up parts of Beirut to try to maintain order as a multinational peacekeeping force. The French had been in Lebanon for decades, so they were given the high-profile job of patrolling the port. The Italians, known for their sociability, took responsibility for South Beirut, an impoverished area with a growing number of refugee camps among the Shiite Muslims.

So the Marines drew the difficult job of guarding Beirut International Airport near the coast in West Beirut. Their mission was to protect the airport and keep the city open to international trade and tourism. This, in turn, would help Beirut start rebuilding itself into the crown jewel of the eastern Mediterranean. The airport seemed like a natural assignment for the Americans since they had the most helicopters to ferry diplomats and envoys for the round-the-clock talks on the nation's seemingly endless civil war.

The airport had one major drawback, one that violated a basic tenet of Marine Corps doctrine—always take the high ground. Instead, low-lying Beirut International was within easy shelling distance of the Shouf Mountains east of the city.

The airport also was within mortar and rocket distance of the Shiite-dominated enclaves of East Beirut. Since the civil war began in 1975, the city's old working-class neighborhoods had become a safe haven for the Shiite guerilla fighters known as the Amal.

Adding to the geographical conundrum, the Marines were under explicit orders to restrict their movements to their assigned area of West Beirut. An exception was made for the Marine guards and patrols that drove downtown to the American embassy. Earlier in the year, the embassy had been hit by a car bomb carrying 300 pounds of TNT, demolishing much of the building and killing sixty-three people.

Joy knew this was a tough and thankless assignment—but an important one nonetheless. President Reagan had told him this in person at Camp Lejeune in late October of 1983, when the chief executive attended a memorial ceremony to honor the dead and wounded from the October 23 truck bombing.

"I know you're going to do a super job," Reagan said. Then he added somberly, "Jim, we can't stand to lose any more Marines over there."

After a briefing in Washington, Joy was given orders to fly commercially to Paris, then on to Beirut aboard the only airline that was still flying to Lebanon—the state-owned Middle East Airlines. Joy had assumed he would be flying incognito along with his staff. But their cover was blown when someone back in Washington booked them on the flight as U.S. Marines. Even their ranks appeared on their tickets. This was not good. The Amal and other factions had spies at the airport who surely would check the passenger manifest and know that the Marines were landing. Joy felt like he had a big target painted on his back.

After the Middle East Airlines jet touched down in Beirut and taxied to the terminal, Joy was met by Col. Tim Geraghty, the commanding officer of the 24th Marine Amphibious Unit, which had been devastated by the terrorist attack.

"We've got to get you out of here," Geraghty said. "We're pretty sure they know you're coming." He whisked them off to a nearby helicopter whose rotors were already spinning. And sure enough, as soon as they lifted off, an explosion rocked the other end of the tarmac—a mortar round welcoming them to Beirut.

Joy was accustomed to such rude introductions, though. He had two tours in Vietnam, including his command in 1972 with Ray Smith during the Easter Offensive. Looking over at Geraghty, he could see the toll the loss of life had taken on the respected ground commander. His eyes had dark circles and he looked like he hadn't slept in days. As they flew to a newly reinforced command bunker near the airport, Geraghty's story poured out about the events of October 23.

He had been sleeping in his field office in a tent about 100 yards from the barracks. The autumn nights were cold in Lebanon, so he was wrapped in a sleeping bag. The explosion was deafening. It blew out dozens of windows and shot shards of dagger-like glass in every direction, including Geraghty's tent. He felt the sting of the cuts as he scrambled to get up, along with a few other men sleeping nearby.

When they stumbled outside into the pale light of dawn, their minds could not process the scene around them: an inferno of smoking rubble rising into the sky like a circle of hell. The barracks, and most of the men in it, were simply gone.

A mushroom cloud lingered above the pile of destruction. At first they thought they'd been hit by a tactical nuclear bomb. But when Geiger counters came up negative for radioactivity, they realized it must have been a conventional, but highly sophisticated, explosive device. Investigators found evidence of TNT mixed with canisters of flammable gas. The explosion lifted the entire four-story structure, severing support columns fifteen feet in circumference with reinforced steel. All that was left behind in the scorched earth was a mammoth crater of thirty-nine feet by twenty-nine feet.[1]

Nobody knew who was behind it, Geraghty said, but there was a long list of suspected terrorist groups that pointed to a number of state sponsors, including Iran.

Considering all he'd been through, Joy realized that Geraghty was holding up pretty well. He was still under investigation by a congressional committee, known as the Long Commission. Chaired by retired Adm. Robert L. J. Long, it had started hearings that week on a ship anchored safely out at sea. The focus of the probe was to find out why so many Marines had been put at risk by living as a garrison under one roof in such a dangerous situation. As the MAU commander, Geraghty was being held responsible— even though he was simply following orders that had been approved all the way up the military chain of command, from the European Command to the Pentagon to the Reagan White House.

Joy had known the colonel for years and hated to see him go through this congressional inquiry that seemed to be searching for a scapegoat. From his own experience in Lebanon, Joy knew the Marines received a steady stream of intelligence from the CIA warning of car bombings and increased terrorist threats. But nobody in authority put the pieces of the puzzle together and warned Geraghty to guard against an explosive-laden truck ramming into his barracks. The ground commander had pleaded for the green light to increase his defenses and let his men launch more active patrols out on the volatile streets of Beirut. But he was rebuffed by diplomatic and government officials stuck in denial about the ticking time bomb facing the Marines.

As Eric Hammel put it in his book on the bombing, *The Root*, "There had been no time when the 24th MAU was ashore that Colonel Geraghty did not feel a sense of unease over the open, 'permissive' nature of his compound. He made guarded entreaties through the chain of command in the hope of being allowed to dig in deeper, but each request was rebuffed with a warning that Beirut International Airport could not be fortified."[2]

Geraghty was a veteran who was stuck in the wrong place at the wrong time, and the lost lives of his Marines would be seared into his heart and mind. The investigation continued from Beirut to Washington, where Congress began hearings. Geraghty was the scapegoat and his career was effectively over—all in the glare of the international media.

The bombing attracted hundreds of print, radio, and broadcast journalists to Beirut to cover the arrival of the replacement troops from America: that is, Ray Smith and the his BLT 2/8. By the time Brigadier General Joy arrived on the chaotic scene, the

Navy ships were still about a week away. Joy, whose rank as a brigadier general gave the Marines more clout in Lebanon, began shoring up the shattered defenses around the airport.

His first grim task was to survey the mountain of rubble at the barracks. He fought back tears as he imagined the boom of the blast, the breaking glass, the cries of agony, the blood, and the confusion. Much of the rubble had been removed by bulldozer and dumped in a nearby pit. Yet even after two weeks of rescue efforts, some human remains remained in the pile of concrete, steel and plaster. The stench of rotting flesh filled the air.

Stifling his own nausea and emotions, Joy walked the line of bunkers and checkpoints to visit the replacement troops who had been brought in for temporary duty. Their esprit de corps made him proud.

Then he toured the rest of the city, where his logistics officer, Chuck Rheinhart, made an interesting find on the waterfront. Beirut's harbor, once bustling with international shipping, had come to virtual halt because of the fighting. But in this frozen scene, Rheinhart saw an opportunity for the Marines. "See those boxes, general?" he said, pointing at the shipping containers piled one on top of the other along the piers. "I think we could use them."

Called "connix" boxes, the metal containers were a staple of international shipping because they made it easier to handle and store goods on docks and aboard ships. "Why not use the boxes when we build our new bunkers?" Rheinhart suggested. "They're just gathering rust here."

"Brilliant, Chuck," Joy said. He requested a team of Seabees, the Navy's engineering arm, to come ashore from the 6th Fleet and help the Marines dig in. The Seabees arrived the next day and started digging deep trenches for the twenty-foot-long containers. Using forklifts to lower the metal boxes into the ground, the resourceful engineers reinforced the connix boxes with plywood and covered them with dirt and sandbags.

Joy marveled at the resourcefulness of the Navy's building crews. For finishing touches, they added doors, steps, and parapets to the bunkers. Smith's men would have better firing positions than the Marines who had been surprised by the bomb-laden truck. The 2/8 would land and set up shop in the reinforced bunkers around the airfield and in the no-man's land between the Muslim-dominated neighborhoods to the east. With the barracks gone, the Marines would approach their assignment with a new, harder attitude, shrugging off the mantle of "peacekeeping" and treating this for what it was: a civil war.

But it was a civil war played out on the evening news. On November 17, 1983, the 2/8 Marines waded ashore on the beach at Beirut. They were met by scores of photographers, reporters, cameramen, and TV correspondents. Smith could see the fish-bowl setting would be challenging. But he'd never had any problem dealing with reporters, and he knew, if he played his cards right, they might even help him better understand the tactical situation around this crazy city.

There was another side to their arrival that nobody expected: an outpouring of support from the American public. It began with a trickle of cards, letters, and packages addressed to "the Marines in Lebanon." The trickle turned into a flood, with mail that was measured in the tons. Smith's name had appeared in some news reports about Grenada, so he received hundreds of letters over the next few months. The messages were a mixture of plaudits for the victory in Grenada to expressions of sympathy for the Marines' plight in Lebanon.

For the first time since Vietnam, Smith sensed a shift of public opinion. Even as Congress sparred with the Reagan Administration over America's ill-defined mission in Lebanon, average Americans were taking time to pay tribute to the Marines.

Smith was struck not only by the quantity of goods but also the quality. People sent Virginia hams, Wisconsin cheese, and plenty of beer to wash them down. One high school class in upstate New York asked a Marine recruiter what would please the men on the front lines. When he said a stereo would be nice, they took him at his word and sent a huge sound system with 500-amp speakers.

The firemen of Schenectady, New York, shipped several large boxes filled with 2,000 canvas shaving kits. The kits were made of top-quality leather and engraved with a message: "To the peacekeepers in Lebanon from the firemen of Schenectady, New York."

Tens of thousands of dollars worth of gifts flowed into Beirut off the Navy ships. The Marines got so much food that every bunker was filled with chips, hams, and cheeses. And there were tens of thousands of letters of support.

Somehow the Pinkerton Tobacco Company of Richmond, Virginia, learned that Smith's call sign was Red Man, in honor of his choice of chewing tobacco. Pinkerton promptly shipped four large boxes filled with tobacco products—enough to addict all 1,200 men in his BLT.

In many ways, the 2/8's arrival had a storybook quality, with citizens pouring out their hearts and cupboards. The simultaneous success in Grenada and tragedy in Lebanon struck a chord across America. The brave young leathernecks digging in around Beirut International Airport were portrayed as "peacekeepers" by President Reagan, strong men willing to face up to terrorism.

"Today, the world looks to America for leadership," the president told Marines and families during a speech in North Carolina. "And America looks to its corps of Marines. Whether humankind will suffer a new onslaught of bloodshed and tyranny has much to do with the American people's strength of character and sense of purpose.

"Let no terrorist question our will, no tyrant doubt our resolve," Reagan said. "Americans have courage and determination, and we must not and will not be intimidated—by anyone, anywhere. Since 1775, Marines . . . have shaped the strength and resolve of the United States. Your role is as important today as at any time in our history."

Despite the proud rhetoric and good wishes from home, the Marines in Beirut knew they had been dealt a bad hand. All the way down the chain of command—from General Joy, to Lieutenant Colonel Smith, to the nineteen- and twenty-year-old men in their sandbagged bunkers—the Marines knew they faced a vague mission from their president "to establish an environment in which the government of Lebanon could exercise sovereignty over their own territory."

It sounded noble enough, but Lebanon's government, ruled by a Christian minority, was shaky at best. Car bombings rocked the city streets daily and militias had nightly gun battles in a region steeped in centuries of tribal hatred and bloody revenge.

Ray Smith loved the Gipper, but he had serious doubts about Reagan's orders to establish a stable environment in such an unstable place. The 2/8 Marines were expected to provide a "presence" in Beirut, like a cop standing on a pedestal on the street corner. This tactic worked for a while, Smith said, until the warring factions saw that "the cop on the corner wouldn't do anything. Somehow just standing there was supposed to stop these criminals from committing criminal acts." The pose could work only until the different factions realized the Americans were just pieces of "cardboard standing up there."

Making matters worse, the Marines were supposed to follow the confusing rules of engagement that had already created an opportunity for a truck bomber to drive past sentries whose rifles were not loaded and ready to fire. Normally, the rules of combat are supposed to be secret. But after meeting with some American newspaper reporters, Smith discovered that they were carrying the same pocket-sized orders as those of the Marines at the embassy (a blue card) and at the airport (a white card). Each card contained instructions for the use of deadly force. While the rules varied for the embassy guards and the airport Marines, the central message was the same: fire only if fired upon, and if you do fire your weapon, employ a "reciprocal" or "proportional" response— that is, return rifle fire for rifle fire, mortar for mortar, and rocket for rocket.

The rules were monitored by the U.S. European Command, whose headquarters was hundreds of miles away in Stuttgart, Germany. It was bad enough that Smith's Marines had to answer to desk jockeys in Germany, but now Smith learned their stupid rules were the worst kept secret in town. Even the warring militias had them. In fact, over time the rules had been revised with the de facto approval of Beirut's three factions: the Amal militia of Nabih Berri, which fought for the underclass of Shiite Muslims; the Druze forces of Wallid Jumblatt, a Muslim spin-off sect that controlled the Shouf mountains above the city; and the Lebanese national army, whose loyalties shifted as often as the wind off the Mediterranean Sea.

The U.S. Embassy, for its part, took a passive stance that discouraged any display or use of force. The cumulative effect of the rules and the diplomatic edicts was to leave the barracks guards paralyzed when the bomb-laden truck came roaring at them on the fateful Sunday morning. They had no time to shoot the driver. The guard at the front gate inserted a magazine into his M-16 rifle, but too late—the truck was already crashing through a guard shack.[3]

★ ★ ★

The first order of business for the new Marine commanders was to get a grip on the security situation. But given the chaotic political environment, and the lack of clear guidance from the European Command, this was easier said than done. The "peacekeeping" role was particularly hard on Smith's frontline officers, the company and platoon leaders whose men were exposed to fire.

Capt. Bob Dobson, Lt. Matt Aylward, and others on the front lines quickly realized that any wrong moves on their part could become an international incident. This wasn't a declared war, and there was a lack of training with the reluctant Lebanese army. The Marines also had to coordinate with the French, Italian, and British forces, and faced a tangled chain of command. Any wrong move would be put under a spotlight, and could easily ruin their young careers.

The notion of a "proportional response" hung over them like some kind of baffling question from a Zen master. When he heard his Marines could insert their magazines and return fire "in kind," Dobson replied, "What the fuck does that mean?"

It seemed to come straight from the pages of *Catch 22*. As Golf Company set up his defenses, Dobson wondered how anyone could keep track of incoming fire, especially in the heat of a battle, and respond "in kind." That sounded more like a gift-giving policy than a military order. Moreover, why should his Marines be hamstrung? He cursed the diplomats and politicians who cooked up such Byzantine rules.

After a brief lull in the wake of the October 23 bombing, Lebanon's civil war started heating up again in mid November, around the time the 2/8 was setting up shop. Dobson noticed that some of the Amal militia seemed to enter Beirut's cafes in late afternoon, after getting off work or whatever they did during the day. Then the mostly young men would fortify themselves with shots of the local liquor, Uzo. Back in the States, drinking men might have played cards or gone bowling. Here they gathered their AK-47s or rocket-propelled grenade launchers and took up positions in the deserted slums to take aim at the fresh troops from the United States.

Dobson's Golf Company drew a dangerous assignment on the eastern perimeter of the airport. They were posted a few hundred yards across an empty field from Hay-as-Salaam, a grim-looking slum dubbed "Hooterville" by the Marines. As he looked in his binoculars at the deserted apartment buildings, Dobson wished he could use more firepower and simply attack whenever firing erupted from one of the broken windows. Perhaps he couldn't justify using artillery, but why not use shoulder-launched Dragon missiles? A Dragon, designed to take out enemy tanks, could easily knock down the concrete walls that protected the drunken idiots taking pot shots at his Marines.

Dobson knew that using the Dragon—whose missiles cost thousands of dollars apiece—might be a hard sell to his bosses. General Joy and Lieutenant Colonel Smith urged everyone to dig in and protect themselves. But for how long and at what cost? Some of Dobson's senior NCOs were asking him the same question, which boiled down was, "What the fuck are we doing here, sir?"

The question of mission began taking on new urgency as the Marines received more and more warnings about terrorist threats.

Sgt. Mike Leiphart wrote in his journal about the warnings. "Most were about possible car bombs. These included a description and sometimes a license number of the vehicle. . . . Soon we had well over one hundred different vehicles to be on the lookout for."

Marine intelligence, the S-2, passed along tips from the CIA, and from the British, French, and Italian forces spread around the city. "Some of the other warnings from the battalion S-2 included packs of dogs or livestock carrying strapped-on explosives," Leiphart wrote. Some of the locals might chase the bomb-laden animals toward the Marines, then blow them up.

When the Marines weren't watching for exploding animals or cars, they were keeping an eye for attacks from on high. "Several times we were told to be on the lookout for a suicide helicopter," Leiphart wrote, as well as "hang gliders from the mountains with suicide bombers aboard."

Terrorists might also tunnel their way into the Marine compounds, or infiltrate the area by wearing Marine-type uniforms. Leiphart considered this the most plausible threat, and kept a close watch on everyone approaching his platoon's bunkers on the northeast side of the airport. Meanwhile, he kept his men busy filling sandbags and reinforcing their bunkers. He tutored them in the fine points of garrison duty—for example, how to stack sandbags so that the seams were not lined up, which would make them more vulnerable to stray bullets slicing through the sand. He taught them to stagger the sandbags like bricks and that it took at least three feet of packed dirt and sand to stop a round from an AK-47.

His men got the message and started stacking their sandbags at a furious pace. As they erected their makeshift fortress, the men of the 2nd Platoon, Golf Company, had trouble finding supports strong enough for a heavy roof. Finally, in the best Marine tradition of scrounging and sometimes stealing, they discovered some twenty-foot-long iron pipes for reinforcement. The pipes, more than a foot in diameter, weighed hundreds of pounds and were too heavy to lift even for Leiphart's men. It took a system of levers, pry bars, and brute strength to move them into place. The heavy lifting lasted from dawn to dusk.

When the construction was done, each Marine had to pull four hours of guard duty. But Leiphart was glad to see the grumbling was kept to a minimum. The men had seen the rubble of the old barracks, and could smell the lingering stench of death. They knew this was a life-and-death situation.

The 2nd Platoon also managed to jury rig a shower using six fifty-five-gallon barrels set up on a platform. The barrels were connected by a pipe welded on the bottom. There was only one shower nozzle, but it was better than nothing. After a few days in country, they were all badly in need of a bath.

All they lacked was water. Beirut's water system was leaky at best, and the outpost was well beyond the reach of any of the city's utilities. But Leiphart's men were creative and stopped a water truck, known as a "water buffalo," as it made its rounds with drinking water. They secured several dozen gallons of water to get their showers going.

This unauthorized utility system sprang a leak, however, when someone on Ray's staff got wind of it and told Leiphart to keep his hands off the drinking water. Undaunted, the Marines slipped over to the truck with five-gallon water cans and kept tapping the mobile water supply.

It didn't take long for the Marines to be glad they had dug in. Each day they faced increasing levels of mortar, rocket, and artillery fire from the nearby tenements and from the Shouf Mountains to the east. Supposedly, the shooting was aimed at Lebanese army positions. But the Lebanese were dug in perilously close to the Marines, apparently clinging for protection. One American outpost was particularly close to the crossfire: known as Checkpoint 76, the Marine observation post was atop a grocery store. During the day, the storekeeper served food and drinks to the city residents who were stuck in the war zone; by night, though, the storeowner closed up shop and hid with his family downstairs. The top of his store had been fortified with sandbags by a squad of Marines led by Manny Cox, the Cuban-born sergeant who distinguished himself in Grenada. His squad also occupied an empty house across the street, where they slept, ate, and kept watch for any suspicious activity.

It was a perilous spot near the Damascus Road, the line of demarcation for government-controlled West Beirut and fractious East Beirut. The Amal militia controlled the maze of streets and slums in the eastern part of the city. The Marines also kept an eye on the Shouf mountains looming farther to the east, where the Druze held sway. Checkpoint 76, in many ways, was like a sentry point between East and West Berlin—an early warning post that would be vulnerable if heavy fighting broke out.

Every night, Cox and his twelve-man squad took turns keeping watch from their second-floor bunkers. Their mission was to pinpoint flashes of incoming fire and help coordinate return fire from Golf Company's mortars or artillery.

"Cox was on the perimeter because I selected him," said Dobson, his company commander. "Because he was the best that I had. Maybe this is kind of unusual thinking, but in the Marine Corps you give the toughest, worst, most dangerous assignment to your best guy."

It was the kind of thinking that set Golf Company apart, and had motivated it throughout the successful mission in Grenada. "We wanted the tough jobs," Dobson said. "That's part of the Marine ethic. If they wanted to be like someone else, they would have joined the Army."

Each day seemed to bring more shooting, and more bullets hit the sandbags protecting Checkpoint 76. Yet, amid the fighting and near-death experiences, life continued below the observation post. Jan "Skip" Wheeler, a twenty-year-old radio operator from Ocala, Florida, tried to make small talk with the shopkeeper's boys.

"*Marahaba*," he said, attempting to say "hello" in Lebanese.

Two dark-eyed lads scurried behind their father. "*Marahaba!*" they called back between giggles.

Their father sold sodas, cigarettes, and the local delicacy of fresh egg sandwiches on pita bread. Some customers were young Shiites from the neighborhood wearing the distinctive red scarves of the Amal militia. "Ragheads," the Marines called them. Wheeler suspected the men quietly munching egg sandwiches were the same guys who were shooting things up every night. He had the feeling they were casing the Marines' defenses.

As one day in Beirut followed another, Ray Smith's battalion fell into a daily routine. In the morning, they would cat-nap, eat, and clean up. By late afternoon they would get ready for the night's action, cleaning weapons, checking ammo supplies, and donning helmets and flak jackets. As the sun started its bronze dip into the Mediterranean, they watched with a mixture of fascination and dread as the first orange tracer bullets started crackling over the Beirut skyline. The shooting would start from anywhere, with no rhyme or reason. The only sure thing was the lethal quality of the bullets and shells. As long as they weren't under fire, the Marines could sit back and watch the light and sound show. But if they were under fire, they had to get to work.

With the city exploding around them, Smith and his boss, General Joy, worked to change the rules of engagement. All along, they contended that they wanted their Marines to properly defend themselves. The Marines gradually began to up the ante when fired upon, employing more mortars and high-caliber machine guns, and occasionally using tanks as well. Some of the reporters on the ground noticed what they saw as a more aggressive posture by the Beirut Marines. But when they asked Lieutenant Colonel Smith about it, the ground commander dodged the question as deftly as he had skirted the RPG in Hue City.

"The rules of engagement are classified information," he said. "I can't discuss them."

The matter made its way back to the White House, where the daily press briefings centered on the Reagan administration's intentions in Lebanon and the ongoing danger for the Marines in the wake of the October 23 bombing. Press secretary Marlin

Fitzwater did his own dance of denial, referring questions to the European Command, who in turn deferred to the Pentagon. It was a transatlantic runaround.

Though Joy and Smith had quietly changed the rules of engagement, it took a while to get the word out to the Marines in the frontline bunkers. Many felt hamstrung by the initial policy of only making a "proportional response" to enemy fire—a rifle for a rifle, and so on. This became evident to Joy one day in early December. He had stopped by Dobson's command post on the northeastern perimeter and asked if he needed help with anything.

"Sir," Dobson replied, "the first thing you can do is get rid of these shitty rules of engagement."

Joy was taken aback. He thought they had done that already. But there obviously was still some confusion about the commanders' intent to defend themselves with every weapon at their disposal. Of course there were limits. As the ranking ground commander, Joy had to approve artillery or naval gunfire.

But the Marines had tanks, mortars, antitank missiles and grenade launchers. Wasn't that a large enough arsenal?

Joy could see this captain felt his hands were tied.

"Sir," Dobson said in his clipped, no-nonsense way, "we are the strongest democratic republic in the history of the free world. I am a company commander in an exposed area of the perimeter. I need to be able to make the appropriate response for the situation."

He paused to see if the general was put off by his straight talk. But Joy nodded and urged him to continue.

"Sir," Dobson said, "if you don't trust me to make an appropriate response, relieve me and put someone out here you trust. These rules of engagement are going to get good Marines hurt."

"What are you suggesting, Bob?"

"I'm suggesting that you allow me to fire any weapons system that I have, if that's what I feel is required," Dobson said.

Joy pointed to the tank assigned to Golf Company. "But Bob, I can't let you fire tank flachette rounds," he said, referring to the "beehive" round that would send out thousands of steel darts.

Such rounds, usually used when a unit was surrounded, could lead to massive civilian casualties.

Dobson said he wasn't suggesting they start raking the enemy with flachette or willy-peter rounds, which could start fires. "But I want to be able to fire the full range of high-explosive ammunition that I have if I think the situation warrants it."

Joy patted the captain's back. "Let me take it under advisement, Bob."

Returning to his headquarters, Joy talked it over with Smith. It was time, they agreed, to send a stronger message to the battalion. The next morning, the lieutenant colonel approached Dobson and told him, "You can fire away."

Dobson called his platoon commanders together. Looking at Aylward, whose men were in an exposed position across from Hooterville, he said, "This one's for you, buddy."

After nearly two weeks in Beirut, the Marines finally had been officially told that the rules of engagement were changed—albeit without any formal notification by Joy to his superiors in the European Command or at the Pentagon. Forget the notion of "proportional response," Dobson told his officers and NCOs." If fired upon, use what it takes to defend yourself, he said. The Amal would no longer get to hide behind the walls of the dilapidated apartments and burned-out cafes.

"Matt," he told Lieutenant Aylward, "the next time they fire from behind that cinderblock wall, I want you to knock it down."

Aylward was listening, but didn't seem to grasp the order.

"Knock it down, Matt," Dobson repeated.

"Yes, sir!"

Aylward passed along the orders to be more aggressive. The next time there was some fire from Hooterville, his 2nd Platoon opened up with thousands of rounds from their M-16s and M-50 machine guns. The Amal were dug in, though, and it was hard to hit them behind the slum walls.

So Aylward called for some shots from the M60 tank assigned to him. Its 105-millimeter shells punched holes in the Amal's defenses, but the hostile gunfire from AK-47s didn't cease. So far no Americans had been killed, but it was just a matter of time.

The tank fire did get the attention of the Shiite's leadership, though. Over at the Marine Amphibious Unit headquarters, General Joy's phone rang. A senior official at the American embassy said Nabih Berri, the Amal chief, was on the other line.

"He wants a cease fire," the official said.

"The Marines are defending themselves," Joy said. "They'll stop firing when the Amal stop."

The Amal may have looked like a ragtag outfit, but they were battle-hardened veterans trained by the Iranians and Syrians—two nations using Beirut and the rest of Lebanon to fight a proxy war against Israel and, by extension, the United States. Shortly before the October 23 bombing, the Marines had battled the Amal at this same place, across a field from a well-known watering hole, Café Daniel, where the fighters often mingled with Western reporters during lulls in the fighting. Near the café was a steel-reinforced wall conveniently fitted with small slits just big enough to fire an AK-47.

Now the wall was shielding Amal fighters who drank Uzo at Café Daniel, then staggered outside to take aim at the Americans. During one particularly heavy attack, Matt Aylward ran up the wooden stairs of his command post, a homemade wooden platform dubbed "the Kool-Aid stand." Peering through his binoculars, he could see the muzzle flashes from behind the steel wall. Several bullets thudded into the sandbags below him. Close. Aylward ducked inside his stand and pondered his options. He'd already used the tank assigned to him, but didn't want to send it out in the field where it could be a sitting duck for the Amal's rocket-propelled grenades. It was time to try something new and let these idiots know once and for all that they couldn't hide behind the wall.

"Bring up the Dragon team," he shouted over the gunfire.

Lance Corp. Matt Collins and two other Marines hustled forward, toting the two-piece missile launcher. Collins's heart was pounding. He'd spent more than a year practicing for a moment like this, when he could finally fire his antitank weapon.

The Dragon was a high-tech descendent of the bazookas of World War II. Its five-foot-long missile had a precision guidance system with remote controls to adjust the missile's trajectory in midflight. The missile stayed connected to the launcher by a tether that transmitted guidance data to its on-board computer. It was known as a "smart" weapon.

Collins knew he was almost assured of hitting the target if he could just keep a clear eye and steady hand. But he also knew the Dragon had its quirks, including its guidance system. Its trajectory was determined by the gunner's eye, so it was possible to get distracted when the missile shot from the tube and look the missile into the ground. When that happened, the gunner looked like an idiot, and the mighty Dragon turned into a gopher.

Collins realized that, for all of his training, this would be the first time he shot an actual Dragon missile. It was a matter of economics: each round cost $5,000. The Marine Corps didn't have enough money in its training budget to let its Dragon gunners fire even one live round in training. Instead, it was done by computer simulation and dummy rounds. Now he hoped he wouldn't look like a dummy.

Rising above the sandbags, Collins exposed himself to enemy fire. But he needed to get a better look across the field at Café Daniel. Breathing deeply, he reminded himself, *Keep it steady, don't look down. Focus, focus.*

The café loomed in his scope like a stucco saloon from the Old West. He could see the steel wall and the Amal racing behind it, keeping their heads down. Little did they know that their red bandanas made them perfect targets for the Marines with high-powered scopes. Collins exhaled, then slowly pulled the trigger. The Dragon shot from the tube with a roar, its rockets popping like firecrackers as it followed the path set by Collins' steady hand and unwavering eye.

A split second later, the missile mashed the wall and blew it up. Several bodies were flung into the air like red-topped rag dolls.

"Nice shot," Aylward said.

The Amal's firing stopped and several men rushed out into the field in front of Café Daniel, furiously waving white flags. The Dragon's fire also prompted a flurry of calls by the Amal's leaders to the American embassy. What happened to the rules of engagement, Nabih Berri wanted to know?

An American embassy official called Ray Smith and asked, "What we do tell them?"

Smith was sick and tired of the whining by Berri, and moreover, by the whole misguided, jury-rigged rules of engagement in Beirut. "Tell them," he said, "if we take fire we are going to respond with whatever weapons systems we feel are appropriate to militarily remove that threat."

The battle at Café Daniel became international news as the Marines appeared to have been given a green light to respond to the ongoing attacks on the airport. Reporters peppered Smith with questions, asking him if his men weren't overstepping the bounds of a "peacekeeping" force.

But Smith felt at ease about taking out the wall in front of Café Daniel. His Marines should be free to defend themselves. Period.

Smith also had an ace in the hole known only to himself and a few top government officials. His radio operator and jeep driver, Lance Corp. Joe Hickey, was the son of Edward V. Hickey, director of the White House military office and a longtime confidante of President Reagan.

Ed Hickey's connection to the president dated back to 1968, when he guarded him as a Secret Service agent during Reagan's failed bid for the Republican presidential nomination. When Reagan bowed out to Richard Nixon, he invited Hickey to take over the security staff of the California governor. Hickey became a trusted aide who later followed Reagan to the White House in 1981.

Marine major general Matthew Caulfield, who served as Hickey's deputy in the early 1980s, recalled his boss's easy access to the Oval Office. Since Reagan had known young Joe Hickey since he was a boy, Reagan took a particularly keen interest in the fate of the Marines serving in Lebanon.

Joe Hickey, an articulate and energetic twenty year old, recalled his father's parting words before the BLT 2/8 shipped out for Beirut: "You're not going to lack any support from this administration and this president to achieve your mission in Lebanon. I tell you that as a father. You have my word."

So when Smith discovered Hickey's back-door access to the White House, he found it reassuring to know one of Reagan's aides—and perhaps the president himself—was getting firsthand accounts of the military situation unfiltered by the media.

Joe Hickey's back-channel communiqués included a letter mailed to the White House *before* the October 23 barracks bombing. In it, he described a speech by Lieutenant Colonel Smith as they set out on their voyage to Beirut. "Come hell or high water, when we get to Lebanon, we are not going to move into those buildings," Ray told the troops. "We are goddamn well going to go tactical. If I have to be relieved, we're going to fight that fight, and we are going to win."

By the time Ed Hickey got his son's letter, the barracks was in smoldering ruins. Whoever this Ray Smith was, Hickey could see he knew what he was talking about. Indeed, the letter had a haunting, even prescient, quality as the Marine leader said he would not move into the barracks once they arrived.

Yet even with the tacit backing of Ed Hickey and the Reagan White House, Smith faced a tricky and shifting tactical situation on the ground in Lebanon. The level of violence began to escalate in late November and early December, and even the local militia leaders were getting worried about the warning signs of an all-out civil war.

On paper Beirut was ruled by the Lebanese government. But in reality, a separate authority, or authorities, ruled the streets. Nabih Berri, the American-educated head of the Amal ("Hope") Movement, represented the Shiite Muslims stuck in refugee camps and slums. They were second-class citizens in the Muslim world dominated by the better-educated Sunnis. The Marines also battled the forces of Walid Jumblatt, the leader of the Druzes, a mountain sect that had split from mainstream Islam in the eleventh century.[4]

After his success in handling the strongmen—and women—in Grenada, Smith was now trying to see through the dark glass of

Beirut's politics. Berri and Jumblad reminded him of village chiefs back in Vietnam, and even mayors he'd run into back in the States. They were smart politicians with constituents to serve, big egos, and self-interest in maintaining a fragile balance of power. Smith had met with them during the early days of the 2/8's occupation. But after his Marines came under fire from both militias, he canceled the meetings. No more games, he told both men. No more dancing with partners who turned on you at the slightest provocation.

As the days passed, Smith also became familiar with a number of war correspondents, and formed friendships that he turned to his advantage. The reporters often returned from East Beirut, where they had been near the Amal fighters. Their reports—and photographs—gave Smith a valuable source of intelligence.

The journalists who helped him filed solid, objective news stories. But they also found ways to quietly help the Marines without compromising their professional ethics. "They were Americans first," Smith said. "They did everything they could to help us." This included providing pictures from the hills that showed him how his positions looked from the enemy's vantage point.

He vowed to never divulge these journalists' names or news affiliations.

By day, the Marines slept, ate, wrote letters and recorded tapes to send home. By night, they fought—or watched the fighting. The action was hottest on the edge of East Beirut at Checkpoint 76, Sgt. Manny Cox's forward observation post.

As the intensity of the firefights grew, Cox did all he could to quell his men's fears. One day he asked Wheeler what he thought about their assignment and the prohibitions on stalking the enemy shooters.

Wheeler shrugged. "It's messed up," he said. The Marines should be allowed to go after their attackers wherever they were, even if it meant chasing them up into the hills.

"Yeah," Cox agreed, "but we'll do the job and go home."

"I hope so," Wheeler said. He wanted to get back to Florida and start college or study for a trade. He had joined the Corps on the advice of some friends after they graduated from high school. The naïve Floridians pictured themselves in fancy uniforms, traveling the globe to exotic places, with beautiful women on their arms.

The reality was a far cry from their youthful fantasy. Their uniforms were dirty, they were stuck in a slum, and there were no pretty women in sight to admire the brave Marines. Every night was getting scarier and most of the men just wanted to go home.

One Marine, in a tape made for friends back home, recorded the sounds of a firefight at Checkpoint 76 as machine gun rounds zipped by like angry bees, and mortar and artillery fire exploded perilously close to their housetop bunker. Young men's voices rose with their adrenalin levels, and one cursed the incoming rounds from their unseen attackers. "Hey, fuck that!"

A radio played in the background and a singer incongruously crooned, *You came when I was happy/in the sunshine.*

"Holy shit!" the Marine exclaimed into his tape recorder after another explosion. "I shouldn't get jumpy," he explained to his friends. "Supposedly we're keeping the peace, but we're still fighting and ain't keeping much peace."

But when the men in the bunker started feeling sorry for themselves, they only had to think of their leader, Manny Cox, and what he was giving up to stay in Beirut. Everyone knew he'd rather be home with his wife, Evi, back in New Jersey. She was close to giving birth to their first child.

In early December, another kind of arrival took the Marine leadership by surprise. On the night of December 3, General Joy got a call from Rear Adm. Jerry Tuttle, deputy commander of the U.S. 6th Fleet.

"Jim, you need to have your Marines hunkered down tomorrow because we're going to fly an Alpha Strike," Tuttle said.

Joy's heart sank. An Alpha Strike meant the Navy was going to launch every fighter plane it had from the USS *John F. Kennedy* off the coast of Lebanon.

"Why?" Joy said. "What's the point?"

Tuttle wasn't sure. The order came straight from the White House and could not be refuted. But the admiral knew what Joy was thinking. "I'm afraid you guys are going to be the ones who are going to suffer," Tuttle said. "Get your Marines to take cover."

Lieutenant Colonel Smith had mixed feelings when he heard about the Alpha Strike. He was glad the Reagan Administration was serious about punishing the Syrians for their ongoing support of terrorists, including those involved in blowing up the Marine Barracks. But he knew Admiral Tuttle was right: the Marines would be in the line of fire for the pro-Syrian forces in town.

"The militias will open up on us and retaliate," he told Joy.

Joy heatedly objected to the 6th Fleet and European Command, but it was too late to stop the Alpha Strike. He was too far down the totem pole to make himself heard. The attack, Joy found out later, was part of a retaliatory strike hatched by Reagan's national security adviser, Robert MacFarlane, a retired Marine who wanted to punish the terrorists behind the barracks bombing.

"The evidence pointed to a previously unknown group, Islamic Jihad, or Holy War, as the perpetrators," Robert Timberg wrote. "Planning and financing had come from Iran. Syria had provided a haven for the training of the terrorists at Sheik Abdullah Barracks, a former Lebanese army post . . . in the Bekaa Valley."[5]

The Alpha Strike on the Bekaa Valley was set to launch at 11:00 A.M. on December 4. But the planning and preparations for launching the Navy bombers proved to be chaotic, with orders to move it up to 6:30 A.M., only one hour from when the Navy's task force commander received the final attack order.

After what Navy Secretary John Lehman called a "mad flail,"[6] the carrier commander won a one-hour delay. But the pilots had to scramble to their planes, which were poorly outfitted for the mission. Radio silence was broken, alerting the Syrians. "Worst of all," Timberg wrote, "because of the change in the launch time, the attacking aircraft found themselves flying into the fiery glare of the early morning sun while the Syrian gunners they were searching out awaited them in the shadows."[7]

The Alpha Strike struck out. The only plane with a full load of bombs was hit by a Soviet-made surface-to-air (SAM) missile and crashed. Both crewmen ejected. The pilot, Lt. Mark Lange, bled to death from a severed left leg. The bombardier-navigator, Lt. Robert Goodman, was taken prisoner. After Goodman was later released to the Rev. Jesse Jackson, Lehman whimsically suggested that aviators' survival gear should be modified "to include a roll of quarters and Jackson's phone number."[8]

And Ray Smith could only order his men to stay close to their bunkers, wondering how the bombing raid would rock the warring tribes of Lebanon.

SEVENTEEN

"Marahaba, Marine"

On guard in Beirut, most of the Marines knew nothing about the debacle unfolding to the east in Syria. Indeed, December 4 began as a joyous day for the battalion. A call came from the American Red Cross with the news that Evi Cox had given birth to a boy in New Jersey. And Sgt. Manny Cox, usually so serious and intent, had a broad grin on his face after he got the news by radio. He jogged from his observation post over to the battalion's headquarters to call his wife.

Evi, recovering from a Caesarean section, was groggy when she first took the call. But when she heard her husband's familiar voice, she sat up and clutched the receiver.

"Oh, my God! Manny! You!"

"Thank you, thank you, thank you," he shouted long distance. "I can't thank you enough for giving me a son. I'm the happiest man."

He was as excited as a kid at Christmas about his newborn son, named Anthony. Before leaving for Beirut, Cox had played his violin beside Evi's pregnant belly, hoping the music would help develop their unborn child. Now his questions poured out like an arpeggio of the heart. "How's he doing? Who does he look like? How much does he weigh? How are *you* doing?"

Evi sighed, cried, and laughed. Her emotions were as wild as a salsa band. "Me? You're asking about *me*? What about *you*?"

Over the past few weeks, Evi had stopped reading newspapers or watching TV. She simply couldn't take any more news from Beirut. Though no one had told her, she sensed that her husband was in grave danger. If there was a hard job, Evi knew her husband would be the first to volunteer for it.

"I'm fine," he said, his voice crackling in the static. "And I love you, Evi. But now I need to leave," he said, becoming more businesslike. "We have been under fire all night. My squad is under fire right now, and I have to get back."

Evi couldn't stop herself from crying out. "Why? What the hell are you going back for, Manny? Don't go back!" She wished she could reach through the phone and pull her man back to the States. She felt like asking him, *Do you want to die?* But she didn't, because she was a Marine's wife and had to be strong.

When he didn't answer her plea, Evi composed herself and said, "Manny, just be careful. Take good care of yourself."

Then the connection ended, leaving Evi with only a dial tone. She lay back, dazed from the surreal experience of hearing from her Marine husband. She wished he would try to apply for emergency leave home, but he wouldn't.

The phone rang again. "Evi?"

"You again?" she said through her tears.

"Honey," Cox said, "let's not waste time. Let's take advantage of this moment to talk."

Evi struggled to compose herself. She knew he was right, and they should talk about their baby boy. She told him how Anthony looked like him and had beautiful eyes like his daddy. She told him things he needed to hear.

When Cox felt himself choking up, he said he had to go. His men were waiting for him. "Take good care of yourself, Evi. I love you."

"I love you, too, Manny," she said.

Back in Beirut, Capt. Bob Dobson talked to his top squad leader about his decision to stay at Checkpoint 76. He had already talked to Cox's platoon commander to let him know the sergeant had every right to catch a flight back to the States to see his wife.

"We'll support his decision," Dobson said.

When the lieutenant objected, Dobson cut him off. "We're sitting in this hellhole here, and the right thing is for Sergeant Cox to go home."

Dobson talked to Cox right after his phone call to Evi. "Sergeant Cox, what have you decided to do about going back home? If you want to go, I support you."

The crackle of semiautomatic gunfire came from the direction of Checkpoint 76, less than a mile away. Cox listened intently for a moment, as though he were listening to a symphony of violence. He had to stay, he explained to Dobson. "My men are here, my duty is here."

Dobson felt a mix of pride and foreboding. But it was the sergeant's call, and he clearly wanted to rejoin his men before nightfall.

Cox double-timed it along the dusty road, past an abandoned Pepsi bottling warehouse and chicken processing plant, and down the street to his home away from home—the grocery store-turned-observation post. Its shutters were closed as the storeowner sensed a rough night ahead.

Bounding to the rooftop bunker, he found his squad on edge. Sporadic shooting had started and their adrenalin was pumping. Cox managed to remain calm, even as some of his off-duty Marines scrambled from the house across the street to join the fray. There were more men than usual on the roof, but Manny decided to let them stay. They might need the added firepower.

By sunset, the pace of the shooting picked up. Small-arms fire was followed by rockets from the Shouf Mountains. Something was up, Cox could see that, since the Druze were joining the fight. Clouds rolled in, making it hard to spot the enemy's muzzle flashes and return fire.

"Stay down," Cox said steadily to his men, "stay down." By now, ten Marines were in the bunker—double the normal size of his observation detail. The bunker had a two-foot-high cinder-block wall around the top, with sandbags on three sides. Only the western side could be left unprotected, since that was the direction of his fellow Marines a mile away.

The pitch of the battle began to rise. Machine guns, rockets, and mortars rained in from the east.

"Get down, get down," Cox said firmly. "Keep your heads down!"

But he didn't heed his own advice. He rose above the sandbags to peer off the roof, desperately trying to spot the enemy gunners. Consulting a map with grids on it, he hollered the coordinates to Skip Wheeler. The radioman relayed them to Captain Dobson.

The company commander called for support fire from the Marines' 81-millimeter mortars and 155-millimeter artillery batteries. But the clouds and darkness gave the enemy a deadly cover.

Sergeant Cox kept directing a steady stream of rifle and machine-gun fire into the Beirut night. The city block was lit up like the Fourth of July. But there was more fire coming from the nearby Shiites and the Druze in the hills than from the Marines or their Lebanese allies. Manny knew this imbalance of power couldn't last for long. He reached for the radio set and pleaded for more artillery support. "Where's my fire?" he hollered above the din. "We need this fire now!"

Enemy rockets zoomed down from the hills like huge fireballs. Then a mortar explosion rocked the nearby Pepsi plant, which caught fire. "Get down!" Cox shouted.

Skip Wheeler left his radio and jumped behind a sandbag bunker on the southeast corner of the roof. Cox was right beside him, looking out the window, desperately trying to spot the enemy mortar positions in the Beirut night.

Boom! A second shell struck nearby.

"Get down!" Cox yelled. "Here comes another one."

It was the last thing Wheeler heard before the world turned a deep and searing red.

Back at his command post, Dobson urgently tried to piece together what was happening to his men. It was impossible in all of the chaos and darkness to know who was firing what, and who was under attack. It appeared that either the Amal or the Druze militias had targeted a Lebanese Army post right up the street from Checkpoint 76. The pro-American Lebanese forces had an old Saladdin tank that occasionally opened fire with little success. The tank became a magnet for mortar fire that was landing too close to his Marines who were now in a life-or-death gun battle.

The first mortar shell hit the Pepsi plant up the street from Cox and men. Another blast erupted about thirty seconds later. After the second explosion, Dobson grew queasy when he understood the enemy's strategy: They were "bracketing" their shots until they finally hit the Marines.

A third mortar shell hit with a loud explosion. Flames erupted from Cox's direction. Dobson tried raising Wheeler on the company radio, but it was dead. Dobson scrambled to form a rescue party to see what had had happened. Several Marines set out in an armored vehicle and fought their way through the streets in an effort to save their comrades.

But it was too late. The single lucky hit obliterated Checkpoint 76. Wheeler awoke to yelling and the smell of burning sulfur and flesh. Cox lay at his feet, curled up as though he were asleep.

"Sergeant Cox, could you move?" Wheeler asked, grinding his teeth from the stabbing pain in one of his legs. "Sergeant Cox, I'm hit. I need to straighten my leg."

Another Marine, Raul Heugas, had shrapnel wounds but was trying to help a comrade hang on. Only now did Wheeler notice that he was sitting in a pool of blood—his own and that of Cox. His brave squad leader was dead.

Since he couldn't help his sergeant, Wheeler pulled a tourniquet from his shirt and tried to tie it around his leg to stop the bleeding. His hands were shaking, though. He heard screams of agony, and realized they were his own. He knew from his training that he must be going into shock, and shouted to Heugas, "Bring me your belt!"

Huegas, who appeared to be one of the only other survivors in the smoking bunker, took off his belt and tossed it to Wheeler. He twisted it around his leg and, remembering his boot camp training, used his rifle to turn this battlefield tourniquet. It worked, and he staunched the flow of blood.

All Wheeler could do now was wait for someone to come and get them. He leaned back and gazed out the window. He thought he could see the nearby Lebanese soldiers looking up at the smoldering ruins. They did nothing to come to the aid of their American allies. Indeed, some ran for cover as the shelling continued. Until now, Wheeler had tried not think ill of the Lebanese, his supposed allies whose government the Marines were trying to rescue. But watching them scurry away, Wheeler felt like grabbing his rifle and picking them off. No one would ever know the difference.

There was something worse than his rage, though. As the pain in his leg became unbearable, Wheeler struggled with the desire to shoot himself. It would put him out of his misery. He could avoid living as a cripple with a shattered leg.

But his brush with suicide was interrupted by the Marines' rescue party.

It was a grizzly sight: six men dead, including Sergeant Cox, and some blown apart. Two other Marines suffered mortal wounds and died on the way to the hospital. Eight Marines in all died that night at Checkpoint 76—the most casualties since the October 23 barracks bombing.

Besides Cox, there was Shannon D. Biddle, Sam Cherman, David L. Daugherty, Thomas A. Evans, J. T. Hattaway, Todd A. Kraft, and Marvin H. Perkins. They were all young men in their late teens or early twenties. Raul Heugas and Skip Wheeler were wounded but made it out alive.

As he was lifted into an armored vehicle outside, Wheeler could see the store owner's boys staring wide-eyed from the first floor window. He had forgotten the children downstairs. How had they endured the hellish night? And what kind of future did they have in such a merciless land?

The pain in his leg was excruciating, and he had a deep thirst. Wheeler reached for a canteen of Kool-Aid mixed earlier in the day. But the corpsman on the scene, Doc Hooper, stopped him.

"Nothing to drink," he said. "Not before surgery."

Wheeler nodded and stifled his urge to scream. The boys from downstairs were watching his every move. He didn't want to scare them.

Instead, he managed to call out, "*Marahaba.*"

The boys waved and returned the greeting. "*Marahaba, Marine*," they yelled back. "*Marahaba.*"

News of the deaths of eight more Marines spread through Beirut, then to the United States, renewing the debate in Congress about the human cost of America's military "presence" in Lebanon.

The next morning, Lieutenant Colonel Smith could see Dobson, normally so stoic, was shaken by the loss of so many men. Still, he had to ask, "Why were so many guys up on that roof at one time, Bob?"

It happened without his knowledge, during the heat of the gun battle, Dobson explained. "Cox's squad wanted to fight, so they all rushed up there to join him. Maybe he could have kept some of them down, but I doubt it."

Smith nodded quietly. He knew Dobson was a straight shooter and had no reason to doubt his explanation. He didn't tell the captain that the loss of American lives had prompted a major investigation and there was bound to be lots of second-guessing.

General Joy spent all night drafting a "flash report" that he sent to European Command in Stuttgart, then on to the Pentagon, White House, and other security and military officials, describing a "direct hit by large caliber incoming."

After sending his top secret cable, Joy lay down around five in the morning. But he was soon awakened by a voice on a secure radio linked to Stuttgart. Normally, a radio operator would stay on to maintain the link, but a stern voice told the operator to get off the line. "I want to talk alone."

It was Ernie Cook, a Marine brigadier general assigned to the European Command. When they were alone on the radio, he asked, "What happened?"

Joy shook the cobwebs out of his head and gave Cook a blow-by-blow account of the firefight that preceded the fatal mortar round.

Well, Cook said, it was front-page news now—on all the radio and TV networks. His bosses were demanding answers. "There's talk of relieving you and Lieutenant Colonel Smith," he said. "They're going to be after your head."

Cook told him he was preparing for a morning briefing and needed answers. Joy masked his annoyance, though he felt too damn tired to care much about the second-guessing in the European Command. Though Beirut allegedly fell under their control, the Air Force and Army officers above Joy on the chain of command rarely visited Beirut. And when they did, they tried to get in and out on the same day, avoiding the escalating firefights at night.

Joy was satisfied that Smith's men had just been doing their job on the front line of Beirut. If they got a little zealous, well, they were Marines. And this was a war, even if nobody in Washington had the guts to call it that.

"It was a lucky hit," he told Cook. "Read my report."

"Okay, Jim," Cook said. "Hang in there."

Joy turned over and dozed off. But he was soon reawakened by a call from Marine Commandant P. X. Kelley. He sat up on his cot and ran through the events of December 4. The Commandant, still hurting from the barracks bombing, told Joy he had his full confidence. There would be no investigation on his end.

"You just keep marching," Kelley said. "Nobody here's lost confidence in you."

But if the outside scrutiny was bad, the self-examination was even worse. Dobson sat alone in his bunker, replaying over and over the last seconds of Manny Cox and his squad. He could still hear the sound of the mortars "walking in" toward Checkpoint 76. *Why* hadn't he seen it coming, Dobson asked himself. Could he have launched a counterstrike to take out the enemy mortars before they scored their lucky, and deadly, shot?

Some men react to grief by exploding outward, releasing their rage and then moving on. Dobson retreated inside himself, becoming numb from sorrow and doubt.

Since he couldn't sleep all night, he started writing the families of the lost Marines. It was especially hard to write Evi Cox, who was alone in New Jersey with her newborn son. It took nearly a week to finish, but he finally sent her a letter dated December 10, 1983:

> Your husband, Sergeant Manuel Cox, was a good man and a fine Marine. He was respected by his peers, seniors, and subordinates. The Marines of this battalion will miss him greatly. . . . Sergeant Cox was what every Marine should aspire to become. He was a loyal warrior, dedicated to his men and devoted to his family. I witnessed the personal turmoil he went through when you notified him of possible trouble at home. He was torn between his love for you and the children and the fact that without him, the men in his squad, who faced danger daily, might need that special brand of leadership that he could give them.
>
> The fact that he chose to stay reflects greatly upon his reliance and faith in your personal strength to bring the family through troubled times. Your strength is being tested again and I'm sure that his faith in you is justified and you will bring the family through—together. If it is any consolation, your husband died on the field of battle. He was with men he loved and trusted and they died instantly with no pain. From talking to him earlier that afternoon, smoking cigars celebrating the birth of your newest son, Anthony, I know he died with the thought of his family foremost in his mind.
>
> Your husband was a great human being and our memories will hold that greatness.
>
> Very Respectfully,
> R. K. Dobson
> Commanding Officer, Golf Company 2/8

He was right about Evi's strength being tested. After losing Manny, she fought a long, lonely battle with grief and postpartum depression as she tried to care for her child. When she learned that her husband was being posthumously awarded the Bronze Star with Combat "V," it didn't seem to matter. She would trade a million medals to have one more day with her tender, violin-playing husband.

Even a letter from the White House took years to bear much meaning—and even then only because it was something to pass along to a son who would never know his father.

> There is a saying that I've often heard about the arrival of a newborn. It goes something like: the birth of a child is God's reminder that He wants life to go on. One day, Anthony will ask you many questions about his father. Let him know that Sergeant Manuel A. Cox was a hero who made the ultimate sacrifice so that a life of peace and freedom would go on for his son and his son's generation. Let him know it was his father and mother who come to mind when I think about the greatness of the American people, who brought tears of sorrow and appreciation to the President and to all his fellow countrymen.
>
> Sincerely,
> Ronald Reagan

In less than a week after the deaths, the early threats of an official investigation faded away. But that didn't stop regular visits from the European Command, along with a steady stream of politicians and government officials eager to bring their collective brain power to Beirut. Sometimes Smith didn't know which was worse, battling drunken Shiites or trying to hold his temper around smug generals. He viewed the visits from the Eucom headquarters as part of a CYA (cover-your-ass) mentality by Army and

Air Force brass, pointing a finger at ground commanders for anything *they* did wrong should the fighting bring more casualties.
Smith also suspected many of the generals were "Marine haters," a
long tradition in American military circles. The same interservice
animus that he witnessed off the coast of Grenada with Gen. Norman Schwarzkopf was resurfacing on the battlefields of Beirut.
He'd held his temper with Schwarzkopf, but after losing Cox and
his men, he wasn't so sure he could control himself.

It happened during an Army general's visit to the Marine
guards at the British Embassy. The American Embassy had been
bombed earlier in the year, so the British were sharing their compound with the U.S. delegation. The Marines built protective
bunkers, but because of limited space, some of their guards had
to sleep inside the British compound. Smith was touring the area
with an Army general who asked about a possible repeat of the
barracks bombing, when so many Marines had died in their sleep
inside a compound. Some of the exterior walls appeared especially vulnerable to a car or truck bombing.

"You're right, sir," Smith said, "but there's nothing we can do
right now. The Brits don't have enough room for us to build
more bunkers."

This sparked a running argument about security precautions
that continued throughout the general's tour of the American
zone in Beirut. Smith didn't mind answering tough questions, but
in the course of the day, he began to bristle at the tone the general took with the Marines on the front lines—men who were
under fire nightly but couldn't actively pursue the enemy because
of fat cat generals like this who failed to push for tougher rules of
engagement.

Things came to a head as they walked near Beirut International Airport, and the general criticized the location of Smith's
reconnaissance platoon position.

"It shouldn't be here, it should be on slightly higher ground,"
the general said, pointing into the distance.

"It is a better piece of ground," the lieutenant colonel agreed,
"but if we move them up there, we can't cover them with small
arms fire." He was making the best of some bad options, Smith

explained, using jeeps armed with machine guns and missiles to patrol a large area at night.

The general didn't let up, though, and kept chewing him out in the presence of several junior officers and General Joy. Finally, Ray kicked a rock that went skittering over the hard, sun-scorched ground.

"Let's go up here where you want me to build this position," Smith said with unmasked sarcasm, his blue eyes ablaze. "I want *you* to mark the spot where you want me to build this position— and then I'm going to build that position. And I'm going to put a sign up on this position . . ."

Some of the junior officers started to smile, because they could see where "E-Tool" was heading. They turned away from the general to cover their grins. They knew that Smith, a mere lieutenant colonel, was way out of line with the brass, but there was no stopping him.

Gen. Jim Joy was also on the tour, and he knew that stopping Ray would be like trying to stop a bull at Pamplona.

". . . and the sign will say this is the general's own memorial recon position," Smith continued, "because the Marine commander didn't want it here."

The Army general was enraged, shouting, "I'll have you court-martialed, I'll have you court-martialed!"

Joy took Smith by the arm and led him away. "C'mon, Ray," he said. "Let's cool off."

Joy spent the rest of the day keeping Smith and the general apart. He managed to convince his Army counterpart that the outburst was understandable, given the loss of Sergeant Cox and his squad. He'd lost some good men and took it personally, Joy said. The general cooled down and didn't bring disciplinary charges against the insolent Marine. And Ray didn't move the recon post.

★ ★ ★

The assaults on the Marines continued. Less than a week after Cox's squad was hit, Matt Aylward's platoon took heavy fire again, this time with a wave of rocket-propelled grenades. The Amal had taken up positions behind an abandoned bulldozer in front of the slums. "Get the dragon," Sergeant Leiphart barked.

Matt Collins already had a successful shot with the antitank weapon a few weeks earlier, so this time he offered to let the other Dragon gunner take aim. But in the face of withering fire, the other lance corporal wouldn't budge from behind the sandbag wall.

Collins couldn't believe his eyes. This was the Marine's one chance to show some balls, but now he was lying on the ground, practically in tears. Matt tried shaming him into to acting like a Marine, grabbing his belt and shouting, "Get your ass up and take your shot. Take that bulldozer out!"

But the kid was frozen in fear. Muttering in disgust, Collins grabbed the Dragon and took aim. "Back blast area all secure," he hollered, a warning to avoid the weapon's backfire.

Keeping the target in his crosshairs, he took aim in the high-powered scope and slowly pulled the trigger. The missile shot across the field and struck the front blade of the bulldozer. The front end collapsed and melted into the sand. Several men appeared to have been killed; the Amal raced around with wheelbarrows collecting their dead and wounded.

The Shiites finally seemed to understand the Marines were adopting a tougher stance when anyone opened fire on their positions. The next day, a militia leader waved a white flag and called for a meeting in the middle of the field separating Golf Company from Hooterville. Dobson warily walked out to meet them.

Through a Marine interpreter, an Amal fighter complained, "Why have the Americans changed rules of engagement? Before, we fire rifle, they fire rifle; we fire main gun, you fire main gun; now we fire rifle, you guys shoot all kinds of things."

Dobson told his interpreter: "You tell him the rules have changed. And if they ever think about killing an American again, I'll kill 'em. You tell them exactly that. I'll hunt them down and kill them."

Upon hearing this, the Shiite fighter shook his head and walked back to the slums, ready to start the fighting again. These

Marines just didn't seem to get the subtleties of Middle Eastern diplomacy.

★ ★ ★

On Christmas, the Navy chaplains dressed up like Santa Claus and handed out gifts to the Marines in the bunkers. There was talk of pulling out of Beirut, even though President Reagan publicly kept expressing confidence in the Marines.

But from Jim Joy on down to Joe Hickey, writing his father back in the White House, whatever "presence" and stability the Marines were providing seemed to be pointless. The factions would keep fighting, and the Marines—along with the French and Italians—would just keep paying the price of this foreign entanglement.

Such was the case on the morning of January 31, 1984, when several Shiites with rifles and red scarves on their heads were spotted on a rooftop. They seemed to be agitated, and one shouted in Arabic about a spotlight the Marines had shot out. One brandished an AK-47.

Aylward kept watch and told his snipers to keep the rifleman in their crosshairs. "If he fires on us, take him out," he said. When the Amal soldier aimed at the Marines, the snipers shot him, and he tumbled to the ground.

Within seconds, the Marines came under fire from up to a dozen other buildings in Hooterville. The ruckus on the roof had been the Amal's way of signaling an assault on the Americans. The battle lasted for hours, and required so much ammo that Leiphart had to dash over to battalion headquarters to plead for more.

"Tighten up," the supply chief replied, unsympathetically. "It takes three days to order and receive more ammo."

Leiphart cursed under his breath. Even when you're under fire, some guys in the back lines could be stingy with ammo. When he returned to the platoon, the sun was setting below Hooterville's crazy quilt of abandoned apartments, stores, and warehouses. Shadows started creeping across the field dividing the two sides, like ghosts rising from the tattered ground.

Matt Collins was returning to his platoon's command post when he heard a cracking sound like a bullwhip. Was the lieutenant hit? Aylward seemed to stagger above him in the Kool-Aid stand.

Collins ran up the wooden stairs, shouting, "The lieutenant's been hit."

But another Marine in the command post seemed agitated. Lance Corp. George Dramas was making a strange gesture, swatting at his chest like he'd been stung by a bee. Dramas turned and looked beseechingly at Collins—then sagged against him. Helping his best buddy down the steps, Collins gently laid him on the ground. Opening the bullet-proof vest, he saw a tiny hole in the middle of Dramas' chest.

"Corpsman!" Collins called.

Dramas was a good kid from Massachusetts, a messenger and a radio operator. He was hot and sweaty from a day of fighting, and had just loosened his flak jacket. In that moment, though, a bullet zipped through a crease in the sandbags around the Kool Aid stand.

Surely, the kid would live, Collins thought. All the Marines knew they would be going home soon as President Reagan wanted to get them out of Beirut. They couldn't leave young Georgie Dramas behind. But the bullet had pierced his heart, and he was gone.

When Aylward saw what had happened, he was furious. He ran down the wooden steps of his command post, picked up Dramas's M-16 and started firing wildly at the Amal. He shot three magazines worth of bullets, exposing himself to enemy fire. He'd had enough of this worthless country and was ready to go down in a blaze of anger.

Leiphart could see his lieutenant had let his emotions get the better of him and rushed down to stop him while Collins laid down some covering fire from above.

"Okay now, lieutenant," Leiphart said soothingly, "we still have thirty-four Marines to worry about."

Aylward looked around, as though coming out of a bad dream. Beirut had finally gotten the better of him, dragging him down to its level of blood rage. Of course Leiphart was right. He threw down the smoking M-16 and set to work taking care of Dramas's body, and writing his mother back in the States.

★ ★ ★

On February 7, General Joy was listening to a short-wave radio broadcast of the BBC. President Reagan had informed the governments of Great Britain, France, and Italy that the U.S. was going to withdraw its forces from Lebanon. This was news to the highest ranking Marine on the ground.[1] Reagan, for all his public pronouncements to the country, had reluctantly agreed that a "redeployment" was necessary. American officials did not officially call it an evacuation or retreat, but one security official admitted, "Redeployment equals failure and retreat with our tail between our legs."[2]

Yet Smith and his men were hardly cowed as they packed up to resume their Med float. Preparing to retreat from the fractured city, they wanted to make sure they made a clean break, leaving behind as little as possible for the Amal militiamen who would swoop into their bunkers. Each platoon did what it could to erase their presence from Lebanon. Leiphart ordered his men to burn everything they could—from electrical generators to typewriters to pallets of meals ready to eat (MREs).

The Marines also burned any letters or packages from home because the Amal and affiliated groups had threatened to send letter bombs to the Americans' home addresses.

Despite the attempted cleanup, the Marines left more than 1 million filled sandbags in Beirut, and plenty of deep fighting holes, according to Marine historian Benis Frank. More importantly, they had lost 238 Marines, with 151 wounded over the eighteen-month-long engagement. No official count was made of the lost Amal, Druze, and Lebanese forces, but the death toll was thought to be in the thousands.

The Marines left Beirut International Airport with mixed emotions. They were glad to be getting back aboard ship, but were dis-

appointed by the lack of a clear victory—especially with the bloodshed in Lebanon. Still, they knew that public sentiment was strong
back home and that the BLT 2/8 had made the best of a bad situation.

"We didn't feel like we tucked our tails between our legs," Ray
Smith said. "We felt like we accounted of ourselves well in the firefights, and when we withdrew, we took everything out. We didn't
flee and leave our shit on shore. We cleaned up the mess, and did
everything as right as you could do it."

With the TV cameras rolling, Smith ordered a color guard to
raise the Stars and Stripes along with the Marines' own battle colors and streamers. The 2/8 Marines marched purposefully onto
the ramp of the landing craft as if to say, *We are not cowed. We are
leaving Beirut on our own terms. We might be back.*

One final incident helped lighten the moment for the weary
troops. As they marched toward the landing craft waiting on the
beach, someone realized a staff sergeant was missing. He had
been carrying his company's guidon. Looking behind them for
signs of the sergeant, the Marines could see the Amal had already
raised their green flags as a sign of occupation.

Then a solitary figure came trudging across the airport tarmac—the delinquent sergeant, bearing the flag like some hung-
over knight who drank too much mead at the inn. When he
arrived, the sergeant sheepishly explained that he had overslept.
He woke up to see a tall, bearded militiaman who nudged his
boot and said in English, "Your friends are gone."

EIGHTEEN

Shades of Gray

To most Americans, the public face of the Marine Corps in the 1980s wasn't Ray Smith, Jim Jones, or Marty Steele. That dubious distinction fell to an earnest-looking lieutenant colonel with a raspy voice, a Clark Kent curl of hair on his forehead, and the boyish habit of winking to win you over to his side:

Oliver North.

North, a contemporary of our trio of Marines, was on the White House staff when he became a central figure in the Reagan Administration's Byzantine plot to try to win the release of six American hostages held by Lebanese terrorists with links to Iran.[1] North's arms dealing to Tehran generated up to $30 million in secret profits that were then diverted to support Nicaragua's Contra rebels in their battle against the communist Sandinistas.

The arms-for-hostages deal, as it became known, sent shockwaves through the Reagan Administration and Congress. But for many veteran Marines, the most galling element of the scandal wasn't the back-door dealings of missiles and bombs to the government of Ayatollah Khomeini. No, they knew that in the shadowy world of despots and deal-making, such things happened. For Marines like Jim Jones, who wanted to see the honor of the service kept out of politics, the worst part of the scandal was watching North testify before Congress in his green Marine Corps uniform in the middle of the summer of 1987.

North was clearly using his uniform—usually left in the closet while he worked in the halls of political power—to project the image of a super-patriot. It was the kind of costume change that may have played well in front of the TV cameras, but one that got bad reviews from some of his colleagues.

In an interview with Robert Timberg, a former Marine and author of *The Nightingale's Song,* Jones described the career climber he met in 1974, when he served with North on Okinawa. "It's generally accepted that Ollie carved out the jobs he wanted—high-visibility, low-risk, high-reward possibilities."[2]

Behind this public face of the Marine Corps, though, there was another face, and personality, that meant more to the average Marine: Al Gray.

Gray had a rugged look, slightly alligator-like, with a raspy voice and accent that showed his roots in the blue collar streets of New Jersey. Smith knew Gray when he commanded the 2nd Marine Division and preached the tenets of maneuver warfare. Smith had toasted Gray before the Marines in Italy, and knew Gray had done everything for the 2/8 while it was under fire in Beirut. Al Gray was known for his personal touch and his personal punches: many Marines to this day tell stories about meeting Al Gray and, before they finished saying hello, getting punched in their arms by the crusty general asking, "How's it going, Marine?"

Marty Steele, for his part, got to know Gray during maneuvers with tank battalions in the high desert of California in the mid 1980s.

Al Gray was the über-Marine, a "mustang" who had risen to the officer ranks after starting as a grunt during the Korean War. At a time when the Marines needed to remember their roots—far from the phony gestures of Oliver North—Al Gray was the real deal.

Yet Jones, for all of his assignments around Washington, had never met General Gray. This would change, but only, ironically

enough, after Jones was sent for a tour on the West Coast with the
1st Marine Division. In 1985, Lt. Col. Jim Jones took over as commander of the 3rd Battalion, 9th Marines, at Camp Pendleton.
Both professionally and personally, living in southern California
was enormously satisfying—spending time on the beach with his
four kids and sitting with Diane on the patio of their home at San
Juan Capistrano, watching the sun set over the Pacific.

Even as he sipped a glass of wine and pondered his future,
Jones—in his forties now—could see that it might be time to
retire. After two years at the battalion's helm, including a six-
month deployment in the western Pacific, he'd learned that his
next job would be as one of the 1st Division's logistics officers. Not
much appeal there, and the Joneses would remain far from their
family and friends back East.

"I think it's time to do something else," he told Diane. Jones
celebrated his twentieth year in the Marines in 1987, which meant
he could soon retire with full benefits. It was also a time when the
national economy was booming (before that fall's stock market
collapse). Many former Marines were pulling in six or seven figure
salaries in corporate jobs in New York, Washington, and Los Angeles. This cadre of successful capitalists often made lucrative job
offers to their friend, Jim Jones, who at age forty-five started thinking that it might be time to move on. He well might have made a
move toward the corporate boardroom if he had not been home
to pick up the phone one Sunday morning that June.

It was Al Gray, freshly picked to be the new Commandant.
"Jim, I want you to consider coming back to Washington to be my
aide," he said. "You've got a great track record here and the Corps
can use you. *I* can use you."

"Thank you, sir," Jones said, his mind racing. How had this
happened? Hadn't he done his time in Washington? Hadn't he
shaken every hand in the Senate and House of Representatives on
behalf of the dear old Corps? Was this his reward, to get called
back to D.C.? After he had escaped the tentacles of power and
politics, why was the Marine leadership yanking him back East? If
anything, he needed to stay out in the fleet, commanding troops,
preferably. Besides, hadn't he just committed himself to retire?

The answer to his questions could be found in Gray's unexpected rise to prominence, and his immediate need for seasoned officers to help him navigate the rocky shoals of Congress and the Pentagon.

Gray, fifty-eight, was the surprise pick to be the Corps' twenty-eighth Commandant. As commander of Fleet Marine Force Atlantic, the three-star general who had worked his way up from private already had submitted his request to retire when he got the call from Navy Secretary Jim Webb. There were a number of other generals ahead of Gray on everyone's short list for Commandant, but not on the only list that counted—Webb's. A noted author and former Marine rifle company commander in Vietnam, Webb urgently wanted to inject a healthy dose of testosterone into the training and attitude of the new Marine Corps.

In *Making the Corps*, Thomas E. Ricks says that Webb saw Gray as a kind of blue-collar Commandant, one who cared more about the grunts in the field than senators in Washington. Gray "struck Webb as the general most likely to 'make Marines feel like the Marines again,'" Ricks wrote. In that vein, Webb set up a secret meeting in Jacksonville, Florida, to ask him to become Commandant.[3]

Al Gray—outspoken, forward-thinking, and gruff, with no time for parlor games—was an outsider who fit Webb's agenda to clean house inside the Corps. It was easy to underestimate the rough-and-ready, tobacco-chewing ex-sergeant. Beneath his redneck exterior, Gray had a shrewd mind shaped by years of working as an intelligence liaison with the CIA and the National Security Agency. After serving as a special operations officer in Vietnam in the early 1960s during the Kennedy administration, he later had a front-row seat on the chaotic pullout of American forces in 1975, directing the placement of demolition charges in the defense attaché's office at Tan Son Nhut Airport.[4]

Whether he was commanding Marine ground troops in Vietnam or serving in delicate staff jobs in Washington, Gray learned to make the best of his humble origins. He developed a Jimmy Cagney persona that kept more educated officers off balance, and charmed leaders like Webb who were looking for Marines reminiscent of Chesty Puller.

Indeed, Webb held his own special appeal to the Marines, especially those who were tired of being portrayed in film and books as psychotic baby killers in Vietnam. In his 1978 novel, *Fields of Fire*, he showed the infantry Marines were neglected heroes, a generation of inner-city and rural kids "at the end of the pipeline" who served their country rather than avoid the war through draft deferments.

In the novel's climactic antiwar rally, where a North Vietnamese flag was flying, Webb's protagonist, Goodrich, rips into the crowd.

"Look at yourselves," he shouts. "And the flag. Jesus Christ. Ho Chi Minh is gonna win. How many of you are going to get hurt in Vietnam? I didn't see any of you in Vietnam. I saw dudes, man, dudes. I didn't see you. Where were you?"[5]

Al Gray was not exactly a street dude, but Webb saw in him a veteran leader who could help the Corps regain its focus, footing, and above all, its "first to fight" esprit de corps.

During Ray Smith's time with the 2nd Marine Division in the early 1980s, he had seen Al Gray as the spiritual guru, chief cheerleader, and—when men died—the kindly uncle who came to funerals, including that of Sgt. Manny Cox when Evi laid him to rest in New Jersey.

Marty Steele knew Gray from many desert warfare exercises. The general's innovative ideas and enthusiasm helped Steele gain support for his own passion—improving the element of surprise for tanks and armored vehicles in combat.

Despite Gray's extensive experience, some Washington insiders questioned his ability to handle the more delicate parts of the job. Could he testify before Congress without alienating powerful senators and congressman who controlled the military purse? Could he work with the Joint Chiefs of Staff? Could he apply a little spit and polish to his tobacco-spitting image, or would Washington's power brokers chew up and spit out Al Gray?

One of Gray's advisers, then Brig. Gen. Jack Sheehan, knew just the guy to be the Commandant's Senior Aide-de-Camp: Jim Jones.

As he considered Gray's out-of-the-blue offer, Jones knew that the Commandant was right. He could help him avoid the political depth charges along the Potomac. In so doing, Jones felt in his heart that he would be helping the Marine Corps. Without further ado, Jones heard himself saying, "I accept, sir."

After hanging up, he looked down at his wife, her big brown eyes open with wonder and consternation. Only then did he realize he had failed to discuss this life-changing decision with Diane. "I guess I'm not retiring," he said with a shrug.

After taking command in mid 1987, Gray promptly started a series of initiatives to bring back the Marines' "warrior" focus. "Everyone is going to be a rifleman," he declared, and he set to work on improving the Corps' combat readiness and toughness. This included an element of intellectual rigor. Beneath his blue collar façade, Gray was an avid reader. He immediately decreed that all Marines should hit the books about history, military tactics, and the best practices in business. He issued a reading list that included works about America's blunders in Vietnam, such as Neil Sheehan's *Bright and Shining Lie* and *How We Won the War* by General Giap, the North Vietnamese military commander. Book sales boomed like never before at the base bookstores from Quantico to Okinawa as everyone scrambled to do the Commandant's homework.

There was a method to Al Gray's madness, of course: He was leading the Corps in peacetime the way he wanted it to fight in war—that is, fighting smart as well as tough. The same principle applied to the Marines' survival in the ongoing trench warfare of Washington, D.C. Each armed service must protect its flanks and focus on winning key battles. To do that, he needed smart tacticians like Lt. Col. Jim Jones.

"The reason I asked him to be my aide was that I really wanted a senior, polished special assistant," Gray explained. "I wanted to get back to the warrior focus, and I knew Jim would understand that."

Some generals use aides as personal assistants and hat carriers, relegating them to carrying out orders with little leeway. But this was not Al Gray's style. "I really turned him loose," he said of Jones. "I made sure he knew my position on certain things, then I let him carry it anywhere he wanted."

Gray's first mission was to do some fence-mending on Capitol Hill. The Marine Corps had never fully recovered from the blow to its pride in the wake of the Beirut barracks bombing. Much of the blame had fallen on the shoulders of Gen. P. X. Kelley, who actually was out of the direct chain of command. As Robert Timberg described it in *The Nightingale's Song,* "Even so, a Marine Commandant denying responsibility when so many of his troops had been killed, was unthinkable. What rankled many was the fact that he maintained that an attack of that magnitude could not have been foreseen and that the Marines had done everything reasonable to prepare their defensive perimeter."[6]

There had been other public embarrassments in the mid 1980s, such as a sex scandal involving a Marine embassy guard in Moscow. So Gray, who many assumed lacked the nuance to effectively lobby Congress, set out to do just that. By his own estimate, he personally visited 90 percent of the members of the Senate and about a third of the 435 members of the House of Representatives. And he sent out a cadre of close aides, including Jim Jones, to lobby the rest.

✯ ✯ ✯

Little had changed in Washington since Jones left in 1985 during the first term of Ronald Reagan. The Iran-Contra affair was brewing, but despite Lt. Col. Ollie North's involvement, this was a problem for the White House, not the Marine Corps.

On the plus side, the Marines had a new supporter in Congress, John McCain, who had been elected as a Republican from Arizona.

Jones knew most of the heavyweights Al Gray wanted to keep on his side to secure enough money to improve the Corps' training, equipment, and education. He reconnected with Sen. John

Tower of Texas, the powerful chairman of the Senate Armed Services Committee, and with other key senators and their staffs, among them Sam Nunn, John Chafee, and John Glenn. He renewed his friendships with the younger leaders like Gary Hart and Bill Cohen.

Jones's people skills were reminiscent of a figure who helped shape the republic: Benjamin Franklin, "the consummate networker," who, as Walter Isaacon put it, understood "the American principle that it pays to be liked."[7]

Many of Jones's friendships had been forged on the earlier trips with congressional delegations—the "codels." While critics in the press sometimes lambasted the taxpayer-funded forays as junkets, the travels abroad did have one redeeming quality: They got the politicians out of their chambers in Washington and put them face to face with some of the world's toughest foreign leaders and situations. Sometimes, the trips even gave them a taste of the dangers that Marines like Jones often took for granted.

Bill Cohen in particular relished telling the story of an earlier trip with Gary Hart and Jones to El Salvador to visit a mountain village that had been attacked by rebel troops backed by the communists of neighboring Nicaragua. As they rode in a helicopter outside of San Salvador, Cohen sat stoically in the front wearing headphones that allowed him to hear the pilot's chatter with his ground controller. Hart and Jones sat in the back, looking out the windows.

Cohen listened with growing alarm as the pilot complained about the strong winds buffeting the chopper as they rose through the clouds above the lush green mountains.

Then the pilot exclaimed, "Damn, we're losing fluid fast." With that, the pilot pulled out a manual and started flipping pages. A look of panic crossed his face as he radioed, "I'm going to park this—now!"

For some reason, though, the pilot kept climbing—much to Cohen's chagrin. If they were going to crash, wouldn't it be better to do so at a lower altitude? And why was the pilot reading a manual?

"Why are we going so high?" Cohen called to Jones over the roar of the engine.

"Probably to get out of range of any small arms fire," Jones shot back.

What? Cohen thought to himself. Nobody had warned him about this before they left on this fact-finding trip. But Jones sounded so cool and untroubled by it all that Cohen was able to stifle his own fears. In the end, they landed safely in the mountain village, no worse for the wear and, at least for Cohen, with a new-found sense of flying into a war zone.

A subsequent trip to the region proved equally dicey, and further tightened the bonds between the senators and their Marine escort. In 1984, as Gary Hart contemplated a run for the Democratic presidential nomination, he traveled with Cohen and Jones again—this time on an unmarked jet. The destination was Managua, Nicaragua, where they were to meet with Daniel Ortega, who had recently been elected president of Nicaragua. The leftist Sandinistas were opposed by the Reagan Administration, which was providing clandestine financial and military support to the Contra rebels. As the American jet prepared to land, the pilot received an urgent order to abort his landing. The airport was under attack from Contras.

The Americans diverted to Honduras, where the jet's nose landing gear broke upon touching down. No one was hurt. As they got out of their damaged aircraft, wondering whether they were jinxed every time they flew in this region, Cohen and Hart got word from the American ambassador in Managua that the rebel attack on the airport was over. They should come back and dine with Daniel Ortega after all.

So the adventurous senators secured another plane from the CIA and landed that evening at Managua's airport. It was bedlam. TV crews and newspaper reporters and photographers greeted what was supposed to be a low-profile visit by the congressional party. But coming on the heels of the rebel attack only hours before, the Americans' visit became a big news story in Central America.

As their CIA jet taxied up to the terminal, Cohen looked out the window at the burning wreckage of a twin-engine Cessna shot down by the Sandinistas. Ortega's troops found a suitcase filled with cash, documents, and bills of lading showing the pilots had flown from Miami—more "proof," they would claim, of America's clandestine war against the freely elected government of Nicaragua.

As soon as they stepped onto the tarmac, the senators blinked into bright lights and flashing cameras and faced a pack of reporters eager to know whether the Cessna was part of a CIA operation. Cohen shrugged and said, "Look, the CIA would not be trying to bomb you in a twin-engine Cessna." To Jim Jones, the whole affair looked like a staged event one would expect to see in a second rate spy movie.

There was nothing more to say, so they jumped into a government car and were whisked across the city to Ortega's home. One of the dinner guests was enchanting, dark-eyed Nora Astorga, the Sandinista Deputy Foreign Minister. The CIA had briefed the delegation about the legendary figure known as "the Spider Lady": Astorga was the mistress of General "the Dog" Vega, who drew his nickname from his cruel treatment and torture of enemies of the previous regime of General Somoza. But Astorga led a double life, working for the underground as a kind of Mata Hari of the Sandinista Revolution. According to legend, she slept with the Dog to set him up for arrest and execution—right in her bedroom.

As they took their seats around an elaborate dinner table in Ortega's candlelit dining room, Jones noticed that Hart had been assigned to sit beside the femme fatale. "The word's out, senator," Jones whispered. "She has a crush on you." It was all Hart could do not to spit out his drink from laughing.

With such personal experiences under his belt, it didn't surprise Washington insiders to see Al Gray beckon Jim Jones back to Washington to put his talents to use. There was plenty of work to do. With the fervor of a new president, Gray proposed a series of initiatives to upgrade the Marine Corps. One of the first was to secure funds for a new library at Quantico to promote more innovative thinking and research. Congress promptly approved $10 million for the Advanced Amphibious Research Center, which was later named for Gray.

Out in the field, the new Commandant made it a point to visit units on the West Coast, who sometimes felt ignored by their commanders back East.

"The message was the same," Gray said, "we're going to be warriors." The Marine Corps overhauled its recruiting efforts to get the best and brightest young men and women who wanted to test their mettle in the Corps. It was the same appeal that had drawn the boys of 1967 into the Basic School, but with some new twists. Hand-to-hand combat was reemphasized, but so were the martial arts. "We're warriors," Gray said at his change of command at 8th & I.[8] "Some people don't like to hear about war—people who fight don't like to have to do it, but that's what we're about."

Al Gray's words sounded as sweet as a bugle to guys like Ray Smith, who had been hamstrung by the internal politics of his Beirut assignment, and Marty Steele, who wanted to push ahead with maneuver warfare for tanks.

Like many colorful leaders, though, Gray had his idiosyncrasies, which could rival those of the last Marine to inspire such devotion: Chesty Puller. Both men inspired love and fear for what they might do in the heat of the moment. In polite Washington circles—where senior officers tried to observe social decorum and smooth the rough edges of the rifleman—Gray could be a bull in a china closet. He was direct, outspoken, and occasionally profane. He became known for chewing tobacco and using a mess kit as his spittoon. His John Wayne style played great with the troops—who prized Gray as one of their own—but it sometimes clashed with the ladies and gentlemen of the nation's capital.

"My theory is very simple," Gray later explained. "What you see is what you get." In political terms, his approach was to tell members of Congress what the Marine Corps needed, "then you, Mr.

Congressman, as the representative of the nation, you'll give us what you give us."

Gray carried his facts, and much of his agenda, in his heart and his head. In four years of congressional testimony, he claimed to never have consulted a note. He also disdained much of the paperwork that most senior military commanders rely on to keep track of their daily decisions, edicts, and policies.

Jim Jones soon discovered the limits of General Gray's shoot-from-the-hip management style. The job of Commandant in the modern era requires a unique set of skills, combining the decisiveness of a corporate CEO with the wisdom of a Supreme Court judge. Everything from budget planning to making the final decision on legal matters comes across his desk—and presents a unique juggling act of paperwork, phone calls, and meetings that can challenge the most organized leader. Al Gray was organized, no question about it, but often he kept his organization inside his own head. As a result, Jones soon started hearing from senior commanders who couldn't get the Commandant to return letters or phone calls. Pressing matters started getting lost in a black, or gray, hole.

"General Gray didn't read informational things," recalled Peter M. Murphy, the longtime chief counsel to the Commandant, who served as Gray's attorney. "You'd send up an action paper, then you'd never see it. Action items, you'd never see them, unless Jim Jones went through them."

Before long, some senior officers started complaining about an administrative logjam. Jones, still only a lieutenant colonel, found himself in the uncomfortable position of hearing from three-star generals beseeching him for help in getting through to his boss. Jones's role became something akin to a powerful young prelate in the Vatican-like hierarchy of the Marine Corps. If a general wanted something to happen—a training program perhaps, or a new way of structuring a division—Jones would tell them "they would have to do it themselves," Murphy recalled.

Things became so clogged that Jones had no choice but to sometimes sign documents on behalf of the Commandant, including important edicts known as "Attention Marines Worldwide." Eventually, Gray learned about his aide taking the initiative and castigated Jones for exceeding his authority. But the crisis would always pass, as did the Commandant's ire. General Gray was smart enough to know he needed someone to keep track of all of the tiresome administrative details.

The feisty Commandant also wasn't one to hold a grudge. For beneath his rough exterior, Al Gray was a thinker, innovator, and visionary in military preparedness and tactics. After the thousands of deaths in Vietnam, and the subsequent losses in Beirut, Gray was determined to prepare the Corps for the twenty-first century. His priority was to achieve better training and equipment to attack the enemy with speed, stealth, and surprise.

Impatient with the Washington bureaucracy, Gray was determined to radically alter the Marine Corps' training regimen, throwing out any last vestiges of 1940s-style amphibious fighting and replacing them with classroom and field training in the audacious tenets of maneuver warfare. As described by a Marine strategist, Lt. Col. H. T. Hayden, "maneuverism" goes beyond battlefield strategies, but actually requires a new way of thinking of combat. "It is a culture. It is a concept of how to deal with the fog of war, chaos, and friction of war," he wrote. Surprise, audacity, and independent decision-making are necessary from every Marine.

Now, it was one thing to speed up the operational tempo on the battlefield, but quite another to try to grease the rusty wheels of the Pentagon bureaucracy. Gray knew it was a daunting task, but for the nation's smallest armed service, it was the only way to focus on its ability to be the quickest, and deadliest, fighting force. He was determined to fight for the Corps' most pressing needs in equipment and funding, even if it meant slogging through some of the long-running battles at the Pentagon and Capitol—political disputes that made the Battle of the Somme look like child's play.

One of the first skirmishes of Gray's tenure was over acquiring adequate funds for a much-needed new generation of troop transports. Starting in the mid-1970s, the Marine Corps lobbied for new technologies that were fast enough and smart enough to attack the enemy from long distances, or "over the horizon." With the Soviets' increasing radar and satellite capabilities—which they were spreading to client states in Asia, the Middle East, and Africa—achieving an element of surprise was crucial.

So Gray pushed for a new kind of aircraft that would provide what he called "deep insert, deep extract" of troops in and out of enemy territory. What he got was the V-22 transport plane, an aircraft designed to take off and hover like a helicopter. With special "tilt-rotor" technology, its propellers could then rotate and allow it to fly like a conventional propeller-driven airplane. Built in a joint contract with Bell and Boeing, the airplane's gawky appearance inspired a nickname—the Osprey.

The fast, multifaceted plane would replace the Marines' fleet of aging Vietnam-era helicopters, some of which were built before many of the current crop of Marines were even born. By combining the strengths of a turboprop aircraft and a helicopter, Gray and other Marine leaders saw the Osprey as the troop aircraft of the future, a lethal bird that could rule over the battlefield. "Twice as fast, twice as far" as the Blackhawk helicopters favored by the Army, and the CH-53s still employed by the Marines, Gray said.

Replacing an entire fleet of helicopters would not come cheaply, and the Osprey would cost billions of dollars to develop and put in production. And the U.S Navy—nominally the Corps' sister service and ally—had its own weapons wish list such as new destroyers and aircraft carriers.

For Gray and his aides, securing funds for the Osprey was nearly as tricky as the physics of the tilt-rotor plane itself. The project hit major turbulence when then–Secretary of Defense Dick Cheney announced his opposition to any more spending on the V-22. In early 1989, Cheney proposed trimming $10 billion out of the $300 billion defense budget. But such trimming was hard when the Air Force was calling for an additional $15 billion for a fleet of 312 B-2 stealth bombers, and the Navy needed $3.6 billion for five Aegis guided-missile destroyers; the Army had its own artillery and tank list costing many more billions of dollars.

Gray argued that the Marine Corps was asking for a paltry $136 million for development costs to hatch its beloved Osprey. But Secretary Cheney, faced with a series of tough calls among the services, put Gray's pet project on the chopping block. As the Osprey was close to being beheaded, Gray mounted a political counterattack, deploying Jim Jones and other aides across Capitol Hill. Gray's men made the Corps' case to all 435 members of the House of Representatives, lobbying Democrats and Republicans alike. In this, they followed Gray's rule of staying out of political partisanship since the Marines had friends on both sides of the aisle.

By presenting a vigorous defense of its vertical-lift airplane, Gray won the day in the halls of Congress, despite the opposition of his boss, Dick Cheney. The Osprey's supporters included Republicans McCain and Cohen and Democrats Glenn and Nunn.

After the funding was restored, he started mending fences, delivering an invitation to Cheney for an upcoming parade at Marine Barracks, along with a model of the Osprey. Cheney grumbled but laughed. "Get that out of here," he said, pointing at the model, "and I'll come!"

Maintaining good relations and avoiding unnecessary fights were keys to surviving the Washington pressure cooker. "There's an important thought here that I think Jim shares," Gray said later. "Don't take this stuff personally. Too often, people do."

Yet Gray himself could take things very seriously indeed, with angry outbursts that Jones couldn't avoid. Senator Sam Nunn's chief of staff, Arnold Punaro, recalled a morning when Al Gray burst into his office and shouted at him, "Get out!"

Since this was Punaro's office, he considered objecting to Gray's absurd demand. But the Commandant was obviously riled up about something, so Punaro, a Vietnam vet and an officer in the Marine Corps reserve, got up and walked away from his desk. Gray slammed the door shut behind him, thus occupying the office of the chief of staff of the Senate Armed Services Committee.

Thirty seconds later, Jim Jones rushed in, looking for his boss. "Where'd he go?" he said, breathing hard.

Punaro pointed into his inner office.

"What's going on?"

Punaro shrugged. "I don't have a clue."

Jones glanced at the closed door and considered his options. "Well, we better not go in there," he said, and joined Punaro on the couch in the anteroom. About forty-five minutes later, Gray opened the door and left without a word of explanation or apology.

For all of his mood swings, Al Gray was not all that different from some of the more colorful leaders through the Corps' history—from John Lejeune to "Howlin' Mad" Smith to Chesty Puller. Lt. Gen. Victor H. "Brute" Krulak once noted that the Corps was "perennially the smallest kid on the block in a hostile neighborhood" of the armed services.[9] It took strong, sometimes irascible, leaders to protect the Corps' turf.

Ultimately, Krulak wrote, "They came to accept, as an article of faith, that Marines must not only be better than everyone else, but different as well. Some of their critics claim they are even eccentric, but as John Stuart Mill explains in his essay, 'On Liberty,' the border between eccentricity and genius is drawn precious fine."[10]

Al Gray walked that fine line. For his aide, dealing with the general's occasional outbursts or eccentricities—including having to walk the general's beloved French poodles—was simply part of the job. By his mid forties, Jones was a self-confident veteran officer with his feet firmly planted in the world of the Corps, and the territory beyond it. He found himself increasingly tolerant of all kinds of personalities and people, and wasn't as quick to judge others as he was in his younger days. His worldview had been shaped to a large extent by his experience caring for his only daughter, Jennifer. She was born with mental and physical disabilities that prevented normal development. The gregarious girl also was medically fragile, requiring many hospitalizations.

While it was hard for Jennifer to connect with the outside world, she found understanding within her circle of family and close friends. She forged deep emotional bonds with her parents and her three brothers.

Jones began to discern Jennifer's special impact on his professional life as he neared his twenty-year mark in the Corps, before the Father's Day call from Al Gray.

"1985 to 1987 was the watershed," Jones recalled, "because for the first twenty years I was focused on the competitive aspects of the profession within my peer group—perhaps too much so. I always knew where I was in the pecking order. I don't know if it's just the testosterone thing or whatever, but from day one, I was aware of my class standing at the Basic School and, later, where I stood at the various commands I was in."

This wasn't all that unusual, Jones added. "Most Marine officers are competitive," and seek the most challenging commands as part of the "natural progression" of a career. "I don't think I was perceived by my peer group as being a jerk about things," Jones reflected, "but I know in my own mind I was a pretty competitive guy."

He was experiencing a change of heart every bit as profound as his brush with death on Foxtrot Ridge, where he first came to terms with his own mortality. For Jim Jones, it was no longer "my" Corps, it was "our" Corps. This infantry officer who once dreamed of being a pilot stopped thinking of his career as a solo flight and instead "started thinking of it in terms of how we can make it better for everybody. Whatever happened to me from that point on became secondary. It was the last time I worried about the next promotion or the next assignment." And for this epiphany he credits Jennifer's "very profound" impact on everyone around her. "Jennifer taught me compassion."

This change of heart allowed Jones to see others in a new, more compassionate, way. "I stopped looking at Marines who weren't big and strong as inferior or second-rate. I stopped being intolerant of Marines who had problems with weight, for example, or people who just didn't look right. I began to understand the heroism of the Marine spouse and the family. I never used the word 'dependent' again as I found it to be demeaning, though unintentionally, to our family members. It was a major change in my life. I genuinely believe that people start off each day by trying to do the right thing, and that given the right guidance, they can all make a contribution. Part of the responsibility of leading is to unlock the key to individual success."

Even gruff Al Gray admired the way Jim and Diane Jones stood by Jennifer, particularly when others suggested it might be better to simply send her away to an institution.

"Having Jennifer," Gray said, "caused him at a younger age to realize there are more important things in life than him or the Marine Corps. There's a wholeness there."

But wholeness can exact its own price—at least in terms of a career. Jones's many years inside the Washington Beltway were starting to pile up, and they weren't necessarily on the plus side of his professional ledger. Staying put helped him deal with Jennifer's needs and care for Diane, who was battling a severe form of breast cancer.

Gray felt confident Jones would be promoted to colonel—at least on his watch. But even the commandant couldn't tell a promotion board what to do when the time came to decide if Jones's career would continue beyond that point. "I wasn't that confident he'd make general," Gray said.

So in the summer of 1989, Gen. Al Gray took it upon himself to do something to jump-start the career of Jim Jones, who by then had become his top advisor, or military secretary. Despite Jones's political instincts and invaluable assets in Washington, it was time to get him back into the field. Gray accomplished this by recommending him for promotion to colonel with orders to Camp Lejeune, where he would take over the 24th Marine Expeditionary Unit. The MEU was deep into training to attain status as "special operations capable."

It seemed like propitious timing for Jones's career. Storm clouds were swirling over the Arabian Peninsula as Saddam Hussein was moving his troops toward the border of Kuwait. The Marines were bracing for a fight.

Diane and the kids could stay put near Washington while he headed out to his new assignment to the south in North Carolina. After kissing them all goodbye, Jones drove south on Interstate 95 toward Camp Lejeune. He could only hope that this new war wouldn't start without him.

NINETEEN

Dust Ups

The day Saddam Hussein invaded Kuwait—August 2, 1990— marked a turning point in the lives of Marty Steele, Ray Smith, and Jim Jones. As Iraqi tanks rolled over Kuwait's borders to seize its oil and other assets, a strange kind of synchronicity seemed to draw them into the drama unfolding on the world stage and the preparations for a large ground war on the Arabian Peninsula.

The battle against the strongman that the first President Bush vilified as Sa*damn* was the largest military operation since Grenada, but with much higher stakes: the hegemony of the United States throughout the world, and, if the president was right, "a war in which good will prevail." Comparing Saddam's invasion of Kuwait with Hitler's 1939 blitzkrieg into Poland, Bush echoed Franklin D. Roosevelt's declaration that America was engaged in a struggle of "good versus evil, right versus wrong, human dignity and freedom versus tyranny and oppression," and the coda to his symphonic speech before Congress: "It is a just war."

Though Saddam had recently been backed by the U.S. to block the expansion of Iran in the mid 1980s, Bush argued that

303

things had changed since America made its uneasy alliance with the Iraqi dictator. Privately, he was intent on punishing Saddam, referring to him as "that lying son of a bitch."[1] The president, while no FDR in the public speaking department, nonetheless managed to rouse a skeptical American public when he told a joint session of Congress that the Iraqis' aggression "will not stand."

The Marine Corps' leadership didn't need to be convinced of the need to jump into the fray. Marty Steele personally witnessed this eagerness early on the morning of August 2, only a few hours after news of Saddam's actions were reported. He had just returned from duty in Korea, where he served as the operations officer of the Combined Forces Command. Now he was reporting for duty at the Marine Air-Ground Task Force Warfighting Center in Quantico. Much to his amazement he found his office was already occupied—by the Commandant of the Marine Corps.

Al Gray looked as casual as though they were shooting the breeze about the Washington Redskins' prospects for the 1990 season. "Have you heard the news about Kuwait?"

"Yes sir," Steele said. "I heard it on the radio driving in." He glanced at his watch: 6:30 A.M. Did Al Gray sleep?

Gray put his feet up on Steele's desk and stuck a pinch of chewing tobacco into his mouth. It was a nasty habit, but he wasn't about to try to change Al Gray at this point in his life. The tobacco came with the package.

Gray chewed thoughtfully for a minute, then said, "I'm going to be dealing with you on a regular basis."

"What do you mean, sir?" Steele could feel his gut churning at the thought of getting caught in a squeeze play between the Commandant and the brigadier general who ran the new Warfighting Center. What would he think of the Commandant commandeering his No. 2 man?

Of course, Al Gray had created the Warfighting Center to give senior officers a time and place to hash out strategic plans outside the confines and conventional thinking of the Pentagon. Now the crusty general appeared to be pulling rank to mobilize his think tank to work on planning for the Kuwait/Iraq crisis.

It was a heady, if confusing, start to the latest chapter in Steele's professional life. He had spent a tense two years working in the joint military command in Seoul, South Korea. Though Korea was largely ignored by the American public, the military was on a constant war footing—a time warp dating back to the earliest days of the Cold War, and the start of a standoff with the fanatical police state of North Korea. Marty's job was to help the joint force prepare for attacks by the Communist north's well-armed, million-man army. He had to think on a broader scale, like a Douglas MacArthur or Dwight Eisenhower, the great Army theater commanders, and less like a battalion commander in the Marine Corps.

He also got to work for some of the Army's new generation of leaders, Vietnam veterans like himself ready to lead the military into the next century. One of his colleagues was Maj. Gen. Bill Carpenter, known as the "Lonesome End" on West Point's football team. He was one of the finest officers Steele ever met. Steele worked with Carpenter in preparing battle plans should North Korea decide to mount an invasion during the 1988 Summer Olympics in Seoul.

This was not simply a contingency plan, he recalled, but rather preparation to meet an implacable enemy who starved its people in order to buy the next generation of weaponry. "I arrived on the fifth of July in 1988 and it was not until the twenty-sixth of July, 1989, that I went to bed for the first time not thinking the North Koreans could come over the wall that night," Steele recalled.

★ ★ ★

Back in the States, he was being thrown into the preparations for another kind of invasion on the other side of the world as the Iraqis plundered Kuwait's oil fields. Steele felt confident he could bring together a group of planners to come up with some creative ideas for the Marine Corps' role in the major engagement. But could he handle Al Gray?

The colorful Commandant was clearly chomping at the bit to get a piece of the action over in Kuwait. But this could be a tricky business within the military hierarchy—both in the Pentagon and over at Central Command headquarters in Saudi Arabia.

It was already presenting special challenges for Steele, and he hadn't even poured himself a cup of coffee yet, much less reported to his new boss, Maj. Gen. Matthew Caulfield, director of the War-fighting Center. Wouldn't Caulfield be a bit baffled, if not peeved, to see his assistant cozying up to the Commandant? But what choice did he have? General Gray outranked them all, and his mind was as focused as a heat-seeking missile. He wanted to be part of the fight. He wanted a piece of Sa*damn*. So he cooked up a special experiment at his military lab.

Pacing around Steele's empty office, Gray rubbed his hands together and warmed to the work ahead. "I want you to pull in the best minds we've got from across the Corps. I don't care what anyone's doing, take them off that assignment and bring them in here. I want you to tell me what the Corps needs to do—right now!—to be as ready as we can be for this fight in the desert."

Technically the Kuwait study group would fall under Caulfield's command, but Gray let Marty know he wanted him to be the point man on the project and report directly to him. "I want you to find the best guys you can, you know, some real out-of-the-box thinkers looking at our preparedness from every angle—infantry, artillery, aviation, logistics, communications, and intelligence."

A nagging question tugged at the back of Steele's mind. "Sir, has the president declared war on Iraq?"

"Not yet," Gray said, chewing his tobacco and lost in thought. "But we are going to war over there, Steele. I feel it in my bones." He spit into his tin cup, which pinged like a bullet. Steele could feel his blood rising as the Commandant got pumped up about the looming battle.

Yet Marty Steele's cooler side told him this special assignment would be one tough challenge—an institutional minefield to rival the barriers that Saddam was preparing for the Americans in the desert of Kuwait. The study group was being asked to tackle a question that normally would take months, if not years, to answer: How should the Marine Corps best prepare for war in the Persian Gulf?

"I want your study group to rank these things, Marty," Gray explained. "What needs to be done now, what needs to be done in the midterm, and what can we put off for a while?"

My God, Steele realized, *he wants an entire review of the working operations of a fighting force of more than 170,000 men and women.*

"How soon do you want this, sir?"

Ping, ping, ping. Gray fired a few more shots into his cup, and then looked up with his crocodile grin. "How about yesterday?"

Marty would have despaired if this monumental task had come from anyone else. But he shared a special bond with Al Gray—a mutual passion for equipping the Corps' tankers for large-scale maneuver warfare. A few years earlier, Gray had helped Steele get a plum job leading one of the Corps' first light armor battalions in the 1st Marine Division at Camp Pendleton. The general later joined him for maneuvers up in the high desert of 29 Palms.

With 932 square miles of territory, the Marine Corps base at 29 Palms is nearly as large as the entire state of Rhode Island. But its rugged, sun-scorched terrain resembles Saudi Arabia more than New England. With summer temperatures soaring above 120 degrees, the desert enclave gives the Marines ample room to roam in tanks and armored carriers, not to mention enough terrain to drop bombs and shoot missiles to their warrior hearts' content. In the 1980s, as turmoil ruled on the Arabian Peninsula thousands of miles away, 29 Palms provided a practice stage for whatever desert warfare lay ahead. All that was missing were oil fields, shepherds, and mosques.

Unlike smaller bases such as Quantico or Pendleton—which were becoming hemmed in by suburban sprawl beyond their fences—29 Palms remained an isolated outpost, a deserted place where the Marines could stage maneuvers on a large scale. With huge movements of troops, vehicles, weapons, and aircraft, the high-desert war games seemed to Steele like training for the Super Bowl. After years of preparation in the use of heavy armor and tanks, he could practice on the big stage.

General Gray seemed especially fond of Steele's revamping of the old "sand table" to show the movement of troops and equipment. Typically, this was a table that supported a relief model of terrain built out of sand for the study of maneuvers.

But at 29 Palms, Steele took the models to a new height by creating sand tables on a grand scale on the rocky desert floor. This allowed his Marines to get a true sense of the battle by walking across the practice field of battle in a space as large as a football field, a hundred yards or more out in the sand. He also ordered his men to spray-paint the sand to show the direction of tank battalions and companies moving to battle objectives. Other arrows showed the speed and direction of jets and helicopters. Boulders were added on this life-sized sand table to represent mountain ranges.

Gray regularly visited these field exercises to savor their size and scope. By rehearsing on such a large-scale stage, the Marine Corps seemed to be coming as close to real combat as possible without killing each other. (Later, after some Marines died in the live-fire training, the exercises were scaled back.)

It was the golden era of war-gaming, a thunderous ballet of bullets and bombs as artillery units fired live rounds, aviators shot rockets, and armored troop carriers opened up with machine guns—all within limits, of course, and without shooting directly at each other. But as much real-time simulation as possible was needed because, with tanks racing along at speeds of thirty miles per hour or more, it would be easy to outrun infantry units moving on foot.

Only by practicing in the high desert dust and heat could the Corps hope to operate in joint exercises with the Army's swift and lethal M1A1 Abrams tanks. As a smaller, quick-strike force, the Marines could never match the size or scope of the Army's massive armored divisions. But if they were smart and resourceful, Steele was sure that the Corps' tank battalions could be elevated from mere "supporting arms" to the Marines' billing as "the tip of the spear" of the American military arsenal.

Marty Steele's opportunity to be a part of a different kind of Marine Corps arrived in 1985, as he worked on General Gray's Maneuver Warfare Marine Corps. Surrounded by phenomenal officers, senior NCOs, and bright, hard-charging Marines, all of his frustrations from the past seemed to melt away in the California sun. Initially, he was selected to command the 1st Light Armored Vehicle (LAV) Battalion. Since it was a brand new eight-wheeled, fourteen-ton armored vehicle fresh from the factory, his Detroit experience would reap great dividends.

The unit had to be built from scratch. Although there were less than twenty people present when he arrived, he increased the team to almost 600 Marines and had the luxury to train, equip, shape, and mold them into the newest war-fighting capability in the Corps. Every NCO came from another unit in the 1st Marine Division. They were all volunteers who reenlisted simply to be part of history. The senior NCOs, survivors of the 1970s, were totally dedicated to the profession of arms. The officers were a mixture of infantry, armor, artillery, and both fixed- and rotary-wing aviation. They were all risk-takers, and men who thought unconventionally and were hungry to lead, to fight, and to take General Gray's maneuver warfare vision to the next level.

Supported by his Division Commander, Brig. Gen. Terry Cooper, LAV Battalion had a year of constant training and maneuvers at 29 Palms, unfettered by the drudgery of higher headquarters' mundane administrative requirements. Steele felt like he'd died and gone to heaven—albeit one with heavy armor around the pearly gates.

Then, much to his surprise, General Cooper and his successor, Maj. Gen. Joe McMonagle, asked him to move to the other side of Camp Pendleton and take over the 1st Tank Battalion. The opportunity to take command of the organization in which he started out as a young private first class in 1965 was a dream come true. Three years in back-to-back commands was an unprecedented move in the Corps at the time. His implementation of combined arms operations on a grand scale with the finest Marines in the Corps under General Gray served as a professional rebirth.

When he ran into Gray later in 1990, Steele felt sure the Corps' tankers would help the Army crush Saddam Hussein's Soviet-made T-72 tanks. But something else was gnawing at him, and it had nothing to do with military power and everything to do with the politics of running the Marine Corps. The more he listened to General Gray, the more he realized that his ultimate boss was overstepping his authority.

As Commandant, Gray had many duties: overseeing the training and preparation of the Marines; issuing policy directives and guidance; serving on the Joint Chiefs of Staff; and representing the Corps' interest in Congress. But his duties did not include direct command and control of the Marines in the field. Ever since the Goldwater-Nichols Act of 1986, the U.S. military had regional commanders—from the Pacific to the Atlantic to the Middle East.

By the time Marty was button-holed by Gray at Quantico, preparations for war with Iraq were already well along at U.S. Central Command headquarters at Riyadh, Saudi Arabia. And the theater commander, or CINC, was the same irascible Army general, Norman Schwarzkopf, who had butted heads with Ray Smith and other Marines seven years earlier before the invasion of Grenada.

For Marty, the prospect of facing Saddam's Soviet-made tanks and Scud missiles wasn't nearly as daunting as the prospect of getting caught between two explosive egos like Al Gray and "Stormin' Norman."

That morning, August 2, 1990, Col. Jim Jones was happy to be out of Washington and its inevitable power struggles over how to conduct the coming war. The day before, Jim had assumed command of the 24th Marine Expeditionary Unit, a force of 2,400 men, at Camp Lejeune, North Carolina.

Dressed in combat utilities, with his helmet strapped under his chin, he stood in the coastal Carolina humidity to accept the 24th MEU's battle flag from its outgoing commander, Col. Ronald R. Matthews. The picture of the change-of-command ceremony that ran in the base newspaper showed Matthews firmly grasping the flagstaff, his forearms and biceps rippling with power. Jim stood straight as a statue, with his hands open as though he was ready to finally get a firm grip on a field command.

The MEU (pronounced *mew*) was a rapid response unit trained to ship out to foreign hot spots on relatively short notice. A decade earlier, when Ray Smith shipped out for Beirut with the 2nd Battalion, 8th Marines, they were called Marine Amphibious Units. Now the 2/8 was part of the larger force of more than 1,000 Marines under Jim's command.

By 1990, the Corps had six permanent MEUs, with three based at Camp Pendleton for deployment in the Pacific, and three stationed at Camp Lejeune ready to ship out to the Middle East and Africa. The 24th MEU, which included helicopter and support units, was a seasoned force that had made eleven practice landings and numerous deployments from Spain to Italy to Egypt. By the time Jim Jones took over, it was in its second month of training to add one more bit of alphabet soup to its resume: SOC—or "special operations capable." The special operations designation provided a kind of postgraduate degree for Marine units, requiring mastery of eighteen special missions, including amphibious raids, civilian evacuations, and hostage rescues.[2]

At the time the Iraqis invaded Kuwait, the 24th MEU was still a few months shy of attaining its special status. That meant it couldn't ship out for the Mediterranean until Christmas—a fact that created a nagging question in the back of Jim Jones's mind: Would the war be over by Christmas?

Across the Marine Corps, men and women were wondering the same thing. After President Bush declared a crusade against Saddam, the top Marines launched their own campaigns to get into combat. It was like a huge game of musical chairs. When the first shots were fired, the music stopped and you stayed put for the duration.

In years past, Ray Smith had mastered this game—and been darn lucky in the process. With the help of Gunny Canley, he had managed to return to one war zone during the Easter Offensive of 1972. In 1983, his timing was impeccable as he assumed command of the 2/8 in the months before the fighting in Grenada and Lebanon.

This time around, though, his timing was all wrong. August 2, 1990, was the day he reported to the Pentagon for a staff job as chief of the Southeast Asia branch of the Joint Staff. Normally, this would have been a perfectly fine assignment—one that allowed Smith to use his Vietnamese language skills and study the strategic issues facing the United States from Korea to Indonesia. He already had improved his academic credentials by getting a master's degree in international relations from the Naval War College in Newport, Rhode Island. But the timing of this Pentagon gig couldn't have been worse. The action was in Kuwait, not Korea.

Adding to his frustration, Smith's oldest son, T. J., had enlisted in the Marines and was serving in the 8th Marine Regiment. Like his father, T. J. Smith had taken the hard road into the Corps—as an enlisted man—and was ready to ship out for the fight against Saddam. Ray sure as hell wanted to follow him.

So E-Tool started hatching a plan that would hook him up with his old pal from Vietnam, Walt Boomer. Lieutenant General Boomer commanded the 50,000 man 1st Marine Expeditionary Force. Back in 1972, he had been bound to Ray by a parachute cord as they marched away from the North Vietnamese during the Easter Offensive. They were brothers for life, and Ray had no doubt Boomer would find a place for him on his staff. Only one person stood in the way—Al Gray.

The Commandant wouldn't budge.

"You might as well just shut up, Ray," he said over the phone. "You're not wiggling out of this joint duty."

Gray knew he had to keep the Corps running smoothly during the upcoming operation against Iraq, code-named Desert Shield. If he let Smith off the hook in the Pentagon, there was no telling how many other colonels would be at his door, asking for similar treatment. Sometimes even the best warriors had to man the home front.

It was Smith's most frustrating moment in the Marine Corps. For once he had to sit on the sidelines while other Marines—his own son among them—went off to war.

Back at Quantico, the special study group on Kuwait was secretly meeting around the clock. Thirty officers had been hand-picked by Caulfield and Steele. They were divided into groups to tap into various fields of expertise—from fire support to aviation to logistics. They had forty days to complete a top-to-bottom study of the Corps' readiness. Then they were to report directly to Al Gray.

As the United States prepared to face off with Iraq's eleven divisions—including three Republican Guard divisions with nearly a thousand tanks—Steele's major concern was the state of the Corps' aging tanks. Would the M60A1 tank, which dated back to the 1960s, defeat Iraq's Soviet-made model, the T-72? The M60 historically had suffered from engine problems caused by ingesting dirt and dust, not a good sign before desert combat.[3] Mechanical improvements had been made, but Steele felt passionately that the real answer lay in equipping and training the Corps with the more reliable and lethal M1A1 tank.

"The M1A1 Abrams, first developed in the 1970s, was a sixty-seven-ton behemoth with thermal sites that permitted its four-man crew to spot targets through smoke and haze at ranges of two miles or more," wrote military historian Rick Atkinson.[4] It could go thirty miles per hour cross country, and nearly double its speed on asphalt. Its speed and accuracy were impressive, but what Steele really wanted for his tankers was the protection afforded by the Abrams, which outweighed the T-72 by about twenty tons. Its added armor could spell the difference between life and death on that windswept desert between Kuwait and Iraq, especially with all of the minefields the Americans would have to traverse.

The Marines Corps, which prided itself on traveling light, never had completely accepted the idea of integrating heavy armor into its operations. The Army, by contrast, maintained a massive presence in Germany, where it represented the first line of defense from an invasion by the Soviets or other Eastern Bloc forces. Before the fall of the Berlin Wall in 1989, "Much of the Corps' leadership viewed the change to mechanized operations on the European continent with considerable trepidation," wrote Kenneth Estes. "The Corps retained its historic paranoia, fearing budget conscious observers in Congress and the Pentagon would view it as a second land Army."[5]

Faced with this identity crisis, some of the old Corps generals rejected the idea of heavy armor in favor of embracing "with new enthusiasm the amphibious capability the Corps had exemplified in World War II."

Colonel Steele was quite sure those generals were wrong. For the Marines to be relevant in an age of large-scale desert warfare, they had to have the best tanks possible. To do otherwise would be like showing up for a football game with a bunch of linemen who had been on a strict diet, while your opponent was knocking back steroids and sirloin steak. He knew he was in the minority on the point, and had already butted heads with old-liners who saw tanks as the Army's business. To those stuck in World War II–era thinking, the Marine Corps' tanks represented "a supporting arm for infantry units to move forward and shoot over their heads as they moved forward."

Yet on the verge of this high-stakes war with Iraq, Steele knew Al Gray would never accept such old-school thinking. His Marines needed the fastest, most lethal tanks to employ the maneuver warfare tactics that everyone had been practicing over the last

decade. During the marathon sessions in Quantico, Steele pushed
the planning group to take a hard look at the sorry state of the
tanks. After much cajoling on his part, the task force agreed with
his radical proposal to replace as many tanks as possible and ship
them over to Saudi Arabia, where the Marines were preparing for
the desert clash.

Gray, for his part, acted with the urgency of Franklin Roosevelt rushing his New Deal through Congress. He gathered his
senior staff at Headquarters Marine Corps and had Steele brief
them on the study group's ideas. After each recommendation, he
looked around the conference table and pointedly asked, "Can
you do this?"

It was hard to turn down the Commandant when he was pressing the ideas of his own task force. "Any opposition?" Gray asked.
Hearing none, he nodded to Marty and said, "Let's do it."

Out of 102 proposals, 101 were immediately approved. Some
were bold initiatives, such as establishing language schools with
crash courses in the Farsi language spoken by many Iraqi soldiers.

But after an intense eight-hour-long briefing before the
Corps' senior leadership in Arlington, Steele looked down at the
list of ideas scrawled on a legal pad on the table. It was time to
present the boldest of the 102 proposals—the replacement of
aging M60 tanks with the high-tech M1A1 Abrams. Given the
Abrams' battlefield superiority, he argued, the Corps should seek
early delivery of scores of M1A1s from the Chrysler production
plant in Detroit. Pushing so many new tanks into service also
would require expedited training programs at 29 Palms.

"It's the right thing to do," Steele said in an impassioned voice.
"It will help us win the war, and save the lives of our tank crews."

Looking around the conference room, he could see the skeptical looks among the generals and their aides.

General Gray, seated at the head of the table, looked up and
said, "Can I see you in the hallway, Marty?"

Steele pushed back his chair and followed the Commandant
out into the hall. He knew full well his pet project ran counter to
the prevailing view in the room: *Let the Army handle the tanks, we'll
win with light armor, cunning, and guts. We are the U.S. Marines, com-*

ing over the top, tank or no tank. Such conformity and bravado was hard to fight, yet Steele was willing to wage this bureaucratic war if it meant saving lives of young Marines getting ready to go turret to turret against Saddam's Republican Guard.

He had known some of the senior officers on General Gray's staff for many years, and he respected most of them. But he also knew that, when it came to tank warfare, they were stuck in the 1960s. The twenty-first century was right around the corner, and it was time to move on. His only hope was the one Marine whose opinion really counted in that conference room, Al Gray.

In a flash Marty Steele's mind raced over the last twenty-five years of his career and all the debates about the need for tanks in the Marine Corps. He had heard the paranoia from his mentors in 1st Tank Battalion when he was only a private first class. He had listened intently to the previous generations of tank officers who had felt under appreciated and misunderstood and turned their anger into swagger and hubris. Like his tanker friends, he had been involved in the debates from the beginning and even argued with his closest friend, Ray Smith, for hours about the utility of the tank.

Now, at a key moment in history, would it come down to old prejudices and ignorant bias, or would his beloved Corps move forward and properly prepare for what could be its biggest tank battle in history? Serious discussions had started almost ten years earlier while Steele was a student at the Marine Corps Command and Staff College. Just back from Detroit, he was keenly aware of the M60's deficiencies. He'd written a paper about the utility of tanks and the necessity for the Marine Corps to deliberately plan to replace the 700 tanks they had just purchased. But who would listen?

Amazingly, the director of Command and Staff College arranged a private meeting for Steele to discuss his rationale with then-Commandant Gen. Robert H. Barrow. After listening politely for forty-five minutes, General Barrow, a highly-respected Marine and southern gentleman, calmly told Steele that "the decision on the tank will not be made while I am your Commandant."

After staff college, Steele was assigned as the Tank Acquisition Officer at Headquarters Marine Corps and briefed Gen. P. X. Kelley in the same room where years later he would meet with General Gray and his skeptical staff. Before briefing Kelley, Steele was told by his boss at the time—Lt. Gen. Hal Hatch—"Marty, you're on your own on this one."

Steele was convinced not only of the requirement for a new tank on the modern battlefield, but also the urgent need to find a way to get the M1A1 into the hands of Marines. In 1984, he solicited the support of the CIA to give a highly classified briefing on the vulnerabilities of the M60 to General Kelly and his assistant, General D'Wayne Gray. Although they agreed on the tank's weaknesses, the classification of the briefing precluded anyone else knowing the rationale for their opinion.

More importantly, procurement money for a possible M1A1 was being utilized on major programs like the LAV and the M198 Howitzer and critical upgrades to the AAV.

When Steele asked the Agency to come and brief Al Gray a few years later, they hesitated, wondering how many times they would have to keep coming to the Navy Annex on this issue. When briefed, General Gray expressed displeasure with his predecessor for not informing him of the information contained in the brief. By now, Steele sensed that Gray understood the superiority of the M1A1 over the inferior M60. Yet the debate continued to rage with his key subordinates on whether the Marine Corps even needed a main battle tank and, if so, why couldn't they do it on the cheap? Why not upgrade the M60 to make it like an M1A1 for much less money?

To answer that question, General Gray had called Steele and a few key tank officers back to Marine headquarters in early 1988. After three years of leading Marines in the field, Steele had been away from the vagaries of the Beltway and the twisted evolution of this issue. Much to his chagrin, well-intentioned members of industry had made a convincing case for a Super M60 which, on paper, looked like it might compete against an M1A1 at far less cost. On paper, the Marine Corps could upgrade its entire fleet of

M60A1 tanks and make them almost as good as an M1A1 and save a bunch of money.

General Gray directed the small but highly qualified study group to first make a case for "Why a Tank?" He gave them a week to recommend one. Gray, as was his habit, was secretive in his approach but very involved in the process, clear in his guidance, and emphatic on the requirement for an objective recommendation.

The group was tireless in their efforts. For Steele, frustration, anxiety, and—for the first time—doubt crept into his psyche. Why was this so hard? Why can't we just move on? Maybe we shouldn't have a tank. Maybe we could get by with a substitute. Generations of great Marines had not only survived but flourished with the second-rate hand-me-down equipment from the Army. What makes this thing so different? But, deep down, Steele trusted in General Gray. He would agree that the trumped-up data on the Super M60 was totally bogus. If General Gray did see through it, he sure didn't let on.

Completely exhausted the day before the briefing, Steele made a phone call to an old friend in Detroit who he believed had to be involved in the Super M60 proposal. Although they hadn't spoken in almost seven years, the old friend opened the conversation by saying he had been waiting for the call. He felt relieved to share with Steele his sadness over being involved and indicated that he had rationalized it as just business. It's the Marines' choice.

The friend confirmed Steele's doubts about the data and asked him to protect the source. He closed the conversation by apologizing and saying he was glad Steele was giving the briefing the next day. His Detroit friend was planning to retire early.

It was a bitter Sunday morning in February. Steele attended Catholic Mass at Fort Myer Chapel, prayed for divine guidance, and started the trek back to Headquarters Marine Corps to make final preparations for the private briefing with General Gray. Filled with grave doubts about his approach and the outcome, he jumped the wall to Arlington National Cemetery to find some solace amongst the graves of heroes, and perhaps some shelter from the ice storm and wind chill.

The conditions worsened and his face and eyes became glazed over with a sheet of ice. Unable to see, stumbling on the icy ground, and pleading with his God for some sign to deliver him out of this seemingly endless quagmire, he fell against one of the tombstones. After clearing his eyes, wiping the snot from his frozen face, and gaining some sense of bearing, he discovered he was on his knees in front of the burial site of Creighton Williams Abrams—the famous namesake of the M1A1 tank.

Stunned to the point of disbelief and trying to figure out if this was God's answer to his feeble prayer, he tried to capture the meaning of the whole thing. Although a man of great faith, the experience seemed too incredible to comprehend. He managed to humbly thank God for the sign and proceeded to break down and cry. After what seemed a frozen eternity, he buoyed himself against the bone-chilling cold and tried to get up off the frozen ground. Just as he was getting to his feet, doubt reentered his mind. This just can't be real! He immediately slipped and fell, landing on the other side of the sacred tombstone. To his amazement, the first thing he saw was September 15, 1914, General Abrams date of birth. Marty Steele's date of birth is September 15, 1946. The tears of joy now flowed down his frozen face.

"I got it, Lord," he murmured.

The religious experience was capped off by a hot shower, a change of clothes, and General Gray's approval of the M1A1 tank.

Now two years later, Marty Steele was briefing General Gray again. The Commandant stopped in a corner of the hall and turned to look Steele squarely in the eye.

"Okay, Marty, now I want you to be straight with me," Gray said in his gruff Jersey accent. "Did this recommendation about the tanks get the same discussion and scrutiny as all the other ideas you've brought me? Or is it just your pet rock?"

"Sir?" Steele said, wondering if the general was mocking him.

Gray patted him on the shoulder. "C'mon, Marty, relax. I know, and everyone in that room knows, you've always had a personal crusade to get the Marines in the same league with the Army and its tanks. Some of my staff thinks you're using this study group as a way to push your personal agenda."

Steele stifled an urge to lash out at the backstabbers going after him. They didn't have the guts to confront him face to face; instead they run to Daddy Gray like kids in a family feud. Taking a deep breath, he returned Gray's earnest gaze. He knew the top Marine was looking for any sign of weakness or wavering, so it was important to maintain self-control.

"Sir," he said, "I can honestly say that this recommendation was fully vetted by the group and has its full support. It's the best way we can send Marines into battle. You can poll the group, sir. They're all behind it not because of some personal ego trip on my part, but because it's the right thing to do for the Corps."

Gray nodded and squeezed the colonel's shoulder. "Okay, I believe you," he said. "But we're going to have to put this one idea on hold until General Sheehan gets back. I know he's going to need convincing, and I want you to personally brief him."

Maj. Gen. Jack Sheehan was one of Gray's most trusted advisors, and widely seen as Commandant material himself. He had served in combat with Gray in Vietnam, and later suggested bringing Jim Jones back to Washington to serve as the Commandant's aide. Sheehan was known as an independent, insightful thinker, and Gray wanted him to weigh the pros and cons of this sweeping—and costly—proposal to replace tanks.

A week later, Marty Steele returned to Arlington to pitch the tank modernization program again. Sheehan was doubtful at first, asking probing questions about the merits of both models of tanks, and the difference each could make in the upcoming clash with Iraq. If the Marines dug into the desert in defensive positions, he asked, wouldn't the old M60 be up to the task?

"You're kidding me, sir, right?" Steele said. "We wouldn't turn this into a drawn-out defensive war, would we? You're pulling my leg."

"I'm not joking, Marty," Sheehan said evenly.

Steele was nonplussed, but kept a lid on his boiling emotions. The M60 had been around so long that it was a kind of fixture that never seemed to get much worse or much better—sort of like an old pickup truck. Marines had a knack for making do and improvising in combat, as they had shown with their lousy M16s and Korean War–era equipment during the Vietnam War. Steele knew this was the subtext of the argument. The Corps was used to being the under-funded and poorly equipped branch of the U.S. military. In a way, it was the victim of its own inferiority *and* superiority complex. Why should anything be different this time around?

Steele knew that his passion for change meant he was viewed by some insiders as a borderline crackpot, a voice crying in the Beltway wilderness, begging and pleading for his damn tanks. But he didn't care how he looked. His time in the field and, on the production line in Detroit, had given him insights into the workings of the tank that were rare for a Marine. He felt in his bones that if he didn't make the effort to secure a safer tank for his brothers-in-arms, then who would? Win or lose, he was determined to press the case for change.

So, as dispassionately as possible, he showed Sheehan a list of reasons for why the M60 should be put out to pasture: Its underpowered engine could not guarantee it would outflank the Iraqi T-72 on the desert battlefield; its armor was too thin to take a direct hit from the enemy, while the M1A1 could; and if the tanks broke down—as some surely would—its spare parts would run out. The Army was prepared to supply replacement parts only for the Abrams.

By the end of the briefing, Sheehan nodded and thought over what he'd heard. "OK Marty, you've convinced me. I recommend the M1A1 as our main battle tank."

Steele heaved a sigh of relief. Sheehan had come down on his side, and the Marines would be ready to fight in the desert. But now it was a race against the clock as General Gray issued orders to acquire the tanks and start training reserve and active-duty units in the care of the Abrams.

Calling up reserve units had also been on the study group's list of 102 things to do to prepare for the Iraqi war. "Everyone was against it except Al Gray," Caulfield recalled. But as a veteran of Korea and Vietnam, Caulfield knew the Marine Corps reserves were a cut above the rest. "The Marines have always treated the reserves much differently than other services," he observed. "Our reserves are not second-class citizens."

The Army, for its part, showed a remarkable degree of cooperation in helping the Corps scramble to modernize its tank units. The Army tank command at Fort Irwin, California lent the Marines fifteen Abrams tanks, which were taken immediately to a reserve unit training at 29 Palms. The first group of trainees was comprised of college kids from Yakima, Washington, whose company commander was a schoolteacher.

Major General Caulfield, visiting them at 29 Palms, was amazed to see how quickly the young reservists mastered the M1A1, with its computerized firing controls and navigational devices.

The crusty warrant officer in charge of training told Caulfield, "These kids are the best troops I've ever had at 29 Palms. They've broken all the records of the gunnery tables." It was proof, he said, of the wisdom of introducing the high-tech tank.

Back at Quantico, Steele was ecstatic to hear about the early success of the expedited roll-out of the Abrams. But he was exhausted after working for weeks on the Commandant's special task force—often having to sleep at the Warfighting Center and not getting home to Cindy and the kids. It would be good to return to some vestige of normalcy. But with Al Gray, normalcy was never an option.

This became even more apparent when Gray ordered Steele and a small team of officers to travel to the U.S. Central Command headquarters in Saudi Arabia to deliver the 102 recommendations—and see if they might influence the planning for the war effort. Schwarzkopf's not being bold enough, Gray confided to Steele. We can employ the element of surprise and mount a rearguard amphibious assault in Iraq, but no one seems to be seriously considering that option.

Steele tried to mask his concern about where the general was going with this. He pictured Walt Boomer, and wondered what he'd think if he knew the Commandant was second-guessing him back in Virginia. Gray would not be denied, though.

When he arrived in Saudi Arabia, Steele said, "There were a lot of pissed-off colonels." But he made it a point to draw Boomer aside and make sure the general knew he was just doing his job. He also made a point to bring up their common friendship with another Marine.

"I was Ray Smith's roommate in Basic School, and you were his senior advisor on your second tour in Vietnam," Steele said. "Ray's told me about your bravery during the Easter Offensive and how you fought on the hills near the DMZ until you were overrun by the communists, and how you led the South Vietnamese Marines off the hill and regrouped to fight another day."

Looking Boomer squarely in the eye, he said, "I'm not sure how this plan will be received here today, sir, "but I'm quite sure that, like you, the Marine Corps will carry on."

Boomer laughed. "True enough, Marty, true enough."

Steele always appreciated Boomer's professionalism. The general accepted the recommendations, and invited Steele and his team to spend several days training the staff of the Marine Expeditionary Force in combined arms planning. The practice later became institutionalized by the Marine Corps as part of its regular MAGTAF—Marine Air Ground Task Force—staff training.

★ ★ ★

Returning to Washington the day before the Marine Corps' birthday, November 9, 1990, Caulfield and Steele briefed Gray on the visit to Saudi Arabia. They sensed the Commandant was not in sync with his field commander, Boomer, and it made both officers uneasy.

"I want you to form another study group, but a smaller one now," Gray told his strategic planners. He gave them some broad ideas for drawing up a battle plan for a surprise attack on one of Iraq's ports. "I want you to keep this all close to the vest," he added. "No sense in letting the cat out of the bag."

"Yes sir," Caulfield said, glancing over at his assistant, Steele. Each man knew they were skating on thin ice, pursuing a plan that not only was out of their realm of authority, but actually out of Al Gray's authority, too.

"Good luck," Gray said. "I'll be waiting to hear from you."

This was going to be tricky. Any plan developed in the safe confines of Quantico, without any invitation by General Schwarzkopf, could be seen as interference by the Marines' high command. If it was leaked to the press or a member of Congress, it could create quite a stink and give a black eye to the Corps.

On the other hand, Gray's challenge of designing a bold plan of attack held a certain degree of appeal. The Quantico Warfighting Center had been created for precisely this reason—creative, "out-of-the-box" thinking about military planning and tactics that might elude those in the regular chain of command. They reconvened a core group of planners from the first task force and started meeting for days on end. They studied the terrain from Saudi Arabia to Kuwait City and along the coast past Faylaka Island. For this task, they could cull through the latest intelligence from the Pentagon, the CIA, and the National Security Agency.

Poring over maps and satellite photos, the task force kept coming back to Iraq's only coastal outlet to the Persian Gulf, where the Euphrates River emptied into the sea at the coastal city of Basra. If the Marines landed there, they might race up the Euphrates in high-speed hovercraft, then strike a blow on the rear guard of Saddam's forces. This, in turn, could tie up the Republican Guard even before they tried striking back at the Americans.

Such an audacious attack was risky, though. Intelligence reports warned of mines in the Persian Gulf, floating like a ring of death east of Kuwait City. The Navy had minesweepers, but they were reluctant to use them. Caulfield sniffed, "Hell, the whole purpose of a warship is to get blown up every now and then. If we can get that son of a bitch Saddam under a Marine's bayonet, it will be worth it."

Caulfield, a Korean War veteran, was reminded of Inchon, the daring amphibious assault led by Gen. Douglas McArthur that helped turn the tide against North Korea. But even MacArthur encountered opposition to his bold initiative.

Caulfield also knew that MacArthur, by being bold and trusting his instincts, scored one of the greatest military successes in history by launching a surprise landing from the Yellow Sea up the Flying Fish Channel.

Scouring the latest intelligence about Saddam's forces, Caulfield and Steele imagined a similar, if smaller, bold stroke at Basra. A backdoor invasion plan began to take shape.

The Marines could make a night raid in their hovercraft, securing key positions along the inland waterway—the Shatt al Arab—and overwhelm any defenses. The night attack on Basra would be buttressed at dawn by larger units in armored amphibious tractors. With help from close air support, they would quickly seize the port city and establish a beachhead on Saddam's back porch.

They would be working in sync with the Army's massive armored divisions rumbling in from Saudi Arabia, with Boomer's Marine Expeditionary Force driving on Kuwait City, his force including the newly-introduced Abrams tanks. The operation would create a pincer movement that would envelope Saddam's forces, ensuring a quick, decisive victory.

A broad smile creased Gray's tobacco-stained lips. "It's good," he said, studying the arrows on the map that showed the Marines driving a dagger into the heart of Iraq. It was called Operation Tiger.

"Now let me talk to Boomer," he said.

In December, Gray visited the Gulf and received a briefing at the Marine's command post about its mechanized combat team.

According to an account by Michael R. Gordon and Gen. Bernard E. Trainor, the Commandant was not impressed. "To Gray, the plan looked like a recipe for disaster," Gordon and Trainor wrote in *The Generals' War*. The Commandant, after hearing the complex plan to attack Iraq's mechanized forces, said, "This is going to be another Tarawa. You are going right in their teeth."[6]

Gray was overruled by the only man whose opinion mattered—Schwarzkopf, who also staved off the Commandant's efforts to set up a different Marine field command structure.[7]

Before the war began, though, Gray took one last shot at trying to inject his own plan into CENTCOM's war effort. That effort in Saudia Arabia included months of round-the-clock planning by Brig. Gen. Harry Jenkins under the cold eye of Schwarzkopf. It had been a long, arduous process—with or without Gray's interference. They already had discussed past large-scale amphibious landings, including MacArthur's bold stroke at Inchon. It was a seductive thing, this business of making history. Yet as the men responsible for the lives of some 50,000 Marines, Boomer and Jenkins quickly realized there were major differences between the challenges of Korea—where the Marines had to quickly mobilize to help rescue the collapsing army of America's ally—and the more limited situation in Kuwait.

By halting his invasion at Kuwait's southern border, Saddam had smartly avoided rushing into Saudi Arabia, where his forces would have been exposed to a rear guard action.

"If the Iraqis had come south, we could have gotten behind them and raised all kinds of hell," Jenkins told his planners. "Now the whole damn coast is fortified."[8]

Despite such formidable obstacles, Jenkins managed to draft a plan with ten options, ranging from selected raids to full-blown amphibious landings.[9] One of the attack options resembled the tactical ploy that the Quantico group had cooked up. The Marines could move two battalions to stand ready to threaten Basra as the Army attacked from the west.

That option was shelved, however, due to Schwarzkopf's concerns about having the war spill over into Iran and Boomer's own intentions to strike inland. An amphibious landing was put on the back-burner as an option to consider should the initial land campaign flounder.

So when Gray began describing his own amphibious plan, Boomer had a sinking feeling. He knew there was no way it would fly at this stage in the run-up to the war, but he could also tell that the Commandant was hellbent on getting into the action. Purely out of deference to Gray, Boomer agreed to meet with yet another delegation he chose to send out to Saudi Arabia. But he tried to let Gray know that he was only going through the motions. It didn't seem to work.

"Can you get Schwarzkopf there?" Gray asked eagerly.

Boomer sighed. Couldn't he take a hint? "I'll see what I can do."

Boomer hung up and shook his head. Gray clearly thought they weren't being audacious enough in their war planning—but what did he know, pacing in his office in Arlington? Schwarzkopf's Central Command staff had come up with a sound, and fairly bold, plan to defeat Saddam. Placating Al Gray, though, was another matter altogether.

The plan called for the 1st Marine Expeditionary Force to breach the mine belts between two oil fields in the boot heel of southeastern Kuwait, then drive north to Kuwait City. The Army, executing a classic left-hook maneuver, would push to the west and north to hit the Iraqi Republican Guard and reach the Euphrates River. Boomer was convinced that if the Marines were clever enough, and the Army properly executed its part of the offensive, they could win the war with minimal casualties.

The Corps' part of the plan was designed by generals Mike Myatt and Bill Keys, along with a rising star named Chuck Krulak. "Schwarzkopf really did take a hands-off approach, and Gray could have learned from him," Boomer observed later. "Schwarzkopf gave me a mission and left me alone."

The USS *Blue Ridge* sliced through the dark blue waters of the Persian Gulf, a hulking destroyer whose guns glistened in the sun. As he rode in the back of a Huey toward the deck of the Navy flagship, Marty Steele remembered his last assignment in Vietnam, when he'd flown as a forward observer off another ship toward another war. Closing his eyes, Steele could picture the *St. Paul* and his crew of Marines who fired the eight-inch shell that scored a bulls-eye on the North Vietnamese weapons cache and turned the mountain into molten lava. Since Vietnam, however, much of America's naval gunfire capability had been lost, Steele reflected as he arrived on the Blue Ridge. Nonetheless, the Navy and Marines remained an awesome fighting force from the sea.

Now he had to fight another kind of battle—one fought with words, not gunfire. He had to deliver Al Gray's audacious plan, normally a role he would cherish. Shortly after Christmas, he felt like a bit like Daniel entering the lion's den.

This time he wasn't alone. Major General Sheehan, who had come to support Steele's tank upgrade, was the senior officer and his new boss. As the ship's first mate sounded the whistle, the delegation stepped out of the copter and onto the deck. The officer of the day was waiting for them. "Welcome aboard," he said with a crisp salute.

January had been chosen as the right time to launch the campaign, before the desert became a foreboding place with *shamal* winds from the north shooting sand into the eyes of the American soldiers and Marines. The unknowns of the weather and the terrain were part of the key points the visitors intended to make: The more they took the Iraqis by surprise, the less chance they had of getting bogged down in a long ground campaign or a war of insurgency. The shorter the fight, the less time Saddam's forces would have to set fire to the Kuwaiti oil fields or to wreak other kinds of destruction. One of the biggest fears was that the Iraqis would launch mobile Scud missiles toward Riyadh or Tel Aviv. If they weren't careful, it could be the start of a wider conflict that threatened to immolate the entire Middle East.

Steele could feel his mouth getting dry as he walked down the ship's gray corridors toward the main board room. Despite his own misgivings, he had to make his best pitch for Gray's plan for a rear-guard amphibious assault. The Commandant simply wouldn't rest until he got his nose under the tent of Schwarzkopf's operation.

General Boomer was waiting inside the comfortable board room, a cup of coffee in hand and an impassive look on his face. He was joined by Vice Adm. Stanley Arthur, the senior Navy commander in the Gulf.

"I trust you had a good flight," Boomer said.

After some formalities, everyone sat at the long conference table and got down to business. Steele knew it was time to brief Boomer and Arthur. He sensed from the flat expressions all around him that this was not going to be an easy sell.

This plan, which they had slaved over for weeks, had about as much chance of acceptance as Saddam Hussein had of getting an engraved invitation to the White House. Still, he had his orders. He pulled out some maps and began the briefing—laying out the case for the backdoor invasion at Basra, the bold use of the hovercraft, the savings in lives and materiel by striking an early blow against the Republican Guard.

The briefing took less than hour, but seemed like an eternity as Boomer and Arthur asked a few perfunctory questions. They acted like gentlemen and thanked Sheehan, Steele, and their group for dropping in. Then, as quickly as genies in the *Arabian Nights*, they slipped out the door. Steele had done his job as well as possible, but Gray's unsolicited invasion plan was doomed from the start.

Boomer later explained why. "Because of the mines, the collateral damage, and what we learned about the Iraqis, Schwarzkopf said we didn't have to make an amphibious landing."

Looking back on the episode, Boomer said, "I got great support from the Marine Corps. But what I didn't need was someone to present me with a plan that I guess they hoped we would execute."

He was reluctant to rehash the issue of interference from the Commandant. But he pointedly said, "Al Gray made two visits during Desert Shield. That was one more than any other" service chief. "And he wanted to come back."

Still, Boomer invited Sheehan, Steele, and their staff to stay on board the *Blue Ridge* to help train his staff in the execution of large-scale operations. Steele, for his part, was happy to do anything he could to help toss the Iraqis out of Kuwait—even if he knew the other men on board referred to them as "Gray's bubbas."

☆ ☆ ☆

As it turned out, this first ground war against Iraq took only 100 hours to win. After unleashing an aerial Armageddon with wave upon wave of B-52s, F-16s, and F-18 bombers, American forces completely outgunned and outmaneuvered Saddam's tank and infantry divisions. The intricate plan devised by Schwarzkopf and his generals worked to bloody perfection. Iraq had once been a black hole for Western forces. The British had died by the thousands as they tried marching up the Tigris River valley in 1914. But Operation Desert Storm was a different story. The American-led coalition decimated Saddam's army, driving it out of Kuwait, and back toward Baghdad. There would be intense debate back home about whether America left the job undone by not overthrowing Saddam when it had the chance. But in the short term at least, Desert Storm could be fairly declared a victory.

Boomer's Marines easily penetrated the minefields laid across the Kuwaiti desert and overran the Iraqis with the cool efficiency they had shown during the training exercises at 29 Palms. Indeed, some Marines called the Kuwaiti invasion a "drive-by shooting."[10] There would be postmortems on the war showing how various units could have been better deployed, and how friendly fire deaths could have been averted.

All in all, though, it was a bright moment for the Corps in which everyone—even Al Gray—could take pride. There was one group of Marines, however, who were bitterly disappointed when the fighting ended so soon.

The 24th MEU was sailing across the Atlantic, two days west of Gibraltar, when its intelligence officer informed Col. Jim Jones and his staff, "Well, the war's started."

The news that the war kicked off without them on January 17, 1991, was a huge letdown. The Marines spent months preparing for battle, hoping against hope that they would get to jump into the desert sandbox.

The weeks leading up to Desert Storm had been especially hard for the 2,200-man MEU as they achieved their "special operations capable," or MEU(SOC), status. As they finished their training, Camp Lejeune became a ghost town, with nearly everyone embarking to Kuwait. Mostly women and children stayed behind— along with the MEU.

After they finally set sail in mid January, the three-ship convoy, manned by 3,000 sailors, passed the Strait of Gibraltar into the Mediterranean Sea when the coalition victory and cease-fire were announced. The disappointment was deepest among the newest Marines, who were chomping at the bit for their first taste of combat.

Colonel Jones was concerned about morale plummeting. It didn't help matters when the task force was greeted by the commander of the 6th Fleet who cheerfully touted the tourism opportunities ahead. The admiral meant well, but it was obvious to Jones that this was not what his gung-ho nineteen- and twenty-year-olds needed to hear. The idea of taking snapshots on the steps of the Roman Colosseum or the Greek Acropolis somehow didn't compare with the idea of firing away at the Republican Guard.

He had to do something to lift their spirits. So he went from ship to ship, talking to his men on deck of the USS *Guadacanal,* the *Austin,* and the *Charleston.* Their long faces told the story of the day. "At ease," he said, squinting into the sun. The waves breaking against the bow of the ship and the salt air were bracing, and under normal circumstances, most of these Marines would have been happy simply to be out on the high seas. But they'd missed the Big One, and now all their colonel could do was level with them.

"Men," he said over the noise of the ship, "a war like this is kind of like an earthquake: You have your initial tremors, and those do the main damage. That's what just happened in Kuwait and Iraq. Our forces have performed exceptionally well there, and they have done the main damage. The first round of the war is over. There's nothing we can do about that."

After letting that reality sink in, he continued in his calm, reasoned way, "As Marines, we know from our long history that wars don't end overnight. Every war has aftershocks, and this one is bound to have its share. So let's remain vigilant in our training, and let's remember that we're Marines, always ready to fight, okay?"

It was a low-key message, devoid of Knute Rockne pep or John Wayne swagger. But the men seemed to take his message to heart, and he noticed some of them nodding approval at his upbeat message. He hoped he hadn't promised too much, though. He had no idea if they would be called on to do anything in the aftermath of Desert Storm.

His sergeant major, William Hatcher, recalled, "It was very disappointing that we were being passed over for this operation. The general feeling was we had trained hard, passed all of our qualifications and were went out as the 'pointy end of the spear,' only to be left out."

But Colonel Jones was "always the optimist," Hatcher added. "He said that maybe there was a reason for it, that we would get something before it was all over."

Steaming across the Mediterranean, Jones worried about the growing risk of taking shore leave in southern France or Italy. Intelligence reports warned of Muslim extremists working in small groups around seaports. There had been some isolated drive-by shootings at sailors and Marines, with warnings of car and truck bombings reminiscent of Beirut. He issued an order that no one would travel on the mainland alone.

On April 9, while the 24th MEU(SOC) was conducting amphibious landing exercises at Sardinia, Italy, Jones received an urgent message from Sixth Fleet. He was to backload his vehicles and troops, return to ship, and set sail eastward to the port of Isk-enderun, Turkey. They were to take part in a massive military and civilian humanitarian relief effort in southern Turkey and north-ern Iraq. People were starving and freezing to death in the after-math of the war. It was time for the Marine unit to show that—true to their alphabet-soup status—they were truly capable of handling special operations.

Jones's prediction had come true. After Saddam's crushing defeat by the Americans, he sent his army to northern Iraq to sup-press a growing rebellion among the Kurds. This proud group of farmers, shepherds, craftsmen, and shopkeepers comprised one-fifth of Iraq's population and claimed northern Iraq as their ancestral home, Kurdistan.[11] They had not knuckled under to tyranny, and paid a great price. On March 16, 1988, Saddam quashed a revolt by the Kurds in the city of Halabja using mustard gas, nerve agent, and possibly cyanide, killing an estimated 5,000 people, mostly women and children.

But after Desert Storm, some Kurds sniffed freedom in the crisp mountain air. The Iraqi army, dispirited from their crushing defeat by the Americans, fled Kurdistan in the face of renewed local resistance. Dancing and singing broke out in the streets. The celebrations proved premature as Saddam regathered his army and returned to the north.[12] The Kurdish Peshmerga ("Those Who Face Death") fighters, with only rifles and pistols, were no match for the tanks, artillery, and helicopter gunships that remained in Saddam's arsenal. In late March, the last Kurdish holdout south of the Turkish border, Zakho, was blasted by artillery fire and strafed by gunships. With Iraqi troops bearing down on the mountain city, rumors of yet another chemical attack spread. Most of Zakho's people fled under the cover of night, beginning a hard four-day trek to the border with Turkey.

The panic spread, and within a few weeks, the Kurdish exodus became an international crisis—a "medical apocalypse" in the words of Doctors Without Borders. About a half million Kurds huddled in sub-freezing temperatures in the mountains of south-ern Turkey, while another 1.3 million refugees shivered in camps in northern Iraq. Measles, cholera, typhus, and dysentery spread. Relief workers estimated that 1,000 refugees were dying each day. Fearing the extinction of his people, a Kurdish leader made a plea for U.S. assistance.[13]

After hesitating to recommit American troops and resources back into the region, on April 5, 1991, President Bush signed the order to launch Operation Provide Comfort. It would become the largest humanitarian relief operation in the history of the Marine Corps.[14]

For Jones's 24th MEU, Provide Comfort offered a kind of final exam to test its new "special operations capable" (SOC) status. Besides the logistical nightmare of trying to help more than a million freezing refugees, there was the distinct possibility of starting Gulf War II.

As MEU commander, Jim Jones's first mission was to establish a forward support base at Silopi, Turkey, a rural village near the Iraqi border too small to warrant a spot on the map. Its people lived in mud brick huts with straw roofs, and lacked electricity. It was, wrote Lt. Col. Ronald J. Brown, "like traveling back in time."[15]

Silopi lacked an airfield, railroad, and barely had any roads. From this rugged staging area, Marine helicopters began moving 450 miles inland to deliver supplies to the refugees in the mountains. Over the next two weeks, the Marines' aviation combat element, the HMM 264, delivered more than 1 million pounds of relief supplies and flew more than 1,000 hours without a major mishap.[16]

As the CH-53E Super Stallion helicopters swooped in with pallets of food, water, and other supplies, crowds of desperate Kurds would rush on the ground below. The helicopter squadron commander, Lt. Col. Joseph A. Byrtus Jr., described "80,000 starving and freezing people tightly congregated on the steep mountainside in a patchwork of garish blue, white, and orange tents. . . . Because every square foot of land suitable for landing was occupied by refugees, the Super Stallions had to land one at a time in one of the few level areas not blocked by the tall, defoliated trees that dotted the camp."[17]

The Marines raced to unload the supplies as the crowd rushed dangerously close to the spinning rotor blades. Some 10,000 Kurds surged toward one Super Stallion, forcing the pilot to escape. In a low hover, the pilot was forced to blow back the throng with his rotor blades. The crew pushed the remaining pallets out of the rear of the aircraft, and the crowd spread to avoid getting crushed.

Working with Army and Royal Marine forces, the Marines built thousands of tents to provide temporary shelter for the freezing Kurds. Hospitals were repaired, electricity rewired, water mains fixed. Even the French, who were part of the Allied Coalition, got into the act, setting up a field bakery that made 20,000 loaves of bread a day

Jones's men also provided a security shield to keep the Iraqis at bay. On April 19, they guarded Army lieutenant general John M. Shalikashvili as he met an Iraqi delegation at the Habur Bridge border crossing. The Army leader let his adversaries know that coalition forces would enter Iraq on April 20 on a humanitarian mission. The Iraqis were instructed to offer no resistance. A special committee would be formed to establish direct communication with Kurdish and Iraqi authorities.

Then Jones and his MEU rode in jeeps and trucks through the snow-covered mountain passes into Zakho. The city of 150,000 was a ghost town, with fewer than 2,000 inhabitants left behind. Many homes had been looted and vandalized by the Iraqi army.

Despite the Americans' show of force, Saddam refused to budge. He ordered 300 soldiers—dubbed "police"—to patrol Zakho's streets, supposedly to keep the peace. Saddam's ruse was obvious, though, and the remaining residents were still being terrorized. Something had to be done.[18]

As he led his Marines into the city, Colonel Jones ordered the Iraqi forces to leave immediately—a moment captured by *NBC Nightly News*. The tall, articulate colonel was an effective spokesman for the Corps as it made a show of force, while also showing a humanitarian face. No shots were fired. The band of Iraqis knew they were outmanned and outgunned. "We showed them what we had at our disposal," Jones said. "It was clear this Iraqi

Army did not want to fight. They turned their artillery tubes station south, and did everything they could to show they had no stomach for a conflict."

First and foremost was the MEU's main combat unit—the 2nd Battalion, 8th Marines, the same unit that Ray Smith had taken into Grenada and Beirut. Now under the command of Lt. Col. Tony Corwin, the 2/8 was more lethal than ever, with four rifle companies and a weapons company. It carried 81-millimeter mortars, 60-millimeter mortars, guided antitank missiles, Dragon antiarmor missiles, four 155-millimeter howitzers, tanks, and light armored vehicles.

The eviction of the Iraqi army along with the arrival of food and medical supplies worked wonders to instill confidence in the Americans' intentions. "These initiatives were key in convincing the citizens of Zakho that this was an army, perhaps the first in memory, that only meant them goodwill," Jones would later write.[19]

As word of the relief effort reached the refugee camps, the Kurds starting streaming down the mountain passes toward Zakho. It began as a trickle, but turned into a flood of humanity—sometimes walking sixty to eighty miles to reach their homes. Other refugees used cars, mule-driven carts, buses, tractors, and motorcycles.

During a flight over the snowy region, Sergeant Major Hatcher could see why they were so eager to leave. Amid the Kurds' makeshift camps, he saw gravesites dotting the cold, hard ground. But the urge to live was strong among this transnational tribe that reached into Turkey and Iran. The Kurds were a colorful and intelligent people that defied easy categorization.

"I was amazed at seeing blonds, brunettes, and redheads," Hatcher said. "They reminded me of children I see all the time in my neighborhood back home. The only thing different was their dress and limited ability to speak English. . . . For the most part they appeared to be well educated and very passionate about their plight, and desire to live as they wanted to. They did not appear to be beaten down, and had lots of fight left in them."

Hatcher spent time with an educated couple—the husband had a college degree in hotel management and the wife had a law degree. Talking to them, he learned how the Kurds had survived their winter of dislocation. "When we first started delivering food to them in the mountains, one MRE was divided up so that three people could live off of it for seven days," Hatcher said. The typical Marine, by contrast, would consume an MRE, or "meal ready to eat," about three times a day, he said.

Operation Provide Comfort demonstrated the ability of military, government, and relief organizations to stave off a larger disaster. It also showed the value of international cooperation, and highlighted Jones's unique abilities, from speaking French to instilling trust in others.

"One thing that always impressed me is his ability to gain the trust and confidence of the other services that were with us during Provide Comfort," Hatcher said. "I'm not only talking about the U.S. Army, Navy, and Air Force, but the French, Brits, and the Spanish. There were others, too. They enjoyed seeing him, and the cooperation of forces was greatly enhanced because of this. The man has charisma."

After three months of grueling and often tense work, the joint operation had successfully prevented any more loss of life and the possible extinction of the Kurds of Iraq. President Bush issued a protective order, prohibiting Saddam's forces from entering the security zone north of the thirty-sixth parallel—what became known as the "no-fly zone."

Unfortunately, Saddam's appetite for despotic control and power was not easily sated. For years to come, he would play a dangerous game of brinksmanship, daring America to come back and fight on his home turf.

Though the future was uncertain, by mid 1991 Col. Jim Jones and the 24th MEU could leave Iraq with a sense of pride in knowing that they helped save thousands of lives and given a freedom-loving people a chance to fight another day.

"On the morning of 15 July," Jones wrote, "Marines from BLT 2/8 along with paratroopers from 3/325 Airborne Combat Team were the last combat elements to withdraw from Northern Iraq. In the early afternoon, the American flag was lowered for the last time at JFT-B headquarters at Zakho.

"Minutes later, U.S. military leaders, who had entered Iraq on 20 April, walked across the bridge over the Habur River, leaving Iraq for the last time."

Two Air Force F-16s followed by two A-10s swooped in over the bridge in a final show of air power for the ground troops.

Four days later, the 2,200-Marine unit backloaded onto amphibious ships and "watched as the city of Iskenderun and the Turkish horizon slipped into the sea," Jones wrote. "After a six-month deployment, it too was finally on its way home."[20]

TWENTY

The Other Side of the Pentagon

*The man who never does more than supinely pass on the
opinion of his seniors is brought to the top, while the really
valuable man, the man who accepts nothing ready-made but
has an opinion of his own, gets put on the shelf.*
—Erwin Rommel

The 1990s marked our trio's third decade of service in the
Marine Corps—a turning point where they could either keep
climbing the promotion ladder or face the uncertainties of life in
the civilian world and the dreaded "r" word, retirement. British
military theorist B. H. Liddell Hart described this tension between
military and civilian identities as the sound of a clock ticking in the
back of a senior officer's mind. "The time factor . . . rules the profession of arms," he wrote. "There is perhaps none where the dicta
of the man in office are accepted with such an uncritical deference, or where the termination of an active career brings a quicker
descent into careless disregard."[1]

Most of the time, Smith, Steele, and Jones were too busy to
think about it. But as they climbed each rung of the ladder—surviving the gauntlet of peer review inherent in the Corps' promotion process—there was that ticking of the career clock. Tick:
brigadier general. Tock: major general.

Making it to the next rung would be a trickier business,
though. Promotions to lieutenant general are uncommon and

somewhat unique in that one is selected not by a promotion board, but by nomination—usually from one's Service Chief to the Service Secretary, the Secretary of Defense, and finally to the President. Finally, the Congress must confirm each nomination, a process that, as history has shown, is not automatic.

Beyond that was the top rung of the Corps' ladder of success—promotion to Commandant. That would be a still harder feat to accomplish. But like a climb up Mount Everest, this professional ascension would bring Smith, Steele, and Jones together to breathe the rarified air of success and, inevitably, the reluctant return down the military's magic mountain.

☆ ☆ ☆

In the fall of 1996, Jim Jones was asked to help roast old friend Bill Cohen to honor his retirement after nearly two decades in the U.S. Senate. A small group of friends gathered for the party at the F Street Club. When it was time for Jones to perform, he was ready. He'd paid a waiter to enter from the wings, announcing, "Phone call from President Clinton."

Taking the phone, Jones asked, "Hello, Mr. President, what are you doing up so late? You're playing solitaire?"

This got a good laugh.

"Yes," Jones continued, "I'm here with Bill Cohen . . . and you say you're interested in offering Senator Cohen some jobs for his consideration. . . . You want him to be director of the CIA?"

Playing along, Cohen shook his head. The crowd booed.

After dangling several more high-level posts, Jones turned to Cohen and asked, "Secretary of Defense?"

Cohen flashed his 100-watt smile and gave a thumbs up; his wife, Janet, gave an even bigger one. His friends cheered—and that seemed to be the end of that. Another respected legislator was retiring to the private sector, where he would make a fortune as an international consultant. It seemed absurd to think a staunch Democrat like Clinton would invite a Republican into his cabinet. Jones's skit turned out to be strangely prescient, however, as two weeks later, right before leaving the Senate, Cohen got a call from the White House: Would he consider replacing Bill Perry as secretary of defense?

With the Senate and House of Representatives firmly in Republican hands—and a tug-of-war between Congress and the White House that had created political gridlock in Washington— it turned out to be a master stroke by the politically astute Clinton. Maine's senator was part of the dying breed of moderate Republicans who favored a tough military and fiscal conservatism, but also valued helping the poor and supporting other social initiatives. As the Republicans tilted to the right and embraced religious causes, Cohen, who had played basketball in college, managed to pivot away from the pressure being applied by the Trent Lott/Newt Gingrich wing.

The former mayor of Bangor, Maine, was a lawyer and a kind of Renaissance man. After election to the House of Representatives in 1972, Maine voters sent Cohen to the Senate in 1978. Somehow he found time to write or co-author eight books, including three novels and two books of poetry. He became known as a consensus-builder who paid his dues in defense matters through years of hard work on the Senate armed services and intelligence committees.

Cohen accepted Clinton's invitation to join his team, knowing he was entering a whole new arena of power, decision making, and politics. Trying to shape policy in the Senate was hard enough, but trying to lead the Pentagon and the global defense network was a mammoth task.

"We'd been around the military enough in eighteen years on the Armed Services Committee to understand a lot of nuance," said Robert Tyrer, Cohen's chief of staff. "But that's an oversight role, which is very different than a leadership role."

Cohen faced the added burden of dealing with Clinton's poor standing within the military. The president who had opposed America's involvement in Vietnam and avoided service was persona non grata among many in the armed services, including a new generation of Marine officers. Some feared he would erode the Corps' identity as a band of warriors—*manly* warriors—that had been so faithfully restored by Jim Webb, Al Gray, and others during the years of Reagan's defense buildup. Unlike the other services, the Marines stubbornly resisted allowing men and women to train together and had no intention of changing.

The most incendiary issue, was President Clinton's early edict to overlook sexual preference among the troops. What became known as the "don't ask, don't tell" policy simply didn't fly in Quantico the way it did in New York or San Francisco. The demons of Jane Fonda and the far left, which appeared to be exorcised by the military's successes of the 1980s and early 1990s, now seemed to be waiting in the wings.

Cohen, a seasoned politician and lawmaker, knew he was walking into a political minefield in the Pentagon. He also faced an added burden: Despite his pro-defense voting record, he never had served in the military himself. Still, he accepted Clinton's offer and, in early 1997, was confirmed by the Senate as the nation's twentieth secretary of defense. His first task was to assemble a team that could give him immediate credibility within the ranks of the armed services. As Cohen considered the right person to serve as his Military Assistant, he and his staff quickly zeroed in on the straight-talking Marine who had taken them on so many trips and helped them in the Senate. Jim Jones had helped them better understand the warrior ethos and, along the way, had become a close friend.

Jones was the natural choice to serve as Cohen's Senior Military Assistant because of their mutual trust. "I think it was Secretary Cohen's instinct that, just as he would be having civilian assistants who had been with him for several decades, it would be important to get good military advice from a similarly trusted source," said Bob Tyrer, his chief of staff.

As luck would have it, Jones was already back in Washington. After a stint at Camp Lejeune as commanding general of the 2nd Marine Division, he had been brought back to the Capital in 1995 as a major general, where he worked for Adm. Mike Boorda, the Chief of Naval Operations. Jones was promoted in 1997 to lieutenant general under Commandant Charles S. "Chuck" Krulak, and he became the Director of Plans, Policies, and Operations at the Marine Corps Headquarters in Washington.

In the past, the position of senior military assistant to the Secretary of Defense was a billet for a one-star or two-star general; Congress needed to give special approval for Jones to take the job as a three-star.

By early 1997, the defense department had 1.4 million active duty personnel and an annual budget of about $250 billion. The balance of power had become slightly unhinged after the end of the Cold War. From the Balkans to Bali, from Kenya to Kabul, the world stage featured a new, increasingly lethal brand of fanatic. The year before, an American base called Khobar Towers was struck by terrorists in Saudi Arabia when a 3,000 pound truck bomb killed 19 U.S. airmen and injured more than 500 people at the Khobar complex. The kind of shadowy killers who had truck-bombed the Marines in Beirut in 1983 were stalking Americans again.

The world was a treacherous enough place for Cohen's leadership team and the internal intrigues of the Pentagon provided another set of challenges. The institution's size alone is daunting—three times the size of the Empire State Building, with 17.5 miles of corridors inside its five-sided walls on 34 acres of land near the Potomac.

It also has 25,000 workers, most of them career military men and women. With the armed services vying for a limited amount of the federal budget, everyone has an angle—whether it's the Army pushing for high-tech artillery, the Air Force coveting a new fighter jet, or the Marines seeking faster troop transports, like the V-22 Tiltrotor.

Jim Jones's role as Cohen's senior military assistant was to familiarize his boss with the new environment. He served as an honest broker in a bazaar of influence, sorting through the agendas of scores of generals, members of Congress, and White House officials. Jones also served as a kind of institutional memory, especially when it came to sending messages from the defense department to military commanders around the world. He provided what Tyrer called "an intuitive understanding of the Pentagon."

This was the case early in Cohen's four-year-long tenure as defense secretary, when a pile of promotion papers landed on his desk. Every week, he routinely reviewed and generally approved the higher ranks for generals and admirals, giving them only a cursory glance. So when another list of names was sent over by the Air Force Chief of Staff, Cohen was inclined to give his stamp of approval. One of the Air Force service chief's recommendations was the promotion of a brigadier general, Terry Schwalier, to major general. The name didn't ring a bell with Cohen or Tyrer, but it did with Jim Jones.

Schwalier had been the base commander when Khobar Towers was blown up in the terrorist bombing of 1996. When he saw the promotion list, Jones flagged Schwalier's sheet.

He proceeded to provide a brief history of the controversy surrounding Khobar Towers: After the bombing, Defense Secretary William Perry requested an independent investigation by a retired general, Wayne Downing. Downing concluded that, while Schwalier had taken some security precautions, he had failed to take other steps that might have prevented the attack, or at least minimized its impact. Downing's report found a number of shortcomings in the ground commander's performance, such as not providing a wide enough perimeter area between a fence on the edge of the base and the Khobar Towers; failing to install an alarm system or conduct evacuation drills; and a lack of other preventative measures, such as installing shatterproof windows that would have protected American troops.

It was a scathing report, and Jones found himself in general agreement with its conclusions. General Downing ranked highly in Jones's opinion as a courageous and forthright warrior. But the Air Force attempted to blunt its impact by conducting two studies of its own that exonerated Schwalier, concluding he had taken adequate security precautions.

Jones looked up from his briefing papers and shook his head. "You need to get a second opinion," he told Cohen somberly. "This defense of Khobar Towers is fundamentally about infantry tactics, and you should try to judge it from that perspective, from a ground commander's point of view." Jones had never met Schwalier and bore him no ill will. "But what you do here is going to say a lot about what the current Secretary of Defense thinks about force protection of all U.S. forces around the world."

Cohen put Schwalier's promotion on hold and ordered his staff to take another look at the events surrounding the bombing. When the Air Force Chief of Staff, Gen. Ronald Fogleman, got wind of it, he went ballistic. He stood behind the Khobar commander, saying Schwalier did everything he could to protect the air base and shouldn't be made a scapegoat. Fogleman testified before a Senate committee that the bombing was an act of war that could not have been prevented.

Contrary to what Jim Jones was telling Cohen, the Air Force chief warned that the Secretary's actions could have a chilling effect on ground commanders everywhere. They would be looking over their shoulders and worry about being second-guessed by the Pentagon.

As much as he would have liked to avoid revisiting the Khobar tragedy—and the B-52-sized beef it generated with the Air Force—Cohen found that he agreed with Jones: a strong message about security had to be sent to ground commanders, especially given new reports of threats by Islamic extremists. Fogleman's anger was understandable: he was protecting one of his own. But for Cohen and Jones alike, there was nothing personal about the promotion decision. It was simply a matter of accountability. Pinning two stars on Schwalier's shoulders would send a message that, in the end, incidents such as these were "business as usual," and this impression was unacceptable to Bill Cohen. Although he did not rush to judgment, he found that the commander had not done all that he should reasonably be expected to have done to protect the base.

Cohen concluded that Schwalier had not made adequate preparations or protections for a terrorist attack. The promotion was denied. But Cohen also found there was nothing deliberate about Schwalier's performance, and ruled out any disciplinary action.

He could also see that Jones was right about the symbolic nature of what should have been a routine decision. Around the globe, the Schwalier case was seen as a litmus test of the Secretary's resolve in addressing terrorist threats, one that was closely followed by U.S. military commanders on the ground.

Despite the threat of losing his Air Force chief, Cohen felt obliged to send a clear signal that the highest-ranking ground commander must do everything in his power to protect the troops.

"We must avoid the temptation to circle the wagon around one of our senior officers," Joint Chiefs Chairman Gen. John Shalikashvili said at a press conference. "We owe nothing less to those young men, and women, that we . . . often lead into danger. We must provide them commanders who are held to high standards."

Pentagon reporters pressed Cohen to explain why only one officer was being punished for the nineteen deaths. "He's not being made a scapegoat," Cohen replied. "He's being held accountable." The general should have better prepared his defenses, Cohen said.

Schwalier, for his part, said he would retire and walk way with his "head held high." His boss, General Fogleman, announced his own retirement, saying he felt out of step with the Pentagon leadership. (Fogleman was "a total gentleman" about his own resignation, Cohen said.)

Cohen took plenty of flack for making an example of the Air Force general who, arguably, was a victim of state-sponsored terrorism. By the mid 1990s, Iran and Saudi Arabia had become breeding grounds for radical Islamic groups, including a new terrorist network masterminded by a Saudi exile named Osama Bin Laden.

Despite his internal struggle with the Air Force, Cohen soon saw that his decision sent the right message to his field commanders. On visits across the Middle East to the Pacific—where the threat was greatest—Cohen saw for himself a dramatic rise in the number of guards, barriers, and training to defend against terrorist attacks. From the moment he stepped off the plane, Cohen recalled, "Every commander I visited said, 'Let's go check it out.'"

Jones had been right: each and every base commander needed to be on high alert and know that the buck stopped with them.

Despite the rising alarm within the military about such threats, the specter of global terrorism remained firmly on the back burner of American interests. There were simply too many other distractions during the mid to late 1990s: from the exponential growth of the Internet industry to the juicy presidential scandal involving a former White House intern.

Cohen and Jones sensed a deadly pattern emerging. "From the bombings in Beirut to Khobar to bombings in West Africa, we knew very well what was coming," Cohen said. But aside from shoring up base defenses and monitoring CIA reports on Bin Laden, the Clinton Administration was not yet ready to take the fight to a well-funded foe that had the United States in its crosshairs.

Around this time, Marty Steele was also working in the Pentagon as the Corps' director of plans, policies, and operations, having relieved Jones after he went to work for Cohen. After Steele's promotion to lieutenant general in early 1997, he started working on improving the Marines' training and force structure under the guidance of Commandant Charles "Chuck" Krulak, a longtime mentor and friend.

Steele was also assigned to improve the Marines' posture for the growing terrorist threat, including possible attacks on the homeland. He'd always felt uneasy about the lack of response to the 1993 bombing in an underground parking garage of the World Trade Center in New York, which killed five people and injured hundreds more.

The depth of Steele's concern was made clear during testimony in Congress in early 1999. "The Marine Corps has long recognized the growing vulnerability of the homeland to asymmetric threats such as chemical and biological terrorist attacks," he told the military subcommittee of the House National Security Committee. "As the Tokyo sarin gas attack proved, these threats are increasingly real, and new concepts of civil-military cooperation and response are going to be required to counter them."

In another briefing in the Senate, Steele raised the possibility of another attack on the 110-floor World Trade Center towers. As he recalls it, the committee hearing was halted and a senator called him over to talk in private. "General Steele," the lawmaker said, "I understand what you're saying, but you're going to scare the hell out of the American people."

"Senator," Steele replied, "I'm not trying to scare the hell out of the American people. I'm trying to scare *you*. We've got so much information that it's going to happen. How many times do I have to come over here and say it's going to happen?"

The hearing was adjourned, and General Steele's testimony ended. Despite his sense of foreboding, Steele managed to maintain his fundamental optimism about America and its Marine Corps. But he saw the need to change the old ways of doing business, with each part of the power structure—military, diplomatic, and relief organizations—operating on their own. The multiplicity of dangers and cross-border threats required a new sense of cooperation to foster democracy and peace. Though a warrior by training, Steele had grown to see the other side of the coin—the need to avoid fighting in the first place.

His philosophy evolved in the mid 1990s when he worked in the U.S. Pacific command as director of strategic planning and policy—normally a job for a Navy admiral in Honolulu. Over two years, he traveled more than a million miles to forty-four countries, including China, India, Japan, and Korea. He met with military leaders and began to master the intricate calculus of each nation's internal and external politics. Most countries wanted some form of U.S. protection. But they also didn't want to be branded as American puppets, so they insisted on keeping such alliances quiet. Steele learned that military and diplomatic ties had to be made as delicately as possible. It was the age of the stealth alliance.

Back in the States, the Marine Corps was changing its training regimen to meet the shifting, almost kaleidoscopic, world situation. The Marine of the twenty-first century would have to be trained in many more roles than was necessary back in the days of storming Japanese pillboxes or rebuffing the North Vietnamese.

They began training for what General Krulak called "the three block war." On the first block, he said, the Marine might be called into a humanitarian crisis, such as helping the Kurds in Operation Provide Comfort. On the second block, the Marine might separate warring factions, as in Somalia. On the third block, the Marines would have to repel foreign invaders such as throwing the Iraqis out of Kuwait.

As Steele traveled with Frank Kramer, an assistant secretary of defense, he helped forge new relationships with foreign leaders that could pay dividends in the future. In Thailand, for instance, he helped negotiate the terms of regular joint operations with U.S. forces—training that would blunt the growing threat from Islamic terrorists operating in Southeast Asia.

In India, they tried—but failed—to talk the military out of conducting nuclear tests. In China, they got to know mid-level Army officers who quietly helped their country implement economic reforms to pry open up the largest marketplace in the world. Kramer and Steele helped funnel American aid to China to build hospitals and enhance goodwill between the two countries. As Kramer noted later, sometimes "the programs aren't as important as the personal relationships you form."

And in a world where huge wads of money often seemed to define defense planning, the Marines still managed to get things done on the cheap. In Romania, Steele and Kramer found a dispirited and disorganized army searching for guidance and training as the nation left the Soviet sphere of influence. Kramer, always impressed by the Corps' training regimen, pulled Steele aside and said, "If I can just get a good gunnery sergeant, I think we can start turning them around."

So Steele called a retired Marine general who, in turn, contacted several retired gunnery sergeants willing to travel to Romania to start a new training regimen from the ground up—bringing as much of Paris Island to Transylvania as possible.

"No one could have done in Romania what the Marines did," Kramer said.

Marty Steele's fondest memory of the 1990s circled back to his early days as an officer, when he stopped cleaning his room at Quantico and was needled for studying too much. After arriving in Honolulu in 1995, he got a phone call from South Korea and heard a familiar twang on the line.

"Hey, Steele, why don't you and Cindy come up for a visit?"

It was Ray Smith, who was working in Seoul on a joint command job with the Korean army.

"We'll come out to see you," Steele remarked, "but from what I hear, you don't need much help from me."

He was alluding to the events of the prior year when Smith was dropped into the middle of a crisis involving the fanatical North Koreans. On December 17, 1994, a U.S. Army helicopter was flying what was supposed to be a routine training mission near the demilitarized zone separating the two Koreas.

The chopper strayed into North Korean air space and was shot down and crashed into a snowy hillside. Chief Warrant Officer David Hilemon perished, while another Army chief, Bobby Hall, was taken captive. The hardliners in Pyongyang declared the incident an "act of self-defense" and demanded an apology for an obvious "act of espionage by the Americans."[2]

Normally, a United Nations representative in Seoul would have handled negotiations for the return of the soldier's body and the release of Hall. However, the U.N. representative on duty at that time happened to be a South Korean. Since the North Koreans denied their neighbors' right to exist, they refused to meet with the U.N.

This brought a call to the senior American duty officer, Ray Smith.

Riding in a jeep up the bumpy road to Panmunjom, the mountain village separating the two Koreas, Smith felt a sense of irony about the prospect of this face-to-face meeting with communist officials. Since the recent fall of the Berlin Wall and the breakup of the Soviet bloc, North Korea now seemed like a relic of the 1950s—the last of the hardline communist regimes. It existed in a time warp, as though Marilyn Monroe was still married to Joe

DiMaggio, "I Like Ike" campaign buttons were being handed out, and A-bomb tests were pulverizing Pacific atolls.

By the mid 1990s, even China was morphing into a free market society. But not North Korea. Its paranoid leaders feared any kind of compromise, since the long-ago war and animosity were the only things that kept them in power over a starving, brain-washed people.

Smith knew all this, as he rode toward the joint security area. Yet he felt almost nostalgic about the old, familiar enemy of international communism. Without the Russian bear breathing down America's neck, Smith just didn't feel the same fire in his belly. His initial mission as a Marine—battling communists to the death—seemed to be done. There could be new enemies looming on the horizon, but nothing on the scale of nuclear-armed Soviets ready to rampage across Western Europe and attack the United States.

His jeep pulled up to the cinderblock building that housed the Armistice Commission, the scene of constant haggling since the Korean War ground to an unsatisfying halt in 1953. Over the years, each side had accused the other of thousands of truce violations, with neither willing to accept any blame.

Smith looked out at the fortified towers on the barren landscape and thought of the two Army officers who had been brutally beaten to death in 1976 by axe-bearing North Koreans while the American troops tried to trim a poplar tree in the DMZ. Since the axe murder, security guards had been forbidden to cross over to North Korea's side of the security zone. He saw the bridge that runs astride the military demarcation line, the Bridge of No Return. He could imagine the exchange of prisoners on the bridge in 1953, where any soldier who voluntarily walked north would never be allowed to return to South Korea.

All around him, he was reminded that even though Korea had signed an armistice, it was still far from achieving a lasting peace.

Entering the austere building, Smith felt remarkably calm. It was like standing in a tomb full of Cold War ghosts—and the North Koreans were the undertakers. This whole exercise over the fate of the downed Army pilot was just one more charade that let them keep living in their war-torn fantasy world.

Smith sat down on one side of a long conference table next to his translator, a bright-eyed American soldier of Korean descent. On the other side sat a stern-faced major general in the North Korean army, a career bureaucrat wearing a green wool uniform. He had a bored, yet angry air about him.

The North Korean immediately began fulminating about "American aggression" and the provocative acts of the Army helicopter pilots.

Smith cut him off. "Hey look," he said through his translator, "I don't know what happened, and you don't know either. You're a soldier just like I am, and you should know that soldiers screw up. This guy made a mistake, that's all."

The North Korean was taken aback at first by Smith's bluntness. But he recovered and shouted, "Your pilot is a spy!"

Smith shook his head and laughed. Then he leaned back in his chair as though the two of them were just playing poker. "Aw c'mon!" he insisted, "the poor guy made a mistake; he flew his helicopter into your air space, that's all. I'm sorry that happened, but you already killed his copilot. There was no intention to do any harm, and he didn't harm anybody. We want you to release Chief Warrant Officer Hall."

The North Korean wasn't buying it. He crossed his arms and pouted—a petulant pose he had down pat. It's funny, Smith thought, that he calls *us* puppets when his act is completely orchestrated, right down to a tirade about the Americans acting as "puppets of the south." The general even took a verbal shot at Smith's translator, calling the Korean-born American a traitor to his people and a "lackey of the imperialist running dogs."

Smith's attention wandered as the general droned on. Such bombastic behavior was tolerated by the U.N. officials at Panmunjom as part of a kind of Kabuki dance that always preceded getting down to business. But Smith, who never claimed to be a diplomat, finally had all he could take.

"Look," he said, leaning across the table, "you're a soldier and I'm a soldier. We're about the same age—right? You're about 50?"

Taken aback by the interruption, the general crossed his arms and glared at the rude American. Nonetheless, when his translator delivered the personal inquiry, he nodded and listened.

"See, it's true!" Smith said eagerly. "You and I both have served our nation's military all of our lives, so it's important we understand where we're coming from."

The general seemed interested in what he had to say, so Smith continued, "All of us who serve in uniform are affected by the significant events of our lives, and we probably were most affected by those things that occurred when we were young.

"For me, the significant emotional event of my life, the thing that my life has been built around, is the Vietnam War. I don't know what you were doing during that time, but I know I was there with the South Vietnamese, and we were fighting communists. We were attempting to stop the spread of communism, a thing which I consider a scourge on the face of the Earth."

Smith's fresh-faced Army translator was gamely trying to make Smith's laid-back soliloquy make sense in Korean, even as the Marine general strayed far from the usual script of these meetings. For in his inimitable way, Smith had launched the rhetorical equivalent of an incursion over North Korean air space, and now he was ready to drop his homemade bombs.

"Now you said something earlier about this young man, slandering him as a 'traitor to his people,'" Smith said, motioning to the Army translator but keeping his pale blue eyes locked on his nemesis across the table. "Let me tell you something, general. When I was in Vietnam, some of those other United Nations countries weren't there with us, even though they also were threatened by the communists. But I remember who *was* there fighting beside us—the South Koreans. And I'll never forget that, general, never! For as long as I live, I will remember the South Koreans. They are our friends, they are our fellow soldiers, we are of one blood. And as long as I live I will fight to the death to keep them at our side. And as long as you threaten them, you threaten *me*."

By now, the other general was simply flabbergasted. Over the decades of negotiating border disputes, no one had ever crossed the line like this, speaking so bluntly and stripping away the cloak of diplomacy. After a few speechless seconds, the North Korean returned to his default position and started spouting off about the proletariat and the people. But he clearly was stumped about how to proceed. He might as well have been talking directly to Douglas MacArthur for all the good his rhetoric was having on this crazy American Marine who appeared slightly bemused by the translation. Finally, the North Korean pushed back his chair, which scraped on the wooden floor, and stomped off. The meeting was over, and the door slammed shut like a gunshot.

Smith's brutal honesty could have backfired, but it didn't. Other Americans were working behind the scenes to secure the pilot's release, including then-Rep. Bill Richardson of New Mexico, who happened to be on an official visit to Pyongyang. A deal was struck to release the downed Army pilot. The State Department signed a written "understanding" expressing "sincere regret for this incident," with a pro forma promise to avoid any such incursions in the future. The official record did not include an account of the tongue-lashing by the Marine duty officer.

As the 1990s drew to a close, Ray Smith, Marty Steele, and Jim Jones all had more than thirty years in the Marines—or together, nearly a century of service. Jones and Steele each had been promoted to three-star general. Smith seemed to be ready to join them as lieutenant generals. In early 1999, Smith assumed command of Camp Lejeune—an important job, but a dead-end assignment if he wasn't recommended for promotion to three-star. Inside the Pentagon, Steele was working to advance the cause of his old roommate, arguing that Smith's experience and legendary status as a warrior were assets that shouldn't be lost by the Corps. He would make a great MEF, or Marine Expeditionary Force, commander. Steele's boss, General Krulak, agreed.

Only one thing stood in Smith's way—approval by the Navy Secretary, John Dalton, who would then pass his name along to be approved by the Senate Armed Services Committee.

"Tell Ray I want to talk to him before he meets with Dalton," Krulak said.

Steele smelled trouble. The main stumbling block to Smith's third star was E-Tool himself. He would have to be careful during the interview with Dalton, particularly on one issue: women in combat.

For more than a decade, as women continued to make strides in the other military services, the Marine Corps was the last holdout in liberalizing its training and combat assignments. It segregated women during boot camp, and kept them out of combat positions. It was a delicate, and perhaps impossible, balancing act for the Marine Corps leadership to recruit women and tout equal opportunity, then not trust them to fight alongside the men.

When Smith arrived at the Pentagon, Steele felt a mixture of pride and trepidation at the upcoming interview. Smith looked every bit the war hero, with a rack of medals that reflected how many times he had risked his life for Corps and country—the Navy Cross for the Easter Offensive, the Silver Star for Hue City, and a host of other medals and commendations, from the Bronze Star to the Purple Heart with two gold stars.

As Smith walked in with his easy cowboy's gait, Steele was filled with a sense of pride at his old roommate. He hoped Smith was ready to climb up to the next rung. He *should* be promoted again. But unlike the old obstacle course back at Quantico, which could be surmounted by hard work and determination, this interview had a more slippery slope—one greased by personality and politics.

Krulak greeted Smith, and Steele pulled up a chair beside him. He wanted to warn his friend that the interview with Dalton might seem strange at first and wanted to prepare him for any curveballs. Steele explained: "He'll have a list of written questions, Ray, and it's going to seem stiff and very official. The most important question will come at the end when he asks you about training for combat."

That would be a loaded question, one that should be treated like a live grenade. Women had carved out a long and distinguished role in the Corps since they formed the Marine Corps

Women Reserves in 1942. But their underlying purpose had been to perform work that would free the men to fight. Even as recently as Operation Desert Storm, the 1,000 women Marines had taken on support roles in communications and logistics.

The Army, Navy, and Air Force had moved toward joint basic training, but the Marines had held the line at Parris Island and San Diego, keeping the men and women in separate programs at boot camp. This often caused heartburn during congressional hearings, since the Corps stood out for not changing with the times. Yet the official Army and Defense Department policy still limited women to support units and away from infantry that clashed with the enemy.

It was a touchy issue that needed to be avoided or soft-pedaled in these hypersensitive times. "Don't be brutally blunt," Steele advised. "Just give the official line: 'Boot camp is challenging enough without the additional challenge and distraction of the gender issue.'"

Smith frowned. "I'm not sure I can buy that."

A voice crackled over the intercom. "Mr. Dalton is ready for General Smith, sir."

"Good luck, Ray," Steele said.

As he walked into the posh office of the Navy Secretary, Smith hoped to have a serious chat about various defense issues, including the Marines' role in the current military regional war-fighting structure. Dalton, a 1964 Naval Academy graduate, was a contemporary of his, so Smith assumed they would find plenty to talk about.

Dalton was a Texas lawyer who had secured the Pentagon post as a reward for fundraising during the second Clinton presidential campaign. For him, the role of women in the Navy and Marines remained a front-burner issue, especially after a sex scandal that had rocked the Navy in the early 1990s.

In late 1991, drunken Navy and Marine Corps pilots attending their annual celebration in Las Vegas—known as Tail Hook—made women run down hotel gauntlets and engaged in all sorts of lewd behavior. This sparked investigations, recriminations, demotions, lawsuits, and a barrage of bad publicity. Against this backdrop, Dalton had to conduct his own litmus test for the promotion of any admiral or general to three stars—especially someone like E-Tool Smith, whose tough-guy reputation preceded him.

After posing a series of innocuous questions he read from a clipboard, the Navy secretary put down his prepared text. "What is your personal opinion about the direction we are all going with regard to women in the military?"

Smith paid close attention to how Dalton phrased the question. By law, general officers testifying before Congress are required to give honest assessments whenever they're asked for personal views on any defense issue. It was a law dating back to the 1960s when military leaders didn't feel comfortable giving straight answers to Congress about the president's policies in Vietnam. The law was supposed to shield any military officer who felt compelled to speak out about national policy.

Smith's mind raced. No, he wasn't testifying before Congress, but this was all part of the vetting process for his name to be submitted for confirmation by the Senate Armed Services committee. So he decided that Dalton's question about women in the military was inextricably bound to that legal process. He also wanted to give a straight answer, even if it wasn't the politically correct one.

"Sir," he said to Dalton, "do you really want my personal opinion on that?"

"Yes, I do," Dalton said.

"To tell you the truth," Smith said with his cragged smile, "I wish we weren't having this conversation."

Dalton looked at Smith curiously. "What do you mean by that?"

Smith took a deep breath and plunged in. "Mr. Secretary, I come from a large family. I have four sisters, my sisters are as capable of fighting as I am. But I damn sure don't want them to. I don't believe the most powerful nation on earth should *want* to send its women to war. In my honest opinion, Mr. Secretary, only losers send their women to war—countries in such desperate situations that they have to send their women to war.

"The entire issue, in my opinion, Mr. Secretary, represents a strain in the American body politic that indicates we aren't really serious about fighting our wars."

Looking Dalton square in the eye, Smith continued, "But Mr. Secretary, more powerfully than I feel that, I feel that those of us that are in uniform have to understand that we don't make the nation's policy. That's up to your boss, the President, and to the Congress of the United States. And I believe that if the people of America *want* to send their women to war, even as infantrymen, if they send them to me, I'll train them the very best that I know how."

When Smith was done, a somber-looking Dalton said, "Is there anything that you want to add that hasn't come up?"

Since he'd been honest thus far, Smith decided to keep going. "Well, I have to tell you that I'm a little surprised that I'm interviewing to take command of the Marine Corps' premier warfighting command and you and I have not talked about fighting wars."

Dalton gave him a blank gaze, but didn't take Smith up on his invitation to have a more substantive discussion. "Thank you for coming in," he said, adding, "and for your years of service to the country."

Walking out of the Secretary's posh office, Smith figured he'd done what he set out to do. He was honest, and said that he would obey orders even if he didn't agree with them. Despite his many skirmishes with authority over the years, Smith was still a small-town boy at heart, a Marine who wanted to serve his country.

Several days later, though, word arrived from the Commandant: Dalton had turned down his promotion, and Smith would have to retire within the year.

Why had Smith given Dalton an answer that might scuttle his career? To Smith, it was a matter of honesty and integrity. But his friend Marty Steele wondered if his old roommate had simply grown tired of dealing with the system. "I was very disappointed," Steele said. "This man who did what he did as a lieutenant and captain in Vietnam, and has the presence of mind to look that North Korean general down the way he did. . . . That he would do this was beyond my comprehension. I was devastated, perhaps more devastated than Ray."

Gen. Al Gray agreed. "Ray Smith should never have been allowed to get out. He is one of the best warriors this country ever had. He's still a national asset."

Dalton said through a spokesman that he could not remember the conversation with Smith.

Not long after Ray Smith's career-ending interview, Marty Steele reached his own professional crossroads. In early 1999, he would either be selected as the next Commandant or he would secure one of a handful of regional commands—the commanders in chief, or CINCs—reserved for four-star generals. He remained close to General Krulak, whose four-year term as Commandant expired June 30, 1999.

Steele knew his prospects to succeed Krulak were slim because the Commandant, while dominant within the Corps, does not get to pick his successor. As part of the government's system of checks and balances, the Secretary of Defense holds the authority to recommend who the President should nominate for the service chiefs.

Besides Steele, there were many qualified candidates to succeed Krulak, including Peter Pace, another lieutenant of the late 1960s. But Cohen was always clear about his choice for leading the Marines into the twenty-first sentury. "We put the handwriting on the wall who Krulak's successor would be," said Robert Tyrer, Cohen's chief of staff. "There was never a chance that it was not going to happen." Jim Jones, his military assistant, would be picked "not because he was Cohen's buddy, but based on the merits," Tyrer said. "He was the logical candidate for the job."

Steele was hoping for a separate path to continuing his career. Krulak proposed making him the first Marine to serve as commander in chief of U.S. forces in the Pacific, or CINCPAC. It would have been a plum assignment, allowing him at age fifty-one to tap his vast network and expertise around the Pacific. In a long memo to Cohen, Krulak noted Marty Steele's visits to forty-four countries and his close ties with political and military leaders around the Pacific Rim.

Nonetheless, Cohen chose a navy admiral for the regional command post. It was a numbers game, and Steele lost: the Marines already had two generals serving as CINCs—Tony Zinni at Central Command in Saudi Arabia and Jack Sheehan at the Atlantic Command in Norfolk. A third Marine in a regional command put Marines in charge of half of the prime leadership positions. This would have been viewed as a slap in the face by the Army, Air Force, and Navy leadership as well as their friends in Congress.

Finally, Steele could see that, despite the well-intentioned support of Krulak, the game was over. He wanted to let Jones know there were no hard feelings. He was tired of the chatter around the water coolers and coffee pots in the Pentagon, and the people saying that the system shouldn't be rigged in Jones's favor. It was time to clear the air.

But for some reason, Jones seemed to be avoiding him. Steele felt like a stalker, trying to linger in the tan corridor outside Cohen's office for a chance to pull Jones aside. Finally, he caught up with him.

"We need to talk," Steele said, drawing him aside. Jones frowned and glanced at his watch.

"Sorry, Marty, this isn't a good time. I've got a meeting with the Secretary on the Hill."

"This won't take long," Steele said. He gathered himself, locking in on Jones's steely gaze. Steele was more than half a foot shorter, but he had a powerful grip from his days on the gridiron. He clasped Jones's arm like a linebacker who won't let go.

"Jim, I know you've heard all the talk about the Commandant pushing my name for the nomination—"

Jones tried to pull away. "Stop, Marty. It's not a good thing to talk about."

Steele leaned closer, and said in a voice that was between a whisper and a growl. "Listen, Jim, I want you to know that I'm disappointed about all the scuttlebutt, and I'm disappointed that General Krulak has been so persistent about this. But I can't convince him to stop his campaign on my behalf."

Jones appeared ready to bolt down the hall, but Steele blocked him. They made an incongruous pair: short, stocky Steele, a former running back and centerfielder; and long, lanky Jones, a former basketball player who still had his hook shot. Steele had him in a full-court press. "You and I go way back, all the way to Basic School. This is me, Marty Steele, we're friends, right?"

"Sure," Jones said, "but—"

For once, the articulate general was at a loss for words.

Steele persisted, "I want to let you know that I think you're the right man for the job, and I support you one hundred percent."

Jones put his hand up, as though warding off an evil spirit. "I'd rather not talk about it," he said curtly. "It's premature."

Steele laughed dryly. "What do you mean premature? It's over. You *are* the nominee to the president."

When Jones protested again, Steele smiled. "Are you superstitious? Do you think I'm going to jinx this, or leak it to the *Post?* I'm not about to do that. I have no hidden agenda. I'm talking to you as my friend, and I don't want this to come between you and me. I'm not going to be Commandant, and you are. I don't even *want* to be Commandant. I would like to be CINCPAC."

For once, he wished his friend would drop his guard. For as long as he'd known Jones, he'd always put up a kind of emotional shield that was hard to crack. Just this once, Steele wished he'd let him in.

"I'm sorry, but I've got to go," Jones said. "We'll talk later." With that, he spun away from Steele, and disappeared into the flow of pedestrian traffic.

After more than thirty years of living and breathing the Marines, Marty Steele knew it was time for him to reenter the civilian world. He knew he could succeed, but it would be hard to say good-bye.

Steele was traveling to South America when he got the news about the CINC's job from someone at U.S. Central Command in

Tampa. He was hurt that Cohen didn't take time to speak to him personally about his decision. Mostly, though, he was saddened to realize that, after thirty-four years of service, his long march as a Marine was coming to an end.

Steele started clearing out his Pentagon office in May 1999, and prepared to move to New York to head the *Intrepid* Museum. He poured his energy into a new organization, building up a non-profit group that promotes military history and values for students aboard the restored aircraft carrier *Intrepid* docked on New York's West Side. He established a new mission to honor national heroes, educate the public, and inspire youth about the price of freedom.

Before Steele left the Pentagon, Jones called to ask him to reconsider his letter of resignation. He knew Steele probably thought that as a Krulak protégé, he would be expected to leave. Everyone knew there was no love lost between the outgoing Commandant and the new one. But that was no reason to resign, Jones told him. He offered Steele several high-level posts, including command of the Fleet Marine Force Pacific and the 1st Marine Expeditionary Force.

But after the disappointment of not getting the Pacific joint command, Steele sensed it was time to go, and he politely told Jones so. Somehow it felt right to report for his new civilian duty aboard an old aircraft carrier, where he could set up a new base of operations and pursue another course in life.

Working at the *Intrepid* would be like being captain of a ship of history: After entering the Navy's fleet in 1943, the *Intrepid* played a key role in the Battle of Leyte Gulf near the Philippines. It survived so many hits by Japanese *kamikazes* that it became known as "the ghost ship." The *Intrepid* stayed in service through the 1960s, when its planes supported American forces in Vietnam and its helicopters snatched up capsules in NASA's Mercury and Gemini space programs.

In his early fifties, Gen. Marty Steele, retired, stood on the flight deck of the Intrepid and wondered what new missions lay before him. For this Marine, the wars were over.

SEPTEMBER 2001

The Commandant's staff works in a set of cramped offices deep inside the Pentagon. On a typical morning, it is a cyclotron of activity as aides, protocol officers, and generals dart in and out, handling the official business of the Marine Corps in and around Washington.

A staff sergeant at the front desk serves as a gatekeeper, greeting visitors and fielding telephone calls. It seems fitting that everyone—congressman, senator, or White House official alike—must get past a duty sergeant to reach the top-ranking Marine, whose office lies somewhere beyond the entry cubicles at the core of this beehive of activity.

The walls are covered with paintings and photographs capturing some of the great moments of the Corps: hollowed-eyed Marines in ponchos, covered in ice and worn down by battle, after surviving the onslaught of the Chinese Communists at Korea's Chosin Reservoir; and further back in time, an oil painting, "Marines Aboard USS *Wasp* engage HMS *Reindeer*, 1814," shows a scene from the War of 1812, as blue-coated Marines take aim at the British red coats.

A more recent photo shows the thirty-second commandant, James L. Jones Jr., looking sharp in his dress blues, chatting with Vice President Dick Cheney.

Out the window, the Potomac River shimmers in the early morning sunshine. Towering above the water, the monuments to Washington, Jefferson, and Lincoln provide quiet testimony to the nation's endurance. And further on, the spire of the National Cathedral is a pointed reminder of the solace sought by presidents and Congress alike during trying times.

The perpetual meetings inside the Commandant's office are orchestrated by his military secretary, Col. George Flynn. The slim, wisecracking native of New Jersey has a peephole that lets him peer into General Jones's office to see if he's ready for his next appointment. Flynn eyes the clock. It's just past 9:30 A.M., and "the boss" must leave for a mid-morning funeral across the river in Georgetown.

A TV in the waiting room is usually on mute. But someone turns it up after they notice a special news report break into *The Today Show*—a commercial airliner has crashed into one of the World Trade Center towers. It's an unbelievable, terrible explosion in the heart of New York City. Nobody can believe their eyes. The general joins his staff in time to see a second airliner burst into flames against the second tower. As the fire and smoke rushes toward the camera, one name crosses his mind: Osama Bin Laden, the subject of recent intelligence briefs on global terrorism.

The phones start chirping. The desk sergeant is trying to keep up with the calls—"Office of the Command—"—when everything goes silent. The entire building seems to shudder as a strange over-pressure fills the hallways. Earthquake? A horn signals an evacuation.

Everyone's ordered out, including Jones. Only George Flynn stays behind to shut down the office computers, which contain classified material. Jones isn't flustered. Evacuation drills are routine at the Pentagon and, despite the disturbing scenes from New York, this could be one more drill. The Pentagon, after all, is a massive structure and a city unto itself. Erected in only sixteen months in the middle of World War II, it was built in a five-sided shape to shoehorn the building onto an open space between Arlington Cemetery and the Potomac River. After using 327 architects and 15,000 construction workers who worked round-the-clock, the Pentagon opened on January 15, 1943—a marvel of American ingenuity and perseverance.[3]

Now the Pentagon seems to exhale as a surge of air rushes through its corridors. Jones hurries outside with his aides and a bodyguard to his car idling in front of the north entrance. Sirens wail and a pungent, burning smell fills the air. Jones slides into the back of the black Lincoln with "1775" on its plates. His driver speeds away and, before they reach the Memorial Bridge, they notice large shards of metal stuck like knives into the grassy banks above Washington Boulevard.

He would turn back, but so far no one has been able to tell him what has happened. He will keep his commitment to attend a funeral over in Washington, and keep in touch with his office by car phone. A column of thick black smoke rises from the Pentagon, snaking ominously into the otherwise spotless blue sky. The unthinkable has happened: America has been attacked on its shores.

An hour later after the funeral, Jones gets back in his staff car and, driving back across the Key Bridge, learns more about the deaths and destruction at the Pentagon. "Take me to the annex," he says somberly. His Lincoln follows detours around the phalanx of fire, police, and rescue vehicles, and slowly makes its way up Columbia Pike to the Navy Annex, which looks down on the Pentagon from a ridge about half a mile to the east. Seeing the black smoke belching from the wounded building, Jones thinks back to 1968 and his night of mortal combat on Foxtrot Ridge. Then, as now, he must take the high ground to regroup.

They pull into the parking lot of the Navy Annex, a beige, nondescript building that was the former Marine Corps Headquarters, and now, among other installations, houses the Marine Corps personnel department. Hustling to a conference room, he orders the evacuation of key Marine functions from the Pentagon to the Annex. He invites both the Secretary of the Navy and the Chief of Naval Operations to also make use of the Annex as a temporary command post. The Navy's new communications center had been wiped out when the hijacked airliner crashed into the Pentagon's newly renovated wing.

Jones learns his general counsel, Peter Murphy, narrowly escaped the subsequent explosion. His fourth-floor office was located directly above the point of impact of American Airlines Flight 77. The impact tossed him into the air, along with his deputy, Bobby Hogue. Both somehow escaped injury and managed to escape through the roiling smoke.[4] Murphy staggered outside and they zigzagged through the thousands of other fleeing workers until they found Hogue's car. The five-mile trip home to Alexandria, normally about a fifteen-minute ride, took three hours this day as traffic was backed up for miles.

When he got home, Murphy found his wife was nearly hysterical from not knowing his fate.

That night Jones called Murphy's home to check on him. The dapper attorney assured him he was fine. But he appreciated the parting words of Diane Jones, who said quietly, "We're praying for you."

🌟 🌟 🌟

The next morning, September 12, Peter Murphy attends the meeting at the Navy Annex. From this vantage point on a hill west of the Pentagon, he can look down upon the smoldering ruins. It is sobering to see the carnage of the terrorist attack; yet even in these early hours after the 9/11 attacks on New York and Arlington, he can see how the hijackers missed a much larger opportunity to strike at the heart of the American command structure: the Boeing 757 hit the recently-fortified side of the Pentagon, missing the side of the nearly sixty-year-old building that would have taken out Secretary of Defense Donald Rumsfeld and the Joint Chiefs, including Gen. Jim Jones.

No one knows what happened inside the commercial airliner before it swooped into the base of the five-sided building. As Murphy ponders the smoking ruins, he wonders what transpired between the hijackers and the passengers inside the stolen airliner. Why had it circled around the Pentagon and plunged into its base when so many other valuable targets lay close by, including the Capitol and the White House? The hijackers, it turned out, had run smack into the most fortified side of the Pentagon.

Still, the building looks like it's been bashed by a massive artillery attack, with airplane wreckage strewn about like so much shrapnel. Someone has draped an American flag to cover the gaping hole in the Pentagon as recovery work continues. Some 125 people, including 59 in the airliner, are reported dead.

Only now does it dawn on Murphy that the plane hit directly below his office. This realization makes him feel woozy, and he sits down in a corner of the conference room as an extraordinary meeting of the top brass of the Navy and Marine Corps gets underway.

More than seventy admirals and generals are on hand, including Navy Secretary Gordon England and Adm. Vern Clark, the Chief of Naval Operations. They start an informal round of discussions about the implications of the attack for both services. The armed forces have been put on DefCon Three, for "defense condition three," the highest state of military readiness since the 1973 Arab-Israeli War.

When it's time for General Jones to speak, Murphy senses the calming effect he has on the room. "We don't know what's happened," Jones says, "but we're going to find out as quickly as we can. Let's pray for those who didn't make it out, and be deliberate and aggressive in what we do to punish the perpetrators."

Rather than waving the flag, or trying to whip up hostility toward the hijackers or their purported sponsors, Jones keeps cool and firm in resolve to take action at the right time and place.

"He didn't bullshit anybody," Murphy said later. "There was no bravado. It was a great message because it was reality."

☆ ☆ ☆

As the reality of September 11 set in, the Marine Corps prepared to be part of a joint operation with the Army to invade Afghanistan. Jones pushed his commanders to work as fast as possible to move men and equipment into place to topple the Taliban and start the hunt for Osama Bin Laden.

But as the plans for war progressed, it was important to keep up appearances to the public. So Jones made it a point to maintain his normal schedule, flying around the country to speak before business and veteran groups, and, even more importantly, visiting his troops from California to Okinawa.

He wanted to let his Marines know that, despite the 9/11 attacks, the Corps would keep its proud tradition and, once again, strive to be the first to fight. And as the 173,000-strong force of leathernecks prepared to take on a shadowy enemy in the mountains of Afghanistan, Jones kept pushing for a leaner, meaner Marine Corps capable of responding to the worst the world can throw at it. These preparations had been in the works since July 1, 1999, when he took over as the thirty-second Commandant. Immediately, he called for a revival of the Corps' vaunted reconnaissance units, which he termed "broken," and for pumping up the morale of junior officers. He also called for an end to a kind of "zero defect mentality" that had trickled down from the top commanders, where one mistake can ruin a Marine's career.

Jones also helped put some new wrinkles into the "warrior ethos" that Al Gray pushed for in the 1980s. This drew the attention of *The Wall Street Journal* which touted his initiatives in a front page article headlined, "A Few Good Men Try Marine Martial Art, And Take on 2 Gurus." In those days before 9/11, the Marines were preparing themselves for peacekeeping duties, the Journal reported. "Worried that the Corps could lose its edge, the Marines' commandant, Gen. James L. Jones, decided to create a new martial art to give his Marines a sense of 'inner peace' even as they get in touch with their inner warrior."

As a result, the Marines hired a psychologist with a fifth-degree black-belt, and transferred a lieutenant colonel with a black belt in judo and put them together with 170 Marines at Camp Pendleton. The goal, *Journal* reporter Greg Jaffe wrote, was to strive for inner peace by mastering a dozen "warrior values," including accountability, integrity, and courage.[5]

The martial arts push was reminiscent of a visit with Secretary Cohen to the Indonesian jungle, where they had witnessed the circus-like feats of bat-swallowing commandos. But Jones's interest actually dated back far longer—to his Vietnam days, when he had seen the South Korean Marine Corps strike fear into the enemy's heart by using its self-defense discipline, *tae kwon do.*

He also initiated the development of a new combat utility uniform, a thoroughly modern attire with a computer-generated "pixelated" pattern. The new combat fatigues provided a distinctively Marine look for the new century and grew so popular that the Army launched plans to redo its uniforms along the same lines.

Another focus of his leadership was to follow in the footsteps of his old mentor, Al Gray, and to give due credit to the Marines the field—and to their noncommissioned leaders. In this spirit,

Jones created a high profile for another exceptional Marine who would play an important role in the Corps' new direction—Alford L. McMichael, a soft-spoken native of Arkansas, would become the first black Sergeant Major of the Marine Corps. He became a proponent of improving education and professional improvement among the troops. McMichael had Jones's ear and was able to present practical advice and suggestions from the enlisted ranks. It was a new channel to the power network in Washington—and one that let the senior NCOs know that their ideas mattered to the Commandant.

On a visit to a base in New Orleans, Jones's fondness for the Sergeant Major was evident as he introduced him to a group of NCOs. "Every day I'm allowed to serve with Sergeant Major Al McMichael," he said, "is a great day in my life."

They traveled together around the world, including a 1999 visit to Jungle Warfare Training Center in Okinawa, where Jones had commanded several infantry companies in the 1970s. In this relatively placid period—nearly two years before 9/11—Jones was cautioning against apathy.

"Don't think things can't happen," he told a rifle company. "In every one of my deployments here, my unit was called to a real-world contingency."

One magazine account of the visit noted, "Despite the sweltering heat, Jones and McMichael tirelessly addressed large and small groups of Marines at mess halls, clubs, and theaters, and in machine shops, office spaces, and training areas."

Shaking hands, answering questions, and posing for photographs, "The pair was warmly received at every stop"[6]

They kept a torrid pace of travel, attending receptions, dinner parties, and ship dedications around the country. When old veterans wearing the red caps of the Marine Corps League shuffled up to shake the Commandant's hand, Jones was unfailingly polite, asking where they had served and thanking them for their service.

In those months after 9/11—before the divisive presidential election campaign of 2004—a wave of patriotism washed over the States. And Jones was riding that wave. On a visit to Seattle in the summer of 2002, the scoreboard at the city's luxurious Safeco Stadium, was lit in golden letters: "Life, Liberty, and the pursuit of all who threaten it."

Along the waterfront of Puget Sound, Jones attended the dedication of a spanking new Aegis-class destroyer—a 9,300-ton behemoth equipped with guided missiles. The USS *Shoup* was named for another Commandant—David M. Shoup, a hero of the battle of Tarawa, but also a controversial figure who rocked the boat in the 1960s when he dared to question President Johnson's mishandling of the Vietnam War.

But on this cool June day in Seattle, everyone and everything seemed to be in harmony. The military has its sacred rituals, and the baptism of a new ship is among them. More than 5,000 of the faithful gathered on the Pacific's edge, with naval officers and sailors looking pure and spotless in their crisp white uniforms. They escorted wives and girlfriends resplendent in flowery dresses and fine West Coast tans.

The ship's bell rang three times, echoing across the waterfront. Then nearly 400 sailors and officers came out of nowhere, double-timing it from behind the viewing stand up to the ship. A brass band played "Anchors Aweigh" and the USS *Shoup* was ready to sail. Some of the Marines chuckled at the sight of the sailors gasping for breath after the short jog.

Afterward, at a dockside reception, the Marine faithful approached Jones like parishioners waiting to greet a visiting bishop. Some were active-duty Marines bringing their children to shake hands with the general and get his autograph. One captain, visiting from Quantico, brought his son, who was confined to a wheelchair. The boy tilted back his head and checked out the man in the blue uniform towering above him.

"How are you today?" Jones asked, touching the boy's head. The captain smiled at this seemingly small gesture. The Commandant was clearly comfortable around the boy in the chair, since one of his goals—along with Diane—was to improve services for families of children with disabilities. Caring for their own daughter, Jennifer, is a constant challenge that gives them special insights that can help other parents who are in the same boat.

As a cool wind blew off Puget Sound, the old salts from the Marine Corps League lined up in their red caps and pressed on to Jones, eager to relive their battles and talk to him about the generals they once knew. Guys like Willie K. Jones and Ray Davis and Al Gray. Standing on the waterfront, the ghosts of generals past lingered like the fog rolling in off the coast.

It was a long reception line, but Jones stayed unfailingly polite, honoring each old-timer who stopped by. One officer looking on approvingly from the wings said, "He's the main event."

During another 2002 tour of the West Coast, the "main event" continued in San Francisco as the first keynote speaker of the George P. Schultz Lecture series. Several hundred local glitterati— CEOs, congressmen, academics, and former Secretary of State Schultz himself—packed the old ballroom of the Marines' Memorial Association downtown. Jones had spent weeks preparing the speech, applying the finishing touches flying out from Washington on a five-hour flight on a converted DC-9 jet he shares with the Chief of Naval Operations. Though it has a separate sleeping section for "the boss" to do his work, the aging airliner is hardly opulent. The flight crew and cadre of aides sit elbow-to-elbow back in coach class seating, while the mess sergeant in charge of the galley makes do with basic accommodations. There's no stove or refrigerator, so the precooked meals are heated on hot plates. Drinks are kept on ice in coolers.

The Spartan business jet has a distinctly Marine Corps feel to it, as does the upbeat attitude of the Commandant's crew awaiting his arrival for takeoff at Andrews Air Force base outside of Washington. He finally arrives from a late meeting at the Pentagon and coming aboard he looks over his support staff and declares, "I need a drink."

The hatch shuts, and within a few minutes the plane is scooting down the runway as Bruce Springstein's "Glory Days" blares over the p.a. system. The jet banks over the Potomac River, shimmering pink and blue in the fading light, and sets a westward trajectory.

Within ten minutes, Jones reappears, looking more relaxed in a dark warmup suit. "I've got my Krispy Kreme Donut shirt on," he says with a grin. There's a big "K" across his chest.

Even as he relaxes, the paperwork of his job is relentless. Colonel Flynn has filled several black briefcases with reports and decision papers that must be completed before they touch down in California. "You wouldn't believe the amount of material he goes through every week," Flynn says.

During dinner in his tiny suite, he's regularly interrupted with updates from Flynn.

"We just lost a Harrier jet off the Tarawa," he says.

"Landing or takeoff?" Jones asks.

"Takeoff." But the pilot appears to be alright, with only a slight injury. "Sorry, sir," Flynn says of the interruption.

Jones shrugs. "It's okay. At least he's not hurt."

After his aide leaves, Jones turns to a visitor and says, "Welcome to my life."

For all the interruptions and constant demands, though, Jones is obviously in his element, primed and ready to lead. The next day in San Francisco is a perfect example. He is introduced by George Schultz, the former Marine captain who fought hard in the Reagan Administration to get the Marines out of Beirut before the cataclysmic terrorist bombing of 1983.

In his introduction, Schultz proudly notes, "The Marines throughout the existence of our country have been there fighting for us, and they're doing it today." He calls Jones "a Marine leader who never asks his men to do anything he wouldn't do."

After the applause died down, Jones scanned his speech on the lectern and, much to his surprise, realized he can't read a word of it. The television crews in the back of the room have set up lights that are so bright—and pointed directly in his eyes—that he's completely blinded. And no one has put a light on the lectern to give him a chance of seeing the work of the past few weeks.

Rather than stop or complain, though, he plunges onward, delivering the keynote address from memory. He starts by reminding the well-heeled audience that the spread of Al-Qaida and other terrorist groups poses new challenges for all free nations. "Things were easier when you had a clearly defined opponent," he says. But post-9/11, "We don't have one enemy, but a series of threats."

Sitting behind Jones on the dais, Schultz looks on with evident satisfaction at his choice of a keynoter. Like most everyone else—except some members of his staff, who know their boss strayed from his prepared text—he doesn't know that General Jones is winging it.

More than ever, Jones says, the nation's armed services must work cooperatively and erase the old interservice rivalries. There's simply no time for such nonsense. After the attacks on the Pentagon and New York, the Marine Corps has shown how quickly it can adapt to a new threat in a distant land. The Corps managed to transport troops and weapons hundreds of miles inland in Afghanistan to support the Army's Special Forces in the overthrow of the Taliban and the smashing of terrorist camps. Once again, the Marines have met the challenge of being "first to fight." He does not mention that one of his own sons, Greg, has enlisted and is now at The Basic School.

He also avoids the matter of Osama Bin Laden's escape from American forces at the battle of Tora Bora. Instead, facing this friendly group, he sticks to the broader theme of facing a decentralized, stateless kind of enemy who can be hard to find and destroy.

The Corps will often be the first into battle, he assures the rich Californians and Marines. But where and who will they fight? Despite all of the unanswered questions, the Commandant sounds upbeat and, moreover, he *looks* commanding, with the stars on his shoulders and the gallery of medals and ribbons on his chest.

"The Marine Corps knows who it is, and where it is going," he concludes, "The Marines are allowed to have only one fear: the fear of failing the nation. And the Corps will not fail.

"God bless you all. Semper fidelis."
He gets a standing ovation.

Earlier that day he had not expected any applause when he dropped in for an interview at the *San Francisco Chronicle*. He expected a grilling. The war in Afghanistan was bogged down, and Bin Laden remained at large, thumbing his nose at the United States and issuing videotaped messages of *jihad*. Rumors of war with Iraq are starting to dribble out of the Pentagon.

Before arriving at the newspaper's downtown offices, Jones was briefed about a variety of issues, including San Francisco's ban on military recruiters at its high schools.

"So what kind of ambush am I walking into this morning?" Jones asked over breakfast with Brig. Gen. Drew Davis, who headed the Corps' public affairs office. They reviewed some of the potentially explosive issues, including a Marine suspected in a recent local murder. On a lighter note, Davis informed Jones that the newspaper's top editor, Phil Bronstein, is married to the actress Sharon Stone.

"I've heard of Phil Bronstein," Jones deadpanned, "but I've never heard of Sharon Stone."

After more than two decades of dealing with the Washington press corps—making such high-powered friends as Sam Donaldson and Bob Woodward—Jones was able to stride into the *Chronicle*'s boardroom looking relaxed and friendly. Sitting down with the editorial board of a liberal newspaper would seem to be a public relations disaster in the making. Certainly, it was a long way from the Commandant's normal audiences of business leaders and veterans.

Yet even in the presence of eight journalists with wire-rim glasses, notebooks, and the intense manner of professional skeptics, Jones seemed at ease and in control of the situation. "I don't have an opening statement," he said. "I've been testifying for three straight days in Congress, and I'm talked out."

Laughter filled the room, and Jones didn't miss a beat, launching into a seemingly off-the-cuff talk about war and combat. First, he told the editorial writers that the military is not omniscient in its planning, and that sometimes the United States "seems to be better at getting into situations than getting out of them."

Then he reeled off statistics about the Corps, its relatively good retention figures, and the average age of today's Marine: twenty-four. He talked about information technology and other ways the leathernecks are keeping up with the times. As a few late-comers arrive, including one writer in blue jeans, he opened the floor for questions.

Is the war on terrorism new?

"Actually, not particularly," he replied. He harkens back to the suicidal aviators of the Japanese Empire—the kamikazes—and other terrorist tactics thrown at the Corps over its long history. The difference today, he said, is that the Corps will not attack the enemy in a direct, or "symmetrical," way, but rather it will "take the fight to them in an asymmetrical way."

Asked about the continuing resistance American forces faced in Afghanistan, he replied, "It's not particularly surprising. . . . Afghanistan is a very tribal region. You're going to find major pockets of resistance."

Some issues, such as land mines, Jones sidestepped with the deftness of a quarterback avoiding a blitz. While saying he understood the desire to rid the world of mines, he said he could not support a total ban because that would take one weapon away from his Marines.

The small group of writers—men and women alike—seemed intrigued when he spoke of the military's obligations to deal with the media. He learned during Vietnam, that "you say what you know when you know it. Bad news doesn't get better with age."

In a democracy, he said, leaders should tell the truth.

Heads nodded all around the conference table. For one shining moment, the U.S. Marine Corps and the liberal press occupied the higher ground together. Still, there were a few tough questions, such as one about the crash-plagued Osprey. The V-22 aircraft, which can land and take off like a helicopter and cruise like an airplane, had become an albatross around Jones's neck. After two crashes in 2000 killed twenty-three Marines, news reports surfaced of an attempted cover-up by Marine aviators in charge of the plane's maintenance.

"You're still fighting for that even though you've had a lot of trouble," one writer said, asking him to explain his reasons.

"I'm fighting for it because two independent panels have recommended it," Jones answered evenly. He then provided a detailed explanation of the engineering problems with the Osprey, including the "chafing of titanium fuel lines" that might have caused the engine failures.

"Those are relatively easy fixes," he said.

The meeting with the *San Francisco Chronicle*'s editorial board seemed to go well. So well, in fact, that Jones said he was surprised that they were so easy on him. He shared part of his secret of success with the press, one honed by many hours testifying before the Senate Armed Services Committee.

"The longer you talk," he said, "the fewer questions they can ask."

Even before the San Francisco trip, he found other ways to show his confidence in the Osprey. After one of the crashes in 2000, he flew to the Naval Air Weapons Station at China Lake, California, to fly on the experimental aircraft. Diane, who was traveling with him at the time, refused to stay behind on the ground, sitting in a hangar in the middle of the desert.

So Jones let her ride along, a moment captured by an Associated Press photographer. They sat side by side wearing flight suits and headgear as Jones spoke to her through a radio microphone. Diane listened intently on her headset. It was an unscripted moment, but better public relations for the Corps would be hard to buy.

Despite their best efforts, though, the Osprey project plagued Jones and cast a shadow over the Corps. Machinery could be fixed, but the core values of a service dedicated to trusting in each other was not something to be tinkered with. The Osprey scandal broke in early 2001 when Navy Secretary Robin Pirie Jr. received an

anonymous letter and audio tape from someone claiming to be a
mechanic in the V-22 squadron based at the Marine Corps Air Station at New River, North Carolina. The letter charged Lt. Col.
Odin "Fred" Leberman, the squadron commander, with ordering
the falsification of maintenance records to keep the tilt-rotor airplane flying.

Along with a letter was a tape, purportedly of Leberman, saying, "The reason we need to lie or manipulate the data or however
you want to call it, is that this program is in jeopardy."[8]

Under pressure from Congress for an independent investigation, Jones turned the matter over to the Pentagon's inspector
general. While denying any bias by the Marines' own investigation,
Jones said, "I am concerned that the nature and gravity of the alle-
gations may invite unwarranted perceptions of command influence or institutional bias."

The Osprey was grounded until further notice.

Privately, Jones said the lies and duplicity surrounding the aircraft was the nadir of his time as Commandant. But using an independent investigator was necessary, he said, because "when you
have a tragic accident such as this with the Osprey, I insist on
absolute honesty and absolute transparency to find out what happened. You don't circle the wagons because you're culturally
under attack. You take a few hits in the press, and if they're legitimate hits, you learn from them and you move on."

He made those observations on March 10, 2001, shortly after
the scandal broke. He had returned with Diane to North Carolina
to visit Jennifer, who was living in a group home. They had taken
her to a pancake house for breakfast in Jacksonville, North Carolina, home of Camp Lejeune.

For all he'd been through, Jones looked rested and relaxed.
He laughed about the sign outside the restaurant, which contained a greeting for someone named "Bubba." Looking around
at all the Marines and families eating breakfast, Jones said, "This is
the kind of place I'd like to own when I retire. A place for Bubbas." He also fantasized about buying a Harley Davidson and hitting the road with Diane riding on the back.

His motorcycle days were yet to come as more work lay ahead. He was sipping coffee to wake up from a long night of revelry. He was the keynote speaker at a rousing mess night hosted by 200 Marine lawyers who were part of the Corps' legal branch, the judge advocate general (JAG). The mess night tradition dates back to the British Royal Navy's formal gatherings to boost the officers' spirits, both literally and figuratively. With dress blues and a brass band playing music, the evening-long celebration combines elements of a Friars' roast with a medieval drinking party. As one newspaper account from 1816 describes it, "The company sat down to dinner at five o'clock and spent the evening with the purest harmony and good humor. . . . Accompanied with songs and music from the Marine Band, and announced by repeated discharges of artillery, many toasts were drunk." The martial celebration is thought to be the origin of "having a shot."

At Camp Lejeune, the shots came fast and furious. After each toast, the speaker was expected to drink from a large silver bowl filled with "grog," a heady brew of hard liquor that contained enough alcohol to launch a fighter jet.

When it was his turn to address the rowdy crowd, Jones duly drank from the ceremonial bowl. Then he went to work on the room as surely as David Letterman. He started by declaring that one of the lawyers, Brig. Gen. Joe Composto, was so "vertically challenged" that he actually had been standing on a chair while he spoke.

"I had a great speech prepared," Jones began, grinning down at Composto, "but I'm going to do like he did."

With that, the Commandant of the Marine Corps got up on his chair. Towering above the diners like the Jolly Green Giant, Jones searched for a major who a few minutes earlier had dared to stand and challenge his elders.

"I just want you to stand up so I can remember your face," said Jones, feigning outrage. "You're obviously trying to draw attention to yourself. You're obviously inebriated. We'll reconsider your pending promotion next year."

The major laughed uneasily and his face seemed to say, *General Jones was only kidding, right?* Jones got down from the chair, delivered a few more funny lines, then settled down to talk earnestly with this flock of legal eagles.

"First and foremost in our Marine Corps we celebrate the fact that we are number one, first and last, and always United States Marines."

A cheer rolled through the dining hall along with another round of toasts.

"That's a very important part of our culture," he continued. "It defines us. It speaks to where we are and everything we do for our nation. We learned that at the Basic School, to be a Marine rifle platoon commander. The Marine and his rifle is paramount in our mind, paramount in our ethos."

The hall fell silent. For all the chatter and the bad jokes and the clinking of glasses, this was the moment they had been waiting for—not a sermon, perhaps, but as close to it as they would come in this modern equivalent of a mead hall.

"We must never forget the transformation we received at the Basic School—the fact that we're a society not a bureaucracy. That social compact we make to each other as Marines is so very important, we must cherish it."

Standing before this roomful of comrades—with a few civilian friends allowed in the inner sanctum—Jones showed a rare bit of emotion. Not tears, perhaps, for as Marty Steele observed back in the Pentagon, he seems to protect his feelings behind a personal invisible shield.

No, his message that night at Camp Lejeune seemed to spring from a deeper place—the memories of a man looking back on a life filled with risk, patriotism, and purpose. It is a connection that allows him to speak so easily, yet with meaning, to each person in the room. Jones knows where the power lies, and it's not with vertical pronoun I. The true power of the Corps—the touchstone of the faith—comes from the strength of another word: we.

"I'm reminded every single day of our lives of that bond, that cultural tie—whether you've become a senator, whether you've become a CEO, or whether you left active duty to become a schoolteacher, it makes no difference.

"You harken back to that time with your formative days at the Basic School, with the classmates who helped make you who you are . . . and how that experience defined you as a Marine officer, and perhaps even more importantly, as a person."

General Jones looked out over his band of brothers and sisters and invited them to treasure their own transformation from civilian to Marine and, eventually, back to society. "Remember," he said, "that is probably the most important experience that happened, up to that point, in our lives . . . and we were changed forever."

Epilogue

Tracing the lives of three Marine generals may not be as hard as trying to keep up with them on the battlefield, but it has been a challenge. My initial assumption that these men in their mid-fifties were at a stage when they were slowing down, with ample time to reflect on their lives, was dead wrong. If anything, their lives—even in so-called retirement—fulfill Henry Adams's "law of acceleration" of history. Jones, Smith, and Steele each entered the twenty-first century like the "man meteorite" that Adams predicted in the early 1900s. They're still blazing new trails, with an uncanny knack for being close to the unfolding drama of history.

On the morning of September 11, 2001, Marty Steele was standing in front of the *Intrepid* Museum on West 46th Street when he looked up to see the first airplane hit the World Trade Center. He immediately called his staff into the *Intrepid*'s conference room, where they turned on a television and watched the second plane strike.

Steele closed the military-themed museum and called the FBI to offer the ship as a secure command post for federal agents. Within forty-eight hours, 750 agents were living aboard the fabled "ghost ship," staying for two weeks as they began investigating the surprise attack on America. The *Intrepid*, which had survived Japan's suicide attacks more than half a century before, sprang to life in this new hour of crisis.

Then Steele reached out to his son, David, who was a twenty-nine-year-old Marine AH-1W attack helicopter pilot. On 9/11, David Steele was serving with the special operations capable (MEU SOC) 15th Marine Expeditionary Unit, training in Australia and preparing to operate in the no-fly zone in Iraq.

Steele let his son know that, like his grandfather and father, he would be entering harm's way to defend his nation. Capt. David Steele and the other 2,200 Marines in the 15th MEU were deployed as the first conventional force to Afghanistan as Task Force 58, joining combat operations against the Taliban. Their landing more than 400 miles inland became the longest amphibious assault in the history of a Marine Expeditionary Unit.

Captain Steele was awarded the Air Medal with Strike Flight 2 for his combat missions over the treacherous mountain terrain. Since then, he has been promoted to major and now serves with the elite aviation group—HMX-1, or Helicopter Marine Experimental-1—that flies the president aboard his Marine One helicopter.

The events of 9/11 influenced the characters in this book—and its writing—in other ways. As I began my research, I discussed with Ray and Colleen Smith the possibility of returning to Grenada, where then-Lt. Col. Ray Smith led the successful air-ground operation of 1983. Ray had already returned to the tiny island-nation to mark America's role in overthrowing the Marxist government, a ceremony also attended by President Reagan. We talked about returning to retrace the footsteps of Battalion Landing Team 2/8 and perhaps find some of the gentle people of St. George's who had helped him sort the bad guys from the good. But because of the problems with air travel and security after 9/11, the trip fizzled out.

However, Ray Smith is never one to get pinned down for long. In 2002, he embarked on a new and remarkable journey that drew on his expertise in urban warfighting in Vietnam. He accompanied an old friend, Bing West, to join the invasion of Iraq. This led to the book *The March Up: Taking Baghdad with the 1st Marine Division*. West, a former Marine infantry officer and Assistant Secretary of Defense for International Security Affairs in the Reagan administration, described the unique way they managed to get into the thick of the action. "Back in December," West wrote, "Ray and I decided to write a book about the upcoming war in Iraq describing the changes in tactics between the fight in Hue City and the projected fight in Baghdad City in 2003. Although initially reluctant to have a retired general and a former assistant secretary of defense on the battlefield, Headquarters Marine Corps kindly issued us orders to serve as unpaid consultants in support of a Marine Corps public affairs film crew, at our own expense."[1]

After arriving in Kuwait, the intrepid duo was allowed to accompany the 1st Division with two stipulations: "First, that we were on our own, and second, that we keep a low profile because as a senior Marine said, 'we want to keep the focus on the young Marines, not us old guys—so don't get yourselves killed, because then you would be a story.'"

They obeyed orders, staying alive and chronicling the remarkable 900-mile trek of the 20,000-man force of Marines. They followed the "march upcountry" of the Greeks 2,400 years ago as recounted in *Anabasis*, the eyewitness account of the historian and military leader Xenophon. The Greek invaders had sided with a challenger to the Persian throne; the Americans wanted to topple a modern-day dictator and nemesis.

For some Marines, it was a chance to fight terrorism on foreign turf. "We want all jihad fighters to come here," Gen. John Kelly said. "That way we can kill them all before they get bus tickets to New York City."[2]

Subsequent events in Iraq—with the many questions about the Bush administration's intelligence failures—would do nothing to sully the accomplishments of the Marines who once again had done their duty and fought in the Corps' finest tradition. The Marines of 1967—those who had lived in O'Bannon Hall—could appreciate the symbolism underlying the first major mission of the twenty-first century. "The task force was named Tripoli, an allusion to the refrain in the Marine hymn 'From the halls of Montezuma to the shores of Tripoli.' In 1805 Lt. Presley O'Bannon had trekked 900 kilometers across the Sahara Desert to attack pirates along the shores of Tripoli."[3] In 2003, the 1st Division followed in the footsteps of Alexander the Great, who had defeated the huge army of Darius, King of Persia, in 331 B.C. That victory "began the long martial ascent of the West over the Middle East and Asia," West wrote.

Whether this latest invasion will ultimately help civilize and democratize the region remains an open question. But Vietnam veterans may have a sense of Yogi Berra's "deja vu all over again" with Iraq: demands for a troop pullout; dire warnings of the consequences of leaving; harsh rhetoric in Congress, with personal attacks that question critics' patriotism. Whatever happens, history-minded Marines know this won't be the last time their missions are subject to national mood swings.

And whatever the outcome in the cradle of civilization, it won't be for lack of effort or sacrifice by the Corps. At this writing, more than 600 Marines (or Marine reservists) have been reported killed in action, with many times that number wounded.

Meanwhile, Gen. James L. Jones keeps pushing to transform the military organization of NATO, working on a broad front that takes him from high-level conferences in Europe to meetings with troops and government leaders in Afghanistan, Iraq, and Africa. Though his current challenges play out on a global stage, some things never seem to change. The young second lieutenant who tried to better clothe and feed his troops is now a sixty-two-year-old general seeking better equipment and intelligence for his NATO forces.

"Strictly speaking, NATO has no organic intelligence," he said at an April 25, 2005, meeting. "We exist in the field on the largess of individual nations."

Something has changed, though. The Cold War of the "twentieth-century defensive, bipolar world" is over, he said, replaced by a murky world of terrorist cells and rogue nations—"a multipolar world requiring a flexible and rapid response to a myriad of threats."

Today, the man who gladly relinquished the nickname "Bulletproof" is creating a quick-action NATO Response Force (NRF). This seems fitting, since quickness and decisiveness are qualities that have defined his career, as well as those of Ray Smith, Marty Steele, Les Palm, and others from their Basic School class. Some fell in combat, some stayed in the Corps, but most took their skills into the civilian world, where they put the indelible stamp of the Marines on universities, companies, and non-profit groups. Their accomplishments, like those of the ancient Greeks, could fill a dozen more books and exhaust a platoon of biographers.

Like all good Marines, these men have never stopped marching.

Appendix

Into the island

The 2nd Battalion, 8th Marines landed north of Grenada's capital and helped free hostages, capture weapons and restore calm after a military coup.

EUROPE

Morehead City, N.C.O   OBeirut

AFRICA

OGRENADA

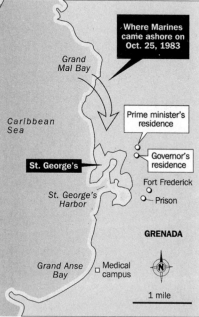

Where Marines came ashore on Oct. 25, 1983

Grand Mal Bay

Caribbean Sea

Prime minister's residence

St. George's

Governor's residence

Fort Frederick

St. George's Harbor

Prison

GRENADA

Grand Anse Bay

Medical campus

N

1 mile

Caribbean Sea

N

Pearls Airport

GRENADA

St. George's

AREA OF DETAIL

Airstrip

5 miles

The Battle of Beirut

The 2nd Battalion, 8th Marines relieved the units that filled in after the lethal attack of Oct. 23, 1983. Fighting continued at a series of checkpoints and positions near the city's airport.

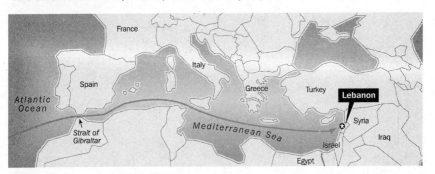

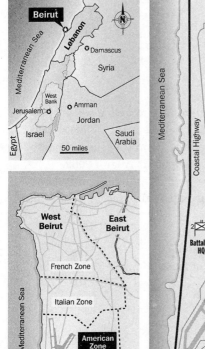

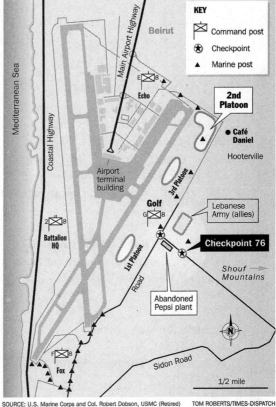

SOURCE: U.S. Marine Corps and Col. Robert Dobson, USMC (Retired)   TOM ROBERTS/TIMES-DISPATCH

Notes

ONE: THE "WARRIOR MONKS"
1. Gen. Tommy Franks and Malcolm McConnell, *American Soldier* (New York: HarperCollins Publishers Inc., 2004), 275.
2. David Rennie and Anton La Guardia, "Top US general attacks hawks' strategy on Iraq," *Daily Telegraph*, 23 August 2002.
3. Bill Gertz and Rowan Scarborough, "Afghanistan Lessons Don't Apply to Iraq, General Says," *Washington Times*, 22 August 2002, A-1.

TWO: THE SCHOOL OF EXPERIENCE
1. Edwin H. Simmons, *The United States Marines: The First One Hundred Years* (New York: The Viking Press, 1976), 108.
2. Ibid., 125.
3. Ibid.
4. Stanley Karnow, *Vietnam: A History* (New York: Penguin Books, 1983), 516.
5. W. M. Cryan, "The Basic School," *Marine Corps Gazette* 51, no. 5 (1967): 18–22.
6. Ibid.
7. Ibid.

THREE: OBSTACLES

1. U.S. Marine Corps, *Small Wars Manual* (Washington, D.C.: U.S. Government Printing Office, 1940), 45.
2. Ibid.
3. Simmons, *United States Marines*, 21.
4. Ibid., 22.

FOUR: UNDER THE ENEMY'S GUNS

1. Jack Shulimson et al., *U.S. Marines in Vietnam: The Defining Year, 1968* (Washington, D.C.: History and Museums Division, Headquarters, U.S. Marine Corps, 1997), 14.
2. Shulimson et al., *Marines in Vietnam*, 19.
3. Karnow, *Vietnam*, 273.
4. Shulimson et al., *Marines in Vietnam*, 11.
5. Ibid., 19.
6. Ibid., 23.
7. Ibid., 31.
8. David Douglas Duncan, *War Without Heroes* (New York: Harper & Row, 1970), 91.
9. Shulimson et al., *Marines in Vietnam*, 72.
10. Karnow, *Vietnam*, 552.
11. Shulimson et al., *Marines in Vietnam*, 260.
12. Karnow, *Vietnam*, 553.
13. Ibid.
14. Ibid., 554.

FIVE: THE ROCKET DODGER

1. Karnow, *Vietnam*, 542.
2. Keith William Nolan, *Battle for Hue: Tet 1968* (Novato, CA: Presidio Press, 1983), 4.
3. Ibid., 11.
4. Ibid., 14.
5. Ibid., 64.
6. Ibid.
7. Shulimson et al., *Marines in Vietnam*, 182.
8. Karnow, *Vietnam*, 547.
9. Ibid., 561.

10. Ibid., 553.

11. Shulimson et al., *Marines in Vietnam,* 312.

12. Ibid., 326.

13. Ibid.

SIX: GREEN FOR GO, RED FOR STOP

1. Mark W. Woodruff, *Foxtrot Ridge: A Battle Remembered* (Clearwater, Fla.: Vandamere Press, 2002), 23.

2. Ibid., 26.

3. Ibid., 5.

4. Ibid., 65.

5. Ibid., 103.

6. Shulimson et al., *Marines in Vietnam,* 320.

7. Woodruff, *Foxtrot Ridge,* xii.

SEVEN: POSITIONS OF AUTHORITY

1. Robert Debs Heinl, *Soldiers of the Sea* (Annapolis, MD: United States Naval Institute, 1962), 4.

EIGHT: MAY DAY MALAISE

1. Victor H. Krulak, *First to Fight: An Inside View of the U.S. Marine Corps* (Annapolis, MD: Bluejacket Books, 1984), xiv.

2. Ibid., xv.

NINE: "YOU SONUVABITCHING AMERICANS"

1. G. H. Turley, *The Easter Offensive: Vietnam, 1972* (Novato, CA: Presidio Press, 1985), 27.

2. Karnow, *Vietnam,* 22.

3. Turley, *Easter Offensive,* 80.

4. Ibid., 81.

5. "South Viets in Retreat Near DMZ," *Washington Post,* 1 April 1972, A-1.

6. Turley, *Easter Offensive,* 165.

7. John Grider Miller, *The Bridge at Dong Ha* (Annapolis, MD: United States Naval Institute, 1989), 151.

TEN: SOUL OF THE NEW CORPS

1. Simmons, *United States Marines*, 301.
2. Ibid., 297.
3. Ibid., 32.
4. Robert Debs Heinl, *Dictionary of Military and Naval Quotations* (Annapolis, MD: United States Naval Institute, 1966), 97.

ELEVEN: DRAWING THE LINE

1. Simmons, *The United States Marines*, 214.

TWELVE: STAR QUALITY

1. Robert Timberg, *The Nightingale's Song* (New York: Simon & Schuster, 1995), 276.

FOURTEEN: MID-COURSE CORRECTION

1. Thomas E. Ricks, *Making the Corps* (New York: Scribner, 1997), 146.
2. Larry Pintak, *Beirut Outtakes: A TV Correspondent's Portrait of America's Encounter with Terror* (New York: Lexington Books, 1988), 10.
3. Timberg, *Nightingale's Song*, 332.
4. Ronald Spector, *U.S. Marines in Grenada, 1983* (Washington, DC: History and Museums Division, Headquarters, U.S. Marine Corps, 1987), 2.
5. Rick Atkinson, *The Long Gray Line* (New York: Henry Holt, 1989), 483.
6. Marine Corps Development and Education Command, newsletter, January–March, 1984, 4.
7. Spector, *Marines in Grenada*, 1.
8. Atkinson, *Long Gray Line*, 484.
9. Ibid.
10. Spector, *Marines in Grenada*, 2.
11. Benis M. Frank, *U.S. Marines in Lebanon, 1982–84* (Washington, DC: History and Museums Division, Headquarters, U.S. Marine Corps, 1987), 3.
12. Robert T. Jordan, "Tribute to Sgt. Manuel A. Cox, USMC," Quantico, VA, June 7, 2000.

392 _____ Boys of '67

13. Spector, *Marines in Grenada,* 10.
14. Ibid., 7.
15. Ibid., 8.
16. Heinl, *Dictionary of Military and Naval Quotations,* 315.

FIFTEEN: THE MAYOR OF ST. GEORGE'S
1. Atkinson, *Long Gray Line,* 485.
2. H. Norman Schwarzkopf, *It Doesn't Take A Hero* (New York: Bantam Books, 1992), 252.
3. Spector, *Marines in Grenada,* 18.
4. Ibid., 22.
5. Ibid., 23.
6. Ibid., 25.

SIXTEEN: BUNKERING DOWN IN BEIRUT
1. Eric M. Hammel, *The Root: The Marines in Beirut, August 1982–February 1984* (Orlando, FL: Harcourt Brace Jovanovich, 1985), 303.
2. *Ibid.,* 213.
3. Frank, *Marines In Lebanon,* 2.
5. Pintak, *Beirut Outtakes,* 22.
6. Timberg, *Nightingale's Song,* 337.
7. Ibid., 341.
8. Ibid.
9. Ibid.

SEVENTEEN: "MARAHABA, MARINE"
1. Frank, *Marines in Lebanon,* 134.
2. Timberg, *Nightingale's Song,* 342.

EIGHTEEN: SHADES OF GRAY
1. Timberg, *Nightingale's Song,* 413.
2. Ibid., 206.
3. Ricks, *Making the Corps,* 143.
4. Ibid., 143.
5. James Webb, *Fields of Fire* (Englewood Cliffs, NJ: Prentice-Hall, 1978), 338.

6. Timberg, *Nightingale's Song* (New York: Touchstone, 1995), 401–2.
7. Adam Gopnik, "American Electric," *The New Yorker*, 30 June 2003, 97.
8. Ricks, *Making the Corps*, 144–45.
9. Krulak, *First To Fight*, 3.
10. Ibid.

NINETEEN: DUST UPS

1. Rick Atkinson, *Crusade: The Untold Story of the Persian Gulf War* (New York: Houghton Mifflin, 1993), 194.
2. Ronald J. Brown, *Humanitarian Operations in Northern Iraq, 1991: With Marines in Operation Provide Comfort* (Washington, DC: History and Museums Division, Headquarters, U.S. Marine Corps, 1995), 14–15.
3. Oscar C. Decker, *Camp Colt to Desert Storm: The History of U.S. Armored Forces* (Lexington: University Press of Kentucky, 1999), 314.
4. Atkinson, *Crusade*, 251.
5. Kenneth W. Estes, *Camp Colt to Desert Storm: The History of U.S. Armored Forces*, 477.
6. Michael R. Gordon and Bernard E. Trainor, *The Generals' War: The Inside Story of the Conflict in the Gulf* (New York: Little, Brown and Company, 1995), 176.
7. Ibid., 177.
8. Atkinson, *Crusade*, 171.
9. Ibid.
10. Estes, *Camp Colt to Desert Storm*, 485.
11. Brown, *Humanitarian Operations in Northern Iraq*, 1.
12. Ibid.
13. Ibid., 2.
14. Ibid., 3. Brown notes that this would be surpassed in size and scope by the Marines' relief efforts in Somalia two years later.
15. Ibid., 26.
16. James L. Jones, "Operation PROVIDE COMFORT: Humanitarian and Security Assistance in Northern Iraq," *Marine Corps Gazette* 75 (Nov. 1991): 100.

17. Ibid., 101.
18. Ibid.
19. Ibid., 102.
20. Ibid., 107.

TWENTY: THE OTHER SIDE OF THE PENTAGON
1. Heinl, *Dictionary of Military and Naval Quotations*, 278.
2. T. R. Reid, *Washington Post*, 30 December 1994.
3. 9/11 Research, "Pentagon History," http://911research. wtc7.net/pentagon/history.html.
4. Timothy Dwyer, "Security Issues Elbow in on Design Work," *Washington Post*, 3 August 2003, C-1.
5. Greg Jaffe, "A Few Good Men Try Marine Martial Art, and Take on 2 Gurus," *Wall Street Journal*, 9 October 2000, A-1.
6. Arthur P. Brill Jr., "'You Are Ready'—Jones Salutes WestPac Marines," *Sea Power*, October 1999.
7. "Marines Turn Osprey Investigation Over to Pentagon," 24 January 2001, http://archives.cnn.com/2001/US/01/24/ osprey.pentagon/index.html.

EPILOGUE
1. Bing West and Ray L. Smith, *The March Up: Taking Baghdad with the 1st Marine Division* (New York: Bantam Dell, 2003), 8.
2. Ibid., 248.
3. Ibid.

Acknowledgments

I could not have written this book without the generous support of the Marine Corps University Foundation, where Maj. Gen. Donald R. Gardner and Lt. Col. John R. Hales encouraged me to apply for a research grant. Thanks to the General Gerald C. Thomas Endowment for Amphibious Warfare Research, and its generous benefactor, Bruce H. Hooper, I was able to take some time to travel and conduct interviews. The Marine Corps Heritage Foundation also provided a research grant.

Fred Graboske, chief archivist at the Marine Corps History and Museums Division in Washington, D.C., was an invaluable source of documents and leads. Col. John Ripley, director of the Marine Corps Historical Center, also helped me get started.

Christopher Evans, history editor at Stackpole Books, believed in *Boys of '67* from the start, providing steady encouragement and suggestions over the past six years. His assistant, David Reisch, has kept it all running smoothly. Literary agent Jody Rein has been a bedrock of support and a fountain of inspiration, along with her assistant Johnna Hietala.

I am grateful to Maj. Gen. Les Palm, executive director of the Marine Corps Association, who has patiently answered my many inquiries. Suzanne Palm also graciously answered questions about the life of a young Marine couple.

Ron Chambers, former publications director at the Naval Institute Press, provided professional guidance, and as a member of The Basic School Class 5-67, told his part of the story.

Former Secretary of Defense William Cohen and his chief of staff, Robert Tyrer, shed light on the workings of the Pentagon and Congress. Sen. John McCain took time out to talk about his early work on Capitol Hill with Jim Jones.

Former Commandant Al Gray was kind enough to discuss his career and his time with these men. Arnold Punaro, former senior aide to Sen. Sam Nunn and a major general in the Marine Reserves, pulled back the curtain on the Washington stage.

I am indebted to Gen. Anthony C. Zinni for writing the foreword.

Thanks to Capt. Gregory Jones for sharing his early experiences as a Marine.

Before his death in 2003, Gen. Ray Davis talked with me about his command of the Third Marine Division in Vietnam and about Jim Jones' time as his aide-de-camp. Thanks to Ralph Larsen and Harold Blunk for reliving the harrowing night on Foxtrot Ridge, and to Vic Noriega and Jerry Martin.

Justice Department attorney Barry Kowalski recalled his high school friendship with Jim Jones and their encounters in Quantico and Vietnam.

Brig. Gen. James R. Joy detailed the dangers of the Easter Offensive and the hard times in Beirut in 1983. Col. James P. Faulkner and Navy Vice Adm. Joseph Metcalf III added their perspectives to the on-board friction off the coast of Grenada. 2nd Lt. John Watts tried to educate me about ship-board logistics.

John Ligato gave me a street-level view of the Battle of Hue City.

Peter Murphy, counsel to the Commandant, described the traumatic events of 9/11 at the Pentagon. Washington attorney Fred Graefe added more details to the early career of Jim Jones.

Thanks to the many members of General Jones' staff who tried to keep me on schedule during his travels, including his military secretary, Col. George Flynn, and Sergeant Major of the Marine Corps Al McMichael.

Frank Kramer, an assistant secretary of defense during the Clinton administration, helped me better understand military and diplomatic efforts in the Pacific Rim in his travels with Marty Steele. Dr. James S. Chase, former chairman of the history department at the University of Arkansas, praised Steele's academic achievements.

Clebe and Deanna McLary showed that gracious southern hospitality is alive and well at Pawley's Island, South Carolina. So did Jim Barta, who served with Clebe as a Force Recon lieutenant.

Thanks to Maj. Gen. Matthew Caulfield for insights into prewar planning for the first Iraq invasion. Jim Jones' sergeant major with the 24th MEU(SOC), Sgt. Major William Hatcher, provided vivid recollections of the Kurds and Operation Provide Comfort.

Maj. Bob Jordan and Evi Cox-Jordan went beyond the call of duty in describing the life and times of Sgt. Manuel A. "Manny" Cox. They also were my point of contact with Beirut veterans and helped me reach a brave, and mostly forgotten, group: Col. Bob Dobson; Lt. Matt Aylward; Staff Sgt. Mike Leiphart; and infantrymen Matt Collins, Skip Wheeler, and Joe Hickey.

Authors Rick Atkinson, Dean King, and Charles Slack delivered professional advice and personal encouragement.

At the *Richmond Times-Dispatch*, business editor Pamela Feibish offered understanding, copy editor Linda Hall helped excerpt the book, and research librarian Kathleen Albers offered information. Mary Boynton, Bill Van Arnam, and other friends at St. Matthias' Episcopal Church have been a continuing source of good humor and support.

I owe an incalculable debt to the three main characters of this book and to their wives, all of whom patiently endured hundreds of e-mails, phone calls, and visits: Jim and Diane Jones; Ray and Colleen Smith; and Marty and Cindy Steele.

Finally, I wish to acknowledge the tireless efforts of my beloved wife, Deborah White Jones, my front-line editor, who provided sound advice and boundless support, and my children, Lauren, Chief, and Mary. They have been a daily reminder that in writing as in life, "love never ends."

Index